Positive Child Guidance

Fourth Edition

Join us on the web at

EarlyChildEd.delmar.com

Positive Child Guidance

Fourth Edition

Darla Ferris Miller

THOMSON

DELMAR LEARNING   Australia   Canada   Mexico   Singapore   Spain   United Kingdom   United States

THOMSON

DELMAR LEARNING

Positive Child Guidance, Fourth Edition
Darla Ferris Miller

**Vice President,
Career Education SBU:**
Dawn Gerrain

Director of Editorial:
Sherry Gomoll

Acquisitions Editor:
Erin O'Connor

Editorial Assistant:
Ivy Ip

Director of Production:
Wendy A. Troeger

Production Editor:
Joy Kocsis

Technology Project Manager:
Joseph Saba

Director of Marketing:
Donna J. Lewis

Channel Manager:
Nigar Hale

Cover Design:
Joseph Villanova

Composition:
Type Shoppe II Productions

For permission to use material from this text or product,
contact us by
Tel   (800) 730-2214
Fax   (800) 730-2215
www.thomsonrights.com

Library of Congress Cataloging-in-Publication Data

Miller, Darla Ferris.
  Positive child guidance / Darla Ferris Miller.-- 4th ed.
      p. cm.
Includes bibliographical references and index.
  ISBN 1-40181-256-2
  1. Child rearing--United States. 2. Child development--
United States. 3. Child psychology--United States. 4.
Parenting--United States. I. Title.

  HQ769.M5325 2003
  649'.1--dc21   2002041324

NOTICE TO THE READER

Contents

Chapter 3   Understanding the Reasons for Problem Behavior   83

Appendices

Preface

Parents and early childhood professionals worry about discipline: "How do I get kids to clean up after themselves?" "How can I keep toddlers from biting and pulling hair?" "What should I do when preschoolers call each other hurtful names?" "Am I being too strict?" "Am I being too lenient?" "How can I manage my own feelings of anger and frustration when children throw tantrums?"

Child guidance is the very challenging process of establishing and maintaining responsible, productive, and cooperative behavior in children. Parents and early educators must devote a great deal of time, effort, and persistence over many years to help children become considerate and self-disciplined members of society. **Knowledge of the natural stages of child development is the most powerful tool adults have to guide youngsters successfully through this process of maturing.** This book provides answers focused on developmentally appropriate guidance.

Self-discipline and self-control do not automatically appear out of thin air. Competent, well-behaved children do not just happen. Dedication and skill on the part of parents and early educators help children reach their full potential. Effective guidance prevents behavior problems, keeps children safe, safely channels emotional expression, and builds a solid foundation for children's future participation in society.

This book has been written specifically for those adults who make an invaluable contribution to society by caring for and teaching the youngest and most vulnerable members of society: our children. The book is intended as a road map to guide adults as they strive to meet the developmental needs of children from infancy through early childhood. **Every child has unique needs. Consequently, no single guidance strategy will be appropriate for all children at all ages.** This book addresses typical characteristics and needs of children as they proceed through chronological and developmental stages. It provides a broad range of practical, effective, and flexible guidance strategies that are based on principles of straightforward communication and assertiveness. The underlying theme is that of respect for the dignity and human rights of the infant and young child.

Much writing in the area of child guidance has focused only on behaviorist learning theory, a view that all behavior can be explained as the result of externally reinforced (or rewarded) learning. This view assumes that because a full understanding of the internal workings of the human mind is impossible, process is, therefore, irrelevant. For too many people, discipline (or guidance) simply means giving rewards and punishments to control children's behavior. Far too many

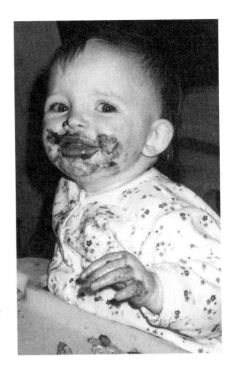

Parents and early childhood educators must devote a great deal of time, effort, and persistence over many years to help children become considerate, self-disciplined members of society.

schools rely exclusively on competitiveness, grades, stickers, and time-outs to motivate and control children. A key problem with exclusive reliance on behavior modification—ignoring negative behaviors and reinforcing positive behaviors—is that it may be carried out in an aloof or manipulative manner.

Additionally, rewarding children for behaving a certain way raises several sticky issues. Since human beings of all ages are infinitely complex, the praise or prize that reinforces one child may embarrass, bore, or alienate another. **Doling out privileges and prizes may place an adult in the role of a stingy Santa Claus rather than that of a democratic guide and role model, and may stimulate competition rather than cooperation among children.** Doling out attention and praise as reinforcement risks implying to children that compliance is a condition for affection and that only "good" children are loved.

Another problem that undermines the effectiveness of behavior modification as a sole strategy for guidance is the contemporary child's frequent exposure to many different adults and settings. Even intermittent reinforcement of a behavior through attention from children or other adults can undo an attempt by a teacher to eliminate that behavior by ignoring it. The behaviorist educator attempts to control the child's behavior by controlling the child's environment, a very helpful tool for guidance in specific situations but not a feasible overall plan for child guidance.

Strategies for child guidance should not rely only on methods for external control, but rather must interact with and extend the development of naturally unfolding internal mechanisms and motivations for self-control. In this way, children can be encouraged to become independent and self-directed rather than dependent and other-directed. As they grow toward adolescence and adulthood, they will begin making more and more critical choices about what to do and how to behave.

Since imitation, or modeling, is a key avenue for early child learning, how adults cope with the stress and frustration of handling children's misbehaviors is critical. Children tend to do what we do rather than what we say to do. **The purpose of child guidance is to support and direct the growth of effective life skills rather than only to bring about the immediate control of annoying behaviors.**

Positive, persistent assertiveness is considerably more painstaking and time-consuming than bullying and intimidating children into compliance by scolding, screaming, or spanking. And it definitely requires a great deal more thought and effort than giving up responsibility for children's behavior, allowing children to bully others, and assuming that maturation will somehow automatically bring discipline and self-control.

In child guidance—as in much of our instant, drive-through, disposable culture of expedience—the slower, more difficult method has special value. In spite of the added skill and effort required to carry out positive, assertive discipline, its impacts on the child's personal growth and on the early childhood setting make it a worthwhile method. **Positive, assertive discipline bolsters self-esteem, nurtures cooperativeness, and models socially acceptable coping skills.** The early childhood program is a training ground in which very young people acquire and practice the skills needed for effective living. The personal characteristics and capabilities needed for survival in an autocracy or anarchy are very different from those needed for participation in a democracy. In an interdependent world, early child guidance should begin the development of self-respect; awareness of and consideration for the rights of others; and recognition that persons of all ages, colors, and creeds should be treated with equal dignity, although each may have very different roles and responsibilities.

The ultimate goal of child guidance is the child's development of responsibility, self-confidence, and self-control. Inner discipline, based on an intrinsic desire to be a cooperative community member, is more functional to adult life in a democracy than sole reliance on external

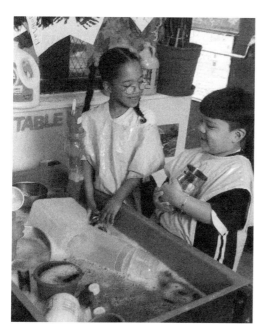

Positive assertive guidance bolsters self-esteem, nurtures cooperativeness, and models socially acceptable coping skills.

discipline based on an artificially contrived desire to gain rewards and avoid punishments. Of course, there is no place in any democracy for laissez-faire anarchy in which people wantonly trample the rights of others in their quest for self-gratification.

This book outlines practical, workable steps for creating a cooperative, respectful community of children and adults. Behavior modification will be addressed, not as the foundation of child guidance, but as a single, carefully placed stone in a solid structure of active guidance. Maturation will be addressed, not as an excuse to relinquish responsibility for child behavior, but as a powerful tool for understanding and responding appropriately to various stages of child behavior. The method presented is one of assertive and respectful enforcement of cooperatively developed rules and persistent protection of individual rights.

Aggression, passivity, and manipulation are identified as hindrances to positive child guidance. They trigger negativity, even rebellion, in children, and they model behaviors that are hindrances to successful participation in democratic community life. **The role of the adult, in this book, is that of one who seeks not to gain control over children but rather to guide them effectively, while setting for them an immediate and tangible example of appropriate coping and assertive negotiation.**

In this model, the adult guards the safety and individual rights of children, and stimulates their development of inner control by creating a functioning democratic community of children and adults. Positive child guidance means guiding children as firmly as necessary, as gently as possible, and always with respect.

This book is meant to be a lively, poignant, warm, and very human look at the process of adults guiding, managing, and coping with children's behavior, and children trying to deal with their own emerging needs and feelings, as well as with persistent adult expectations. Although the book is readable, and at times even funny, it is based on a solid theoretical foundation drawn from the empirical study of social and emotional development in infants, toddlers, and young children.

NEW TO THIS EDITION

- The sequence of chapters has been adjusted to stress the importance of relying on the basic principles of child development to more effectively guide children and support appropriate behavior.
- New information has been integrated throughout this edition to emphasize inclusion and cultural sensitivity in guiding children and resolving behavior problems. New material addresses individual differences in child behavior and adult expectations related to culture, gender, age, birth order, disabling conditions, and philosophical perspectives.
- There is a greater focus on the role of positive guidance in developing children with the self-discipline, self-reliance, and respect for others necessary to thrive in a global society.
- Extensive updated resources are featured at the end of each chapter and include related readings, helpful Internet sites, and listings of children's books dealing with problem issues.
- This edition addresses new research findings, emerging social issues, and special challenges confronting contemporary families and early childhood professionals.

ANCILLARY MATERIALS

INSTRUCTOR'S MANUAL

Available with the fourth edition is an updated instructor's manual, a chapter-by-chapter plan for organizing a course using *Positive Child Guidance*. In addition to chapter overviews, outlines, key terms, resource lists, and teaching tips, this manual will include a complete list of PowerPoint masters, which are arranged by chapter in the Online Resources™. Instructions for using the Online Resources™ are also part of the manual.

ONLINE RESOURCES™

A special accompaniment to this edition of *Positive Child Guidance* is an Online Resources™, which integrates Internet technology and child guidance and developmentally appropriate practice. You'll spot the Online Resources™ icon next to Web references throughout the text, indicating where additional information or activities on that topic can be found in the Online Resources™. The Online Resources™ also contains critical thinking questions and activities for each Practical Application section found in the text, and questions relevant to chapter learning objectives, which are presented for individual or group consideration. Web links and other resources are included along with PowerPoint masters for instructor use.

The Online Resources™ can be found at www.earlychilded.delmar.com.

COMPUTERIZED TEST BANK

An updated computerized test bank on CD-ROM allows teachers to create student exams composed of multiple choice, true/false, short answer, and completion questions for each chapter. The CD-ROM provides upward of 1,000 questions in addition to the following features: multiple methods of question selection, multiple outputs (print, ASCII, and RTF), graphic support, random questioning output, and special character support.

WEBTUTOR™

WebCT and Blackboard courseware, designed to help instructors create an on-line teaching and learning environment, is available for purchase with this edition of *Positive Child Guidance*. The courseware offers an easy-to-use, common interface with integrated tools and content for on-line course creation. Instructors can customize the course as much or as little as they wish as there is a pre-built and class-ready course requiring minimal or no modification. Components of the courseware include:

- Course Information Section—course description, required materials, recommended materials, course learning objectives, policies, testing, attendance, and grading.

- Contents Section—chapters organized according to core text

- Communication—chat, e-mail, calendar, white board, and discussion area

- Tools—calendar, search, content compile, change password, and white board options

- Student Progress Section—my records and progress

- Resources—glossary of terms and Web links resources

Acknowledgments

I am indebted to many colleagues who assisted in the development of this text. I especially thank LaTrella Thornton, Karen Burkhardt, Andre Perez, Juan Primo, Laura Dupree, Grace Hively, Susan Thornton, and Alice Quiroga for their help and support. Many of the beautiful photographs that appear on these pages were graciously provided by the families and staff of:

- Children at Risk, Inc. of Houston
- City College Child Development and Family Services Center of the City University of New York
- Echo Park-Silverlake People's Child Care Center in Los Angeles
- Belle Johnson Child Development Lab School Program of North Harris College in Houston
- Montessori Country Day School of Houston

I received encouragement and inspiration from my husband Tommy and our two daughters, Michelle Denise and Cynde Allyson. Michelle holds a doctorate in cognitive psychology from UCLA and is on the faculty of Northern Arizona University. Cynde holds a masters degree in fine arts from UC Irvine and is on the faculty of Chaffe Community College.

Erin O'Connor, Alexis Breen Ferraro, Amy Simcik Williams, Ivy Ip, and many other professionals at Delmar Learning have been of great assistance. Additionally, I sincerely thank the early childhood faculty listed below who contributed significantly to the readability, accuracy, and usefulness of this book by critiquing it and adding their own ideas and suggestions:

Alice D. Beyrent, Department Chair
Hesser College
Manchester, New Hampshire

Elaine Camerin, Ed.D
Daytona Beach Community College
Daytona Beach, Florida

Carol P. Fontana
Keystone College
Scranton, Pennsylvania

Teresa Frazier
Thomas Nelson Community College
Suffolk, Virginia

Tracy Keyes
Kutztown University
Kutztown, Pennsylvania

Margaret King, Ed.D.
Ohio University
Athens, Ohio

Frances Langan, Ed.D
Keystone College
Scranton, Pennsylvania

Elaine Wilson, Ph.D
Oklahoma State University
Stillwater, Oklahoma

DEDICATION

This book was inspired by and is dedicated to my parents, Evolee and Roy Ferris. "Papa Roy" did not live to see the book completed, but he had great interest in and enthusiasm for its writing. Because he grew up the youngest child of a troubled single parent during the Great Depression, he spent much of his adult life struggling to learn how to be a good parent and to let his children know that he loved them. When he read the beginning draft of this book, his eyes got a bit misty, and he said, "You've said some important things in here. I'm really proud of you." Of course, no child ever outgrows the need to know she has made her parents proud!

As my husband, Tommy Miller, and I have reared our daughters, we, too, have struggled to learn how to be good parents and let our children know they are loved. Today we feel awe as we watch the beginning of our next generation emerge. Our beautiful second granddaughter, April Myra McDonald, slips her chubby baby feet into her mommy's high heels, dons her daddy's big baseball cap, and wobbles off toward the future.

ABOUT THE AUTHOR

Darla Ferris Miller holds a doctorate in Early Childhood Education, Texas and Mississippi teaching credentials, and the American Montessori Society Preprimary Certification. She is presently Vice President for Community and Institutional Advancement at North Harris College. Dr. Miller has served in a wide range of roles within the field of child care and development. She has been caregiver, teacher, center director, teacher trainer, professor, and consultant, and she has worked with children from infancy to school age. Dr. Miller's publications include:

Miller, D. F. (1990). Toddlers. In L. Ard & M. Pitts (Eds.), *Room to grow: How to create quality early childhood environments.* Austin, TX: Texas Association for the Education of Young Children.

Miller, D. F. (1989). *First steps toward cultural difference: Socialization in infant/toddler day care.* Washington, DC: Child Welfare League of America, Inc.

Miller, D. F., & Ginsberg, M. B. (1989). Social reproduction and resistance in four infant/toddler daycare settings. *Journal of Education, 171*(3) [31–50].

Chapter 1
Introduction

Every child represents a new beginning full of bright possibility.

OBJECTIVES

After reading this chapter, you should be able to:
- Identify contemporary practices in child guidance.
- Define responsibility for healthy child growth and development.
- Recognize the purpose of child guidance.
- State the criteria for creating early childhood rules.
- Describe ideal early environments.

CHILD-REARING IN TODAY'S WORLD

At dawn every weekday morning all across the country, from bustling cities to tiny rural communities, mothers and fathers struggle to begin another workday. In millions of homes and apartments, parents hurry to feed and dress babies and young children. Without a minute to spare, they grab diaper bags and satchels, buckle little ones into car seats, climb onto buses, or push strollers into elevators. They head for a variety of child care arrangements ranging from homes of relatives to registered family day homes to proprietary, religious, and government funded child-care centers, early childhood programs, and schools. Stress begins early for today's parents and children. The world is changing dramatically, but children still need protection, nurturance, love, and guidance. Whether mommy is a full-time homemaker or a business executive with an urgent 8 A.M. appointment makes little difference to a toddler who plops in the middle of the floor and cries because he doesn't want oatmeal for breakfast. Child guidance is a challenging task for any parent, but if parents work outside the home, managing their children's behavior may be more complicated, and they may rely a great deal on early childhood professionals to support their children's social and emotional development (Brazelton, 1985; Curran, 1985; Bond, Galinsky, & Swanberg, 1998).

Practical day-to-day responsibility for guiding the next generation is shifting from parents alone to parents, communities, and early childhood personnel working together. Today, there are fewer full-time homemakers caring for children and rapidly increasing numbers of exhausted dual-earner couples, single parents, grandparents, stepparents, and other arrangements of employed households juggling work while rearing young children (Barnett & Rivers, 1998; Bond, Galinsky, & Swanberg, 1998; Daly, 1996; Francke, 1983; Hochschild, 1997; Thorpe & Daly, 1999; Yarrow, 1991). At the same time family structures are changing, more and more research has surfaced highlighting the critical importance of early experiences for the long-term development of a child's personality, character, values, brain development, and social competence (Adlam, 1977; Anyon, 1983; Banich, 1997; Bandura, 1977; Cook-Gumperz, 1973; Elman, et al., 1997; Greenenough, Black, & Wallace, 1993). Never before has there been such acute awareness of the impact early caregivers have on young lives, and never before has there been such need for people outside the family to assume major involvement in the process of child rearing (Bronfenbrenner & Morris, 1998; Chugani, 1993; Galston, 1993; Hamburg, 1992; Marshall, 1991; National Commission on Children, 1991).

Decades ago, "baby-sitting" provided a brief break from the real business of child-rearing (which was most often handled by mothers). Having someone other than a family member look after the children represented only a brief interruption from day-to-day caregiving. It was assumed that any untrained but reasonably responsible teenager or adult could be relied on to sit with the baby or child for a short time just to assure that the child was safe and that basic physical needs were met. Now, however, over half of all babies and young children live in homes where the adults in the family work part or full time outside the home. Child care is not a brief interruption from routine caregiving but rather a major portion of it. Many children spend most of their waking hours in some form of child care by someone other than parents from as early as the first weeks of life (Blau, 1998; Skolnick, 1991; Hamburg, 1992).

These changes place new pressures on parents and on early childhood professionals. Employed parents must face the stress of juggling family and career obligations. Fathers find that modern lifestyles present a new level of paternal involvement in caring for and managing young children. Early childhood educators find that more and more is expected of them by parents who depend on them to be skillful in supporting wholesome growth and development in the children. Today, more households than ever are being shared by three or even four generations. Adult children often stay at home or return home, and the elderly live to such advanced ages that many families care for parents as well as children (Center for Policy Alternatives, 2002; Daly, 2000). Working parents' time and finances are often strained to the breaking point. Welfare reform means more parents are required to be employed, although their earnings may be meager and their child care costly.

Even parents who are full-time homemakers find that contemporary lifestyles bring new stresses and strains to child-rearing. Many feel that their toddlers and preschoolers benefit from participating in professionally run early childhood programs, even if a parent is home full time and child care is not linked to employment.

WHY PARENT AND PROFESSIONAL TRAINING IN CHILD GUIDANCE IS IMPORTANT

In today's world, many children do not spend the first years of their lives sheltered in cocoon-like home settings. They are up with the alarm clock, their days are structured and scheduled, they come

KEY FACTS AND STATISTICS

- Forty-two percent of employed workers are responsible for children under 18 years of age (AFL-CIO, Bargaining for Child Care Fact Sheet)

- Sixty-three percent of women with children under the age of six work, and 78% of women with children between six and 18 work (AFL-CIO, Bargaining for Child Care Fact Sheet)

- Sixty-two percent of working parents say that their main problem with child care is finding high-quality care (AFL-CIO, Bargaining for Child Care Fact Sheet)

- About 13 million preschoolers (including six million babies and toddlers) spend some or all of their day being cared for by someone other than parents (Children's Defense Fund, The State of America's Children, 1999)

- Nearly 5 million school-age children spend time as latch-key kids without adult supervision (Child Care Bureau, 1997)

- Seventy-six percent of school-aged children with working mothers spend time in at least two different child care arrangements during a typical week in addition to their time in school (Child Care Bureau, 1997)

- Seven out of 10 public schools have no after-school programs (AFL-CIO, Working Together for Kids)

The teacher of little children is not merely giving lessons. She is helping to make a brain and nervous system, and this work which is going to determine all that comes after, requires a finer perception and a wider training and outlook than is needed by any other kind of teacher.

Margaret McMillan (1930)

---

in contact with many caregivers, and they must learn to get along with other young children in groups. Modern parents need help in developing the skills they need to guide young children effectively and prevent behavior problems since they may have limitations in their flexibility and time to deal with a tantruming toddler who refuses to get dressed, or a pouting preschooler who insists that everyone in the whole world hates her. Parents need support with child guidance so that behavior problems do not place additional strain on family life structures that may already be stretched thin simply from the stresses of contemporary living (Amato, 1997; Coontz, 1997; Copeland & McGreedy, 1997; Salk, 1992; Stringer-Siebold, et al., 1996). (See Appendix A for additional resources.)

Early childhood professionals need help in developing effective child guidance strategies so that they can truly meet the social and emotional needs of the children in their care, so that they provide much needed support to family life, and so that they can assume a reasonable portion of the responsibility for teaching the next generation how to be responsible, cooperative, and competent citizens. Teachers and caregivers can never replace the important role of caring parents.

Every child, every moment, is in the process of creating the adult she will become.

Parents have an irreplaceable impact on their children's lives simply because of the emotional bonds that are a part of being a family. While caregivers must never compete with or infringe on this special parent-child relationship, they can be a tremendous support to both children and their families. Parents are the first and most important teachers children will ever have.

Changing attitudes and expectations in society bring dramatic changes in contemporary child-rearing practices.

WHO SHOULD BE RESPONSIBLE FOR THE WELL-BEING AND GUIDANCE OF CHILDREN?

We are all responsible for the well-being and guidance of children. In past centuries, children were thought to be their parents' property. In Western Europe only a century and a half ago, babies were not considered to be real persons. It was not even thought necessary to report their deaths (Aries, 1962). In a modern democracy, however, children are not viewed as property of their parents but rather as human beings with inalienable human rights. Governmental agencies hold responsibility for the welfare and guidance of young children because children are the future citizens of the country. Failure to address early needs later costs government millions of tax dollars in remedial education, indigent support, and crime (Hernandez, 1997; Jackson, 1997; Lindjord, 1997; McAlister, 1997; White, 1995). Business and industry hold responsibility for the welfare of young children since they will be the workforce of the future, and competitiveness in world markets depends on the availability of competent, cooperative, responsible workers. Civic groups, churches, schools, and each of us are also responsible. Good citizenship obligates us to look toward the future well-being of humanity rather than just our own personal interests. You can help your community build a brighter future by joining with other interested parents and professionals to support advocacy groups that inform and encourage better child care and education.

AMERICA'S CHILDREN: 2000

- The family structures of children have become more varied. The percentage of children living with one parent increased from 20 percent in 1980 to 27 percent in 1999. Most children living with single parents live with a single mother. However, the proportion of children living with single fathers doubled over this time period: from two percent in 1980 to four percent in 1999. Some children live with a single parent who has a cohabiting partner: 16 percent of children living with single fathers and nine percent of children living with single mothers also live with their parents' partners.

- Many children live in households that have housing problems such as physically inadequate housing, crowded housing, or ones with a high-cost burden. The percentage of households with children that have these problems has been increasing since 1978: 36 percent had one or more housing problems in 1997, up from 30 percent in 1978.

- The percentage of children experiencing food insecurity decreased in 1999. However, nearly one-third of children in poverty experienced food insecurity.

- Death rates for children continued to drop in 1998. For children ages one to four and five to 14, the death rates were 34 and 20 per 100,000 children in each age group, respectively. The leading cause of death in these age groups was unintentional injuries, with most of these fatal injuries resulting from car crashes. Birth defects, cancer, and homicide were also leading causes of death for children ages one to 14.

- Between 1996 and 1999, the percentage of children ages three to five not yet in kindergarten who were enrolled in early childhood centers rose from 55 percent to 59 percent. The largest increases were among children living in poverty, children with mothers who were not in the labor force, and black, non-Hispanic children.

(continues)

America's Children 2000 *(continued)*

America's Children: Key National Indicators of Well-Being, 2000 is the fourth report in an annual series prepared by the Interagency Forum on Child and Family Statistics. Copies are available through the Health Resources and Services Administration Information Center while supplies last. The Center is located at, 2070 Chain Bridge Road, Suite 450, Vienna, VA 22182. Telephone 1-888-Ask HRSA, e-mail ask@hrsa.gov. or visit their Web site at http://www.childstats.gov/

Throughout the country, there is growing recognition that investing efforts and resources to better the lives of children is not only humane but also very cost-effective. Children are open to ideas and experiences. It is possible to bring about meaningful changes in their lives, and to have real influence on their long-term development of values and character traits. Adults, on the other hand, tend to be more rigidly set in their habits and potentials. If we are to continue to enjoy the benefits of living in a democracy, then we must begin by helping children learn personal responsibility and respect for others so that they will know how to function properly as adults.

"Be safe—sand is for digging, not for throwing. Sand hurts if it gets in your eyes."

SHORT-TERM OBJECTIVES FOR CHILD GUIDANCE

The short-term objective for child guidance is deceptively simple. Children will be helped to follow the same basic rules for decent and responsible behavior that are applicable to all persons living in a democracy. To accomplish this, we can use the following guidelines to determine the appropriateness of children's day-to-day behaviors and help them learn the difference between right and wrong:

- Behavior must not infringe on the rights of others.

- Behavior must not present a clear risk of harm to oneself or others.

- Behavior must not unreasonably damage the environment, or animals, objects, or materials in the environment.

> *In the sweep of seven decades, the image conveyed is one of children, smaller than anyone else, lighter in physical weight and political clout, easily picked up and blown wherever the winds of economic, political, and social movements were heading.*
>
> *Rochelle Beck (1973)*

To communicate these rules effectively, to translate them to the comprehension level of young children, they must be greatly oversimplified. By oversimplifying them, young children can be guided to make sense of what otherwise may seem to them to be an endless number of unrelated little rules. By lumping rules into three basic categories, young children can be helped to remember and understand the basic guidelines for appropriate behavior: be *kind*, be *safe*, and be *neat*. These ground rules can be stated as reminders before more specific and practical instructions are given. For example:

- Be *kind*! Wait for your turn.

- Be *safe*! Go down the slide feet first.

- Be *neat*! Put your paper towel in the trash can.

Stating the guidelines for appropriate behavior is easy. Evaluating real behaviors in real children is a great deal more difficult and it requires some critical thinking on the part of the adult. A very well-coordinated five-year-old is leaning back on two legs of his chair. Does this behavior infringe on the rights of others? (For example, is the walkway between tables blocked for other children?) Does this behavior risk an injury? (Could the child fall? If he fell, would he hit soft carpeting or a cement floor?) Does it appear that equipment could be damaged by this behavior? (How sturdy is the chair? Are breakable things nearby?) Personal judgment, practical experience, and knowledge of individual children and their capabilities will determine how different adults answer these questions, and how they go about setting rules and enforcing discipline. I hope you will answer these questions with enough compassion to see every situation through children's eyes, enough courage to be true to your sense of fair play and good judgment.

WHAT ARE THE RIGHTS OF CHILDREN?

Children Have a Right to Be Safe.

Adults should be very conscientious about protecting every child's right not to be hit, kicked, bitten, or shoved. It is never okay to allow a child to be kicked because he did it first and "deserved to get a taste of his own medicine." It is never okay to bite a toddler back "so that he will learn what biting feels like." An old cliché that happens to be true is: "Two wrongs do not make a right." The only thing that revenge really does is set the stage for more hurtful behavior. Adults should monitor children carefully and consistently so that aggression can be prevented or interrupted immediately when it does occur.

Children Have a Right to Avoid Unnecessary Discomfort.

They have a right to eat lunch peacefully without an unnerving noise level caused by children around them screaming and yelling. They have a right to listen to a story without being squashed by others who are struggling to see the pictures. And they have a right to build sand castles without getting sand in their eyes because gleeful playmates are shoveling sand into the air just for the fun of it. Although all young children begin with a kind of thinking that limits them to a self-centered (or egocentric) view of the world, adults can help children begin to recognize that others have feelings. In time, children begin to get a sense of what it feels like to be someone else. A one-year-old may try to give his pacifier to an older child who is crying, or a preschooler may run to tell a teacher that his friend got pushed off the swing. Adults who are consistently sensitive to the comfort needs of children set an emotional tone in which children are much more inclined to be sensitive to each other.

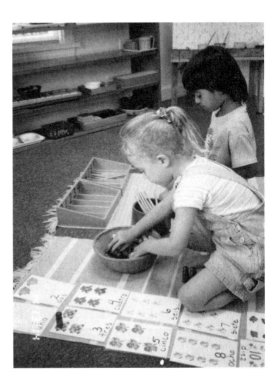

Young children appreciate pleasant and comfortable surroundings.

Children Have a Right to Their Possessions

Adults sometimes impose very strange views of sharing onto children. In the adult world, government provides very precise laws related to possession and ownership. Law forbids others from tampering with one's possessions without permission. Even social customs follow the same rule. If I take a cart in a grocery store and begin doing my shopping, it would be extremely rude and surprising for another shopper to snatch that cart away and dump my groceries because she wanted "a turn" with the cart. I would greatly appreciate a store manager (authority figure) who intervened politely but assertively, and redirected the offending shopper to other available carts. Oddly enough, a child in preschool who complains because another child grabbed the tricycle or snatched the container of crayons he was using is often not helped but instead chided for "tattling" and for "not sharing."

A child's personal possessions are his own, and no one—not even a parent or teacher, should tamper with them without asking the child or at least letting the child know that, for example, "I'm going to put your sweater away now." Objects that are available for shared use belong to the person using them at any given time (until, of course, that use infringes on the rights of others). In a home setting, if one child is watching television, another should not be allowed to march in and change channels without asking. In a group setting, a puzzle belongs to the child who chose to work with it, and no one else should be allowed to touch that puzzle without permission from the child who chose it first. Sharing is only really sharing if it is voluntary.

This little boy has a right to explore his art materials without unnecessary interference from other children.

Children Have a Right to Fairness

Fairness is a concept that emerges slowly in children during the preschool and early elementary years. Even before that concept is well developed, however, children deserve fair treatment, and they need to observe role models of integrity and fairness. If one child is allowed to have a picture book during naptime, then it is unfair to deny that privilege to another child without some logical reason or explanation.

By the time children are around kindergarten age, they can sometimes be heard proclaiming loudly, "Hey, that's not fair." Although their logic is still rather limited and their actual concept of fairness may be hazy, they are likely to complain if the action of an adult or another child appears to them to be blatantly unequal or out of compliance with a rule. Sometimes, if an adult carries out a disciplinary action that appears arbitrary and capricious to a child, the child will immediately begin enforcing that action on other children, partly as revenge and partly in imitation of the adult. For example, a teacher angrily snaps at a child and yanks his lunch box out of his hand because it is not yet time for lunch. A few minutes later, the child mimics the adult's behavior and tone of voice, yanking away a smaller child's toy and snapping, "Gimme that, you baby!"

HOW DO WE TELL THE DIFFERENCE BETWEEN ENFORCING REASONABLE SAFETY RULES AND BEING OVERPROTECTIVE?

Just about every interesting activity or environment has some element of risk. Imagine for a moment trying to create an environment that had absolutely no possibility for any kind of accident. Unfortunately, a child can potentially misuse, fall off of, throw, choke on, or bump into just about any kind of equipment or material that can be named. The only perfectly safe environment would probably be a an empty room with padded walls and floor, and some child would undoubtedly find a way to get hurt there, too. Of course, a padded cell would not offer many opportunities for exploration and skill development. So, in an interesting, challenging environment, safety is always a matter of compromise. The difficulty for many teachers and parents seems to be in deciding what level of risk management is acceptable and reasonable, and what level is not.

Children feel a sense of pride and dignity when they succeed in mastering a difficult challenge that has a bit of risk involved. No baby ever learned to walk without risking a fall, and no child ever learned to jump off a step, climb a tree, roller skate, or ride a bicycle without risking a bump or bruise. Some pediatricians assume that if a child makes it through early childhood without so much as a broken finger, then he has been overprotected. The acceptability of risk must be weighed against the severity of possible outcomes. If the worst thing that could reasonably result from a behavior is a two-foot fall onto a thick gymnastic mat, then the risk seems very acceptable. If the child could possibly fall 10 feet onto brick pavement, then there is a clear risk of harm; that kind of accident could result in serious or permanent injury to the child.

Adults must be diligent about safety for young children. Environments in which young children play should be checked and double-checked routinely for hazardous equipment, toxic plants or substances, and dangerous but tempting situations. Then, but only then, can adults step back and allow children the latitude to negotiate challenges independently, under a watchful eye but without hovering control.

Responsibility and independence develop when children learn to care for themselves and their environment.

WHY SHOULD CHILDREN BE INVOLVED IN MAINTAINING AND PROTECTING THEIR ENVIRONMENT?

In order to learn, children need the freedom to make mistakes, to know that it is really not so awful to break a glass or spill paint on a shirt. Most things can be restored or replaced. Stained clothes will soon be forgotten, but a child's first painting may be treasured for many years, and the benefit of the experience of painting may stay with a child for the rest of his life.

Although it is essential to keep a reasonable perspective about neatness, one cannot lose sight of the fact that responsibility, manners, and good citizenship require one to have respect for his surroundings. We all share the resources of this planet and have an obligation, therefore, to use them wisely and well. Early child guidance prepares children for good citizenship. When a child remembers to use one paper towel at a time and then throw it away, he is preparing for membership in adult society where everyone benefits if forests cut for paper mills are replanted, water used in factories is cleaned before being dumped, and fish and game are taken according to lawful limits and seasons.

In the first years of life, children can gradually learn to take only what they need, use it with care, then restore it (put it away) when they have finished using it. Toys, games, and learning materials should be arranged in an orderly manner on low shelves that are accessible to children. Even a very young child can learn to replace a puzzle if it has its own place on a shelf or in a puzzle rack. A stack of ten heavy puzzles crammed on a shelf makes it difficult or impossible for a child to select and take any but the top puzzle. There should be no more materials available at any one time than those with which children can deal. And adults must set an example for care of the environment and assist children consistently in learning that things are easier to find if they are always returned to the same spot.

Children should be stopped firmly but kindly when their behavior is damaging to the environment. While playing outdoors, children may innocently break limbs off shrubs, smash birds' eggs, or peel bark off trees. Teaching them about nature and the value of plants and animals assists them in building respect for living things and in accepting responsibility for their own actions. Indoors, children playfully smash riding toys into table legs and stuff tissues down the sink drain just to see what happens. These actions should immediately be interrupted in an understanding but matter-of-fact way. If the child is shown how tables are built, sanded smooth, and painted, or how pipes bring water into and out of our homes, he will be more likely to understand and care for his environment.

LONG-TERM GOALS FOR CHILD GUIDANCE

If children are to become responsible adults, they must learn to control their actions and impulses. Unfortunately, self-control is not an easy thing to teach. Children begin life without any self-control whatsoever, so our most critical long-term goal is to assist them in their journey to responsible adulthood by nurturing their mastery of self-control.

Children are not simply lumps of clay to be shaped by caregivers. They are born with individual potentials and personality traits. They are also, however, profoundly influenced by the people, experiences, and events they encounter, especially during the first years of their lives (Baillargeon, 1997; Begley, 1997b; Begley & Springen, 1997; Berk, 1997; Bodrova & Leong, 1996; Eddowes & Ralph, 1998; Jackson, 1997; Stevenson & Lee, 1990). The effect of the environment on children, interestingly, is reciprocal. Children have tremendous impact on the behavior of the adults in their lives. Instead of being passively shaped by adults, children are actively involved in the experiences that influence their own development. Adults behave differently with different children. The actions and appearances of individual children trigger different emotions and reactions in individual adults.

Children are born with individual and distinctive behavioral patterns (Collins & Gunnar, 1990; Rutter, 1976; Santrock, 1997; Sroufe, 1996; Thomas & Chess, 1977; Thomas, Chess, & Birch, 1970). These clusters of personality traits are referred to as temperament. The temperament of an infant or child has an influence on how adults will care for him. Also, the quality and style of the care that adults provide have a strong influence on that continually developing temperament. He affects his caregivers and they affect him; both change and are changed by their interactions. All these influences, both internal and external, ensure that no two people will ever be exactly the same. We must help children celebrate and appreciate their differences.

Furthermore, even if two children's behavior is similar, their gender, size, or appearance may trigger different adult reactions. A thin, frail infant girl may evoke more protective, nurturing behavior in adults than a loud, robust infant boy who may evoke more roughhousing and active playfulness in caregivers. A child who appears defiant may be treated sternly while a child who appears contrite may be treated indulgently after an identical incident. A cycle emerges in which the child begins to anticipate a certain kind of interaction with others so he behaves accordingly, actually triggering the expected interaction. What began as incidental action and reaction settles eventually into habit, attitude, and personality. The bottom line is, of course, that early experiences make a difference in children's lives.

We play a critical role in shaping children's future lives. Our long-term goal for guidance is our most important contribution: equipping children with the skills and attitudes they need for happy, responsible, and productive adult life. The early childhood setting, whether in the home or in a child care center, is a miniature community in which children develop and practice the rudimentary skills they will need to cope with the larger community they encounter as they go through school, then Îfinally the big, wide world when they are grown. Child guidance builds a foundation on which everything else in the child's life is built including social interaction with others, academic learning, and personal development. By their very nature, babies come into this world helpless, self-centered, and dependent. Guidance transforms them into full-fledged, functioning members of society.

THE NURTURING ENVIRONMENT AND LONG-TERM DEVELOPMENT

High-quality early childhood settings look so simple that it is easy to underestimate the importance of the interactions there. An appropriate environment for young children is relaxed and playful. Children follow their own curiosity as they freely but respectfully explore objects, toys, and materials in the environment. They move about, chatter peacefully, laugh, and occasionally argue as they explore human social interactions and learn reasonable limits. A home where children are expected to be seen and not heard, or a formal school setting with pupils sitting rigidly and silently following teacher instructions or listening to lectures, are not examples of optimum early environments.

The rote memorization typical in lessons with workbooks, flash cards, and ditto sheets is definitely something many young children can master if coerced, pressured, and bribed. The abstract concepts this memorized jargon represents, however, are totally unrelated to young children's level of brain development and, therefore, rather meaningless for them. Even a very young child can memorize and repeat chants and rhymes with long words, but he is unlikely to have a clue as to their meaning. If too much time is spent in such questionable ventures as rote memorization, the loss of time for more wholesome experiences can interfere with the really essential business of early childhood; that is, healthy development of the whole child, socially, emotionally, and physically. The foundation of early learning is exploring, practicing, constructing, pretending, and problem-solving (Gestwicki, 1999; Gordon & Browne, 1996a). Experience truly is the best teacher for young children. If a child's early environment does not fully support these experiences, it will be impossible for the child to reach his full potential.

Properly matching early childhood settings to the natural stages of growth and development seen in infants, toddlers, and young children has been termed developmentally appropriate practice. Detailed information about developmentally appropriate practice can be obtained through the National Association for the Education of Young Children (NAEYC) (Bredekamp & Copple, 1997). (Further description of methods to "set the stage" for positive behavior by creating a developmentally appropriate early childhood environment is provided in Chapter 5.)

In family settings where parents feel strong bonds of love and attachment to their child, they will quite naturally respond to that child's cries and smiles when he needs attention or care. A healthy, well-developing baby or child gives many signals or cues to indicate what he needs, and a sensitive, caring parent uses trial and error to discover what will work to stop the child's crying, and to keep the child happy and comfortable. This same give-and-take can be the heart of group care. If we see child care as a tedious chore that can be made easier by ignoring the child's cries and refusing to become emotionally attached, then nature's way of ensuring healthy development is undone. Caregivers and teachers who do not find joy in working with children may well be advised to seek different careers.

Affection and attention foster the long-term development of children's potential to become competent, confident, cooperative people.

CHILDREN—OUR INVESTMENT IN THE FUTURE

In some child care situations where working conditions are stressful, pay bottom-of-the-barrel, training inadequate, and staff turnover never ending, teachers/caregivers may not be able to function consistently at a level parents want their children to emulate. Parents, early educators, and public policy makers are becoming acutely aware of the significance of early experience on long-term development. Too often in past years, it has been assumed that child care need be little more than a kindly but custodial parking lot for youngsters. Growing evidence from the study of human development indicates that the first years of life may be the most, rather than the least, critical years in a child's emotional, physical, and intellectual growth (Carnegie Corporation of New York, 1994).

Child care centers, preschools, mother's-day-out programs, and other early childhood settings have the potential to help parents create a better future for children and for society in general. To have resources, support, and high expectations from communities, the child care profession must come to be viewed as an integral part of our educational system, as well as a necessary service to support the economic well-being of low-income families (Adams & Rohacek, 2002; Families and Work Institute, 1993).

Because early experiences are so important to healthy development, child care outside the family takes on special significance. The first question parents should ask as they examine child care alternatives is, "Are the adults in this setting warm, nurturing, and emotionally available to the children?" And, since modeling (imitating) and first-hand experience, rather than direct teaching, are the major avenues for learning in young children, the next crucial questions parents might ask are, "Do I want my child to absorb the personality traits, communication styles, and problem-solving behaviors of the adults here?" and "Do these adult role models set an example for behavior that I value and want my child to imitate?"

Do adults in the child care center appear to genuinely enjoy and appreciate the individual qualities of each child in their care?

POSITIVE ADULT ROLE MODELS . . .

- treat everyone with dignity and respect at all times.

- rely on communication, persistence, and patience rather than on force.

- respond assertively to misbehavior with both firmness and gentleness.

- use problem-solving strategies to identify the causes of misbehavior.

- plan and prepare appropriate activities, materials, and routines.

- give unconditional affection and affirmation.

- are polite, honest, and straightforward in communications.

- protect every child's individual rights.

- celebrate differences.

- really listen.

POINTS TO REMEMBER
- Contemporary family life brings special stresses and strains to children and families.
- The basic rules for responsible human behavior are simple; respect the rights of others, take only reasonable risks, and protect and maintain the environment.
- Positive guidance is the process of proactively, assertively, and respectfully supporting the development of responsible, self-disciplined children.
- Spoiling refers to overindulging and overprotecting children, shielding them from responsibility for their own behavior and rewarding inappropriate conduct.
- Caregivers should never worry about spoiling babies and toddlers. Attention and interaction helps babies develop to their full intellectual, physical, emotional, and social capacity.
- Ignoring infants' cries interferes with healthy development and undermines the foundation of trust that is critical to later development of self-control and self-discipline.

PRACTICAL APPLICATION

THE SPOILED CHILD—MYTH OR REALITY?

It is a glorious day at the park. Bright sunshine is radiating just enough warmth to balance a flag-snapping breeze. This sudden evidence of spring has drawn families and children outdoors like a magnet. Sitting on the grass alongside a large sandbox is a cluster of grown-ups who are laughing and talking as they watch their youngsters squealing and running or digging eagerly in the sand.

Al and Tamara's four-year-old son Joel makes gleeful whooping sounds as he chases his two-year-old brother Eddy with a wriggling bug he has found in the sand. Eddy screeches and dives onto his dad for protection as his mother beseeches Joel to "stop being so wild."

As he skids to a stop, Joel inadvertently smashes into a double stroller holding the Rodriguez twins. While Al escorts his boys back to their buckets and shovels, Tamara bends down with Elena Rodriguez to make sure the one-year-old twin girls are okay.

Several other parents have stopped talking and are watching attentively as Elena adjusts the little girls in their stroller and smoothes their crisp red dresses with identical embroidered collars.

Other mothers are amazed that the twins have not cried. Tamara takes one little girl by the hand and says, "Shall we get them out and let them play for a while?"

"Oh, no," says Elena, "They would get filthy. They know that they have to stay in the stroller." Al comments that his boys were never that "good." They would have pitched a fit to get out and get right in the middle of the dirt.

Several other parents chime in with awe-struck comments about how good the twins are. Elena responds, "I knew with twins and me working that they had better not get spoiled. In the child care center I use, they are very strict about not spoiling the kids. They only pick up the babies to change and feed them. The babies cried for a few days right at first, but now they're just no trouble at all."

The conversation about Elena's twins trails off as other parents scatter to chase after straying toddlers and to respond to their children's cries of "Watch me," "Push me in the swing again," and "Look at my sand castle." As Tamara rushes to Eddy to remind him not to eat sand, she feels a surge of envy for Elena and her "good" babies who are never any trouble.

DISCUSSION QUESTIONS

1. What do people really mean when they label babies either "spoiled" or "good?"
2. What appear to be Elena's priorities and values in caring for her children? What are her daughters learning about their role in the world?
3. Why do you think the staff in Elena's child care center were opposed to holding, rocking, and playing with babies? Does frequent holding and cuddling create a setting in which adults are "warm, nurturing, and emotionally available to the children?" Why is this important?
4. How do you feel about Al and Tamara's relationship with their children?
5. List, in order of importance, the ten characteristics you personally value and admire most in a person (for example, kindness, sense of humor, energy, intelligence, enthusiasm, and so on). Are these the same characteristics you expect caregivers to model in their interactions with babies and young children? Describe a real situation in which you modeled the characteristic you most value.
6. List the ten characteristics you like least in a person. Are these characteristics that you have seen caregivers demonstrate in their interactions with youngsters? Describe a real situation in which you modeled a characteristic you would not want children to imitate.

RELATED READINGS
CONTEMPORARY PARENTING

Aidman, A. (1997). *Television violence: Content, context, and consequences.* Champaign, IL: ERIC Clearinghouse on Elementary and Early Childhood Education.

Amato, P. R. (1997). Life-span adjustment of children to their parents' divorce. In E. N. Junn & C. Boyatzis (Eds.), *Annual editions: Child growth and development 97/98* (4th ed.). New York: McGraw-Hill. (Original work published in *The Future of Children*, spring 1994.)

Paul Amato provides information on children's adjustment to divorce, including their academic, social, and psychological well-being in childhood and as adults. Amato also describes how children's adjustment depends on many factors and explains that differences are generally small between children of divorce and children from intact families.

Barnett, R. C., & Rivers, C. (1998). *She works, he works: How two income families are happy, healthy and thriving.* Cambridge: Harvard University Press.

Blankenhorn, D. (1997). Life without father. In K. M. Paciorek & J. H. Munro (Eds.), *Annual editions: Early childhood education 97/98* (18th ed.). New York: McGraw-Hill. (Original work published in *USA Weekend*, February 24–26, 1995.)

The increase in divorce and in single-mother families has led to a situation that David Blankenhorn calls "disappearing dads." Children without two caring and supportive parents are at risk of future failure in a number of areas.

Bond, J. T., Galinsky, E., & Swanberg, J. E. (1998). *The 1997 national study of the changing workforce.* New York: The Families and Work Institute.

Bozett, F. W. (1987). *Gay and lesbian parents.* New York: Praeger.

Christian, L. G. (1997, May). Children and death. *Young Children, 52*(4), 76–80.

Cooksey, E. C., & Fondell, M. M. (1996). Spending time with his kids: Effects of family structure on fathers' and children's lives. *Journal of Marriage and the Family, 58*(3), 693–707.

Coontz, S. (1997). Where are the good old days? In K. M. Paciorek & J. H. Munro (Eds.), *Annual editions: Early childhood education 97/98* (18th ed.). New York: McGraw-Hill. (Original work published in *Modern Maturity*, May/June 1996.)

Throughout our nation's history, families have always been in flux. Economic changes have resulted in increasing poverty, homelessness, and distress for young children.

Copeland, M. L., & McCreedy, B. S. (1997, January–February). Creating family-friendly policies: Are child care center policies in line with current family realities? *Child Care Information Exchange, 113*, 7–10, 12.

Council of Economic Advisors (1999, May). *The parenting deficit: Council of economic advisors analyze the time crunch.* Council of Economic Advisors, with commentary by Brian Robertson. Available at http://www.whitehouse.gov/WH/EOP/CEA/html/famfinal.pdf

Crouson, R. L., & Boyd, W. L. (1993, February). Coordinated services for children: Designing arks for storms and seas unknown. *American Journal of Education, 101*, 141.

Daly, K. (1996). *Families and time: Keeping pace in a hurried culture.* Thousand Oaks, CA: Sage.

Denby, D. (1997). Buried alive. In E. N. Junn & C. Boyatzis (Eds.), *Annual editions: Child growth and development 97/98* (4th ed.). New York: McGraw-Hill. (Original work published in *The New Yorker*, July 15, 1996).

In this essay, David Denby argues that "an avalanche of crud" from popular culture television, films, toys, and video and computer games buries today's youth. He offers insight into the impression this culture may leave on children's character and their views of reality.

deToledo, S., & Brown, D. E. (1995). *Grandparents as parents: A survival guide for raising a second family.* New York: Guilford.

More than a million American grandparents today are the primary caregivers for their grandchildren. Most have found their lives altered, their finances spread thin, and their parenting techniques old-fashioned. They find themselves challenged by a new, different, and sometimes traumatized generation. The book is a useful resource for professionals who work with parenting grandparents, and a good reading recommendation for grandparents and family members who need some encouragement and advice.

Duis, S. S., et al. (1997, Spring). Parent versus child stress in diverse family types: An ecological approach. *Topics in Early Childhood Special Education, 17*(1), 53–73.

Ehrensaft, D. (1997). *Spoiling childhood: How well-meaning parents are giving children too much— but not what they need.* New York: Guilford.

In this book, Dr. Ehrensaft discusses the difficulties and stresses that today's parents are creating for themselves and their children. She describes the absurdities, frustrations, and possibilities of contemporary child-rearing. She argues that parents today are all too often caught up in a guilt-driven pendulum swing between parenting too little and parenting too much. They are always in a hurry yet anxious for their children to succeed, aware of children's autonomy yet fearful of losing their love. Our culture has created a new kind of child, half miniature adult, half innocent cherub, whose new set of problems creates a divided sense of self and chronic anxiety.

Elkind, D. (1981). *The hurried child.* Reading, MA: Addison-Wesley.

Elkind, D. (1997). School and family in the postmodern world. In E. N. Junn & C. Boyatzis (Eds.), *Annual editions: Child growth and development 97/98* (4th ed.). New York: McGraw-Hill. (Original work published in *Phi Delta Kappan*, September 1995.)

David Elkind describes how schools and education have undergone, in the postmodern era, major changes due to broader changes in the family and society. One such change is that schools now assume many parental functions.

Frieman, B. B. (1993, September). Separation and divorce: Children want their teachers to know—Meeting the emotional needs of preschool and primary school children. *Young Children, 48*(6), 58–63.

Galinsky, E. (2001, April). What children want from parents—and how teachers can help. *Educational Leadership, 58*(7), 24–28.

Galinsky argues that the source of difficulty for modern families is not that many mothers work outside the home but that our society undervalues parenting. She identifies how schools can help parents manage their guilt and stress, value both working and stay-at-home roles, involve more fathers, and raise community awareness.

Gillis, J. (1996). *A world of their own making.* New York: Basic Books.

Helburn, S. W., & Bergmann, B. R. (2001). *America's child care problem: The way out.* New York: Palgrave.

Well-researched review of current problems associated with child care and a bold proposal for solutions.

Henderson, A. T., & Berla, N. (Eds.). (1994). *A new generation of evidence: The family is critical to student achievement.* Washington, DC: National Committee for Citizens in Education.

Hernandez, D. J. (1995, Winter). Changing demographics: Past and future demands for early childhood programs. *Future of Children, 5*(3), 145–60.

Hildebrand, V., Phenice, L. A., Gray, M. M., & Hines, R. P. (1996). *Knowing and serving diverse families.* Upper Saddle River, NJ: Merrill Education/Prentice-Hall.

This book responds to the growing need for programs to work comfortably with all people and to help solve critical societal problems of relating to today's people at home, in the community, the nation, and the world. It examines both ethnic and structural diversity in families in the United States.

Hochschild, A. (1989). *The second shift.* New York: Avon Books.

Hochschild, A. R. (1997). *The time bind: When work becomes home and home becomes work.* New York: The Henry Holt and Company.

Howe, M. B. (2000). Improving child care and promoting accreditation: The military model. *Young Children, 50*(5), 61–63.

Gives a brief history of factors leading to dramatic quality improvements in the military's child care system, how the military's child care system has promoted quality, and policies supporting its high ac-creditation rate.

Isenberg, J. P., & Jalongo, M. R. (Eds.) (1997). *Major trends and issues in early childhood education: Challenges, controversies, and insights.* New York: Teachers College Press.

Jackson, B. R. (1997, November). Creating a climate for healing in a violent society. *Young Children, 52*(7), 68–70.

Jacobs, J., & Gerson, K. (1998). Who are the overworked Americans? *Review of Social Economy, 4*, 442–459.

Kagan, S. L. (1997, May). Support systems for children, youths, families, and schools in inner-city situations. *Education and Urban Society, 29*(3), 277–95.

Kagan, S. L., & Neuman, M. J. (1997, September). Highlights of the Quality 2000 Initiative: Not by chance. Public Policy Report. *Young Children, 52*(6), 54–62.

Kagan, S. L., & Neuman, M. J. (1997). *Solving the quality problem: A vision for America's early care and education system. A final report of the Quality 2000 Initiative.* New Haven, CT: Yale University.

Lakey, J. (1997, May). Teachers and parents define diversity in an Oregon preschool cooperative—Democracy at work. *Young Children, 52*(4), 20–28.

Larson, R. W., Richards, M. H., & Perry-Jenkins, M. (1994). Divergent worlds: The daily emotional experience of mothers and fathers in the domestic and public spheres. *Journal of Personality and Social Psychology, 67,* 1034–1046.

Leland, J. (1997). Violence, reel to real. In E. N. Junn & C. Boyatzis (Eds.), *Annual editions: Child growth and development 97/98* (4th ed.). New York: McGraw-Hill. (Original work published in *Newsweek*, December 11, 1995.)

John Leland looks at the debate on violence in film and television, and challenges the research conclusion that there is a clear causal relationship between televised violence and real-life aggression. Leland critiques many of the famous studies on the topic, as well as discussing the recent controversy over the V-chip.

Lewin, K., Lippitt, R., & White, R. (1939). Patterns of aggressive behavior in experimentally created social climates. *Journal of Social Psychology,* 271–99.

Three leadership styles—authoritarian, democratic, and laissez-faire (permissive)—were studied. Authoritarian leadership resulted in higher discontentment and aggression among the children, but also in more work production. Children in the democratic model showed less hostility, more enjoyment, and more independent self-direction in their work. The laissez-faire group accomplished relatively little and the children evidenced boredom.

Lindjord, D. (1997, November–December). Child care: The continuing crisis for working families and child care teachers. *Journal of Early Education and Family Review, 5*(2), 6–7.

McAlister, B. G. (1997, Spring). Growing up in a violent world: The impact of family and community violence on young children and their families. *Topics in Early Childhood Special Education, 17*(1), 74–102.

McLanahan, S., & Sandefur, G. (1994). *Growing up with a single parent: What hurts, what helps.* Cambridge, MA: Harvard University Press.

McMath, J. S. (1997, March). Young children, national tragedy, and picture books. *Young Children, 52*(3), 82–84.

Mitchell, S. (1997). The next baby boom. In K. M. Paciorek & J. H. Munro (Eds.), *Annual editions: Early childhood education 97/98* (18th ed.). New York: McGraw-Hill. (Original work published in *American Demographics*, October 1995.)

The nearly 76 million baby boomers born between 1946 and 1964 have produced 72 million children of their own, born from 1977 through 1993. This next generation of boomers is very different from the first. These new children and their families often do not have a father living at home. Parent lifestyles and responsibilities have changed tremendously.

Moore, W. E. (1963). *Man, time and society.* New York: John Wiley.

Newman, S., Brazelton, T. B., Zigler, E., Sherman, L. W., Bratton, W., Sanders, J., & Christeson, W. (2000). *Fight crime: Invest in kids* (2nd ed.). Washington, DC: Fight Crime: Invest in Kids, Inc.

Demonstrates how investing resources in quality early childhood care and development programs would yield such significant crime reductions and other benefits that governments would have more money for Social Security, tax cuts, or any other purpose in the years ahead.

Pallas, A. M., Natriello, G., & McDill, E. L. (1989). The changing nature of the disadvantaged population: Current dimensions and future trends. *Educational Researcher, 18*(5), 16–22.

Pleck, J. (1996). Paternal involvement: Levels, sources and consequences. In M.E. Lamb (Ed.), *The role of the father in child development.* New York: John Wiley and Sons.

Provenzo, E. F., Jr. (1992, March). The video generation. *American School Board Journal, 179*(3), 29–32.

Roberts, P. (1997). Fathers' time. In E. N. Junn & C. Boyatzis (Eds.), *Annual editions: Child growth and development 97/98* (4th ed.). New York: McGraw-Hill. (Original work published in *Psychology Today*, May/June 1996.)

Paul Roberts presents evidence on fathers' roles in the family, their influence on children's emotional and intellectual development, and their distinct interaction styles. Roberts also describes how fathers have only recently received attention from researchers, showing that they are no longer subservient in the parenting realm.

Russell, P. (1992). *The white hole in time: Our future evolution and the meaning of now.* San Francisco: Harper.

Seefeldt, C., & Glaper, A. (1998). *Continuing issues in early childhood education* (2nd ed.). Upper Saddle River, NJ: Merrill Education/Prentice-Hall.

This book contains discussions, debates, disagreements, and disputes, with the expectation that these will lead the reader to explore and question various points of view.

Shores, E. F. (1991). *Prenatal cocaine exposure: The south looks for answers.* Little Rock, AR: Southern Association on Children Under Six.

Stabiner, K. (1997). Get 'em while they're young. In E. N. Junn & C. Boyatzis (Eds.), *Annual editions: Child growth and development 97/98* (4th ed.). New York: McGraw-Hill. (Original work published in *Los Angeles Times Magazine*, August 15, 1993.)

Karen Stabiner describes how advertisers set their sights on young children, using sophisticated tactics to shape their consumer habits and tastes to cultivate lifelong loyalty to their products. Also discussed are techniques that parents can use to protect children from the early onslaught of advertising aimed at those too young to understand that commercials are designed to sell a product.

Stengel, R. (1997). Fly till I die. In K. M. Paciorek & J. H. Munro (Eds.), *Annual editions: Early childhood education 97/98* (18th ed.). New York: McGraw-Hill. (Original work published in *Time*, April 22, 1996.)

The shocking April 18, 1996, death in a plane crash of Jessica Dubroff, her father, and a flight instructor led many people nationwide to question the parenting skills and knowledge of child development of her parents. Should there be a time when decisions made by families are questioned by the government? Just how much are young children today being pushed to achieve goals that may or may not be their goals?

Stoney, L. (1999, May). Looking into new mirrors: Lessons for early childhood finance and system building. Public policy report. *Young Children, 54*(3), 54–59.

Reviews research on public policy in housing, health care, higher education, and transportation to evaluate how these policies can be applied to improve early childhood care quality and availability.

Stringer-Seibold, T., et al. (1996, Fall). Strengths and needs of divided families. Research Highlights. *Dimensions of Early Childhood, 24*(4), 22–29.

Stroud, J. E., et al. (1997, Summer). Understanding and supporting adoptive families. *Early Childhood Education Journal, 24*(4), 229–34.

Swick, K. J. (1997, Spring). Strengthening homeless families and their young children. *Dimensions of Early Childhood, 25*(2), 29–34.

Thorpe, K., & Daly, K. (1999). Children, parents and time: The dialectics of control. In C. Sheehan (Ed.), *Through the eyes of the child: Revisioning children as active agents of family life.* New York: JAI Press.

HELPFUL WEB SITES

http://www.childstats.gov/   This Web site offers easy access to federal and state statistics, and reports on children and their families including demographics, health, behavior, and education.

http://www.childrennow.org/   Children Now uses research to inform the public and supports positive change for children. They offer a directory of children's issues and hundreds of Web sources.

http://www.childrensdefense.org/   The Children's Defense Fund advocacy site offers news, statistics, reports, job information, and links to other Web sites addressing the needs of poor and minority children, and those with disabilities.

http://www.childcarerr.org/   The National Association of Child Care Resource and Referral Agencies is a nonprofit organization dedicated to providing up-to-date information to parents seeking child care, child care professionals, NACCRRA members, and child care advocates. Includes information on how to select a child care provider and links to related Web sites.

http://nccic.org/   The National Child Care Information Center, (NCCIC) contracted by the U.S. Department of Health and Human Services, disseminates *Childcare Bulletin*, works closely with state and national organizations related to child care, and offers forums and conferences.

http://www.futureofchildren.org/   The Future of Children is a publication of the David and Lucille Packard Foundation that provides information on critical issues affecting children and families.

http://www.childrensdefense.org or http://www.nsaca.org   Children's Defense Fund National School-age Care Alliance.

http://www.usakids.org/sites/ccac.html or http://www.dol.gov/dol/wb   Child Care Action Campaign Women's Bureau.

http://www.usakids.org   Coalition for America's Children.

For additional information on positive child guidance, visit our Web site at
http://www.earlychilded.delmar.com

Chapter 2
Understanding Children's Behavior

OBJECTIVES

After reading this chapter you should be able to:
- Recognize typical ages and stages of early childhood.
- Identify developmental milestones that affect behavior.
- Identify relationships between maturation and guidance strategies.
- Outline changes over time in adult-child relationships.
- Trace the development of positive self-esteem.

TYPICAL AGES AND STAGES

The most important thing to remember when considering the typical ages and stages of childhood is that no child is completely typical. Every child is unique. Although typical or average patterns can be identified, real children have individual patterns and rates of development that may be normal but not at all average. The most valid reason for comparing a child's rate of development to standard rates is to be alert to any consistent pattern of differences, or "red flags," that indicate a need for professional screening and possibly the need for therapeutic intervention.

Typical behaviors change quickly as children grow from one developmental stage to the next. Look at the changes in Cory over the first year of his life (clockwise starting on the top left): at three days, four months, seven months, and eleven months.

Sometimes, by comparing a child's individual behaviors with typical behaviors, we can better understand the child, recognize that the child is only going through a normal phase, and anticipate phases that the child will soon be entering. Adults are often comforted to know that many children at a certain age behave the same way as the child with whom they are dealing. Babies shy away from strangers, toddlers become stubbornly assertive, preschoolers worry about who is or is not their best friend at any given moment, and

Identifying individual levels of social, emotional, physical, and intellectual development is intended to assist us in creating developmentally appropriate environments for children. It must never be used to label or stereotype children.

school-agers reject everything that is not considered "cool" by their friends. Adults are also relieved to realize that most children tend to outgrow whatever phase is at issue, regardless of how adults try to respond to it.

Typical behaviors tend to be consistently clustered together and in a sequential order, so a child's behaviors might be matched to those at a specific age level although her chronological age may actually be younger or older than that listed. A seven-year-old who is developmentally delayed may show a wide range of typical toddler behaviors. However, a gifted four-year-old who can already read may act a bit like a school-ager in some behaviors, but like a preschooler or even a toddler in other behaviors. The value of assessing each child individually is to match guidance strategies to the individual child's developmental capabilities and needs, and never to label or stereotype the child.

If, for example, a toddler is discovered trying to poke an object into an electrical outlet, the adult may look very concerned and say, "Ouch, that could hurt you. Come play with your toys." But the primary discipline strategy would be to change the environment to protect the toddler more effectively. A specially designed safety guard could be installed to prevent access to the outlet, or the child could be removed to a safer, better supervised, area.

A five-year-old, however, who is discovered exploring and trying to insert an object into an outlet should be handled quite differently. The adult must determine whether the child is curious, misinformed, or feeling rebellious. When the adult has a sense of why the behavior has occurred, she might firmly discuss the cause-and-effect dangers of playing with electric outlets. She should then redirect the child's curiosity by helping the child explore the characteristics of electricity using a safe six-volt battery, wires, and a tiny flashlight bulb. The child's curiosity could be channeled into a whole new area of interest and knowledge by reading books about electricity. She can be taken outside to look at power lines, to talk about how workers protect themselves when they repair dangerous electrical wires, and to make pretend wires out of strings to attach to the child's playhouse.

The innate temperament of an individual child, the temperament of parents and early caregivers, the environmental setting, the culture, and even the child's role in the family all affect development. The important thing to remember is that every child is a unique human being.

PIAGET'S DEVELOPMENTAL STAGES

Sensorimotor Stage (Infant)

Development is largely nonverbal.

Main concern is developing motor control coordinated with information from the senses.

Gradual emergence of object permanence concept (looks where a hidden object has gone).

Preoperational Stage (Toddler-Preschooler)

Understands and predicts simple cause-and-effect sequences ("If I touch something hot it will hurt").

Develops ability to think symbolically and use language.

Thinking is largely intuitive (egocentric perspective).

Confuses words with the objects they represent.

Child is unable to take the viewpoint of other people.

Concrete Operational Stage (Young Schoolager)

Mastery of the concept of conservation of matter (now realizes that Santa's bag couldn't really hold enough toys for everyone at once).

Concepts of time, space, and numbers develop, and categories and principles are used in thinking.

Child can think logically about concrete objects or situations.

APPROPRIATE GUIDANCE METHODS

Birth to 1½ Years

Provide responsive, affectionate caregiving.

Provide consistent, predictable routines.

Nurture the development of trust by responding promptly to the child's needs.

Ages 1½ to 3 Years

In a caring and consistent way, teach self-help skills such as self-feeding, toilet learning, and dressing.

Give children opportunities to make choices within reasonable limitations.

Provide a developmentally appropriate environment for the child to explore that challenges emerging skills.

3 to 5 Years

Help the child set goals, plan, carry out activities, and then talk about what has happened afterward.

Help the child learn that actions have consequences, and it is always best to think before acting.

Discuss frequently why certain behaviors are not allowed, and why other behaviors are better.

6 to 8 Years

Provide experiences in building, creating, and accomplishing to gain a feeling of adequacy.

(continues)

PIAGET'S DEVELOPMENTAL STAGES
(continued)

Ability to reverse thoughts or operations (if 4 x 2 = 8, then 2 x 4 = 8).

Formal Operations (Older School-ager)

Thinking becomes based on more abstract principles and is less egocentric.

Can consider hypothetical possibilities (uses more complex strategies in games).

Begins to develop deductive reasoning and knowledge depending on educational opportunities and the willingness of the child to participate.

APPROPRIATE GUIDANCE METHODS
(continued)

Provide encouragement and deserved recognition to support the development of competence and healthy self-esteem.

Frequently use group discussions to talk through and solve problems and disagreements.

Nurture each child and help her discover and develop her own special talents and abilities.

9 to 12 Years

Provide children support in developing positive self-identity as their bodies begin to change and mature at very different rates.

Provide opportunities for the development of close peer relationships and friendships.

Give children responsibility for tasks that genuinely contribute to the family, classroom, or community.

Provide guidance and supervision to prevent the child bullying or being bullied.

Donohue-Colletta, N. (1995). *What parents should know about school readiness.* Washington, DC: National Association for the Education of Young Children.

Schaefer, C. E., & Digeronimo, T. F. (2000). *Ages and stages: A parent's guide to normal childhood development.* New York: John Wiley & Sons.

INFANTS (BIRTH–12 MONTHS)

Babies are fascinating. Their big eyes and rounded contours are specially designed to turn grown men and women to mush (Alley, 1981). Babies are soft and warm and cuddly, but few parents are prepared for the powerful emotions that well up inside them when they, for the first time, have their own child. Some parents feel a jumble of emotions such as outrageous pride, a protectiveness as passionate as a tiger for her cubs, jealousy of any imagined competition for affection, overwhelming fatigue, fear of failure, even grief over the loss of infancy as the child grows and matures so quickly.

Parenting is one of the most significant and challenging adventures adult human beings undertake (often with little or no preparation). If additional caregivers are involved in infant care, parents may be relieved of some stresses and strains, but other complex feelings or tensions may emerge. Many a mother has left her baby in a carefully chosen child care center for the first time only to sit in the parking lot, collapsed in tears on the steering wheel of her car.

Fathers, grandparents, even siblings also fret over the adequacy of anyone helping to care for the new baby. Jenny, a kindergartner in a child care center, talked her teacher into letting her go to the nursery where her two-month-old brother was newly enrolled. There, she held her baby brother's tiny hand through the bars of his crib for a long time as she carefully watched every move made by the nursery workers. The employees listened smilingly as the little girl pointed out to them, "you mustn't touch his head right up there where it's soft." Although Jenny was only five, she felt protective and concerned about her baby brother.

Who can resist the soft, endearing face of a baby?

DO INFANTS INTENTIONALLY RESPOND BY CRYING?

Usually, the first kind of upsetting behavior adults must cope with in caring for infants are bouts of crying. A typical scenario pictures the adult trying all the usual problem-solving strategies: warming a bottle, changing a diaper, or rocking. Soon, the adult has done everything she knows to do, but the infant cries even more frantically. Some adults hear the infant's wails as a personal indictment of their competence, integrity, or authority: "How dare this baby accuse me of being a bad father (or mother, or caregiver)!" A howling baby can quickly fray the nerves of even the most patient and devoted adult.

A temptation for many of us is the tendency to project intentional motives on the baby for her crying. We say things like, "She's just crying because she knows I'm a pushover," "She always cries when I try to cook, because she thinks she should be the center of attention," or "She's only crying because she's mad at me. She was born with a fiery temper." These rationalizations may make us feel vindicated for angry or resentful feelings that surge through us as we try to deal with the screaming baby, but they are, nevertheless, inaccurate. Infants do not intentionally do much of anything. They simply react spontaneously and unconsciously to their environment.

Sadly, some adults with virtually no understanding of the processes of child development see infant crying as such a clear example of intentional "bad" behavior that they attempt to punish the infant for her crying. Child protective service workers and other social agents often deal with parents who begin shaking, hitting, and spanking babies in the first year of life—a very dangerous and inappropriate practice—in the mistaken belief that they are helping their babies learn to be "good."

CAN BABIES MISBEHAVE ON PURPOSE?

Regardless of many common misconceptions, in the first months of life, infants have no capacity for consciously intentional behavior. They are not able to think about or plan actions to get desired results. Until they have **object permanence** (the mental ability to envision persons, objects, or events that are not in sight), they cannot "think" or "know" that any action will bring about a desired result. They can only react or respond in a very unconscious way to internal feelings such as pain or hunger, and to external **stimuli**, sensations the infant sees, feels, hears, tastes, or smells (Piaget, 1968).

INFANT BRAIN DEVELOPMENT

- Brain development that takes place before age one is more rapid and extensive than previously realized.

- Early brain development is more vulnerable to environmental influence than was previously known.

- The influence of early environment on brain development is long-lasting.

- The environment affects not only the number of brain cells and number of connections among them, but also the way these connections are "wired."

- There is new scientific evidence for the negative impact of early stress on brain function (Mustard, 1999. Adapted from Starting Points, Carnegie Corporation of New York, 1994).

Key Facts about Brain Development—Every Child Magazine, Autumn 2000
Australian Early Childhood Association, Inc.
Every Child Magazine, Volume 6, No 1, Autumn 2000
For more information/subscription, call (02)6241 6900 or visit http://www.aeca.org.au

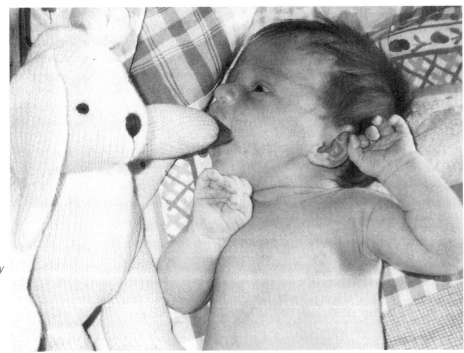

The newborn baby comes into the world equipped to learn by looking, listening, feeling, tasting, and smelling.

Even in toddlers, some behaviors that may seem intentional are actually **unconscious reactions** based on the child's having absorbed connections or relationships among day-to-day experiences. Unrelated objects, events, and sensations become connected. We might expect any nine-month-old to show curious interest in a brightly colored, shiny can. If the child immediately fusses and struggles for the can of soft drink she sees in her mother's hand, though, it is pretty clear her experience has led her to expect a sip whenever she sees a soft drink can.

WHAT ARE REFLEX RESPONSES, AND WHAT IS UNCONSCIOUS CONDITIONING?

In newborns, almost all actions are simple reflexes over which the child has no control. Infants blink, startle, grasp an object placed in the palm of the hand, and root toward a nipple, but not because they choose to do those things. They do them simply because their brains are designed to make certain behaviors happen automatically. From the moment of birth, however, babies carefully study their environment, at first by staring and eventually by using all their senses. Babies gradually progress beyond reflex behavior. They begin to recognize and associate things they see, feel, hear, taste, and smell with other meaningful sensations or events. A hungry, breast-fed infant will become very agitated when she is held near her mother's breast. The feel, smell, and sight of the breast is closely associated with the memory of the sweet taste of milk.

WHAT IS CLASSICAL CONDITIONING?

To a baby, hearing keys rattle means someone is leaving, being placed in a stroller means going for a walk, or hearing the rustle of plastic wrap means getting a cookie. This kind of learning is generally categorized as **classical conditioning**. Looking at a balloon does not normally make babies cry (seeing a balloon is an unconditioned stimuli). Loud noises, however, certainly do make them cry (crying in response to a loud bang is a naturally occurring stimulus-response connection). If a baby has been frightened and has cried on several occasions when balloons have popped, then the baby may begin to cry whenever she even sees a balloon. This is a conditioned stimulus-response connection.

Researchers have, for decades, attempted to document classical conditioning (pairing an unconditioned stimuli with a naturally occurring stimulus-response connection) in newborns. The best that has yet been documented is a rather rough kind of learning now called pseudoconditioning. Studying early responses is difficult since so little of the newborn's movement can really be classified as voluntary (Rosenblith & Sims-Knight, 1985; White, 1995). However, by the middle of the infant's first year, classical conditioning is clearly a part of the child's learning.

WHAT IS OPERANT CONDITIONING?

Operant conditioning is quite different from classical conditioning. It occurs when the child's spontaneous actions (such as crying) are reinforced by pleasurable rewards (such as food). This type of conditioning has been studied and documented in infants from the first days and weeks of life (Sameroff & Cavanagh, 1979). Newborns automatically cry as a response to the discomfort of being hungry. Older babies and toddlers learn to whimper or make a "fake" crying sound to signal that they are hungry. In the classical conditioning example previously described, babies became excited by sensations that unconsciously reminded them of being fed. In operant conditioning, however, hungry babies learn to repeat whatever behaviors have in the past resulted in their being fed. For example, if a breast-fed infant is nursed whenever she roots and pulls at her mother's blouse, then that action (rooting and pulling) may become an unconscious but **learned behavior** that she repeats whenever she is hungry.

A baby first turns toward a nipple in response to an unconditioned rooting reflex. Then, over time, the pleasurable reward of warm milk stimulates more active and goal-oriented rooting. Eventually, the sight of the nipple, recognizing the feel of being placed in a nursing position, or other sensory cues (the smell of milk or the sound of a voice) will trigger rooting and sucking. An adult who is unfamiliar with a specific baby may inadvertently cause her to become frustrated and cry simply by holding her, without feeding her, in a position that she associates with nursing.

WHAT IS METACOGNITION?

Young infants need many repetitions of unfamiliar sensations, actions, and events in order to form associations. By the end of their first year, however, they have learned, through conditioning, to expect many specific responses to accompany certain actions and sensations (Papousek, 1967). This kind of learning is an unconscious process. Although unconscious, conditioned learning continues to take place throughout life. Months and years will pass before the child will develop an ability to consciously and intentionally control her own behavior, a process we call **metacognition**.

When a child has developed metacognition, she will be able to think about her own thinking processes and develop strategies to help her manage her own behavior. Children between three- and six-years-old are only beginning to develop metacognition. School-aged children have a much better developed ability to plan strategies, for example, to say, "I'll hide the candy where I can't see it, then I won't be so tempted to eat it before supper." Babies and toddlers possess none of these skills; they just spontaneously react to the positive and negative sensations in their world.

HOW DO BABIES DEVELOP CONTROL OF THEIR ACTIONS?

The first muscles babies can actively control are those around the face and head. The newborn can move her eyes to follow objects, she can suck effectively, and she can turn her head. Muscle development proceeds from head to toe and from the trunk to the extremities: **cephalocaudal** (top to bottom) and **proximodistal** (close to far). At first, infants are only able to control a few mouth, eye, and neck muscles. Gradually, the infant expands body control downward into the trunk (she learns to turn over), outward through the arms to the hands (she learns to bat at objects and then to grasp them), and finally down the legs to the feet (she learns to crawl and then walk). Tiny muscles of the hands and fingers will not be fully developed for years (then she will finally be able to use her fingers to button her sweater, tie her shoe laces, and write her name).

RECOMMENDED READINGS FOR OVERWHELMED PARENTS

Sears, W., & Sears, M. (1995). *The discipline book: How to have a better-behaved child from birth to age ten.* New York: Little Brown & Co.

William and Martha Sears believe that discipline starts at birth. They discuss guiding infants and toddlers, mother-father roles in modern parenting, saying no to children, self-esteem as the foundation of good behavior, helping a child learn to express feelings, the constructive expression of anger, good nutrition for good behavior, and good sleep habits. In addition, they address the development of healthy sexuality and child guidance in special situations such as after divorce and in the single-parent household.

The American Academy of Pediatrics (1998). *Caring for your baby and young child: Birth to age 5.* Rev. ed., S. P. Shelov & R. E. Hannemann (Eds.). New York: Bantam Doubleday Dell Publishers.

The American Academy of Pediatrics represents the nation's pediatricians, and the most advanced research and practice in the field of child care. This book answers medical and parenting questions, and gives sound, reassuring advice on child-rearing that covers everything from preparing for childbirth to toilet training to nurturing children's self-esteem.

Pantley, E., & Sears, W. (2000). *Hidden messages: What our words and actions are really telling our children.* New York: Contemporary Books.

Pantley and Sears help caregivers better understand how children learn appropriate behavior. Caregivers are guided to *choose* what they teach their children rather than allow children to learn through accidental, unintended, random examples that may or may not reflect the intended values and messages. This parenting book, which is intended to inspire and motivate parents, uses stories to demonstrate how adults make mistakes in their everyday interactions with their children. Each anecdote is followed by reflection on and discussion of possible interpretations by children, and concludes with practical ideas for improving communication.

Pantley, E., & Sears, W. (1998). *Perfect parenting: The dictionary of 1,000 parenting tips.* New York: Contemporary Books.

This is a simple, straightforward book of answers for parents. It is alphabetical and cross-referenced, offering practical, positive solutions for issues such as whining, complaining, back-talk, lying, teasing, fighting, anger, disrespect, interrupting, sassing, nose-picking, laziness, fussiness and other behaviors.

Pantley, E. (1996). *Kid cooperation: How to stop yelling, nagging & pleading and get kids to cooperate.* Introductions by William Sears and Louise Bates Ames. Oakland, CA: New Harbinger Publications.

This book is intended to help parents get children to cooperate more willingly, to end the typical yelling, nagging, and pleading that take place in many families. The tools and skills presented emphasize the development of children's self-esteem and self-discipline, and address strategies to reduce marital stress related to child behavior.

Sears, W., & Sears, M. (2002). *The successful child: What parents can do to help their kids turn out well.* Contribution by Elizabeth Pantley. New York: Little Brown & Co.

Dr. William Sears and his wife, Martha, a nurse, understand that instilling a moral code in one's children is among the most daunting, yet vital, of all parenting tasks. To develop trust and

(continues)

RECOMMENDED READINGS FOR OVERWHELMED PARENTS *(continued)*

self-esteem, the Sears advocate "attachment parenting," the practice of being sensitive to baby's needs. By having her needs met immediately, the child learns to trust adults, and in turn, mirrors this behavior by acting sensitively to the needs of others later on. But the most important thing parents can do for their kids, the Sears say, is to hold high expectations: "Let her know that you expect her to do her best, no less and no more, and that you will love her no matter what."

WHY DO BABIES CRY?

In the child's first year of life, behaviors result almost exclusively from internal developmental characteristics along with gradually increasing conditioned learning. If a baby cries for a prolonged period, that behavior does not stem from manipulativeness, maliciousness, or any other kind of conscious intention, but rather from internal discomfort, stress, or fatigue, or from externally conditioned routines. Babies cannot be held responsible or blamed for their behavior. It is more realistic to think in terms of relieving the cause of a crying infant's unhappiness if the problem is internal, or of gradually changing adult routines to bring about a different kind of conditioned behavior if the problem has been caused externally.

Adults are the ones who establish routines and habits in infants through day-to-day basic care patterns. Infants become **habituated** (accustomed) to those patterns and object loudly when routines are abruptly broken. If an infant is accustomed to being in constant contact with her mother's body, she will cry pitifully when she is left unexpectedly in a play pen. If an infant is accustomed to quiet isolation, he may be terrified by sudden placement in a noisy, bustling child care center. Psychologists define *stress* as the process of recognizing and responding to threat or danger (Fleming, Baum, & Singer, 1984). While working directly with infants over the years in

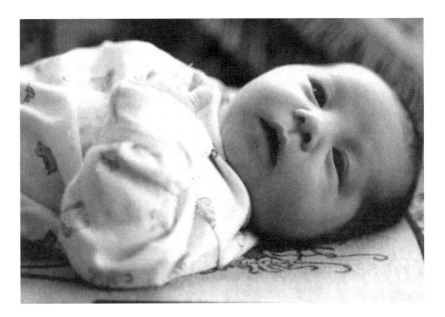

Babies naturally respond to such things as discomfort, hunger, boredom, and fear.

various child care facilities, I have, on several occasions, seen babies who seemed especially upset by a separation or by a stark upheaval in their care arrangements. In spite of attentive caregivers, the infants (ranging from three to nine months of age) appeared to slip from a long period of anguished, relentless crying into a period of quiet depression with only languid whimpering.

The infants withdrew from social contact, avoided eye contact, lost appetite, refused to play, slept too much or too little, and, apparently as a result, appeared noticeably less healthy after a time. After various lengths of time (ranging from days to months), each of these babies eventually recovered spontaneously and became responsive, robust, and playful. Today, almost a decade later, the most severely affected of these infants gives every appearance of being a bright, healthy, and well-adjusted young girl. Nevertheless, stress should be considered in dealing with children of any age, and avoided or eased whenever possible.

Careful planning of basic care and nurturing routines that can be maintained consistently will help protect the child from abrupt and upsetting changes. When changes in routines must occur, careful planning and gradual orientation should take place—especially before drastic upheavals in child care arrangements occur—in order to avoid subjecting babies to unnecessary stress (Trad, 1986, 1987, 1991, 1994; Provence & Lipton, 1967).

HOW DOES TRAUMA AND CHRONIC STRESS AFFECT THE INFANT'S BRAIN DEVELOPMENT?

Constant exposure to stressful environments can dramatically change the way an infant or young child's brain develops, making the child more prone to emotional disturbances and less able to learn. Children exposed to severe, prolonged stress often develop learning disabilities, and emotional and behavioral problems (for example, attention deficit disorder, anxiety, and depression).

Secure attachment to caregivers is critical to healthy emotional development.

They also become more vulnerable to various medical problems such as asthma, immune-system dysfunction, and heart disease (Poussant & Linn, 1997; Pransky, 1991; Prothrow-Stith & Quaday, 1995; Shore, 1997).

HOW BABIES DEVELOP TRUST

According to Eric Erikson (1959, 1963, 1982), trust developed in infancy is a primary foundation for the development of healthy emotional attitudes that must be built on throughout life. Basic care patterns offer our first opportunity to demonstrate our trustworthiness to an infant. Whenever the infant experiences internal distress, she automatically responds by crying. In time, through operant and classical conditioning, she can come to expect a dependable and pleasurable response from the adult caregivers in her life. This trust in the predictability of her environment and in the responsiveness of her primary caregivers helps the baby develop a sense that she is valued and that she can have impact on her surroundings, the first step toward the development of positive self-esteem.

KEY PROBLEMS THAT PUT CHILDREN AT RISK

- Inadequate Prenatal Care. Nearly one quarter of all pregnant women in America, many of whom are adolescents, receive little or no prenatal care.

- Isolation. More divorces, more single-parent families, and less familial and community support have made parents feel more isolated than ever before in raising their young children.

- Substandard Child Care. More than half of all mothers return to the workforce within a year of their baby's birth, but many of their infants and toddlers spend thirty-five or more hours per week in substandard child care.

- Poverty. A quarter of all families with children under age three live in poverty.

- Lack of Attention. Only half of infants and toddlers are routinely read to by their parents, and many parents give insufficient attention to their children's intellectual development.

Carnegie Corporation of New York. (1994). *Starting points: Meeting the needs of our youngest children—The report of the Carnegie Task Force on Meeting the Needs of Young Children.* Waldorf, MD: Carnegie Corporation of New York.

WHAT IS LEARNED HELPLESSNESS?

Babies who are caught in a flow of events that are unpredictable and clearly outside their control may develop an unfortunate style of response termed **learned helplessness** (Honig, 1986; Honig & Wittmer, 1997). Heartbreaking but very instructive studies of the Creche, a Romanian orphanage run by French nuns, helped researchers more fully understand the devastating impact of learned helplessness. Babies in this orphanage were adequately fed, clothed, and kept warm and dry, but the babies stayed in cribs with only uninteresting white crib bumpers and white ceilings to look at. There were few playthings and no structured activities. Caregivers were not aware that talking directly to and interacting with babies was necessary.

Because the babies were fed and changed on a schedule, there was no motivation for caregivers to respond to the babies' cries, so the babies soon learned that there was no use in crying. In effect, the children had no impact on their environment. Nothing that happened to them hinged on either spontaneous or learned actions on their part. They had no incentive to function in any way other than as passive objects in the environment, and, in fact, their behavior was soon not much livelier than that of a potted plant. These babies did not learn to sit up until a year or walk until four or five years. By age six, their IQs were about 50, which is half the normal IQ and well into the range of serious mental retardation (Dennis, 1960, 1973).

Adults who care for babies should be down on the floor laughing, talking, singing, playing, and interacting with the babies, not sitting in rocking chairs watching television programs while babies are isolated and bored in cribs or playpens. Sometimes, adults rationalize this inappropriate behavior by saying, "You shouldn't hold babies and play with them all the time. They'll turn into spoiled brats! It's better for them to learn to entertain themselves."

Obviously, the fundamental needs of an infant for the kind of care that will foster development of social, emotional, intellectual, and physical growth must take priority over questions of convenience for adults. Quality child care, like most other quality endeavors, involves a great deal of effort and hard work. Although overindulgence and overprotection do, indeed, undermine child guidance, lazy or haphazard care and teaching is never in the best interest of children.

> ### *The Concept of Spoiling*
> *Sometimes, caregivers are tempted to leave babies in cribs or playpens for the sake of convenience, or to put them on a predetermined schedule for feeding, changing, and sleeping, regardless of the child's day-to-day rhythms or preferences. A long-standing folk belief in many modern cultures is that responding quickly to babies and holding or playing with them will result in "spoiling," and will make the child excessively demanding and dependent. We know now that lots of holding, touching, talking, and playing with babies is critical for them to grow and learn properly, so do not ever be afraid of giving positive attention.*

Giving babies lots of positive attention is critical for their growth and learning.

RECOMMENDED READINGS FOR PARENTS WITH CHILD SLEEP QUESTIONS

Sears, W. (1996). *The fussy baby book: Parenting your high-need child from birth to age five.* Contribution by Martha Sears. New York, NY: Little Brown & Co.

The Sears identify the high-need baby as one having intense feelings, hyperactivity, persistence, high demand for sucking and for touch, and hypersensitivity to stimuli. To nurture, guide, and cope with such a child, they recommend the approach they label "attachment parenting," which includes on-demand feeding and weaning; nighttime parenting; sharing sleep; soothing through motion, sound, visual distraction, and physical contact; and learning through observation how to anticipate the baby's needs. They give many tips on how to care for oneself, stay positive, and avoid worry, exhaustion, and burnout.

Sears, W., & Sears, M. (2001). *How to get your baby to sleep: America's foremost baby and childcare experts answer the most frequently asked questions.* Charlottesville, VA: LB Collection Books.

Practical tools to help develop good sleep habits based on babies' natural sleep patterns, what sleeping through the night really means, and what to do when nothing seems to work.

Pantley, E. (2002). *The no-cry sleep solution: Gentle ways to help your baby sleep through the night.* New York, NY: Contemporary Books.

Typically, caregivers assume that there are only two ways to deal with getting a baby to sleep through the night: the hotly debated technique of letting the baby "cry it out," or wait patiently until the baby begins to sleep on her own. Pantley explains that when a frequent night-waking baby wakes up and starts to cry, often not because she's hungry or thirsty or wet or even lonely, she's "just plain tired, as desperate for sleep, perhaps, as her parents but, unlike them, clueless as to how to fall back asleep." She guides parents in techniques to gently, respectfully, and carefully change the baby's behavior to match her sleeping patterns to the parent's sleeping needs more closely.

American Academy of Pediatrics (2000, March). Pediatrics, Policy Statement. 105, 3, pp. 650–656. Available on-line at http://www.aap.org/policy/re9946.html.

Bed sharing or co-sleeping may be hazardous under certain conditions. As an alternative to bed sharing, parents might consider placing the infant's crib near their bed to allow for more convenient breastfeeding and parent contact. If a mother chooses to have her infant sleep in her bed to breastfeed, care should be taken to ensure that the baby sleeps on her back, does not come in contact with soft surfaces or loose covers, and the sides or edges of the bed do not present any entrapment possibilities. Adults (other than the parents), children, or other siblings should avoid bed sharing with an infant. Parents who choose to bed share with their infant should not smoke or use substances such as alcohol or drugs that may impair arousal.

Additional resources available on-line:
Elizabeth Pantley http://www.pantley.com/elizabeth/
Dr. William and Martha Sears http://iparenting.com/sears/

WHICH IS BEST—FLEXIBLE SPONTANEITY OR PREDICTABLE ROUTINES?

Two opposing priorities for infants have been described so far in this chapter. The reader might well ask at this point, "Should I provide consistent, reliable routines or respond flexibly and spontaneously to cues from the baby?" The relationship of these two opposite needs is something like that of the contrasting philosophies described in Chapter 10. On one hand, the **external environment** (the infant's physical surroundings, daily routines, and patterns of interacting with others) is important because infants tend to shape future expectations through conditioned learning. On the other hand, the infant's **internal sensations** and needs are important as a basis for adult responses because that process stimulates the child to initiate self-directed behaviors and to assume responsibility for making things happen.

There is a third alternative, however. The "developmental interactionist" perspective describes an interweaving between external forces and internal processes. In terms of guiding young children, this process is called positive child guidance, the assertive but gentle nudge method. A caregiver can be very responsive to and respectful of **cues** (indications of interest or need) from a baby while, at the same time, gradually nudging the child toward routines that are appropriate and convenient for the adult.

Babies explore the physical properties of objects they find in their environment.

A six-month-old may be allowed to follow her inner drives to explore the sensory qualities of her environment by feeling, squishing, pounding, and smelling her food as she tastes it. However, she can also be gently but persistently nudged over time to handle food in a more traditional manner, gradually to use eating utensils, and eventually, years later, to exhibit polite table manners.

In a domineering (authoritarian) setting, the baby would be forced to eat neatly with a spoon or not touch the food at all. In a setting where adults abdicate responsibility (permissive), they would shrug and passively accept the belief that children are hopelessly slovenly in their eating habits and nothing can be done about it. In a respectful (authoritative) setting, adults set very reasonable but slightly challenging expectations for the child based on needs, interests, and abilities. They assist the interaction between the child and her environment by allowing her freedom to explore, modeling appropriate behaviors for her, and encouraging her first clumsy attempts to master skills.

PARENTING STYLES

Parents and early childhood educators who are **authoritarian** are overly strict and controlling. They believe that children should be unquestioningly obedient at all times.

Adults who are **permissive** are overly lenient, hesitant to intervene in misbehavior, and are uncomfortable setting and enforcing reasonable limits.

Authoritative adults set reasonable limits and follow-up to ensure that they are followed consistently. They engage children in developing appropriate rules, and talk about the consequences of positive and negative behaviors on others. They take into account the individual needs and interests of children, and adapt as needed to adjust expectations to children's ability level. Authoritative adults encourage children to assume responsibility for their own behavior.

To learn more, read:
Baumrind, D. (1971). Current patterns of parental authority. *Developmental Psychology Monographs, 4*(1).
Baumrind, D. (1980). New directions in socialization research. *Psychological Bulletin, 35,* 639–652.
Kochanska, G. (1997). Mutually responsive orientation between mothers and their young children: Implications for early socialization. *Child Development, 68,* 94–112.
Kochanska, G., & Aksan, N. (1995). Mother-child mutually positive affect, the quality of child compliance to requests and prohibitions, and maternal control as correlates of early internalization. *Child Development, 66,* 236–254.

WHAT DO WE MEAN BY SECURE ATTACHMENT TO CAREGIVERS?

The attachment of babies to their adult caregivers is a critical part of their overall healthy social and emotional development. Early studies looked only at mother-infant relationships since that was the only interaction that was considered to be of any importance. Freud focused on the attachment of infants to the mother and theorized that the baby considered her a "love object" simply because she provided pleasurable sucking and warm milk. He believed that the process of weaning, whether it was too rigid or too lenient, set the emotional tone for all of the child's future relationships with people and institutions.

Erikson (1963) extended, revised, and updated Freud's theory. He believed that experiences in the first year of life established in infants a general point of view for perceiving the world, either the positive and accepting reaction of trust or the negative and rejecting reaction of mistrust. He theorized that not only interpersonal relations but also competence in learning to use objects was affected by the baby's relationship to the mother. Exploration is essential for skill development, but babies only have the confidence to function competently in exploring the environment when they have an adult who serves as a "secure base" from which to explore.

Konrad Lorenz (1966) discovered a kind of attachment in certain birds (ducks, chickens, and so on) that he called **imprinting**. The ducks he studied became attached to whatever, or whomever, they saw moving near them when they hatched. Baby ducks that attached to "Papa" Lorenz not only followed him around as they grew up but also tried to mate with his leg when they reached maturity. The ethologists (scientists who study behaviors in naturalistic surroundings) do not pretend that human beings behave simplistically and instinctively as ducks do, but they do theorize that some early experiences or attachments have long-term impact on human behavior.

Bowlby (1958) and Ainsworth (1973) studied the processes of human attachment as researchers experienced a dawning awareness that biological mothers were not the only people who could develop important emotional relationships with infants. Writers began to use the word *parent* instead of *mother* when discussing attachment to reflect awareness of the impact of father-child relationships. Gradually, the term *caregiver* came into use to indicate awareness that babies could develop multiple, loving attachments to grandparents, older siblings, and other consistent child care providers outside the family as well as to adoptive and biological parents.

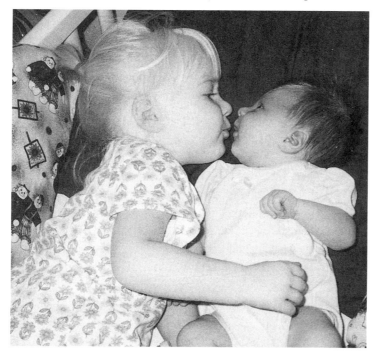

Babies begin to develop emotional bonds to the "significant others" in their lives.

WHY DO BABIES CLING?

It is essential that the process of early attachment be recognized by adults as a valuable occurrence in babies' early development rather than as an inconvenience to be avoided. Elise, a highly successful career mother, picked up her 11-month-old son from his child care center one afternoon. The little boy eagerly crawled to his mother and pulled up holding onto her legs. As he clutched at her skirt, clung to her legs, and whined to be picked up, Elise breathed a dismayed sigh, looked helplessly at the infant-room teacher, and said, "Look at him. He just clings to me. What am I doing wrong?"

Elise was not aware that her son was only showing the normal indications of healthy emotional ties to his mother, which Ainsworth called "secure attachment." When babies brighten at the sight of a caregiver, visually follow that caregiver's movements, smile or vocalize to get attention, hold out their arms to be picked up, or cling to the caregiver, they are showing the typical signs of healthy attachment. Babies who turn or crawl away when a caregiver returns after an absence may be expressing the angry, rejected feelings that accompany a disrupted or poorly formed attachment. Babies who alternately cling and reject, or show a push-pull relationship with the caregiver, may not have built a really secure attachment to the caregiver. Developing secure attachments is an essential step in the growth of normal social and emotional skills.

The positive child guidance concept (assertive but patient nudging) applies well in the area of attachment. Caregivers can best assist infants' healthy social and emotional development by allowing and supporting closeness, but also by gradually, as the child seems ready, nudging the child to move out on her own in exploring the environment. A newborn (or a baby in a new child care setting) may need to be held a great deal of the time at first, but gradually she can be enticed to spend increasing amounts of time occupying herself by looking at or playing with interesting mobiles, toys, and other surroundings. By getting down on the floor to play with the baby, a caregiver can be readily available to serve as a the "secure base" to facilitate the baby's moving out into more and more independent explorations of the surrounding environment.

SEPARATION AND STRANGER ANXIETIES

Attachment to caregivers serves as a survival mechanism for the species because an infant's safety depends on staying close to a caregiver. Therefore, it follows logically that an infant would quite naturally resist being separated from the parent figure who provides comfort and security. Sometime between six months and a year, separation and stranger anxieties begin to appear in many children because of their newly developed cognitive adeptness in visually distinguishing between familiar and unfamiliar faces. Coincidentally, many parents first begin to rely on occasional or regular child care at about this same time. We adults are able to think and talk about child care arrangements. We may have studied a substitute caregiver's references or investigated carefully a center's license to provide care, but a baby has no way of comprehending all this.

When a baby looks up and sees that her daddy is not in sight, she feels the same way she would feel if she suddenly realized she was alone in the middle of a big department store. The swarms of strangers hovering around trying to be helpful would, at first, only be more frightening. Amazingly, it is not uncommon for parents or child care workers to be heard chiding a crying baby, "Hush! There is no reason for you to cry." If I were riding in an airplane that made an unexpected landing, or if I were pushed out kicking and screaming and left in a strange land with strangers who did not speak my language, I might cry, too, as I watched the plane carrying my family fly away. When the parent is out of sight, the child is unable to realize that daddy is not gone forever.

The more positive experiences a baby has had with meeting new people, the less uncomfortable she will feel when she separates from parents or encounters strangers. In time, the baby develops a concrete understanding that strangers can be relied on to provide care and that after a while, parents reappear. Pushing the baby into frightening situations is not helpful, but avoiding encounters with strangers altogether is also counterproductive. Gently nudging the baby into pleasurable and trusting relationships with adults other than parents will assist her in developing confidence and an open, positive attitude toward the world.

HOW DO BABIES PERCEIVE THEMSELVES AND THEIR SURROUNDINGS?

In the first months of life, babies have not yet gained a mental conception of themselves as separate individuals. Their perception of their own existence is limited to that which they see, feel, taste, smell, and hear. They unconsciously perceive their surroundings as if they were the center of the universe, and the people and objects around them were extensions of their own existence. They make no distinction between their own physical being and the surroundings they perceive through their senses.

Caregivers take on a very important role in this context. Caring for a baby means that they literally become a part of that baby's life. Adults facilitate and guide older children whose interests are focused on each other and on their own activities as much as or more than on adults. In the first year of life however, infants focus an enormous quantity of their interest and energy on interacting with adult caregivers. They depend on adults for every aspect of physical care and

Some healthy, well-developing babies cry whenever an unfamiliar adult approaches them.

safety, as well as for entertainment and affection. Their interest in peers is purely **egocentric** (centered on one's own needs and desires). A seven-month-old will crawl onto a younger baby and casually grasp a handful of hair to feel and taste, then look quite puzzled by the sudden loud, piercing noises emitted by the little friend.

By rushing to rescue the younger baby and by **modeling** (demonstrating) appropriate behavior—softly stroking the offended baby's head while saying to the offender, "Gentle, gentle. Be gentle"—babies can eventually **internalize** (adopt as their own) more appropriate ways of behaving. Since the baby identifies so closely with the adult caregiver, the baby will automatically mimic behaviors of that adult. Caregivers who respond harshly or aggressively reinforce inappropriate behaviors in babies by modeling loud or rough interactions.

> *In each stage of child development . . . there is a central problem that has to be*
> *solved . . . if the child is to proceed with vigor and confidence to the next stage.*
>
> *Erik H. Erikson (1971)*

Some health, normal babies experience little stranger anxiety, and cope surprisingly well with separation from primary caregivers.

TODDLERS (12 MONTHS TO 3 YEARS)

Burton White (1975) has termed toddlers "a force to be reckoned with." Any parent or caregiver/ teacher who deals with toddlers probably knows exactly what he means. Young toddlers, the one-year-olds, are phenomenal human beings. For the first time in their lives, they have become upright bipeds like the rest of us. Also, for the first time, they do not depend on us to bring rattles or tacky squeak toys to them for entertainment. They can walk through, wriggle under, or climb over any obstacle a grownup can devise in order to get to the really interesting things that attract their curiosity. While the young toddler can be an adorable timid rabbit one moment, sucking a thumb while peeking from behind a well-worn but snuggly piece of blanket, she can in an instant raise the rafters, crumpled on the floor in a full-fledged tantrum.

CAN TODDLERS CONTROL THEIR FEELINGS AND ACTIONS?

Young toddlers are totally transparent in their feelings. They are openly affectionate, easily delighted by attention, and full of wonder about their surroundings. They also become confused, frustrated, and overwhelmed by their newfound freedom. One moment they are amazingly grown up and ready to take on the world; the next they regress into helpless clingy babies again. Their needs are simple. They want food, comfort, affection, approval, and to learn about the huge, booming, wide world around them. As babies, they still respond to their sensations of need by crying for caregivers, but as growing children, they also begin responding to their own desires by literally moving out into the environment to get what they want.

They use senses (touch, sight, smell, taste, and hearing) to explore the physical attributes of their environment, and both small and large muscles to practice physical skills. They still do not consciously plan or think about their actions much. They just act. If the toddler feels hungry and the box of cereal in the grocery cart with her looks delicious, she may just rip it open and have a snack, then look hurt when her parents seemed shocked by her behavior.

Safety is a major concern in the care of toddlers.

HOW AWARENESS OF CAUSE AND EFFECT DEVELOPS

Toddlers have made a huge cognitive leap since infancy in their ability to remember things and in their first crude ability to manipulate ideas mentally. Cause-and-effect relationships become a focal point for their learning. They are fascinated by light switches and will flip the light on and off many times, if they are allowed, alternately watching the switch and the light fixture and mentally connecting the cause-and-effect relationship between the two.

They also tirelessly explore cause-and-effect relationships in social interactions. The toddler will stick her little pointed index finger out to touch the electrical outlet (covered, of course, with a plastic safety cap) and look up at her caregiver/teacher expectantly as she patiently repeats for the hundredth time, "No, no. That's not for touching." Finally, the little girl will touch the outlet, shaking her head and repeating soberly, "No, no. No touch." She is preoccupied with connecting the cause-and-effect relationship between her action and the adult's words, and has totally missed the point that he would rather she did not touch the outlet. With just a bit more time and patience, she will be satiated in her curiosity about the cause-and-effect connection, will be able to remember the connection each time she sees an electrical outlet, and will probably be quite willing to respect her caregiver/teacher's rule.

TODDLERS NEED TO EXPLORE THEIR SURROUNDINGS

Healthy, well-developing toddlers have a curiosity that is boundless. Their desire to explore at times overshadows all other needs. A toddler who is totally immersed in the miseries of teething will stop crying when her mother carries her to the refrigerator and opens the freezer to get her frozen teething ring. For the moment, her pain is forgotten as she watches the frosty air roll out of the freezer and feels the brisk difference in temperature from this strange part of her environment she has never explored before.

Toddlers learn to walk because their fascination with this form of locomotion outweighs their fear of falling or being hurt. They move out into the environment, away from the security of caregivers, because the exhilaration of discovery causes them to throw caution to the wind. Babies might stay in the comfort of their mother's arms forever if it were not for the powerfully motivating activator we call curiosity that drives toddlers out into the scary but exciting world. Baby birds are comfortable, secure, safe, and well-fed in the nest. At some point, however, nature intends them to leap precariously into the air and to flap their little wings until they figure out how to fly—a frightening and exhilarating experience for babies, of course, but also a frightening and exhilarating experience for grown-up birds to watch.

SAFETY IS A MAJOR ISSUE IN TODDLER CARE

During toddlerhood, a child's motor development far outstrips her capacity to understand, remember, or abide by rules. Since she has not yet developed metacognition, she cannot look at a situation and then think about and plan for the potential consequences of her own behavior in that situation. Toddlers are still a bit unsteady in their walking, running, and climbing, and they are compelled to taste, feel, smell, and manipulate every interesting object or phenomenon they encounter. All this adds up to toddlers being in the most vulnerable period of their lives for accidents.

Unless toddlers are constantly and diligently supervised, they can inadvertently swallow objects and poisonous substances, fall off or bump into things, and touch things they should not

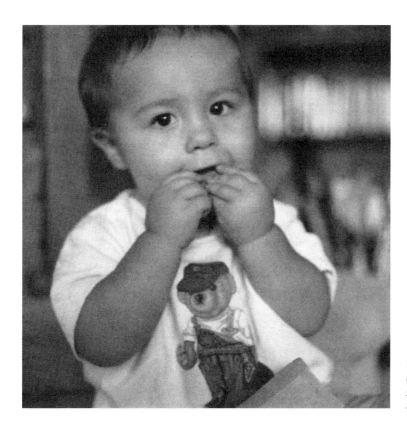

Toddlers may swallow objects or dangerous substances if they are not carefully supervised.

touch despite warnings. If crying is the first major area of potential confrontation between infants and adults, then keeping toddlers from harming themselves or the environment is surely the second big area of stress and difficulty for parents and caregivers.

In past years, parents often bragged that their toddler was so well behaved that the most expensive, fragile, or even dangerous bric-a-brac could be left on the coffee table and the baby would never so much as touch it. They sometimes accomplished that feat by slapping the baby's hand or saying "no" sharply whenever the child attempted to touch the forbidden items. These adults believed that by teaching the baby to be still and not touch anything, they were helping her become well disciplined and polite.

Information about the processes of cognitive development, generated by research over the past two decades, has changed this old perception. A delightful poster that is very popular among child care workers pictures a young toddler standing forlornly in a play pen. The caption reads, "What do you mean, 'Don't touch'? Touching is how I learn." In order to create a richly stimulating environment conducive to optimum development while at the same time protecting toddlers from unreasonable risk of harm, adults must set about "babyproofing" all accessible areas of children's environments as soon as they develop the motor skills to move about. (See Appendix C for additional resources.)

White (1975, 1995) theorized that the period from 10 months to three years is a critical period in the child's life for social, intellectual, and motor skill development. He also theorized that direct sensory exploration of the physical environment serves as a key requirement for optimum

Toddlers need safe, interesting things to explore.

development. In his view, keeping toddlers in play pens or restricted in environments that are "hands off," excessively tidy, not baby-proofed, or downright boring risks losing the child's most valuable opportunity for early learning.

THE KINDS OF SURROUNDINGS TODDLERS NEED

Toddlers thrive in settings that are made appropriate to their needs and abilities so that they can move about freely and safely, exploring and testing every aspect of their surroundings. Of course, they still need careful supervision, even in the most carefully planned environment, but they are provided a much more stimulating range for their play when swallowable objects, toxic plants and substances, sharp corners, and electrical cords are simply put out of their reach.

Rather than struggling to force toddlers to behave safely and appropriately, adults should simply change the child's environment to make interaction in it safe and appropriate. As toddlers become older and more compliant, sometime around their third birthday, toys with parts small enough to be swallowed, blunt scissors, water-based marking pens, and other materials requiring special care can be introduced. Gradually, as children are developmentally ready, they can then be gently but firmly guided to understand and follow appropriate safety rules.

CAN TODDLERS READ BODY LANGUAGE?

From birth, children respond to facial expression, tone of voice, and body movement. Long before a child understands language, she will react to cues such as the nonverbal body language, inflection, tone, and volume that is a part of an adult's speech.

Toddlers can be guided in new activities they can learn to do themselves.

Betty Jo, the lively young mother of 12-month-old Jeremy, comes to pick up her son from the family day home where he is cared for during the day. She chats with other parents picking up their children as she zips Jeremy into his snow suit. Jeremy makes a funny sound and his cheeks turn red as it dawns on Betty Jo that she will have to change his diaper.

Everyone downwind of Jeremy is, by this point, quite aware that the diaper is definitely more than just wet. As other parents chuckle, Betty Jo jokingly but energetically scolds Jeremy for being so rude after she has gone to all the trouble of bundling him up to go home. While the little boy clearly does not understand all her words, he unmistakably interprets her fake scowl and sharp tone to mean that she is angry with him. He turns his face away from her and sobs. Betty Jo is quite startled by his reaction. Since he did not know how to talk, she assumed he would not have any idea what she was saying.

The ability of very young children to make some sense of our feelings from our body language and tone of voice gives us an opportunity to communicate with them nonverbally. Before children have mastered **expressive language** (the ability to speak), they have begun to develop **receptive language** (the ability to understand language). Therefore, if we are honest and sincere in the words we speak to babies and toddlers, our body language will quite naturally convey our feelings and attitudes to the child. If we speak to the child for the benefit of other adults, as if the child were not really present or listening, we may miss an important opportunity to build communication with the child.

Adults can start from the very beginning speaking to babies as if they were (because they definitely are) worthwhile human beings. This has two important benefits for long-term child guidance. First, the child will learn early in life to pay attention to adults, since they seem to say what they mean and mean what they say. Second, adults have plenty of time to practice appropriate communication skills so that they will be prepared when the child really does have a command of language.

Using a kind facial expression and a caring tone of voice, an adult can speak reassuringly to a young toddler who resists going to sleep, "I know you would rather play with your toys, but it's time for nap now. Would you like me to rock you for a minute before you lie down?" Even though the child will not understand all the words, she will sense the adult's caring attitude. She will also have an opportunity to hear language and associate it with objects and events in day-to-day living.

HOW VERBAL COMMUNICATION BEGINS

Toddlers seem to explode into language. At a child's first birthday, she may only know words like "mama," "dada," and "baba" for bottle. Within a few months, the child may know many more single word labels plus a number of holophrases (phrases made of words that are joined like Siamese twins and used as if they were inseparable single words). "Gofieys" may mean, "Go to a fast food restaurant and get French fries." "Sousite" may mean, "Let's go outside to play." The child soon learns to mix and match words or holophrases to create two-word sentences. Soon, the child's speech begins to sound like abbreviated telegrams, including key words but leaving less critical words out: "Paw Paw doggy big!" "No touch daddy gwas [glasses]." By age three, the child's speech begins to sound surprisingly like our own (with a few quirks here and there): "My daddy goed to work an he gots a big office."

The child's language changes each day as she adds new vocabulary and new levels of expression and understanding. At birth, the child had no muscular control of her lips and tongue and no comprehension that language existed or had significance. In only three short years, she has learned how to create many different sounds with her lips, tongue, and vocal cords; amassed hundreds of words in her vocabulary; and grasped the basic syntax (structure) of her native language. Her language comprehension is complex but not at a conscious level. For example, she has simply absorbed an intuitive sense that the "s" sound on the end of a naming word means more than one, and that the "d" sound at the end of an action word means that the action has already happened.

WHAT KIND OF LANGUAGE EXPERIENCES ARE GOOD FOR TODDLERS?

Infants and children of all ages need to hear the rich, lyrical words of adult conversational speech, as well as the musical word patterns in rhymes, songs, and jingles. These kinds of language experiences especially enrich and stimulate language learning in toddlers. For maximum comprehension, however, the child must hear language that is very close to her own level of development. This language should be at or slightly ahead of the child's own level. For example, in developing music appreciation, young children are allowed to hear a wide range of classical, folk, and pop music for enrichment, but for learning actual singing, they are introduced to extremely simple songs like "Here We Go 'Round the Mulberry Bush."

If a baby's language development is still limited to the cooing and babbling stage, the adult can effectively communicate through facial expression, tone of voice, and body language. If the child is using single words, the adult can best achieve communication through holophrases ("All-gone") or two-word sentences ("More milk?").

Toddlers may hear and comprehend only a few words in sentences that are above their comprehension. Often, they catch a few accentuated or familiar words from the beginning or from the end of the adult's speech. The toddler may innocently respond to the words "You . . . candy . . . mouth" from the adult's complicated sentence, "You need to make very sure you don't put that whole big piece of candy into your mouth." To maximize the toddler's comprehension of important communication, choose key words, speak slowly and clearly, and use facial expression and body gestures to emphasize your meaning.

We might use more elaborate enrichment language to say to a toddler, "I believe you need to have your shoe lace tied. It could make you trip and fall down." But, if a response is needed from the child, bend down, take the child's hand, deliberately establish eye contact, and then pat the floor expectantly as you articulate carefully, "Sit, please." We can then reinforce the child's cooperativeness the instant she looks as if she will comply by smiling warmly and saying, "Thank you!"

STRANGER ANXIETY

Toddlers show a wide range of reactions to strangers, depending on their own experiences and temperament. Some children go through a distinct phase in which they are terrified of strangers. When confronted by a stranger (or even a less familiar caregiver), many toddlers cling to their parent's or caregiver's clothing, hide their faces, and cry. Other children, especially those who have had broad exposure to many friendly adults since infancy, may show curiosity about new adults, attempt to make friends, and never give any indication of separation or stranger anxiety. To experience stranger anxiety, the child must be able to distinguish familiar from unfamiliar faces, which usually happens around six or seven months of age.

SEPARATION ANXIETY

Stranger anxiety is often coupled with separation anxiety, the distress children show when they cry on separation from a parent or primary caregiver. Separation anxiety can be seen at any time from infancy through preschool, but it is usually most pronounced in the second year of life.

HOW CAN I MAKE FRIENDS WITH A SHY TODDLER?

In order to establish a relationship with a "shy" toddler, it is essential to understand and respect that child's discomfort in interacting with a new adult. Rather than approaching the child directly with a big smile and immediately attempting to touch or hold the child, avoid eye contact with the child at first. Speak quietly and pleasantly with others around the child while moving a bit closer to the child. If the child is standing or sitting on the floor, sit nearby to be at the eye level of the child. Glance briefly in the child's direction occasionally to see if she is evidencing curiosity or stress at your presence. Smile, but avoid looking directly into the child's eyes until you are confident she feels comfortable with your presence.

After allowing the toddler plenty of time to stare at you, it may be helpful to touch the child's hand casually for a moment while glancing briefly in her direction with a smile. Eventually, she will probably indicate her willingness to make friends and allow eye contact. At this point, a diversion in the form of a game or toy may be a perfect way to cement the budding adult-child

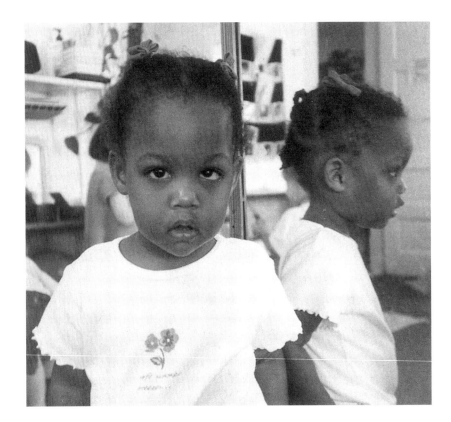

"I need safe, interesting things to explore by looking."

relationship. In a child care center, the teacher may be able, at this point, to interest the toddler in petting the class bunny rabbit, looking at a book, or watching the teacher make a puppet tell jokes and eat pretend cookies. If no toys are available, sing a song, make up a rhyme, or talk about the child's clothing: "Look at those blue sneakers. You can run really fast in those." An effective diversion at this point will hold the child's interest but not require a great deal of sustained eye contact or active response from her.

WHY ARE TODDLERS SO POSSESSIVE?

Young toddlers callously step on each other to get what they want, take toys from each other, and scramble to grab food. Two-year-olds walk into their child care center in the morning, look suspiciously at their peers, tighten their grip on dad's hand, and announce defiantly, "My daddy!" Very young children's behavior is not particularly civilized or polite because they do not yet have a well-developed ability to put themselves in the place of others. Some toddlers who have observed and experienced a great deal of **empathy** (kindness) may show concern for others, but their way of expressing concern is totally egocentric. For example, the toddler may try to give her pacifier or teddy bear to an adult who is crying.

There is little to say about toddlers and sharing except that it cannot be expected of them. Instead of attempting to coerce toddlers into behaving in a way that is developmentally incompatible, adults can rearrange the environment, change the routines, or increase their supervision to protect toddlers from inadvertent rough or rude treatment by their peers. In time, children develop the ability to recognize that other people have feelings and rights, and they develop the ability to imagine how others would feel if they were treated a certain way. Then it will be possible to teach them manners. Until then, setting a good example and tactfully but assertively protecting children's (and others') rights are all that adults can do. Having a wide variety of choices available to toddlers will ease this problem. It will also help to have multiples of the most popular objects such as shovels, balls, and dolls.

WHY DO SOME TODDLERS BECOME SO ATTACHED TO SECURITY BLANKETS, PACIFIERS, AND SO FORTH?

Toddlers use many "crutches" to help them cope with being very little and very powerless in a big, fast, scary world. Some adults call toddlers' worn blankets, tattered stuffed animals, pacifiers, or whatever else they hold onto, the child's "cuddlies." Child psychologists call them objects for "cyclical self-stimulation." Caregivers are sometimes tempted to just call them nuisances. Whatever they are called, when they are lost, they can cause the toddler's emotional world to come crashing down around her. As strongly as children are attached to these comfort items, they generally begin to lose interest in them by the time they turn three. Some preschoolers hang onto

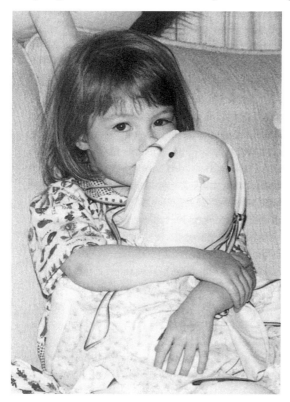

Some toddlers rely on a special cuddly toy to help them cope with the big, confusing, overwhelming world around them.

their cuddlies a while longer, but for many of them, their attachment at this point is more habit than emotional need.

In many primitive cultures, children stay in physical contact with their mothers' bodies much of the time during their first three years of life. In modern industrialized societies, children are separated from their mothers at birth to be placed in a hospital nursery, put to sleep in a separate bed (enclosed with bars) in a separate room at home, and buckled into high chairs and car seats. It is not surprising then that many babies improvise "caregiver replacements" to cling to for a while and to help them cope (nipple-shaped objects to suck and soft, warm, fuzzy, or silky objects to hold). The child's need for these objects should be respected, although she can be nudged gently to do without them for gradually increasing periods of time when they have become little more than habit.

Children especially need to be helped to cope without having a pacifier or thumb "plugged in" too much of their day. It is very difficult for toddlers to practice language with their mouths immobilized. It is equally important, on the other hand, to foster language development early in life by allowing infants plenty of sucking to develop the mouth, lip, and tongue muscles necessary for later speech. Since bottle feeding requires less muscular effort and coordination to produce milk than breastfeeding, many babies benefit emotionally and physically from the availability of nonnutritive sucking. Pacifiers are healthier for teeth and thumbs, and usually easier to wean children from than thumbs.

Although some authorities still encourage mothers to wean babies from breast or bottle at about 10 months of age, weaning in the first year of life will often cause the child to seek some form of replacement sucking or self-stimulation. We can take good advice from our grandmothers who have been saying for generations, "If you baby a baby when he's a baby, you won't have to baby him all the rest of his life."

WHY ARE TODDLERS STUBBORN ONE MINUTE, THEN CLINGY THE NEXT?

Erikson (1982) focused on the development of autonomy (self-sufficiency) as the second step in his eight stages of **social** and **emotional** (affective) **growth**. After trust has been established in infancy, toddlers become immersed in the conflict between autonomy and shame and doubt. Toddlers are able for the first time to do many things that adults consider naughty or destructive. For the first time, adults hold the child responsible for bodily elimination and controlling impulses. The child is torn between assertively resisting adult guidance and feeling fearful and ashamed for getting into trouble so often. She feels she can conquer the world with her new capabilities, but she is constantly getting into scrapes, making messes, and needing adult help and reassurance.

Adults can help toddlers through this period by being very supportive of the child's need to break away from infancy. In order to foster autonomy, we should not do anything for the toddler that she could be helped to do for herself. Toddlers can learn to peel their own bananas for snack, pull up their own socks once the adult gets it started, and choose their own clothing from two appropriate choices. At home, they can be allowed to stand on a chair at the sink to wash unbreakable dishes (although mom or dad will undoubtedly have to rewash them later for sanitary reasons). They can even be given a small bucket with a little water, a squirt of liquid soap, and a small piece of sponge or rag to help wash the car or the windows. In early childhood programs, children can be provided small sponges for table wiping, small brooms for sweeping, and other utensils to help maintain the classroom.

Toddlers are interested in having the freedom and independence to be involved in the processes of grown-up activities. They are not at all interested in achieving specific end products to those processes, and are confused and discouraged by adult concern over end products or results rather than processes. Adults usually do things the most expedient way to get the result that they want. Toddlers spend long periods of time in the process of dipping, pouring, and splashing dishes in soapy water, but lose interest before the dishes are actually rinsed and dried. Sensitive adults will foster the child's involvement in independent processes but wait until the child is older to expect results. They will redirect unacceptable behavior rather than make the child feel inadequate or naughty for following her curiosity and desire to attempt things she sees adults doing.

ARE TODDLERS AWARE OF THEMSELVES?

When babies look in a mirror, they do not necessarily recognize that the image reflected there is their own. At some point in toddlerhood, they finally discover that the face in the mirror is theirs. If they see an unexpected smudge on the nose in the mirror, they touch their own nose to find out what is there. A younger child will only touch the mirror. Toddlers who are not yet aware of their own separate identity seem to think that they cannot be seen by anyone if their own eyes are closed. A toddler being reprimanded for misbehavior may cover her eyes, assuming (because of her egocentricity) that the adults will not be able to see her since she cannot see them.

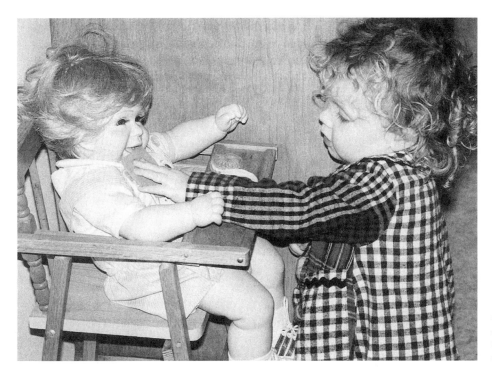

Toddlers try to imitate the actions and events they see around them.

WHY DO TODDLERS GET SO EXCITED AND HAPPY WHEN THEY IMITATE EACH OTHER?

Toddlers who have just begun to get a sense of their separateness tend to be very "full of themselves." If a caregiver gathers two-year-olds around him to read a storybook, she will often discover that they are more entertained by each other than by the book. They giggle and poke each other, and inevitably one toddler will begin a gloriously spontaneous action like vigorously shaking her head until her hair stands out all around her head. In an instant, this action spreads like a contagion, leaving the poor adult sitting rather foolishly, book in hand, watching a band of toddlers laughing uproariously as they shake their heads (and perhaps wiggle their bodies and stamp their feet for good measure).

As toddlers begin to recognize their existence as a separate person like the people they see around them, they begin to develop a **concept** (or picture) of who they are based on feedback, primarily from the adults around them. Sometimes, adults make casual comments that are very cutting such as "You are as fat as a pig." "Why are you always so mean?" "I think you like to make me mad", things we would probably hesitate to say to another adult. Sometimes, these hurtful comments come from siblings or other children. Toddlers are very naive. They tend to believe what we tell them about themselves through our actions and words. As an older toddler's self-image begins to take shape, we can help her develop a healthy and confident view of herself by being very careful about what we say to her (and what we allow other children to say to her). "What a big girl you are." "Everybody makes mistakes sometime." "I really like your smile." "I didn't like the hitting, but I will always like you." The toddler's budding self-esteem will serve as a foundation for her growth as a confident, competent, cooperative, and productive human being.

COMPETENT THREE-YEAR-OLDS ARE . . .

- self-confident and trusting.
- intellectually inquisitive.
- able to use language to communicate.
- physically and mentally healthy.
- able to relate well to others.
- empathic toward others.

Given consistently nurturing and responsive care, healthy babies develop a high level of "competence" by age three. Competent preschoolers are much more likely to be successful and well adjusted in school and throughout life.

Carnegie Corporation of New York. (1994). *Starting points: Meeting the needs of our youngest children—The report of the Carnegie Task Force on Meeting the Needs of Young Children.* Waldorf, MD: Carnegie Corporation of New York.

ADLERIAN OVERVIEW OF BIRTH ORDER CHARACTERISTICS

Adapted from a Chart Developed by Henry T. Stein, Ph.D.

POSITION	*CHILD'S CHARACTERISTICS*
ONLY	Likes being the center of adult attention. Often has difficulty sharing with siblings and peers. Prefers adult company and uses adult language.
OLDEST	May become authoritarian or strict. Feels power is his right. Can become helpful if encouraged. May turn to father after birth of next child.
SECOND	Is more competitive, wants to overtake older child. May become a rebel or try to outdo everyone. Competition can deteriorate into rivalry.
MIDDLE	May be even-tempered, "take it or leave it" attitude. May have trouble finding a place or become a fighter of injustice.
YOUNGEST	Wants to be bigger than the others. May have huge plans that never work out. Can stay the "baby." Frequently spoiled.
TWIN	Can have identity problems. Stronger one may become the leader.
ADOPTED CHILD	Child may become very spoiled and demanding. Eventually, the child may resent or idealize the biological parents.

According to Stein, simplified charts like this one are appealing because they help explain behavior. He emphasizes, however, that they do not do justice to Adler's principle of the uniqueness of each individual (http://www.pir.org/main2/John_Henry_Stein.html). **These concepts should only be used to provide insight, never to label or stereotype!** Additionally, Adler speculated that birth order differences would begin to disappear when child-rearing became less competitive and autocratic, and more cooperative and democratic.

To learn more, read:

Stein, H. (1988). Twelve stages of creative Adlerian psychotherapy. *Individual Psychology, 44,* 138–143.

Ernst, C., & Angst, J. (1983). *Birth order. Its influence on personality.* Berlin, Germany: Springer.

Sulloway, F. J. (1995). Birth order and evolutionary psychology: A meta-analytic overview. *Psychological Inquiry, 6*(1), 75–80.

Sulloway, F. J. (1997). *Born to rebel: Birth order, family dynamics, and creative lives.* New York: Pantheon.

Lansky, V. (1990). *Welcoming your second baby.* Minnetonka, MN: Book Peddlers.

PRESCHOOLERS (3 TO 5 YEARS)

CAN PRESCHOOLERS MAKE PLANS AND DECISIONS?

Toddlers are only able to conceive of objects in terms of the way those objects actually feel, look, taste, smell, or sound. Preschoolers have a new mental ability. They can conceive of objects both in terms of what they are perceptually and what they stand for symbolically. For example, a toddler sees a block only as something to bite, hit, throw, or stack. The preschooler can see the block both as a physical object and as a "pretend" bar of soap to bathe a doll, or a "pretend" car to zoom around the floor. The block can stand as a symbol for something else.

Preschoolers also become more consciously aware of their own interests and intentions. They look over the toys that are available to them and make intentional choices. While toddlers function primarily by impulse, playing with whatever toy catches their eye for the moment, preschoolers are more inclined to select an activity very carefully and then stay with it longer, sometimes even coming back to play the same game day after day until they finally become bored with it.

Older preschoolers can verbalize what and how they want to play. For example, they may say, "Let's play like this is our house and you are the daddy and he is the baby and that box is the baby bed." They can become very frustrated or angry if things do not turn out the way they expect. Preschoolers often squabble over their conflicting perceptions of how their play should proceed: "I don't want to be the baby. I want to play Masters of the Universe!"

Preschoolers become fascinated with toys that require thinking that is more complicated. The begin to anticipate cause and effect. "I wonder what would happen if I did it this way?"

Adults can help preschoolers during this stage by focusing the children's attention on the probable consequences of their actions. Questions should never be used as verbal battering rams, but adults can gently nudge cause-and-effect thinking by asking, "What might happen if someone ran out into the street without looking?" "Hmmm, I wonder what could happen if you paint without putting a smock on over your clothes?" "How would your friend feel if she never got a turn to be the pretend mommy?" Preschoolers are just beginning to be able to manipulate ideas in their heads, and eventually can learn to weigh consequences and make appropriate decisions before acting.

MEETING PRESCHOOLERS NEEDS FOR COMMUNICATION

Because preschoolers have an increasing command of their native language, they benefit from talking about their own actions and events that have taken place or will take place in their lives. Before an event takes place, they can be helped to understand that event by parents or teachers talking about it in advance in very simple, concrete terms. Parents often try to shield preschoolers from adult concerns by not talking directly to their children about sensitive issues.

A three-year-old, whose parents often affectionately called her "our sweet baby girl," cried hysterically when an aunt said, "I hear there's going to be a new baby at your house." She had overheard her parents saying that they thought it best for her not to know yet that there was going to be a new baby. She knew, of course, that when they got a new car, the old car vanished, and when they got a new refrigerator, the old one was hauled away, and when she got new shoes, the old ones were dropped unceremoniously into the trash can. She could only guess what happened to little girls who she imagined were so naughty that their parents decided to get "a new one."

A four-year-old boy developed nightmares and bed wetting after he heard family members crying and talking in somber but hushed tones about how his expectant mother had lost the baby she was carrying. His problem behaviors increased until a psychologist was consulted and discovered that the little boy had been nervously searching in closets and under beds to find the lost baby. He knew that those were places to look when you lost something. He worried that his parents might lose him too!

COMMUNICATING SUCCESSFULLY WITH PRESCHOOLERS

By talking to preschoolers in honest but simplified terms, we can help them understand and deal with events. We cannot take for granted that just because something is obvious to us it will be obvious to young children. There are many things about this world that preschoolers simply do not know yet. A caregiver can use very simple but clear sentences to say, "Marcus, your dad just called on the telephone. He will be late picking you up today. His car won't go so he has to get it fixed. It may be dark when he gets here, but it's okay. I will stay with you. We'll get some cheese and crackers and apple juice and play until he comes." Sometimes, adults become so preoccupied with their own problems and plans that they forget to tell children what will happen to them. Modeling through dramatic play can help children visualize an expected behavior. Talking through a puppet is a nonthreatening way to get a point across or model appropriate language.

A parent can prevent potential problems by anticipating and planning for them. Being especially careful not to communicate negative expectations, the parent could say, "Shelley, your friend Jamie will be here soon. Sometimes when she is here it is hard for you to share your favorite toys. That makes Jamie feel sad. Would you like to choose the toys you want to share and put them in this cardboard box? We can take the toys you choose into the back yard, then Jamie will know which toys you want to share and play with." By helping the child positively think through this potential problem before it happens, the child may be able to consciously behave in such a way as to avoid the conflict before it erupts. While a child is angry and upset, it is unlikely that she will be able to listen to logic or behave rationally.

TEACHING PRESCHOOLERS TO USE WORDS TO EXPRESS THEIR FEELINGS

Democratic societies create laws allowing citizens to use physical force only as a last resort when other reasonable steps to defend themselves have failed. Law enforcement officials are empowered to use physical force—not to hurt, punish, or humiliate people—to protect people and property. In the child's world, this same principle should apply. Children prepare to participate as good citizens in society by learning the skills needed for peaceful conflict resolution. Adults should physically restrain a child only when absolutely necessary to prevent the child from hurting herself or others.

Preschoolers can be guided firmly to use words to get a point across rather than relying on kicking, scratching, and hair pulling. They can be helped to practice appropriate words and allowed to express strong emotions, even anger, through their words. When a preschooler runs to tell parents or teachers about another child's action, instead of being chided for "tattling," the child can be encouraged to talk to the other child: "Did you tell Kirin that it was your turn for the swing? Would you like me to go with you to talk to her?"

Adults sometimes try to squelch children's negative feelings. We say things to quiet children like, "Don't cry." "Don't make a fuss." "She didn't really mean to hit you." Maybe the other child really did mean to hit. A child deserves to express her feelings in an honest but respectful way: "I feel angry. I don't like it when you push me off the swing." Preschoolers especially need to be allowed to express their feelings. They can learn that it is okay to feel angry and it is okay to say so, but it is not okay to lash out in a way that verbally attacks or physically hurts others.

Preschoolers can also be helped to verbalize their feelings by having adults **mirror** (reflect) those feelings. Young children may not realize that they are cranky because they are hot and tired or cold and hungry. Adults can put words to those feelings and assist preschoolers in learning to identify and express what they feel inside by saying, "Brrr, I feel cold! Look at the chill bumps on my arm. Are you cold? Let me feel how cold your hands are."

This mirroring of feelings is called **active listening** (repeating what you understood the child to mean). The adult refrains from lecturing, instructing, commanding, or telling. Instead, she listens and sincerely reflects or restates what she thinks the child is feeling at the moment. In active listening (a useful communication tool for any age), the adult says things such as, "It sounds like you are really feeling angry with Tommy." "In other words, what you are saying is that you feel hurt and sad when you don't get to play." "You seem pretty frightened when the other children pretend to be monsters." The point of active listening is not to solve the child's problem for her, but only to let her know that she has been heard and to give her a chance to talk about, think about, and confront her own feelings.

DOES STRESS STRAIN YOUR PATIENCE WITH CHILDREN?

Perfectionism can be a stress trap for educators and parents. Children have bad days. Adults have bad days. In an environment that is basically nurturing and respectful, children learn to deal with occasional shortcomings in their teachers and parents. Adults must learn to cope with their own lapses in meeting the standards they have set for themselves. They must not shrug their shoulders and give up, but admit and accept that they "blew it" and consciously take steps to do better tomorrow. It is helpful to say to the child, "I made a mistake. It's not okay to shout angry things at others. I was wrong. I'm going to really try to remember to talk calmly about problems so we can solve them the right way."

The need to always be in control can also be a stress trap. Teaching and learning is an inter-active process. In the learning-centered environment, there is a great deal of give and take. Sensitive, responsive adults are willing to put aside planned activities when they observe that children are simply not interested or ready for them. Nurturing adults offer choices within rea-sonable limits, allowing children to feel control in choosing their preferences. It is not a sign of failure or weakness for an adult to admit that he or she was wrong and the child was right in a given situation. Children who listen, question, and speak up for themselves are better suited to thrive in today's world than blindly obedient children who would never question authority.

People pleasing is another potential stress trap. Codependent people depend on other peo-ple's opinion of them for their own self-esteem. They have an impaired sense of their own worth and spend their lives trying to please others. Remember, you can't please everybody all the time. Work on defining and trusting your own philosophy and values. Learn to listen to your own conscience and trust yourself. Force yourself to use "I messages" to express your feelings to others, and remember to take good care of yourself. You can't really nurture chil-dren if you allow yourself to become exhausted trying to please others. Take proactive steps to avoid physical, mental, and emotional exhaustion.

Self-doubt clouds judgment and increases stress. Avoid comparing yourself to others. Set your own standards and work every day to achieve them. Be a life-long learner. Open your mind and take advantage of books and other resources to expand your skills and confidence. Learn to trust your judgment. If you make mistakes, learn from them and move on. Don't be afraid to take reasonable risks. Remember, nothing ventured, nothing gained. When others compli-ment your accomplishments, just say thank you rather than explaining that what you did was not really very good. It's okay to feel proud of your own achievements. It's most important that you feel good yourself about what you've done, not that others notice or approve of your ac-complishment. Doubt and shame get in the way of being a responsive, nurturing caregiver.

To learn more, read:

Thurman, C., Meier, P., Flournoy, R., Hawkins, D., & Minirth, F. B. (Eds.) (1997). *Beating burnout: Balanced living for busy people: How to beat burnout, before burnout beats you.* New York: Arrowood Press.

Reinhold, B. B. (1997). *Toxic work: How to overcome stress, overload, and burnout and revital-ize your career.* New York: Dutton/Plume.

Hull, R. (2002). *Drive yourself happy: A motor-vational maintenance manual for maneuvering through life.* Canada: Cypress House Nonfiction.

Moran, V. (2002). *Fit from within: 101 ways to change your body and your life.* New York: Contemporary Books/McGraw-Hill.

Carlson, R. (1997). *Don't sweat the small stuff . . . and it's all small stuff: Simple ways to keep the little things from taking over your life.* New York: Hyperion.

American Institute of Stress, http://www.stress.org/
Centers for Disease Control, http://www.cdc.gov/
Healthy People, http://www.healthypeople.gov/
Stress Busters, http://www.stressrelease.com/
Stress Management Through Humor, http://www.stressed.com/

FRIENDSHIPS ARE IMPORTANT TO PRESCHOOLERS

Babies and toddlers are very curious about other children but are most concerned about the adults in their lives. Preschoolers, on the other hand, begin to be interested in their relationships with other children. Throughout the rest of childhood, they will rely more and more on their friendships with peers and less and less on their attachment to adults. Between three and five, children need to learn how to be a friend and how to have friends, a very important kind of learning for the child's long-term social and emotional adjustment in life (Corsaro, 1981).

This can be a very trying stage for adults. Children are elated when they feel liked by peers and emotionally crushed when they imagine that no other child in the whole world wants to play with them. Although some children quickly find a best friend or group of friends whom they get along with very well, other children experience a daily emotional roller coaster as they struggle to establish friendships and deal with peers who barter, "I'll be your best friend if you give me your piece of chocolate cake." Paley (1992) suggests creating a class rule that requires inclusion: "You can't say you can't play."

Some preschoolers become very cliquish as they decide who is or is not a friend. They say things like, "You can't be our friend because you don't have a football shirt on." "We don't want you to play because you're a boy." "You draw scribble-scrabble so you can't color in our color book." Adults can feel very frustrated trying to decide when or how to intervene in these troublesome and hurtful interactions. Children need proactive guidance, however, to learn to treat others the way they want to be treated. Cruelty cannot be tolerated.

Friendship becomes an important part of the day-to-day lives of preschoolers.

Some preschoolers may still rely on sucking their thumbs from time to time, but it has usually become more of a comfortable habit than a coping mechanism.

HOW DO PRESCHOOLERS LEARN TO ACCEPT RESPONSIBILITY?

Erikson (1963) focused on the need of four- and five-year-olds to resolve the emotional conflict of initiative versus guilt. Preschoolers are struggling to become independent of adult caregivers and to find their own limits. Still, however, they want to please adults and feel very guilty when they disappoint or anger parents and teachers. An excessive amount of guilt causes discomfort, which the child may relieve by withdrawing from any situation that involves a risk of failure, or by adopting a rebellious "tough guy" facade and appearing to be immune to guilt.

To develop initiative, children must be encouraged to achieve independence from adults. Instead of doing things for preschoolers, adults must tactfully make it possible for the children to do things for themselves. Adults can simplify tasks and then teach simple skills like how to refill the gerbil's water bottle, how to cut safely with a blunt knife, how to clip paper to an easel with clothespins, and how to get a jacket zipper started.

ALLOW PRESCHOOLERS TO DO THINGS THAT ARE DIFFICULT

Preschoolers relish the opportunity to be in charge of their own environment. They make many mistakes and often forget to carry out tasks they have agreed to perform. Adults can respond best by remembering that the process of learning is much more important for preschoolers than the end products resulting from their efforts. Some adults become perfectionists about tasks and say, "It's easier for me to do it myself than to hassle with the kids trying to do it." It may be easier, but it definitely is not better for children who need encouragement and success in accepting and carrying out responsibilities.

With a great deal of practice, encouragement, and patient teaching (one tiny step at a time), preschoolers can learn to carry out fairly complex tasks responsibly and well. They will feel so confident about their accomplishments that they will eagerly show initiative (inner drive) in tackling new tasks or projects without having to be prodded or coerced every step of the way like a child who has fallen prey to feelings of guilt.

HELPING PRESCHOOLERS FOLLOW RULES

Preschoolers are ready for simplistic rules such as "Be kind! Wait until it's your turn to go down the slide." "Be safe! Stop at the gate so a grown-up can walk with you across the street." "Be neat! Use a sponge to wipe up the tempera paint that has spilled." Preschoolers are **preoperational** (in Piaget's terms) so they perceive rules in a superficial way. They follow rules more to please adults than because they comprehend the relationship between actions and possible consequences. Preschoolers still must be supervised closely because they are not yet able to follow rules consistently. In their play, they make up rules on a whim and then break the rules they have made with total abandon when a rule no longer suits them.

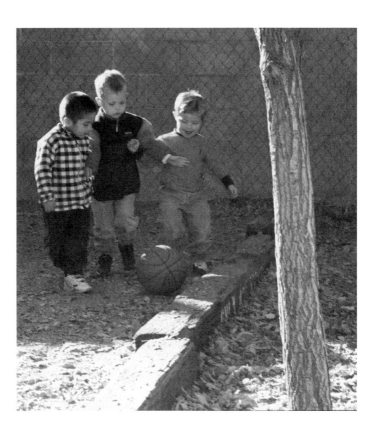

Overwhelming preschoolers with picky or complex rules will alienate them and trivialize the whole idea of following rules.

They begin to make sense intuitively of adult expectations and anticipate what will or will not be allowed in various situations. They tell each other, "Oh! You're gonna get in trouble." They begin to enforce rules on each other, "You didn't flush. I'm gonna tell on you." Adults can redirect this sudden enthusiasm for rules by setting a good example in their own respectful enforcement of rules. If adults are punitive and critical, and seem eager to "catch" wrongdoers, children will imitate that. If adults remind children of rules in an assertive but polite tone and then help them comply, children will imitate that, too.

Adults can maintain children's interest in rules by making very few rules but making sure that children know and respect the rules that are given. Rules always mean more to children if they played an active role in developing them and in deciding on logical consequences that should be enforced when the rules are broken. Overwhelming preschoolers with picky rules will alienate them and trivialize the whole idea of following rules. Children's perception of the value and importance of rules can be greatly enhanced when they are allowed to be part of the rule-making process. At group or circle time in a group setting, or in a family council meeting at home, children can be invited to think of new rules to solve simple problems like pushing and shoving or taking other people's things without asking. Also, adults can help children by patiently explaining the reasons for rules rather than just saying, "It's a rule because I say so." Understanding the reasons for rules helps children develop moral values (see the section on moral development in Chapter 3).

Stating rules—"No one is allowed to climb on that fence!" —and then proceeding to ignore children who climb on the fence will convince children that grown-ups do not really mean the things they say and rules are not really to be followed. It is important to remember that following rules is not only to be "kind, safe, and neat" today, but also to develop habits that will result in the child obeying laws as an adolescent and as an adult.

HOW DO PRESCHOOLERS DEVELOP A POSITIVE SENSE OF SELF?

Although the child's self-esteem (or lack of it) has been developing unconsciously since birth, preschool-aged children begin to develop a clear, conscious idea of who and what they are. Self-esteem and self-concept are two closely related concepts. **Self-concept** is one's idea or image of oneself. **Self-esteem** means that one's image of oneself includes a sense of being worthwhile and valuable. Children's ideas about themselves come from others around them, particularly from parents (Coopersmith, 1967; Cotton, 1984). As preschoolers become more adept at language, they also become more susceptible to the opinions of teachers, peers, and others outside the home.

Preschoolers become increasingly aware of their own identity in terms of larger groupings within society. The child may, for the first time, become aware of her ethnicity. Self-esteem can grow from pride in one's ethnic, regional, and religious heritage. Sadly, exposure to prejudice devastates self-esteem, and creates a cycle of prejudice and low self-esteem since low self-esteem is one of the causes of prejudice in the first place (Bagley et al., 1979). Every child deserves to know that she is special, but, of course, no more special than anyone else!

Preschoolers also become aware, for the first time, that their gender is fixed for life; girls will grow to be women and boys will grow to be men. Toddlers may distinguish between girls and boys or mommies and daddies, but they think they can turn into the opposite sex simply by wearing different clothing. Preschoolers identify with their own gender and may begin playing only with boys or only with girls.

Parents worry about their physically active daughters who prefer playing with the boys or their quiet, sensitive sons who prefer playing with the girls. Preschoolers worry about playing with toys that their friends consider to be "girl toys" or "boy toys." Preschool teachers often worry about making sure boys feel okay about playing in the housekeeping center with dolls and dressups and girls feel okay about playing in the block center with trucks and cars so that all the children will have well-rounded educational experiences. Everyone worries, but children generally persist in play that reflects the real world as they know it. If they see daddy having a good time feeding the baby and cooking, little boys will probably play house more comfortably than if they have only seen women doing these things. The same is true for little girls who have seen their mothers repair a leaky pipe or wear a police officer's uniform.

SHOULD CHILDREN BE ENCOURAGED TO COMPETE?

Another factor that affects preschoolers' development of self-concept and self-esteem is competitiveness. Preschoolers have become aware of themselves in comparison to others, so competitiveness reaches a peak during the preschool years (Stott & Ball, 1957). It can be very tempting for adults to exploit that tendency by saying things like, "Whoever can be the quietest at naptime will get a special treat." "The one who puts away toys the fastest will get to be first in line to go outside." "See if you can get dressed faster than your brother."

These challenges may strongly motivate some children to behave as the adult wishes, but the competition also stimulates friction rather than cooperation among children. Additionally, whenever there are winners, by definition, there will be losers. Winners may feel stressed and compulsive about continuing to win, and losers may feel more and more inadequate.

A more appropriate strategy to motivate desired behavior is to encourage children to work together as teams to accomplish tasks. Ideally, a classroom is a **community of learners** who share ideas, talk about and solve problems together, help each other, and cooperate as a team to clean up the classroom so that everyone can have more time for the next activity. In a true community of learners, children see themselves as valued members of an inclusive team.

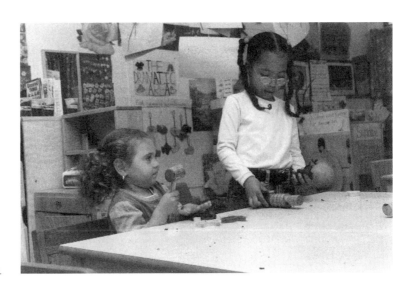

Every individual preschooler can be helped to appreciate her own special talents.

EARLY SCHOOL-AGERS (5 TO 8 YEARS)

Five- through eight-year-old children are very different from younger children, not only because of their gap-toothed smiles and taller bodies, but also because their thinking and language skills are different.

WHY EARLY SCHOOL-AGERS ASK SO MANY QUESTIONS

As school-agers become more aware of the world around them, they want to know a simple answer to every puzzling phenomenon encountered. Preschoolers physically explore things that puzzle them such as "Do rocks always sink in water?" "What's inside my toy car?" "How high will a swing go?" They ask simple, concrete questions about things around them like "What's this?" "What's that?" "What's your name?" Early school-agers question everything, and often ask questions that are really hard to answer, for example, "Why can't I have pizza for breakfast?" "What if gravity stopped and everything flew off the earth?" "Why do things look small when they're far away?" "Why did Grandma die?" "What makes the car go?"

Early school-age children are less gullible than preschoolers. They are quick to see discrepancies in adult actions: "You said that nobody could eat or drink unless they sat down at the table. You're somebody and you're drinking coffee." Preschoolers believe just about anything you tell them, but early school-agers become more critical. For example, if you say, "You can't eat candy because it is not good for your teeth," a preschooler might protest and beg, but a school-ager will think about that explanation logically and answer with her own rationale, "Okay, then I'll brush my teeth after I eat the candy." After the early school-ager has asked a persistent series of logical why or why-not questions, parents and teachers often find themselves snapping with exasperation, "Because I said so!" Of course, this is the phrase we hated to hear as children and promised we would never say when we grew up.

WHY DO THEY GET SO ANGRY IF THEY DO NOT ALWAYS WIN?

Early school-agers make observations and judgments about everything around them. Because of their immaturity, however, their judgment is limited to a simplistic, good-or-bad, win-or-lose view of the world. Naturally, they begin to compare themselves to others. Competition rears its ugly head as children struggle to best each other. They constantly fight over who likes whom best. Adults sometimes throw fuel onto this fire by encouraging competition. For example, teachers say, "Let's see who can be first to get their table clean." "The quietest person will get to go first." "I will put gold stars on the very best papers and put them on the bulletin board for parents night." This tactic is tempting because early school-agers will practically trample each other to be first or best at anything. However, we should find ways instead to help children get along and cooperate more rather than less. Learning to be a collaborative team member is an important prosocial skill for children to learn during these years. In early childhood, competition should be focused on improving oneself, not on "beating" others.

Why do they call each other names and say such hurtful things? Early school-agers have gained skill in expressing themselves verbally. They use more descriptive words to express their anger, frustration, or jealousy than preschoolers. Preschoolers simply shove or hit someone who upsets them, or bluster, "You're a pooh-pooh head an' I hate you." School-agers are more precise in their words, "Why do you act so bossy? You're not my mother." Their responses become more rational and logical. Angry words hurled at early school-agers can wound them deeply, though, so it is important to help them think about the effects their words have on others. Effectively expressing negative feelings in words is an important part of learning to communicate effectively, but cruel or demeaning taunts or epithets must never be allowed.

HOW CAN I EARN THE RESPECT OF SCHOOL-AGERS?

Early school-agers can be intimidating to adults. Younger children who misbehave can be picked up and carried (kicking and screaming) away from a problem situation. School-agers are becoming too large. They can no longer by controlled by physical restraint. We must be able to rely on the child's inner control.

Parents who used spanking to control younger children discover school-age children may be so emotionally immune to being hit that by this age they only respond with apathy. Or, they may be so angered by being treated like a "baby" that an attempt to spank them could trigger outright defiance. Teachers and caregivers will encounter an occasional school-aged child who has been subjected to a great deal of rough treatment in her life and has become aggressive, toughened, cynical, and very difficult to manage. Our best hope for breaking through this tough outer shell is assertive rule enforcement tempered with unconditional affection and open, respectful communication.

Spanking is always an inappropriate and ineffective method for disciplining children. Hitting or hurting children is *never* developmentally appropriate. The powerful negative effect of spanking lies in its ability to frighten and intimidate a child. Although corporal punishment may seem to work quite well at first, when children are tiny and easily intimidated, it models aggressive behavior and accustoms children to being controlled by external physical force. After a child has

The school-aged child begins to worry about her popularity among peers.

been spanked on many occasions, she becomes so accustomed to the way it feels that it no longer has the same effect. It may make her furious, but it probably will not scare her. This creates a difficult situation for everyone, as children grow bigger and stronger. Eventually the child will be too large to control physically.

The surest way out of this emotional trap is for the adult to break the cycle by finding some way to prove to each individual child that she is liked and respected by the adult. Then, and only then, can the adult begin to gain the children's respect and loyalty. External control methods do not work reliably for bright, capable, thinking children who will feel they are being manipulated into doing things they do not want to do by someone who does not really like them.

Inner control depends completely on the child wanting to be a cooperative group member. If school-aged children see the adult as someone who is absolutely fair, has a sense of humor, is reasonable, and who really cares about the needs and feelings of the children, they will be more willing to comply with that adult's wishes.

WHY DO EARLY SCHOOL-AGERS RESIST GOING TO CHILD CARE?

Child care workers can especially be intimated by school-aged children who have not yet developed inner control. Often, the youngest and least experienced workers are assigned to care for school-aged children who attend the facility only during the early morning and late afternoon hours, summers, and holidays. After school, these children can be exhausted from long hours of sitting on hard desks, and feel pressured to meet adult expectations. During summers and holidays, they may envy friends who are at home or away on vacation. They may come into the child care setting with resentment for having to be in a "child care for babies." They may especially feel frustration over being expected to play quietly with blocks and puzzles they have outgrown in a room filled with all the trappings of a preschool.

In a typical scenario, school-aged children begin to behave a bit wildly. Perhaps they start to throw pine cones at each other on the playground or stir their graham crackers into their milk, giggling and making a disgusting mush. Adults may respond in an abrasive and humorless attempt to stop this silly behavior. The children, feeling their oats, become sassy or perhaps stop the behaviors just long enough for the adult to turn her back for a moment. The angrier the adult becomes, the less compliant and cooperative the children will be. This situation can cause the adult to feel frighteningly out of control or helpless, a phenomenon that has an effect on older children similar to sharks smelling blood. Effective adults are able to model inner control, even in difficult situations.

Early school-aged children will feel more cooperative about rules they have helped to create. Family council or class meetings provide an opportunity for school-aged children to think about potential rules and to give their own opinions. If class meetings are run democratically, with real input from the children, then the children can begin to see rules not as inconveniences capriciously imposed by adults but as necessary protection for the rights and safety of all group members. Of course, it is critical that after-school programs are well planned, with opportunities for homework, sports, arts, music, dance, and interesting special projects. Bored children are not likely to exhibit self-control and self-discipline, no matter how caring the teachers are.

WHY DO EARLY SCHOOL-AGERS GET SO UPSET ABOUT FAIRNESS?

Early school-aged children are able to see discrepancies in adult behaviors and so do not gullibly accept everything adults say like younger children do. "But that's not fair" seems to be the battle cry of early school-aged children as they go about daily business. Even though they sometimes gleefully break rules themselves, they may become furious when it seems to them a rule is being enforced inconsistently: "But you didn't make Jerrod go back inside when he threw his book."

At this age, children's concrete operational perspective prohibits them from considering abstract extenuating circumstances that are important to adult decision-makers. The school-aged child may not it as fair when a child who is new to a setting breaks the rules and is simply given an explanation of them while a child who is expected to know the rules is given a stiff penalty for the same offense. Adults must constantly examine their own biases to determine if there is any possibility that their treatment of the children is unequal.

Adults should be meticulous not only about their fairness but also about their appearance of fairness. If a situation seems unfair to a child, the adult may assist the child's understanding by giving a concrete explanation for the action taken: "When you were younger, you needed many chances to remember rules. Now that you're seven, you know that throwing books is not allowed. Jerrod is only five now, but when he is seven, he will have to stop playing, too, if he forgets the rule."

WHY DO THEY INSIST ON PICKING THEIR OWN CLOTHES?

The early school years are an important period for children to develop their own identity. They develop a sense of personal identity by observing how others perceive them. They are especially sensitive to criticism or teasing about their appearance or clothing. Early school-agers also begin

Early school-agers are especially sensitive to criticism or teasing about their appearance or clothing.

to worry about their status with other children. They assert their autonomy with parents by insisting on dressing like peers or heroes.

Since physical development hinges on the active physical involvement of children in their environment by climbing, jumping, painting, gluing, and so on, parents and teachers can encourage (or require) clothing that is comfortable, washable, and not physically or socially restrictive. It is impossible to be "lady-like" in a frilly, short dress while climbing a jungle gym, and it is dangerous to climb the jungle gym in heavy, slick cowboy boots. Whatever steps adults take, it is essential to remember how desperately children want to belong, to fit in, and to be viewed as special by their friends.

HOW WE CAN HELP EARLY SCHOOL-AGERS BECOME PRODUCTIVE

Erikson (1963) identified the emotional crisis for school-aged children as one of **industry** (being productive) versus **inferiority** (feeling incapable). One of the enjoyable characteristics of school-aged children is their ability to function independently. Younger children need direction and help to do new things. School-aged children have the capacity to think of their own projects, to gather the needed materials, and then to work eagerly. They make miscalculations, messes, and mistakes, but they take great delight in having built their own crooked airplane or art object.

School-aged children want to dress like their friends and their role models.

Unfortunately, if they receive criticism instead of encouragement for their efforts and accomplishments, they may develop feelings of inferiority ("I'm no good," "Everything I try fails," "My ideas are stupid") and may be discouraged from trying new things.

Adults should not compare children's work to adult standards. One child's cookies may turn out tough and strangely shaped, but who cares? The purpose of the activity is for children to experience and learn from the process. The only importance of the activity outcome is that it makes children feel the pride of accomplishment.

HOW WE CAN SUPPORT THEIR SELF-ESTEEM

The big, wide world begins to have tremendous impact on the school-aged child. Once she can read, whole new avenues of information are opened. She may see toothpaste ads on television and worry that her teeth have plaque monsters chomping away, or see billboards about fire safety and worry that she will burn up in her bed at night. It is not unusual for school-aged children to experience nightmares or develop irrational fears: "I'm not going to eat that chicken noodle soup because it has mushrooms, and they might be the poison kind that'll make you die."

School-aged children look to each other for approval and recognition.

OLDER SCHOOL-AGERS (9 TO 12 YEARS)

WHY DO OLDER SCHOOL-AGED CHILDREN ARGUE SO MUCH?

As early school-agers become **concrete operational** (at about seven), they spend more time thinking about the things and events in their world. Preschoolers are just barely able to manage thinking through processes or mentally manipulating symbols that represent real objects or events, but by eight or nine, school-agers are usually able to manage manipulating thoughts about entire concrete processes. This enables them to mentally replay an event to evaluate it carefully and logically. Gradually, they begin to detect inconsistencies and gaps in logic. For example, an 11-year-old is likely to say, "Why do I have to wear my bicycle helmet?" A lot more people have accidents riding in cars, and they don't have to wear helmets. Besides, if a car ran over my stomach, I'd be squashed anyway and a helmet wouldn't help." Most children will be adolescents or young adults before they can effectively manipulate abstract ideas and symbols, so they are not yet able to evaluate complex situations. Eleven- and 12-year-olds may look very mature physically, but emotionally and intellectually, they still need a great deal of adult guidance and attention.

Older school-aged children love to talk and listen to each other. Younger children are more inclined to play together in a physically active way, using language as a supplement to running, jumping, climbing, and playing make-believe games. School-aged children still enjoy active play but will sit under a tree or get on the telephone and talk excitedly for long periods about themselves, school events, and authority figures. They have discovered there really is no Santa Claus, and

School-agers begin to focus their attention on gender roles and expectations. The may giggle around the opposite sex, pester them, chase them, or avoid them like the plague.

are beginning to realize grown-ups are not omnipotent deities but simply human beings who can make mistakes. When talking privately with a trusted friend or group of age-mates, school-agers may give an earful of complaints about parents, teachers, and siblings.

HOW CAN I GET OLDER SCHOOL-AGERS TO TRUST AND RESPECT ME?

Older school-aged children can be delightful conversationalists. They will listen attentively and respond appropriately in conversations that hold their attention. They can also build new, more mature bonds of affection and loyalty to adults who are willing to listen to them and treat them fairly and respectfully. Older school-aged children are especially sensitive to being "talked down to" by adults. School places new pressures on them. They are expected to assume a higher level of responsibility for their behavior and schoolwork. They will especially appreciate adults who will really listen to their thoughts and feelings in an open-minded, nonjudgmental manner.

WHY DO OLDER SCHOOL-AGERS TRY SO HARD TO BE "POPULAR"?

School-aged children have a powerful urge to belong to a peer group. They sometimes make up their own clubs or cliques with some semblance of rules and rituals, or even special taboos or requirements in clothing. Younger children may be oblivious to clothing; they wear whatever their parents buy for them, or they may have picky, but individual tastes in clothing. School-aged children become very concerned about wearing clothing that their friends approve. Even first and second graders today seem to know the popular (and unpopular) brand names for blue jeans and sneakers, as well as for dolls and bicycles.

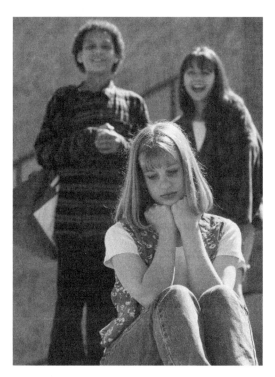

As school-aged children become adolescents, school-agers often go through periods of moodiness and insecurity as they cope with their changing bodies and increasing need for peer acceptance.

The fact that mom, dad, or teacher prefer a certain style of clothing, shoes, or haircut may mean that the children automatically prefer something else. This tendency to dress for peers gradually increases but does not reach a climactic peak until adolescence. Perhaps some entrepreneur will ease the discomfort parents feel by selling buttons for children to wear that say, "My parents are not responsible for the way I look, I dressed myself."

Adults should first help children feel secure, valued, and accepted, because self-confidence and self-esteem assist children in resisting inappropriate peer pressure. Adults can also help children keep material possessions in a proper perspective by respecting the children's anxiety about peer approval, but also by deemphasizing the value of objects. They can strengthen children's character by focusing attention on valuing people for their character rather than for their expensive clothing or toys.

WHY DO OLDER SCHOOL-AGED CHILDREN LOVE PRANKS AND JOKES?

Older school-aged children are becoming more adept at controlling their impulses. Although they may lapse from time to time into less mature behavior such as throwing a tantrum or pouting, they are finally able to wait for a while even though they are bored, hungry, or need to go to the bathroom. As they spend more time conforming to the social and behavioral expectations of authority figures and peers, they eagerly take advantage of opportunities where they feel safe being silly and whimsical. For example, when the teacher walks out of the room for a moment, a child might say, "Hey, wouldn't it be funny to pour this paint into the fish tank and then all the fish would turn purple?" Then, they laugh uproariously and (we hope) resist the urge to really do it. Preschool-aged children are not quite as able to weigh consequences and resist temptations. For toddlers, thinking is doing. Preschoolers can barely resist following their impulses. As children move toward adolescence, they should be developing the ability to persist toward longer-term goals. At this stage, they should not be so easily tempted by instant gratification that keeps them from accomplishing a specific task or project.

HOW WE CAN SUPPORT OLDER SCHOOL-AGERS' SELF-ESTEEM

As children leave early childhood and move toward adolescence, life becomes complicated and stressful. Their bodies seem to take on a life of their own, growing adult genitalia often far too quickly or far too slowly to suit the confused and disoriented owner of the body. We begin to see little children walking around in very adult-looking bodies, and suddenly we expect them to act like a grown-up. Just as in toddlerhood when two-year-olds were torn between the security of infancy and the allure of childhood, preadolescents are likely to waver in their feelings about whether to be a little kid or a teenager. One minute the child is sitting on a curb crying over a skinned knee and the next she is choosing her favorite color of lipstick.

Adults must provide a great deal of support, affection, and patience during these years so that school-agers' self-esteem and confidence stay intact. Babies, toddlers, and preschoolers get many hugs because they are little and cute. Adolescents and adults get romantic hugs from the opposite sex. Older school-agers are at an awkward stage and, especially young boys, may be left out of shows of affection altogether. Everybody needs an **appropriate** (nonexploitive) hug now and then to feel valued and special, and there are many excellent ways other than hugs to express affection. A big smile, sincere recognition, and listening all let the child know we care (American Academy of Pediatrics, 1995; Charlesworth, 1996; Gartrell, 1998; Gronlund, 1997; Meece, 1997; Steinberg, 1995).

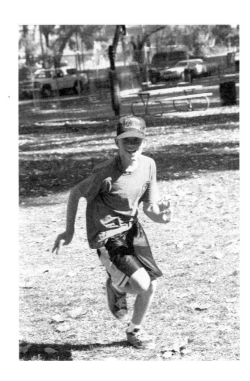

Behaving in a productive and responsible manner fosters feelings of self-worth.

POINTS TO REMEMBER

- Children have individual patterns and rates of development.

- Comparisons should never be used to label or stereotype a child.

- Trust developed in infancy is a primary foundation for the development of healthy emotional attitudes.

- Toddlers strive to achieve autonomy.

- Preschoolers can be helped to express strong emotions or feelings of anger.

- Early school-aged children develop an ability to replay events mentally to evaluate experiences carefully and logically.

- Older school-agers have a powerful urge to belong to a peer group and be well liked by friends.

PRACTICAL APPLICATION

"I'M NEVER GONNA 'VITE YOU TO MY BIRTH'AY!"

Sarah and Lupita, both five-year-olds, have claimed a shady spot under a thick magnolia tree on the playground. It is their favorite place to play. They have staunchly defended their little territory against small bands of marauding playmates by insisting, "You can't play. We got here first. This is our house."

As school-aged children become adolescents, it is critical for them to have opportunities to practice their prosocial skills in settings where they are really needed and appreciated. They can establish the lifelong habit of giving back to their community by organizing food drives, planning school projects, tutoring other children, and other such activities.

Although their teacher does not allow toys from home in the classroom, they have been allowed to bring their dolls outside with them for their outdoor play period. Sarah has a well-worn Raggedy Ann doll and Lupita has a new, soft plastic baby doll in a pink blanket that looks just like a newborn baby.

They have rocked their dolls to sleep and carefully placed them beside the trunk of the tree while they scurried around gathering leaves and sticks to outline a boundary for their playhouse. Sarah finds a large stick and announces that it is the door, "Nobody can come in unless they open this door. Tick tock. Now it's all locked up."

Robby, also five, has been watching and listening to the girls as he climbed and jumped off a climbing structure "fort" nearby. He cannot resist Sarah's challenge. "I can too get in," he taunts as he dances around the line of leaves and sticks that is the pretend wall of the girls' playhouse. He pokes his foot over the line and darts just out of their reach as he sticks his tongue out, laughing and chanting, "Nanny, nanny, boo, boo!"

Sarah chases and yells at Robby while Lupita furiously mends the pretend wall. Robby retreats to the top of the climbing structure, insisting, "Uh, huh! I could get in there. It's not really your house."

Lupita plants her feet firmly in the grass and stares viciously at Robby, guarding hearth and home, while Sarah runs to tell on Robby.

Robby, of course, loses all interest in Lupita's mean look. He is perched behind a post at the top of the fort watching carefully to see what his teacher, Miss Gresham, will do next.

Miss Gresham bends down on one knee and listens intently as Sarah rants and raves about Robby's alleged offenses. Quietly, Miss Gresham says, "Did you tell Robby how you felt when he messed up your house? Would you like for me to come with you to talk to Robby?" Sarah takes Miss Gresham's hand and quickly leads the way back to the scene of the crime. Robby, meanwhile, is huddled on the fort hoping no one can see him. He forgets that Miss Gresham is tall enough to talk eye-to-eye with him at the highest part of the fort.

With a gentle and reassuring voice, Miss Gresham says, "Robby, let's talk with Lupita and Sarah. I think they're feeling very angry." Robby pauses for just a second, but Miss Gresham holds her hands out and says, "It's okay, Robby. Sometimes I make mistakes and people get mad at me, too." Robby leans off the fort and Miss Gresham hoists him to the ground. She looks right in his eyes and pats him as she says, "Thanks, Robby." Then she assumes the role of objective referee as the girls tell Robby, in no uncertain terms, "Don't you break our house no more!"

Robby's lip quivers and a big tear begins to slide down his grimy face as he pulls back his shoulders and announces, "You ain't my best friend and I ain't never gonna 'vite you to my birth'ay party!"

DISCUSSION QUESTIONS

1. Identify characteristics and behaviors of Lupita, Sarah, and Robby that are typical of five-year-olds.
2. List all the reasons you can think of for Robby's interference with the girls' play. Why were the girls so angry?
3. Do you agree with Miss Gresham's handling of the problem? Explain. What would you have done differently?
4. What might have happened if Miss Gresham had responded to Robby with an angry voice and negative punishment?

RELATED READINGS

GROWTH AND DEVELOPMENT

Baillargeon, R. (1997). How do infants learn about the physical world? In E. N. Junn & C. Boyatzis (Eds.), *Annual editions: Child growth and development 97/98* (4th ed.). New York: McGraw-Hill. (Original work published in *Current Directions in Psychological Science*, October 1994.)

Based on the pioneering work of Jean Piaget, researchers once assumed that infants lacked a sense of object permanence. René Baillargeon describes her well-known and ingenious research indicating that young infants do, in fact, possess more fundamental and elaborate knowledge about physical objects than once thought.

Bainer, C., & Hale, L. (2000). From diapers to underpants. *Young Children 50*(4), 80–84.

Two teachers offer guidance on readiness, parent communication, giving children a foundation of support and confidence, and preparing the environment to support toilet learning.

Banich, M. T. (1997). *Neuropsychology: The neural bases of mental function.* Boston: Houghton-Mifflin.

Begley, S. (1997). The IQ puzzle. In E. N. Junn & C. Boyatzis (Eds.), *Annual editions: Child growth and development 97/98* (4th ed.). New York: McGraw-Hill. (Original work published in *Newsweek*, May 6, 1996.)

Scores on intelligence tests have risen dramatically in many countries. Does this mean that children today are smarter than ever? Sharon Begley discusses the possible reasons for these gains—including the popularity of video games and cereal boxes with mazes and puzzles for children—and addresses the debate on whether IQ tests truly measure intelligence.

Begley, S. (1997). Your child's brain. In K. M. Paciorek & J. H. Munro (Eds.), *Annual editions: Early childhood education 97/98* (18th ed.). New York: McGraw-Hill. (Original work published in *Newsweek*, February 19, 1996.)

This article discusses recent research that suggests the human brain is sensitive to experiences very early in life, which influence brain development for skill in language, music, math, and other learning. Sharon Begley describes "learning windows" when children may be most influenced by environmental stimulation.

Behrman R. E. (1995). (Ed.). *The future of children: Long-term outcomes of early childhood programs* (Vol. 5, No. 3). Los Altos, CA: Center for the Future of Children.

Berk, L. E. (1997). Vygotsky's theory: The importance of make-believe play. In E. N. Junn & C. Boyatzis (Eds.), *Annual editions: Child growth and development 97/98* (4th ed.). New York: McGraw-Hill. (Original work published in *Young Children*, November 1994.)

This article describes the view of Lev Vygotsky, a Russian psychologist who emphasizes the importance of pretend play as a forum for learning. In particular, children learn through guidance from parents and teachers that creates a scaffold for experiences, allowing youngsters to take over more responsibility as their skills increase.

Bornstein, M. H., & Lamb, M. (1992). *Development in infancy: An introduction* (3rd ed.). New York: McGraw-Hill.

This overview of infant development is intended for experienced infant and child development professionals who want more information about research issues related to infant development.

Brazelton, T. B. & Greenspan, S. I. (2000). *What every child must have to grow, learn, and flourish.* Cambridge, MA: Perseus Publishing.

Brazelton, T. B. (2001). *Su hijo: La referencia esencial.* Cambridge, MA: Perseus Publishing.

Brazelton, T. B. (2001). *The Children's Hospital guide to your child's health and development.* Cambridge, MA: Perseus Publishing.

Brazelton, T. B. & Sparrow, J. D. (2001). *Touchpoints three to six: Your child's emotional and behavioral development.* Cambridge, MA: Perseus Publishing.

Bronfenbrenner, U., & Morris, P. A. (1998). The ecology of developmental processes. In W. Damon (Series Ed.) & R. M. Lerner (Vol. Ed.), *Handbook of child psychology* (Vol. 1). *Theoretical models of human development* (5th ed.), (pp. 993–1027). New York: Wiley.

Campos, J. J., Bertenthal, B. I., & Kermoian, R. (1997). Early experience and emotional development: The emergence of wariness of heights. In E. N. Junn & C. Boyatzis (Eds.), *Annual editions: Child growth and development 97/98* (4th ed.). New York: McGraw-Hill. (Original work published in *Psychological Science*, January 1992.)

How do we become afraid of heights? Are we born with the fear or do we learn it through life experiences? This article by prominent researchers describes careful experiments designed to determine whether babies are born with a fear of heights or if they acquire it only after learning to crawl and the experience of moving around in the world.

Caulfield, R. (1996, fall). Social and emotional development in the first two years. *Early Childhood Education Journal, 24*(1), 55–58.

Daniel, J. E. (1998). A modern mother's place is wherever her children are: Facilitating infant and toddler mothers' transitions in child care. *Young Children 53*(6), 4–12.

Discusses the importance of supporting mother and child through the critical transition to out-of-home care. Identifies stressors that await mothers and ways providers can ease these stressors.

Eddowes, E. A., & Ralph, K. S. (1998). *Interactions for development and learning: Birth through eight years.* Upper Saddle River, NJ: Merrill Education/Prentice-Hall.

This book emphasizes the importance of different types of interaction for supporting early development and learning. Research is described showing the importance of appropriate interactions between an adult and child, between a child and older and younger peers, or between a child and an object.

Elkind, D. (1996, May). Early childhood education: What should we expect? *Principal, 7*(55), 11–13.

French, L. (1996). "I told you all about it, so don't tell me you don't know . . ." *Young Children, 5*(2), 17–20.

A developmental psychologist and mother of young children discusses the development of the ability of two-year-olds to comprehend information from language alone. She also explains the negative effects of developmentally inappropriate teaching when inappropriate language expectations are made of children.

Gibbs, N. (1997). The EQ factor. In E. N. Junn & C. Boyatzis (Eds.), *Annual editions: Child growth and development 97/98* (4th ed.). New York: McGraw-Hill. (Original work published in *Time*, October 2, 1995.)

Recent brain research suggests that emotions, not the traditional IQ rating, may be the true measure of human intelligence. This article examines this latest trend in the assessment of human ability to cope successfully with challenges.

Gowen, J. (1995). Research in review. The early development of symbolic play. *Young Children 50*(3), 75–84.

Reviews research on early development of symbolic play and ways its development can be promoted. Symbolic play is also called pretend play, fantasy play, dramatic play, or imaginative play.

Honig, A. (2000). Psychosexual development in infants and young children: Implications for caregivers. *Young Children 55*(5), 70–77.

Reminds teachers that young children's sexual curiosity and activity are perfectly natural, and gives tips for promoting healthy psychosexual development. Discusses anatomical differences, Freudian stages, sexual identity, and play choices.

Howard, V., Williams, B. F., Port, P. D., & Lepper, C. (1997). Very young children with special needs: A formative approach for the 21st century. In E. N. Junn & C. Boyatzis (Eds.), *Annual editions: Child growth and development 98/98* (4th ed.). New York: McGraw-Hill.

Using a formative, holistic, family-centered approach, it provides comprehensive coverage of normal childhood development—from birth to age six—and a description of over 50 of the most common medical conditions that early childhood educators should understand before working with families and professionals in other fields.

Hunter, T. (2000). Knowing things before we know them. *Young Children 55*(4), 85.

Explores stages of learning and addresses key factors in designing a lively environment focused on child learning.

Kantrowitz, B., & Wingert, P. (1997). How kids learn. In E. N. Junn & C. Boyatzis (Eds.), *Annual editions: Child growth and development 97/98* (4th ed.). New York: McGraw-Hill. (Original work published in *Newsweek*, April 17, 1989.)

Between the years of five and eight, children absorb an enormous amount of information. New research indicates that learning is best facilitated when active hands-on exploration, cooperation, and problem-solving are emphasized over more traditional forms of passive rote learning of information. Implications for teachers and parents are discussed.

Leong, D., & Bodrova, E. (1996). *Tools of the mind: A Vygotskian approach to early childhood education.* Upper Saddle River, NJ: Merrill Education/Prentice-Hall.

The authors' objective is to enable future teachers to arm young children with the mental tools necessary for learning. The authors view mental tools as a cycle in which ideas are (1) learned from others, (2) modified and changed, and (3) passed back and on to others.

Marose, N. R. (1997, November). Successful toilet learning: At a child's pace. *Young Children 52*(7), 81.

An early childhood professional discusses practical tips for supporting toilet training when the child is ready.

Nash, J. M. (1997, February 3). Fertile minds: From birth, a baby's brain cells proliferate wildly, making connections that may shape a lifetime of experience. *Time Magazine, 149*(5), 48–56.

Newberger, J. J. (1997, May). New brain development research—A wonderful window of opportunity to build public support for early childhood education! *Young Children, 52*(4), 4–9.

Novick, R. (2002). Learning to read the heart: Nurturing emotional literacy. *Young Children 57*(3), 84–89.

Argues that social and emotional school readiness is critical to successful kindergarten transition, early child success, and later adult accomplishment.

Peterson, R. W. (1994, April). School readiness considered from a neuro-cognitive perspective. *Early Education and Development, 5*(2), 120–140.

Powlishta, K. K. (1995). Research in review. Gender segregation among children: Understanding the "cootie phenomenon." *Young Children 50*(4), 61–69.

Reviews research into gender segregation (the preference for same-sex playmates among children). The author focuses on why it occurs, its consequences, and its implications.

Raikes, H. (1996). A secure base for babies: Applying attachment concepts to the infant care setting. *Young Children, 51*(5), 59–67.

This article explains the basic principles of attachment theory and shows how these principles can be used in infant programs.

Reinsberg, J. (1999). Understanding young children's behavior. *Young Children 54*(4), 54–57.

Guides parents and caregivers in identifying underlying causes that might explain children's behavioral actions, adopting reflective rather that reactive approaches to achieve more positive outcomes, and establishing environments that support and nurture children.

Rushton, S. P. (2001). Applying brain research to create developmentally appropriate learning environments. *Young Children 56*(5), 76–82.

Argues that brain research confirms the validity of developmentally appropriate practice and the relevance of child-centered constructivist ideas of Dewey, Piaget, and Vygotsky.

Sameroff, A., & McDonough, S. C. (1997). Educational implications of developmental transitions: Revisiting the 5- to 7-year shift. In K. M. Paciorek & J. H. Munro (Eds.), *Annual editions: Early childhood education 97/98* (18th ed.). New York: McGraw-Hill. (Original work published in *Phi Delta Kappan*, November 1994).

The years between five and seven mark an important milestone in the lives of young children. Educators who have a clear understanding of child development are able to assist children as they make a smooth transition into the primary grades. The onset of this developmental shift depends on the environment, culture, previous school experiences, and the child's unique characteristics.

Schiller, P. (1997, September–October). Brain development research: Support and challenges. *Child Care Information Exchange, 117*, 6–10.

Sroufe, L. A. (1996). *Child development: Its nature and course.* New York: McGraw-Hill.

Gives information on gender socialization; emotional development, prenatal effects drugs; genetic research; post-natal development; brain growth; infant intelligence, assessment, bilingualism, early roots of morality, cross-cultural education; and mixed gender social relationships.

Thorne, B. (1997). Girls and boys together but mostly apart. In E. N. Junn & C. Boyatzis (Eds.), *Annual editions: Child growth and development 97/98* (4th ed.). New York: McGraw-Hill. (Original work published in *GenderPlay: Girls and Boys in School*, Rutgers University Press, 1993.)

Gender segregation—boys playing with boys, girls with girls—is very common during the elementary school years. How might this affect boys' and girls' social and interpersonal development? Barrie Thorne describes how not only peers but teachers as well contribute to gender segregation.

U.S. Department of Education. (1997, Spring). What new research on the brain tells us about our youngest children: Summary on the White House Conference on Early Childhood. *Dimensions of Early Childhood, 25*(2).

HELPFUL WEB SITES

http://www.mentalhelp.net/poc/center_index.php?id=28   Child and Adolescent Development. Mental Health Net's list of Internet resources on child development includes Web sites, Internet mailing lists, newsgroups, professional journals, organizations, and behavior checklists.

http://ericeece.org/   ERIC Clearinghouse on Elementary and Early Childhood Education offers links to ERIC/EECE publications and to other related sites in the ERIC (Educational Resources in Education) system.

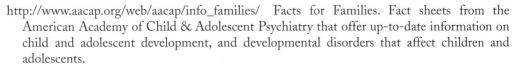

http://www.aacap.org/web/aacap/info_families/   Facts for Families. Fact sheets from the American Academy of Child & Adolescent Psychiatry that offer up-to-date information on child and adolescent development, and developmental disorders that affect children and adolescents.

http://162.129.72.40/poi/   Harriet Lane WWW Links (formerly Pediatric Points of Interest). From the Department of Pediatrics at Johns Hopkins University, this searchable collection of links to resources in pediatrics and child health is intended for health care professionals, but the site also has useful links to resources for parents and caregivers.

http://www.iamyourchild.org/   I Am Your Child provides resources for parents and caregivers on early childhood development that emphasize the importance of the first three years of life.

http://www.nncc.org/Child.Dev/child.dev.page.html   NNCC Child Development Database. From the National Network for Child Care, this site addresses infant, toddler, preschool, and school-aged child care.

http://www.srcd.org/   Society for Research in Child Development is a multidisciplinary professional association with an international membership of researchers, practitioners, and human development professionals.

http://www.wellesley.edu/WCW/CRW/SAC/   National Institute on Out-of-School Time is an organization devoted to the needs of school-aged children before and after school hours.

http://www.zerotothree.org   Zero to Three. National Center for Infants, Toddlers, and Families.

RESOURCES FOR KEEPING TODDLERS SAFE

http://www.aeclp.org   Alliance to End Childhood Lead Poisoning is a national educational, policy, and advocacy organization dedicated exclusively to ending the epidemic of childhood lead poisoning.

http://www.aap.org   American Academy of Pediatrics (AAP) is a "voice for children" dedicated to the health, safety, and well-being of infants, children, adolescents, and young adults. The academy supports breastfeeding and offers medical updates, information, and services for peiatricians and health professionals, as well as for parents and educators.

E-mail: aidsinfo@cdcnac.aspensys.com and http://www.cdcnac.org   Centers for Disease Control and Prevention (CDC), National AIDS Clearinghouse, U.S. Department of Health and Human Services is an agency that makes a collection of scientific and educational HIV/AIDS materials available to people working in the HIV/AIDS field as well as those living with HIV/AIDS.

For additional information on positive child guidance, visit our Web site at
http://www.earlychilded.delmar.com

Chapter 3
Understanding the Reasons for Problem Behavior

OBJECTIVES

After reading this chapter, you should be able to:
- Define characteristics of inappropriate behavior.
- Articulate subjective perceptions of behavior.
- Recognize children's behavioral limitations based on normal stages of moral development.
- List underlying causes of problem behavior.
- Examine causes of misbehavior.
- Prevent misbehavior by correcting its cause.

DEFINING PROBLEM BEHAVIOR

The process by which children learn acceptable behavior is called socialization. Infants have no comprehension of proper or improper behavior. They would have no ability to inhibit their impulses even if they knew what was expected. Gradually over the first few years of life, however, children develop self-control and learn how to get along with others, and how to follow the accepted rules of their family and community. Before self-control develops, children are totally impulsive in

Maturity and practice are needed for children to learn what adults expect of them.

following their feelings and desires. They act like children (of course), making mistakes, acting on impulse, and stubbornly resisting external control, actions we consider to be problem behaviors. Chapter 1 identified three specific categories of problem behavior and recommended interrupting or redirecting any child behavior that:

- infringed unfairly on the rights of others (Be kind).

- presented a clear risk of harm to the child or anyone else (Be safe).

- resulted in the mishandling of objects or living things (Be neat).

Those three guidelines were used for defining basic ground rules for children: Be kind! Be safe! Be neat! Next, we need to ask ourselves why children might behave in an unkind, unsafe, or careless manner. *Misbehavior*, *problem behavior*, and *inappropriate behavior* are used interchangeably, and all three terms tend to be misinterpreted as meaning naughtiness and mischief. Many inappropriate behaviors, however, are not at all mischievous in intent. A child may not even realize that a specific behavior will be viewed as "naughty" by adults. Positive child guidance requires that adults gauge their reaction to misbehaviors by looking at the child's level of understanding, the severity and frequency of the behavior, and possible underlying causes.

A baby who has innocently climbed on top of a coffee table must be dealt with differently than a five-year-old who knowingly uses the couch as if it was a trampoline, although both must be redirected since the behaviors present a clear risk of harm to the children and involve the mishandling of objects in the environment. To get positive results, we must have reasonable expectations for children at various ages, and recognize whether or not they can really be expected to control their actions in particularly difficult or tempting situations.

In many cases, it is far more effective to change the situation than to try to stop a child's behavior. By removing the baby from the coffee table and taking him to a safe piece of play equipment designed for climbing, we can change an inappropriate behavior to an appropriate behavior (even though the child may not yet recognize any difference in the two situations). We assume that the five-year-old knows the difference between a living-room sofa and a trampoline, so our emphasis is on giving the child a clear understanding of pertinent facts, choices, and consequences. For example, we might say, "The couch is not for jumping. If you want to jump, you may jump outside on the soft grass." If the action continues, we should give the child our close, undivided attention at eye level and add in an assertive but sincere tone, "I know jumping on the couch is fun, but it could break the couch, or you could fall on something hard or sharp in here. If you jump on the couch again, then you will not be allowed to play in the living room for the rest of the afternoon." Most importantly, we have to follow through and see that what we say will happen, actually happens.

Assessing the appropriateness of any individual child's behavior requires us to step into his shoes and see the world from his perspective, and requires accurate insight and wise judgment.

We sometimes fail to see the world from the child's point of view.

We are prone, sometimes quickly and flippantly, to label actions that are inconvenient, annoying, or embarrassing to us at the moment as misbehavior, regardless of reasons the child might have for behaving in such a manner.

Children are confused when they do not expect a negative reaction from us and when they cannot make sense of our logic in requiring different behaviors in different situations. They are bewildered when a behavior is praised in one setting but reprimanded in a situation they do not recognize as being very different. Mrs. Perez was exasperated with three of her toddlers who persisted in climbing up on the picnic table in the toddler playground. She had not realized that the wood of the picnic table looked exactly like the wood of the climbing structure nearby. Although the adults were quite clear about the differences between a climbing structure "fort" and a picnic table, a closer look would reveal that both objects are just boards nailed together. Young children's inexperience and naiveté are just a couple of the many reasons they behave in ways that adults perceive as naughty.

Three-year-old Allison Jones' mother opened her dishwasher one morning to discover a pile of dirty towels stuffed where dishes ought to be. Mrs. Jones yelled, "Who put these towels in the dishwasher?" The look of guilt on Allison's face instantly gave her away as the culprit. Although Mrs. Jones asked repeatedly, "Why did you do this? What would possess you to do such a silly thing?" Allison just hung her head and mumbled, "I dunno."

Mrs. Jones never realized Allison intended to surprise her mother by cleaning the bathroom. Her intentions were good, but she was just a little bit confused about which "washing machine" one used to wash dirty towels. Allison's behavior was inappropriate (towels should not be put in the dishwasher) but she certainly was not misbehaving. Her behavior did not deserve a reprimand but rather some gentle redirection. An excellent adult response would be for her mother to say, "Thank you so much for wanting to help. Come with me and I'll show you the right place to put dirty clothes."

WHAT DO WE MEAN BY FUNCTIONAL AND DYSFUNCTIONAL BEHAVIORS?

When children evidence a compulsive and chronic pattern of very inappropriate or self-destructive behavior, the behavior can be termed **dysfunctional**. On the other hand, **functional behaviors** are

The nurtured child is helped to become a responsible adult.

various appropriate actions that serve some productive or positive function in a child's life. Functional behaviors help the child get his needs met. Dysfunctional behaviors produce a negative reaction that may be opposite to the outcome desired by the child. The child's strategies for coping and for interacting with others simply do not work, causing the child increasing stress and unhappiness, and creating a vicious cycle. A lonely child lacking in social skills may relentlessly tease other children to get their attention, but the teasing is dysfunctional because it does not attract friends; instead it causes the child to be disliked. Consequently, the child becomes more isolated and lonely, and even more trapped in the existing cycle of dysfunctional behavior.

THE ADULT-CENTERED DEFINITION OF MISBEHAVIOR

Adult-centered definitions of misbehavior focus on the effect a child's behavior has on the adult. Individual actions are evaluated according to the seriousness of their impact on things the adult cares about, as well as the adult's emotional state or mood. If a child spills his juice in the grass during a picnic, the adult may hardly notice since nothing has to be cleaned up. If the same child spills juice on the kitchen floor, the adult may be annoyed and may reprimand the child. If, however, the spill is grape juice on brand new, light-colored dining room carpeting, the adult may be very angry and punish or spank the child.

The child learns that his behaviors are not always met with a consistent or predictable adult reaction. Children may learn that they can "get away with" inappropriate behaviors when their caregiver is in a relaxed and playful mood. They may also perceive that nothing they do makes any difference when the adult is in a bad mood. They may believe that they will get in trouble regardless of what they do or do not do. (Remember the definition of learned helplessness? We never want children to think they have no control over their circumstances, that things just happen to them randomly.)

Since adult-centered definitions of misbehavior focus only on the adult's needs and desires, desirable behaviors are perceived to be actions that are convenient and desirable to the adult. Being quiet, staying out of the way, and performing the role of a cute (but undemanding) little kid on cue may be seen as the hallmarks of a "good" child. Crying, squealing with joy, being frightened, or being a chatterbox may be perceived as naughty misbehaviors if they are annoying, embarrassing, or inconvenient for the adult.

THE CHILD-CENTERED DEFINITION OF MISBEHAVIOR

In contrast, a child-centered definition of misbehavior focuses on the ability level, motives, and long-term well-being of the child in evaluating the appropriateness or inappropriateness of actions. If an action is wrong or inappropriate, it is judged to be wrong because it infringes on the rights of others, is unsafe, or is unnecessarily damaging to the environment, not because the action is a bother or because the adult happens to be in an intolerant mood. Defining behaviors this way brings about consistency and a sense of fairness. Children learn to be responsible for the consequences of their own actions. They learn that there is a direct relationship between their actions and the reaction they receive from authority figures. (Remember, no learned helplessness, please.)

By taking into consideration the ages and developmental stages of children, adults can recognize that exploring or "getting into things" is normal and beneficial learning behavior for a baby or toddler, not misbehavior. It is the adult's responsibility to baby-proof the environment so that everything accessible to the baby is safe and appropriate. If the baby gets into something inappropriate, the baby is simply moved to an area that is safe for exploration.

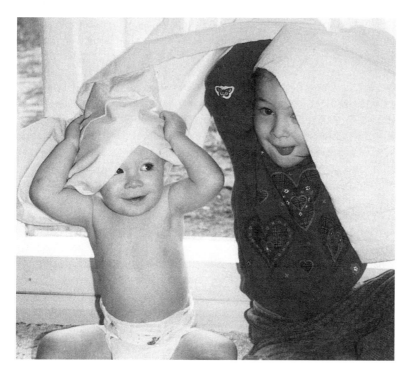

Children explore their world because they want to learn, not because they want to be naughty.

Children who are allowed to become actively involved in daily processes will undoubtedly make mistakes more often than children who are encouraged to stand by passively while things are done for them. Allowing young children to help with food preparation, for example, may be messy and time-consuming. It is quicker and easier for the adult to complete such tasks alone, but the confidence and skill development children gain from such experiences are well worth the extra effort. Dropping an egg or inadvertently spilling flour are not seen as mischief from the child-centered perspective, but rather as important opportunities for children to learn responsibility and independence. Instead of being scolded for making a mess, the child is taught how to accomplish daily tasks successfully and how to clean up after himself.

STAGES OF MORAL DEVELOPMENT IN YOUNG CHILDREN

A critical priority for parents, schools, communities, even entire countries, is the moral development of their children and future citizens. Morality is the ability to distinguish right from wrong and to act accordingly. Moral development is the process by which human beings learn to monitor their own actions, and to decide whether a tempting behavior is a "good" or "bad" thing to do and then to inhibit inappropriate impulses. In other words, morally developed people are able to stop themselves from doing things they know are wrong.

Although the guidance children receive early in life is essential to their moral development, moral behavior is not exclusively a concern of early childhood. Adults who are quick to respond harshly to a young child's misbehavior may forget their own difficulty in inhibiting the inappropriate impulses they have in their own daily lives. Even adults with well-developed morals experience difficulty resisting the temptation to gossip, smoke cigarettes, indulge in foods that are bad for them, or tell "fibs" to get out of tight spots. Remember that one of the key avenues for early childhood learning is imitation. It is essential for adult caregivers consciously to set the best possible example in their day-to-day actions of integrity and strong moral character (Grusec, Kuczynski, Rushton, & Simutis, 1979; Toner, Parke, & Yussen, 1978; Toner & Potts, 1981).

As children observe adult behaviors and experience the cause-and-effect sequences that are a part of interacting with others, they internalize (adopt as their own) the character attributes and ethical standards of the important role models in their lives. Attachment, love, and respect for an adult trigger the child's internalization of that adult's values. When a child has internalized the standards of his adult role models, he begins to experience the emotional component of morality or **moral affect** (the feelings associated with a guilty or clear conscience). Having moral affect means that when he behaves in a way that he knows to be wrong, he has feelings of guilt and shame. When he behaves properly, he feels pride. Moral affect serves as an internal regulator that guides one toward appropriate behavior and away from misbehavior.

Feelings of guilt play a role in regulating moral behavior, but it is not helpful to push guilt on a child by saying such things as, "Aren't you ashamed of yourself, you naughty boy?" Forcing guilt on a young child may actually harden him emotionally and delay his development of moral affect. Conscience that comes from inside us is always more meaningful than guilt imposed on us by someone else. Two specific child-rearing practices are known to help children internalize values and prosocial moral judgment. They are:

- nurturing and affectionate adult guidance.

- consistency in explaining reasons for rules and commands.

Adults help children develop moral behavior by being loving and gentle, and by putting into words the rationales for imperatives. Instead of just saying, for example, "Don't touch that!," they say, "Please use a different crayon because that one belongs to someone else" (Eisenberg-Berg, 1979).

Another important component of moral development is **moral reasoning** (the thinking processes that guide people in deciding what is or is not moral behavior). The way children think about right and wrong changes dramatically as their intellectual capacity matures (Piaget, 1952). Children younger than seven years old tend to focus on the concrete consequences of actions rather than on the abstract motivations or intentions behind them. As they get older and their moral capacity increases, they are better able to take into consideration complicated rationales for various actions (Ferguson & Rule, 1982).

We must see childhood as a stage of life, not just the anteroom to life.

David Elkind (1981)

COMPONENTS OF MORAL DEVELOPMENT

Adapted from Berkowitz, M. W., & Grych, J. H. (1998).

Empathy

To develop empathy in young children, talk frequently with them about behavior and feelings. Talk about the consequences of the child's positive and negative actions on others. Help the child identify and talk about how others' actions affect them. Empathy has been identified by Kagan (1984) as one of the "core moral emotions." Damon (1988) considers it "one of morality's primary emotional supports" (p. 14) and argues that, "Because morality is fundamentally concerned with one's obligations to others, it cannot be developed solely through introspection and recognition of one's inner feelings. . . . Children must learn to become attuned not only to their own emotional reactions but also to those of others" (p. 128).

Conscience

A powerful influence on children's moral development is something researchers call "induction." Induction is the process of stimulating children's understanding of the reasons for choosing one behavior over another by thinking about the impact that behavior will have on another person. When children disobey, adults have the opportunity to teach children what is right and wrong, and more importantly, *why* certain behaviors are preferable to others. This rather simple process is a powerful force for shaping children's moral development because it helps children internalize standards for moral behavior. As Lickona (1983) points out, children "need to see us lead good lives, but they also need to know why we do it. Children develop a conscience best in an environment of mutual respect, empathy, and affection." Parents and early childhood professionals can support conscience development by making sure children know that they are willing to listen, really care about her feelings, and respect her individual needs and interests (Hoffman & Saltzstein, 1967; Kochanska & Aksan, 1995; Kochanska, 1997; Allinsmith & Greening, 1955).

Altruism

To support altruism development, consistently use an authoritative guidance style (Baumrind, 1971), and regularly talk with children about the differences between right and wrong (Zahn-Waxler, Radke-Yarrow, & King, 1979). Oliner and Oliner (1988) found that altruistic adults were motivated by "values learned from their parents which prompted and sustained their involvement" (p. 143).

Moral Reasoning

Baumrind (1971; 1980) and others (e.g., Hoffman & Saltzstein, 1967) have identified three predominant child guidance styles. *Authoritarian* adults are highly controlling and demanding but affectively cold and hostile, and generally uncommunicative. *Permissive* adults tend to be caring and communicative but wield little control and set few demands for mature behavior, incorporating either a warm "best buddy" style or a more distant neglectful style. *Authoritative* adults are affectionate, appropriately controlling, communicative, and have high expectations for children. It is those parents whom researchers have found to produce the most positive child characteristics, including higher moral functioning. Authoritative guidance, especially with its focus on open supportive communication, most effectively nurtures children's moral

(continues)

COMPONENTS OF MORAL DEVELOPMENT *(continued)*

reasoning development. Parents' use of induction, expression of nurturance and support, use of limit-setting, modeling of socio-moral behavior, and reliance on democratic open discussion and conflict resolution style are each positively related to the fundamental "building blocks" of morality.

To learn more, read:

Berkowitz, M. W., & Grych, J. H. (1998). Fostering goodness: Teaching parents to facilitate children's moral development. *Journal of Moral Education, 27*(3), 371–391. Available on line: http://parenthood.library.wisc.edu/Berkowitz/Berkowitz.html.

Eisenberg, N., & Mussen, P. H. (1989). *The roots of prosocial behavior in children.* New York: Cambridge University Press.

Kohlberg, L. (1976). Moral stages and moralization: The cognitive-developmental approach. In T. Lickona (Ed.), *Moral development and behavior: Theory, research, and social issues* (pp. 31–53). New York: Holt, Rinehart and Winston.

Lickona, T. (1983). *Raising good children.* New York: Bantam Books.

Piaget, J. (1965). *The moral judgment of the child.* (M. Gabain, Trans.). New York: Free Press.

Sroufe, A. (1995). *Emotional development: The organization of emotional life in the early years.* New York: Cambridge University Press.

HOW DO YOUNG CHILDREN LEARN RIGHT FROM WRONG?

Sarah, a four-year-old, was told that Jimmy broke four plates and three glasses while trying to help, and Annie broke one cookie jar lid while trying to steal cookies. She insisted that Jimmy was naughtier and deserved more punishment than Annie. Sarah has focused on the idea that breaking a lot of dishes is worse than breaking one dish. The child is not yet able to think about all aspects of the dilemmas presented or to consider such things as motive. Piaget (1952) studied children's sense of right and wrong through a series of interviews in which he confronted children of various ages with moral problems like the one described above. He found that young children's responses contrasted sharply with the responses of older children. The moral reasoning of young children tends to be simplistic and limited to enforcing the letter of the law (or rule) rather than interpreting the spirit or intent of the law.

Kohlberg (1969; 1976) described the stages through which human beings develop moral reasoning. His three levels and six stages are listed below:

Level One—Preconventional Morality

• Stage One
One obeys rules only to avoid punishment and to gain rewards.

For example, a toddler examining an electric outlet may reach for it, then look up at the adult while saying, "No, no. No touch." The toddler will probably resist the urge to touch the outlet only if the adult appears attentive and ready to enforce the rule (or if the child has unfortunately discoverd the pain of an electric shock).

- Stage Two
  One bargains to get one's needs met. Prosocial behaviors are intended to bring about favors from others.

For example, "If you let me ride the tricycle, I'll be your best friend."

Level Two—Conventional Morality

- Stage Three
  There is an emphasis on gaining approval from others by being nice because the focus is on being a "good girl" or a "good boy" to get praise and approval.

For example, when an adult tells one child to taste just a bite of green beans, another child nearby may hurriedly stuff her mouth full of beans, saying, "See me? I'm eating my vegetables!"

- Stage Four
  The focus is on "law and order." At this stage, one is concerned that everyone do his duty and follow the letter of the law. It is only okay to break a rule if everyone else is doing it.

For example, school-aged children become very indignant when rules are broken. They may resent the fact that a child suffering from diabetes is given a candy bar by the teacher. Never mind that the child is ill; it just is not right.

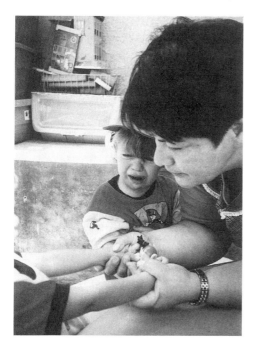

Young children lack the self-control necessary to consistently control their impulses.

Level Three—Postconventional Morality

- Stage Five
  At this stage, correct behavior is defined in terms of individual rights according to widely held moral beliefs of society.

For example, a teacher at this level would recognize that the urgent health need of a diabetic child is more important than usual rules about candy at school that are normally fair and reasonable. Protecting the health of a child is more valued in this situation than following a rule.

- Stage Six
  One decides whether a behavior is moral or not based on a personal decision of conscience in accordance with personal ethical principles that are logical, consistent, and universal.

For example, a child care center director might risk the solvency of her business by testifying in accordance with her conscience in a child abuse case against a powerful and popular community member.

One distinct characteristic of more advanced levels of moral reasoning is one's ability to consider motivation and intention when evaluating the outcome of a behavior. Young children rarely achieve this, but adult caregivers must achieve this if they wish to be effective in positive child guidance. Adults are also functioning at a low level of moral development when they blindly enforce rules just because rules are rules, regardless of circumstances, motives, or effects on individual children. Adults are also functioning at a very low level of moral behavior if they enforce rules only when it is convenient or in their own best interest to do so. Morally mature adults focus on the intents and motives of children, not on the outcomes of their behaviors. If, for example, Alicia tries to knock someone off the jungle gym but nobody gets hurt, and Albert is being silly and accidentally knocks someone off who is hurt badly, the morally mature adult will recognize that Alicia's behavior was more inappropriate than Albert's.

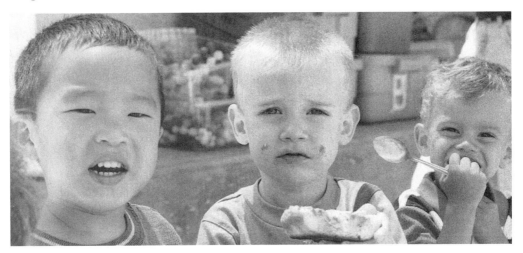

Caregivers should ask themselves: "Are my expectations reasonable? Does the child really understand what I expect?"

METHODS TO SUPPORT CHILDREN'S MORAL DEVELOPMENT

Adapted from Berkowitz, M. W., & Grych, J. H. (1998).

Provide Nurturing and Support

Authoritative guidance supports the development of morality (Baumrind, 1980). Baumrind's research has shown that authoritative guidance fosters social sensitivity, self-awareness, and respect for rules and authority (Baumrind, 1978; Damon, 1988). Authoritative child guidance provides a perfect balance of nurturing and limit-setting, and it is both gentle and firm. This style of guidance is very different from authoritarian disciplinary interactions with children, which tend to be more negative and sometimes antagonistic or combative in nature (Berkowitz & Gibbs, 1983). Warm, responsive guidance communicates to children that they are valued and appreciated. As children learn they are worthy of such treatment, their self-esteem blossoms. They also learn that people in general deserve respectful treatment, and that it is wrong to hurt others. Authoritative adults routinely discuss moral issues with children in a respectful and emotionally supportive way (Powers, 1982; Walder & Taylor, 1991).

Set Limits

An important part of authoritative parenting is something called **demandingness** (requiring certain behaviors from children). Effective demandingness requires three major ingredients.

1. First, adults must set high but realistic goals. Children whose parents have low expectations for them develop low expectations for themselves. Children whose parents set unreasonably high expectations for them become frustrated, angry, and develop a sense of failure.

2. Second, adults musts help children achieve these expectations by carefully supporting, encouraging, and monitoring progress.

3. Third, adults must provide consistent follow-up to evaluate whether or not children achieve the goals. Children recognize when expectations will be forgotten if they stall long enough. High but reasonable standards that are consistently and caringly enforced will develop self-control, altruism, and self-esteem in children.

Model Appropriate Behavior

How we live our lives in front of children, how we treat others, and how we handle our own frustrations and problems all shape children's behavior (Lickona, 1983, p. 20). Children observe the adults in their lives and model their behavior. Adults can model respect and compassion toward others, or they can model behavior that is harmful and abusive by belittling, coercing, or physically dominating others (Grych & Fincham, 1990, 1993). Even if children do not directly imitate the specific behaviors they observe, their beliefs and attitudes about how to treat other people may well be shaped by these experiences. The fact that these "lessons" are unintended makes them no less powerful. Adults who model prosocial behaviors teach their children to treat others with respect (Damon, 1988).

(continues)

METHODS TO SUPPORT CHILDREN'S MORAL DEVELOPMENT *(continued)*

Teach Democratic Decision-making and Discussion

Teach children to rely on group processes—negotiation, consensus, compromise, and discussion—to solve problems. Decisions and rules developed this way are more likely to be just, and participating in the process helps children learn the skills necessary to function in a democracy (Power, Higgins, & Kohlberg, 1989). Using democratic processes produces compliance, moral reasoning development, conscience, higher self-esteem, and altruism in children (Lickona, 1983). Children begin to develop a "fairness approach."

To learn more, read:

Berkowitz, M. W., & Grych, J. H. (1998). Fostering goodness: Teaching parents to facilitate children's moral development. *Journal of Moral Education, 27,*3 371–391. Available on line: http://parenthood.library.wisc.edu/Berkowitz/hofsal67.

Berkowitz, M. W. (1997). The complete moral person: Anatomy and formation. In J. M. DuBois (Ed.), *Moral issues in psychology: Personalist contributions to selected problems* (pp. 11–42). Lanham, MD: University Press of America.

Colby, A., & Damon, W. (1992). *Some do care: Contemporary lives of moral commitment.* New York: The Free Press.

Forehand, R., & Kotchik, B. A. (1996). Cultural diversity: A wake-up call for parent training. Behavior *Therapy, 27*, 187–206.

Harter, S. (1997). The development of self-representations. In N. Eisenberg (Ed.), *Handbook of child psychology* (5th ed., vol. III). New York: Wiley.

Kochanska, G., & Akasan, N. (1995). Mother-child mutually positive affect, the quality of child compliance to requests and prohibitions, and maternal control as correlates of early internalization. *Child Development, 66*, 236–254.

UNDERLYING CAUSES OF PROBLEM BEHAVIOR

Lying on a couch and watching cartoons for hours on end is not a desirable use of a child's time. In order to redirect the behavior, an adult may need to think through any potential reasons the child is not involved in healthier, more active play. Is the child reinforced for being quiet and passive? Does the adult respond negatively to active play that is sometimes messy or noisy? Are interesting toys and challenging play equipment accessible to the child? Does the child need someone with whom to play? Adults must always take into account possible reasons for undesirable behavior in order to have a chance at changing the situation and preventing the behavior from happening. In child guidance, as in health care, the best cure is always prevention! (See Appendix D for additional resources.)

INAPPROPRIATE EXPECTATIONS

Sometimes, children's misbehavior is the direct result of inappropriate expectations on the part of adults. We expect children to be able to do things that they simply are not capable of doing.

Helena and Ray are sitting in the pediatrician's waiting room with their 18-month-old son, Billy. The little boy is dressed in his very best clothes with shiny black shoes and a tiny bow tie. He is sitting on his dad's knee looking like a fashion model for baby clothes. Billy sits silently for a while, then looks around at the room and at his mom and dad who are preoccupied in their discussion of the questions they want to ask Billy's doctor.

After a few more minutes of sitting, Billy points to a large aquarium with huge tropical fish swimming around and says, "Yook!" (his word for look). After a few seconds, he gestures insistently and looks at his mother, repeating, "Yook, wha' dis?" (What's this?). Helena straightens Billy's tie and says, "Yes, they're fish. Shhh, be still now. You'll get your clothes all messed up."

Billy stares at the aquarium a few seconds longer, then scrambles to get down off his dad's lap. His dad pulls him back in his lap and says firmly, "Those aren't for you to touch. You need to stay here and sit still. If you get down, you'll break something for sure." Billy begins to whine and rub his eyes with his fist, periodically struggling to get down from his dad's lap. His mother pulls a bottle out of her diaper bag and offers it to Billy, but he throws the bottle on the floor and begins kicking and crying loudly.

As the nurse comes in to announce that the doctor is ready to see Billy, Helena and Ray seem to be at their wit's end. With great frustration in her voice, Helena says, "Why does he act like this? What are you supposed to do when they get like this? He's just impossible to deal with sometimes."

Little can be done to resolve the situation at this point in time except to remove Billy from the setting and wait for him to wind down. A great deal, however, could have been done to prevent the situation. If Helena and Ray had known, in advance, more about what to expect from a toddler, they might have anticipated that he really could not sit still for thirty minutes to an hour. Perhaps they could have brought one of his favorite toys or books with them, or they could have distracted him by playing peek-a-boo or by allowing him to scribble on a notepad from his mother's purse. Or perhaps his dad could have followed up on his interest in the aquarium by supervising him closely and talking with him about the fish as he looked at and touched the aquarium.

MISUNDERSTANDING EXPECTATIONS

Sometimes, children misunderstand what is expected of them.

Miss Jean, a preschool teacher, was dismayed to discover that her preschoolers had left the bathroom in a mess. Water was all over the floor and paper towels were everywhere except in the trash can. She turned to three-year-old Misha and said, "I'm going to go get a mop. Can you please put all of the paper towels into the trash can where they belong?"

When Miss Jean returned with her mop, she found poor little Misha struggling to pull clean paper towels out of the dispenser and stuffing them by the handfuls into the trash can. In a pitiful voice, Misha said, "It too much, Teacher. It too much paper towels."

> *Luckily, Miss Jean recognized that although the outcome of Misha's behavior was not the desired one, her intentions were good. Misha simply took her teacher's instructions literally when she said, "put all the paper towels into the trash can." Miss Jean had not specified "wet paper towels on the floor."*
>
> *Miss Jean thanked Misha warmly for trying to help and then proceeded to say matter-of-factly, "Let's put the wet, dirty paper towels in the trash can. The dry ones are good for us to use next time we wash."*

If Miss Jean had scolded Misha or snapped, "Now look what you've done, you silly thing," Misha might not have been so eager to cooperate the next time someone asked her to help. Instead, she would have felt shamed for her good intentions, hard work, and inability to read the adult's mind.

IMMATURE SELF-CONTROL

Sometimes, it seems that children really want to abide by an adult's request, but somehow they just cannot seem to manage the self-control needed to accomplish what the adult expects.

> *Eloise provides child care for six children in her licensed family day home. She is committed to being an early childhood educator, not just a babysitter. To help her children learn about science and nature, she has bought a furry baby guinea pig.*
>
> *The guinea pig caused a flurry of excitement on Monday morning as the children arrived for the day. Eloise sat by the cage with two of the toddlers on her lap and talked with the preschool-aged children about the new pet. While the guinea pig ran around in circles making high squealing sounds, the older boys decided that he should be named "Squeaky."*
>
> *Eloise explained that Squeaky would be frightened if people made too much noise or shook his cage. She also explained that although Squeaky was very gentle, he might be confused if he saw a finger sticking into his cage and think it was a carrot or something good to eat, and try to nibble on it. The preschool-aged children talked excitedly about Squeaky and managed to keep their hands behind their backs or in their pockets so they did not forget about shaking the cage or sticking their fingers through the bars.*
>
> *Eloise stepped into the bathroom to help one of the toddlers. Suddenly she heard a commotion with shrieks and squeals from the room with the guinea pig. In her absence, the children had gotten a bit too excited, and pushing and shoving in their eagerness to see Squeaky, the children had accidentally tipped the cage off the table, knocking the cage open. Squeaky was running around squealing, the children were running around shrieking, the toddlers were crying, and water and guinea pig food were spilled everywhere.*
>
> *Eloise quickly captured the terrified guinea pig and then, gently stroking the shaking Squeaky, said in a calm voice, "Listen boys and girls, can you hear the little sound Squeaky is making? He's very scared. Let's sing a quiet lullaby to Squeaky so he won't be frightened." Softly, the older children joined Eloise in singing "Rock-a-Bye-Baby" to little Squeaky. The toddlers watched wide-eyed. When everyone was calm and quiet, Eloise put Squeaky back into his cage and said, "We'll put Squeaky's cage in the storage room for a while so he can rest. After naptime, we'll get him out and watch him again."*

Eloise realized that the children had not maliciously intended to harm or frighten Squeaky; they simply were so excited that they could not manage the necessary self-control to deal with the situation successfully. Eloise felt confident that with enough time, patience, and practice, the children could eventually develop the self-control they needed to watch the guinea pig properly. She also knew that until that time, she needed to remove Squeaky, except during the times that she was able to supervise the children very closely as they watched him. Eloise recognized that reprimanding or punishing the children for their lack of self-control was not appropriate or helpful, since the children, at that point, were simply not yet capable of behaving in a more mature or controlled way. Instead, she helped them identify with Squeaky's feelings and needs so they could understand why they needed to watch without touching. She also knew that it was better to change the environment temporarily rather than trying to change the children's behavior.

GLEEFUL ABANDON, GROUP CONTAGION

Close your eyes for a minute and try to remember the exhilarated sensations you felt as a young child at a terrific birthday party, in a basement full of laughing cousins at a big family celebration, or maybe at a school Halloween carnival. Can you remember you and your friends or siblings going

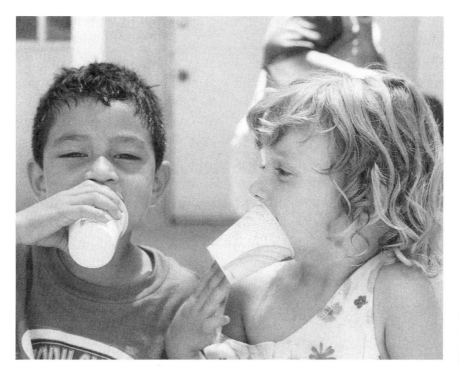

Children's innate desire to explore every possibility around them stretches their learning, but also stretches adult patience!

a little berserk? You knew you would get a stern lecture from your parents later, but it just felt so good you could not stop yourself. Whenever we have come to the end of our ropes with gleeful, goofy children, it may help for us to pause for a second and remember those magical moments in our own childhoods. I know I would love to feel that way again—totally uninhibited and free.

Tuesday mornings are always a little strange at the Elm Street Public Library. The sleepy little library comes to life as neighborhood children troop in for the children's story hour and other events scheduled especially for youngsters, such as movies and puppet shows.

Mrs. Asaad, the children's librarian, spends hours each week choosing just the right books and practicing reading them over and over to make sure her program is interesting and fun for the children. One Tuesday morning, Mrs. Asaad was helping an unusually young group of children get seated on the floor and ready for storytime. She positioned a row of the youngest children, a half-dozen particularly enthusiastic two-year-olds, right in front of her as she began singing a song about three little ducks.

One of the toddlers folded his hands under his armpits (to make duck wings) and helped her with the "quack, quack, quack" part of the song. The other toddlers caught on and began wagging their arms and quacking too, whereupon the first quacking toddler began giggling and falling over on the floor. Of course, all the other toddlers imitated by giggling and falling down and kicking their feet in the air.

Mrs. Asaad finished her song and good-naturedly helped Chris, the toddler who appeared to be the leader of the gang, to sit up. "Are you ready to hear a story about a little duck named Ping?" she asked. Chris vigorously shook his head yes. Of course all of the other toddlers began vigorously shaking their heads, too.

Mrs. Asaad, with great suspense in her voice, began the story. "Once upon a time in a faraway land, there was a little duck named Ping." All of the children, even the toddlers, leaned forward to hear every word. When Mrs. Asaad, however, got to the very exciting part of the story where Ping gets into mischief, the toddlers were overcome with their enthusiasm. Several began stamping their feet on the floor and Chris let out a squeal. As the other toddlers joined into the squealing, Chris began shaking his head so vigorously that his hair stood out all around his head.

Mrs. Asaad stood watching helplessly as the toddlers, and even some young threes, seemed possessed by this gleeful group contagion of head shaking and foot stamping. Suddenly, it dawned on Mrs. Asaad that the toddlers were more excited about the social presence of the other children than they were about her planned story. She realized that the story was simply not working at that particular time, so she laid down the book and stood up, saying, "Who can stretch high toward the sky? Great! Now, who can stamp your feet? Terrific! Let's sing 'Head and Shoulders, Knees and Toes.'"

After a few rousing choruses of active movement songs, Mrs. Asaad dismissed the group early, with an invitation to anyone who wanted to hear the end of the story about Ping to come sit with her. Some of the older children clustered around her (after the wild toddlers had left) and listened quietly to the end of the story.

Mrs. Asaad was very insightful to recognize that the toddlers' rowdy behavior was not a personal affront to her. Chris and the other twos were not naughty but just immensely happy. They were thrilled to be in a group of children at an exciting event, and did not have a clue about the life of a duck from a faraway land. Singing and moving as a group met their needs at this particular time, not hearing good literature.

BOREDOM

Boredom is one of the most predictable causes of misbehavior.

Neighborhood Nursery School was closed for the day, but staff members' children hung around, waiting for their parents' staff meeting to end. The nursery school staff took pride in their professionalism and high standards, and in order to reach their goals for quality, the staff met every Thursday afternoon after nursery school closed to discuss concerns.

Since most of the staff members were also parents, their own children had no alternative but to wait around while the parents met. Staff members took turns bringing a snack for the "staff kids" and attending to their problems and disagreements during meeting times, but it was clear that the staff kids dreaded the long Thursday afternoons. In early December, a meeting went on for hours as the staff planned special Christmas events. The staff kids had eaten their snack, colored pictures, and gone through stacks of puzzles and books. Shelley, five, and Jasmine, four and a half, were terribly bored and beginning to get a little silly. They were going through familiar books, making up ridiculous things for the characters to say, and then laughing uproariously at themselves.

Next, they decided that they were "Harriet the Spy," so they sneaked around under tables and behind furniture, trying to get a peek at the adults without being seen, then retreating to the restroom to roll on the floor in laughter. The spies decided that the next time they forayed into the enemy territory (the staff meeting room), they would attack the grown-ups' coffee table. Ever so slowly, Shelley crept under the refreshment table while Jasmine crouched excitedly in the hall, watching with both hands clasped over her mouth to stifle her giggles. While the adults talked on, a little hand slowly made its way up to the box of sugar cubes by the coffee pot and a strange sound—a muffled giggly sort of chortle—burst from Jasmine in the hall. The adults droned on, not noticing a thing.

The little hand (now grasping a whole handful of sugar cubes) slowly made its way back down the table. Unfortunately, it snagged the cord to the coffee pot on its way, and abruptly, the whole great adventurous fantasy came crashing down around little Shelley.

While Jasmine watched from the hall in horror, Shelley huddled under the table, her hands full of sugar cubes, surrounded by a dented coffee pot and huge puddles and rivulets of coffee. Her face flushed with embarrassment as the room full of astonished adults rushed toward her. Her mother looked the most shocked of all. Shelley was the kind of child no one ever expected to misbehave. Fortunately, no one was injured in this mishap. The adults' assumption that their children would behave appropriately without supervision, however, might just as easily have resulted in tragedy.

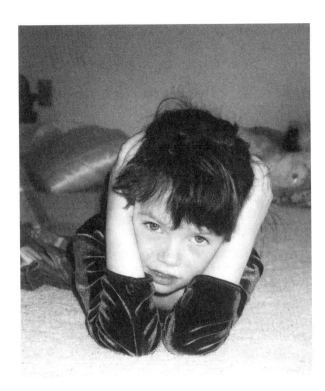

Boredom and fatigue have a definite effect on children's behavior.

Boredom, especially when coupled with lax supervision, is an open invitation to errant behavior (as well as to some extraordinary bursts of "creativity"). Diligent supervision is essential to positive child guidance. Attentive adults can identify the first indications of boredom and take steps to correct it.

FATIGUE AND DISCOMFORT

If we do not feel well, we may have difficulty behaving appropriately.

The Jacobsons had spent a wonderful day at the zoo. They had left home before sunrise and had driven several hours to a large city nearby to expose their four children to the wonders of a first-class zoo. The youngsters, three boys and a girl, ranged in age from fifteen months to eight years. They had enjoyed a near perfect day. The weather was great, the orangutan had hung upside down and delighted the children with wonderful ape tricks, and Allison, the toddler, had learned to say "monkey" and "bird" and make lots of new animal sounds. By the end of the day, the car trip home seemed particularly long and tedious. Al drove, and his wife, Regina, and the kids fell asleep shortly before the family reached home.

As they pulled into the driveway and everyone woke up, it was clear that the children were hungry, crabby, and generally exhausted. Al said, "I think I'll make pancakes for supper. That won't take long at all." Regina got the children bathed and dressed for bed, and everyone sat down to big fluffy pancakes, applesauce, and bacon, usually one of the kids' favorite meals.

Regina collapsed into a chair as Al lifted Allison (in her cute little "footy" pajamas and thick overnight diaper) into her high chair. He began to cut her pancake. Suddenly, Allison began to whine, shake her head, and push the high-chair tray. Al said, "What's wrong? Didn't you want me to cut up your pancake?" Allison stiffened and struggled, getting louder and louder. Al said, "Here, I'll trade pancakes. Mine isn't cut up." Allison took a swipe at the pancake and it landed on her brother William, causing him to start crying.

Al tried to calm William as Regina lifted Allison out of the high chair and said, "Honey, I know you're tired. We're all tired, but you may not throw food." Allison stiffened, struggled, and screamed even louder. Over her screams, Al and Regina wracked their brains to figure out what to do. Nothing they tried seemed to help, and every effort just seemed to make matters worse. They finally decided that the only thing to do was just to put Allison in her crib for the night. She sobbed herself to sleep, finally making the little rhythmic gasping sounds children make after they have cried hard.

After the boys were fed and asleep, Al and Regina puzzled over Allison's tantrum but could not decide whether this was a new stage or just the result of her being overstimulated and exhausted from the busy day.

The next morning, Regina leaned over Allison's crib to say good morning. Allison was all smiles while her mother unsnapped her damp pajama bottoms and pulled off the plastic pants. Then Regina stopped. She discovered to her dismay that a diaper pin was open. Allison had several bright red scratches and pin pricks on her left side. Regina removed the offending pin, then just stood there with tears filling her eyes. "Why," she asked herself, "didn't I think to check her diaper pins last night?"

Fatigue or anything that causes discomfort can cause children (and adults) to lose control and act aggressively, defy rules, or behave inappropriately. Being hungry, cold, hot, sick, or hurt are all reasons for children to be cranky and uncooperative. Very young children usually do not even realize that the source of their misery is a waistband that is painfully tight, a sock thread twisted around a toe, or scratchy sand in a wet diaper. Even older children sometimes become negative without recognizing that they just do not feel good. We need to remember that what appears on the surface is not always the whole story.

DESIRE FOR RECOGNITION

Being ignored hurts at any age.

At three, Kelley was the middle child. His big sister, Kathryn, brought home papers from her elementary school teacher saying how smart and good she was. She also had lots of girl friends who came and knocked on the door asking to play with her almost every day. Whenever Kelley tried to play with Kathryn and her friends, they would tell him to go away, and Kathryn would yell, "Mother, make Kelley go away and leave us alone!"

Kelley's baby brother, Nick, on the other hand, always seemed to be in mommy's arms, getting fed, or burped, or bathed, or rocked. When Kelley asked his mother to read him a book or push him on the swing, she said, "Kelley, please go play with your toys. The baby's crying and I can't play with you right now." Kelley thought his mother did not love him any more, only that stupid baby (and Kathryn with all her important homework and prissy friends).

Kelley wet his pants. His mother said, "Kelley! You're such a big boy. You know how to go to the potty." Kelley sneaked a bottle and climbed into baby Nick's crib. He pretended to be a baby and drank the bottle even though it tasted pretty nasty. His mother said, "Kelley! What are you doing in there? This crib isn't built for a big boy like you. It's for the baby. Look, your shoes have gotten the sheets all dirty."

Kelley pushed an old lawn chair against a tree and climbed up into the tree. Even though it was very scary, he climbed higher and higher until he could not climb any further. Then he started to cry. Kelley's mother ran outside when she heard Kelley crying. "Oh, my soul!" she yelled, "Kelley, how in the world did you get up there?" She called Kelley's dad and it took two hours and the help of several neighbors to get Kelley safely out of the tree. When his dad got him to the lowest branch, he handed Kelley down to his mother. She hugged him so hard he could hardly breathe, but he did not mind. He was just glad to be out of that tree.

Kelley's dad sat down on the grass. He was still panting and sweating from all the climbing and worrying. He motioned for Kelley to come sit on his lap. "Son," he said, "your mother and I love you. You're the only Kelley we have. We can't ever get another boy just like you. Kathryn is special and Baby Nick is special, but Kathryn can't ride on my shoulders and Baby Nick can't sing all the words to 'I've Been Working on the Railroad.' You are the only one who can do those things."

He gave Kelley a playful squeeze and said, "Did you think we could put a penny in a gumball machine and out would roll another Kelley just exactly like you? That I could just go down to the grocery store and put a shiny new penny in there and, POP, out would come a new Kelley? No siree! We couldn't get a new Kelley that way. You're the only one exactly like you in the whole world."

Kelley sat in his dad's lap, encircled by his dad's strong arms, his face snuggled so close to his dad's chest that he could hear the sound of his dad's big heart thumping, the deep voice, and rumbly laughter. Kelley imagined brightly colored gumballs with his face on them rolling out of a grocery store gumball machine. He took a deep breath and grinned.

Feeling ignored is far more painful and frightening for young children than being in trouble and having everyone angry or upset. All human beings need to feel a sense of belonging, to feel that they are wanted and needed. If a child feels unwanted or left out, he may not be able to cooperate and follow rules.

DISCOURAGEMENT

Becoming overwhelmed by discouragement can cause anyone to feel depressed and angry.

Fiona's family moved to a new neighborhood. In her old school, she had already started second grade and had really liked the teacher there. She had made good marks on her schoolwork, and the teacher often let her help other children when her own work was finished.

The teacher had especially praised Fiona for her careful block printing and often put Fiona's papers on the bulletin board for all to see. In her new school, however, Fiona did not think the new teacher, Miss Crane, was very happy to have her in class. On the first day she attended the new school, Miss Crane acted annoyed, and Fiona heard her complain bitterly to another teacher about having to take a student from a different school district in the middle of the year. When Fiona began carefully printing her name in the new workbook Miss Crane gave her, Miss Crane snapped, "Young lady, in this school, second graders do not print! We write in cursive."

Fiona hung her head and stared at her feet, wondering what cursive was. She knew she had heard her mother say many times that she did not like cursing at all. She wondered if her mother would approve of Miss Crane (with her long, blood-red fingernails, bright purple eye-shadow, and high heels). Miss Crane gave Fiona a little workbook filled with grown-up writing and pale blue straight and dotted lines. She said, "I don't have time to teach you everything I've already gone over it with the rest of the class. Just go through this workbook and write the words on each page like the ones in the examples. I don't ever want to see you doing printing in this class again. Do you understand?"

Fiona sat at the back of the room by herself, feeling terribly dejected but struggling to copy the weirdly shaped letters in the workbook. Finally, it began to make sense to her that some of the words were made of familiar letters. The letters were just hooked together in a long string like beads on a necklace. She carefully printed the letters she knew and then tediously connected them to make them look like the examples.

Miss Crane did not like Fiona's work at all. She yelled and told Fiona, "This is not how you write in cursive! You will not be allowed to do another thing until you apply yourself and do this work right. Can't you see how the other children are writing?" Fiona was too embarrassed to look around. She hoped none of the other children were staring at her.

Fiona became very quiet at home. She did not bubble with stories about her day. She stopped looking forward to school and began to have stomach aches almost every morning. She begged her mother to let her stay home. She also seemed unusually irritable, and often had angry fights with her sisters and brothers. Her mother wondered if Fiona was ill. At school, Fiona went to the pencil sharpener every time she thought Miss Crane was looking or walking in her direction. With so much sharpening, the pencil lead was always too pointed so it snapped every time she nervously pressed down on the paper. She erased until she finally wore holes in the sheets of paper in her workbook, which began to look like Swiss cheese and made her work look even more awful. Miss Crane became exasperated with Fiona and began to wonder if Fiona was a slow learner or just a difficult, uncooperative little girl.

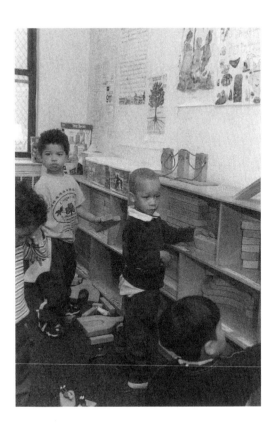

Feelings of discouragement cause children to be less, rather than more, cooperative.

Actually, Fiona was not sick, slow, or difficult, just very, very discouraged. Her self-esteem had slipped, leaving her vulnerable and disorganized, and not at all able to do competent schoolwork, make friends, or live up to the teacher's expectations. Being harshly criticized and "put down" makes it harder, not easier, for a child to accomplish difficult tasks.

FRUSTRATION

No matter how old or how young, we all risk losing control when we hit a certain level of frustration.

Benny was two years old. Hardly a day went by without his mother, Virginia, pointing out to someone that he was a "typical terrible two." He vacillated between acting like a baby and trying to act like a grown-up. He whined, "Me do it," whenever his mother tried to tie his shoes. When Virginia became exasperated with him over the shoelaces, she said, "Okay, you tie them." Of course Benny did not know how to tie them, but he stubbornly worked for fifteen minutes, twisting the laces into a scrambled mass of knots.

Virginia said, "Now look what you've done. I told you that you didn't know how to tie them. Be still so I can get these knots out and tie them right." Benny kicked and fought hard to keep his mother from touching his shoes. She finally spanked him to make him let go of his shoes so she could tie them.

Even though Virginia was a single mother with a demanding job and classes two nights a week, she kept her apartment perfectly clean, and went to garage sales and re-sale shops on weekends to see to it that Benny had all the toys and clothes a toddler could need. Every day, he was dropped at his child care center looking freshly scrubbed and starched, with every hair in place.

When Virginia got Benny home on the weekday evenings that she did not have to go to class, she always had a lot of work facing her. She usually put Benny on the floor and told him to play with his basket of toys while she cooked, cleaned, and studied. Most often, Benny abandoned the toys and followed his mother around getting into her school books or the kitchen cabinets and making messes. When her patience with him wore thin, she would smack his hand and say "no" or give him a firm swat on the bottom.

Tension built in their little household between the busy, frazzled mother and the clingy, insistent toddler. At his child care center, Benny began biting other children when they re-fused to give him a toy or let him have a turn on the tricycle. Even being made to sit on the "thinking chair" for a "time-out" by his teachers seemed to have absolutely no effect on stopping his biting. In fact, it actually seemed to make him more stubborn and agitated.

One day, Benny had been in trouble several times so he was sitting by himself playing with a jack-in-the-box. He cranked the tiny handle and listened to the tune as it played "around and around the cobbler's bench the monkey chased the weasel . . ." until out popped the little clown.

Benny watched attentively, then tried to push the little clown back into the box to close the lid so that he could do it again. He pushed the little clown's head down into the box and mashed hard on the lid, but the toy clown's two little flat, plastic hands were sticking out and the lid would not close. Benny pushed on the lid as hard as he could, but his hand slipped and the little clown popped back out.

Benny glared at the uncooperative toy clown then bent down and bit the little clown's hand. Benny bit so long and hard that his whole body shook with the effort, and he left a clear imprint of his teeth on the plastic hand.

Much of Benny's aggression probably stemmed from the stress and pressure he was encoun-tering in his daily life. His mother, Virginia, had a lot of frustration building up in her as she tried to survive financially and emotionally as a single parent, a working mother of a toddler, and as a student. She felt frustrated in her efforts to be a perfect mother while also trying to deal with her own personal and social needs. Benny "caught" some of her stress like a contagious illness. He did not know why he felt so tense and stubborn all the time, and he did not know how to make the feelings go away.

Stress is a very real crisis for many children and families today. Children can absorb stress un-knowingly from their parents and caregivers, or develop stress symptoms directly from their own lifestyles. Today, there are children who, from earliest childhood, spend their days going from classroom to tutoring to individual lessons to social events, virtually every day from dawn to dusk. Whatever the cause of stress, its symptoms often include inappropriate behavior (along with health, appetite, and concentration problems).

REBELLION

Under repressive enough circumstances, even the most docile of us might be inclined to rebel.

Coach Sam, a tall, muscular nineteen-year-old, had just been hired as the gymnastics instructor in a large, inner-city community center that provided after-school care for six-through twelve-year-olds. His childhood dreams of reaching the Olympics had been dashed by a troublesome back injury, so he found himself teaching gymnastics to small children, something he had never particularly wanted to do.

He decided that in order to create discipline in his class, he would start from the very beginning with his class by being very tough and demanding. He assembled his group of first, second, and third graders on the floor and, towering in front of them with his hands on his hips, announced in a booming voice, "If you talk without my permission, you're out of here. If you don't pay attention and follow my instructions, you're out of here. And, if you even think about being lazy or careless, you're history. Is that understood?" The children chorused back in unison, "Yes, Coach."

At first the children seemed very intimidated by Coach Sam and did everything he said. They were serious and attentive and jumped when he said jump. Gradually, their obedience became more and more strained. Coach Sam never praised the children's accomplishments other than to make a curt comment such as, "Well, finally you're paying attention." He was, however, very quick to mete out caustic criticism such as, "If that's the best you can do, just go sit by the wall. You're not worth me wasting my time." These comments hurt, and the children grew to dislike Coach Sam intensely.

They began to do little things when Coach Sam's back was turned. It became a game for them to see if they could break rules without getting caught. They smuggled candy and gum into the gym. They giggled and whispered whenever Coach Sam tried to give individual attention to a child. Coach Sam yelled and threatened and punished, but the children continued to become even more open in their unruliness.

The children wondered why Coach Sam so frequently threatened to kick them out of class but never followed through on the threat. They did not know that he lacked the authority to expel students from class. They did, however, begin to recognize that most of his threats were empty gestures. In his annoyance and frustration, Coach Sam became colder and more demanding with the children. They became more callous and uncooperative with him. Coach Sam regularly punished children by making them sit by a wall for long periods. Some of the children seemed to be sent to sit by the wall so often that they almost never were allowed to participate. They found ways to use their "sitting" time to create more mischief and disruption for Coach Sam. They expressed their dislike of him and his tactics by causing him endless frustration and interruption. Several children even talked their parents into letting them walk home after school and stay alone rather than go to the community center program at all.

One day, the children in the gymnastics class staged an outright mutiny. They were totally out of control in spite of Coach Sam's yelling and threatening. He ordered a little girl who seemed to be a ring leader to "go sit by the wall for the rest of class." She yelled back, "You can't make me! You're not my mother!" Several other children joined in the confrontation, shouting, "That's right, you can't make me either!"

Coach Sam was filled with feelings of rage and helplessness. He knew he would be fired instantly if he struck any of the children, but he was overwhelmed with the urge to show them he had control over them. If he could not use physical force to control them, then he simply did not know how to maintain discipline and order. Coach Sam did not know that positive discipline can best be achieved by establishing an atmosphere of fairness, trust, honesty, and mutual respect, not by trying to create fear and submission.

The stage is set for rebellion when:

- children feel anger and contempt rather than affection and respect for the authority figures in their lives who set and enforce rules.

- a situation exists in which it is overly difficult for children to abide by specific rules or live up to expectations.

- children realize that rules are just hollow threats that will not be consistently or fairly enforced.

- children reach such a point of discouragement that they feel they are in so much trouble that nothing else they do can make things any worse for them.

Frustration triggers misbehavior. Feeling cornered and threatened can trigger rebelliousness.

These conditions not only trigger rebellion in young children, but in a more general way, are the same kinds of conditions that trigger rebellion and defiance of law and order in segments of adult populations in society at large. Alienation, discouragement, and outrage at inequity are not feelings limited to adults, but on a much smaller scale, also tempt children to defy authority in spite of the risk of punishment (Crockenberg, 1997; Edwards, 1997; Fields & Boesser, 1998; Gallo, 1997; Gartrell, 1997; Katz & McClellan, 1997; Leach, 1996; McCloskey, 1997).

POINTS TO REMEMBER

- Positive child guidance focuses on the child's ability level, the severity and intent of the behavior, and possible reasons for the behavior.

- Adult-centered definitions of misbehavior focus on the effect a child's behavior has on the adult.

- Child-centered definitions of misbehavior focus on the ability level, motives, and long-term well-being of the child in evaluating the appropriateness or inappropriateness of actions.

- Moral reasoning is the thinking that guides children in deciding what is right or wrong.

PRACTICAL APPLICATION

IS A "REALLY GOOD SPANKING" REALLY GOOD?

Edna and Wilbert stopped at a neighborhood fast-food restaurant for a quick hamburger on Saturday afternoon. The place was buzzing with activity and children of all ages were everywhere. Edna and Wilbert had no children of their own, but they watched in amazement as many different types of adults talked to, played with, and reprimanded children.

Wilbert was especially curious about one harried woman who seemed to be in charge of a half-dozen youngsters. One of the children, a six-year-old, shook salt into her hand, licked it, then laughed as she brushed her salty hands over the children near her. They shrieked with laughter as they dodged the salt, throwing napkins to defend themselves. The woman looked sternly at them and threatened to make them sit in the car if they did not settle down.

Wilbert leaned over and whispered to Edna, "What those children need is a really good spanking!"

DISCUSSION QUESTIONS

1. What could be some possible reasons the children Wilbert was watching were behaving the way they were?
2. Why do you suppose Wilbert believed spanking would be helpful?
3. What do you think would be the most effective and appropriate thing for the woman to do in the situation described above?

RELATED READINGS

NURTURING AT-RISK CHILDREN

Aidman, A. (1997, December). *Television violence: Content, context, and consequences.* Champaign, IL: ERIC Clearinghouse on Elementary and Early Childhood Education. Document #EDO-PS-97-26.

Barko, N. (1997). Labeled for life? In K. M. Paciorek & J. H. Munro (Eds.), *Annual editions: Early childhood education 97/98* (18th ed.). New York: McGraw-Hill. (Original work published in *Parents*, September 1996.)

Special needs children are often labeled at an early age to initiate services for remediation. Problems can occur when the label is not accurate or the child's development progresses to the point where the special services are no longer required.

Begley, S., and Springen, K. (1997). Life in a parallel world. In E. N. Junn & C. Boyatzis (Eds.), *Annual editions: Child growth and development 97/98* (4th ed.). New York: McGraw-Hill. (Original work published in *Newsweek*, May 13, 1996.)

An increasing number of children are diagnosed as autistic. Autism is a disease; the cause is unknown, but it leaves children socially withdrawn with poor communication skills, compulsive behavior, and, occasionally, savantism. This article describes recent changes in the definition of autism and some theories of its cause.

Benard, B. (1991). *Fostering resiliency in kids: Protective factors in the family, school, and community.* San Francisco: Far West Laboratory for Educational Research and Development.

Blankenhorn, D. (1997). Life without father. In K. M. Paciorek and J. H. Munro (Eds.), *Annual editions: Early childhood education 97/98* (18th ed.). New York: McGraw-Hill. (Original work published in *USA Weekend*, February 24-26, 1995.)

The increase in divorce and in single-mother families has led to a situation that David Blankenhorn calls "disappearing dads." Children without two caring and supportive parents are at risk of future failure in a number of areas.

Bozett, F. W. (1987). *Gay and lesbian parents.* New York: Praeger.

Brooks, R., & Goldstein, S. (2001). *Raising resilient children: Fostering strength, hope, and optimism in your child.* Lincolnwood, IL: Contemporary Books.

Brophy, J. (1996). *Teaching problem students.* New York: Guilford.

Brown, J. L., & Pollitt, E. (1997). Malnutrition, poverty, and intellectual development. In E. N. Junn & C. Boyatzis (Eds.), *Annual editions: Child growth and development 97/98* (4th ed.). New York: McGraw-Hill. (Original work published in *Scientific American*, February 1996.)

The authors describe research from around the world demonstrating that a poor diet influences children's intellectual development in many ways. The article also addresses other effects of poverty on children's mental growth.

Budd, L. (1993). *Living with the active alert child.* Seattle, WA: Parenting Press, Inc.

Bullock, J. R. (1997). Children without friends. In E. N. Junn & C. Boyatzis (Eds.), *Annual editions: Child growth and development 97/98* (4th ed.). New York: McGraw-Hill. (Original work published in *Childhood Education*, Winter 1992.)

According to research, having friends is crucial for normal development. This article describes the sociometric status of different kinds of children—the popular, rejected, and neglected—and the implications of not having friends. Suggestions are given for teachers to identify and help children without friends.

Cantor, J. (1998). *Mommy, I'm scared: How TV and movies frighten children and what we can do to protect them.* Fort Washington, PA: Harvest Books.

Christian, L. G. (1997, May). Children and Death. *Young Children, 52*(4), 76–80.

Coiro, M. J. (1997). *Maternal depressive symptoms as a risk factor for the development of children in poverty.* Phoenix, AZ: Oryx Press.

Cooksey, E. C., & Fondell, M. M. (1996). Spending time with his kids: Effects of family structure on fathers' and children's lives. *Journal of Marriage and the Family, 58*(3), 693–707.

Copeland, M. L., & McCreedy, B. S. (1997, January–February). Creating family-friendly policies: Are child care center policies in line with current family realities? *Child Care Information Exchange, 113*, 7-10, 12.

Crouson, R. L., & Boyd, W. L. (1993, February). Coordinated services for children: Designing arks for storms and seas unknown. *American Journal of Education, 101*, 141.

Davis, M. D., Kilgo J. L., & Gamel-McCormick, M. (1998). *Young children with special needs: A developmentally appropriate approach.* Needham Heights, MA: Allyn & Bacon.

This book proposes that children with disabilities are more like their peers without disabilities than they are different, and that we need to provide programming from that perspective. Both beginning students and experienced teachers are facing the reality that early childhood classes reflect increasingly more diverse children as time goes on. Child diversity in terms of race, culture, religion, experience, family, and national origin is related to social and economic realities. Increasing emphasis on inclusion promises to add even more complexity to teachers' decision-making processes.

Denby, D. (1997). Buried alive. In E. N. Junn & C. Boyatzis (Eds.), *Annual editions: Child growth and development 97/98* (4th ed.). New York: McGraw-Hill. (Original work published in *The New Yorker*, July 15, 1996.)

Argues that television, films, toys, and video and computer games overwhelm children with violence. Author offers insight into the impact popular culture may have on children's character and perception of reality.

Eichstaedt, C. B., & Kalakian, L. H. (1993). *Developmental/adapted physical education.* Needham Heights, MA: Allyn & Bacon.

This book focuses on the individual learner rather than on the disability, and encourages teachers to emphasize what learners can do rather than what they cannot do. It is based on the belief that a sound developmental approach to physical education is fundamental to all good learning experiences, both for pupils with disabilities and for those who are ablebodied. Adaptations should be made only to the extent necessary to accommodate a learner's unique developmental needs. It includes children from birth to age three, and discusses developmental milestones in one-year increments, offering guidelines for motor assessment, program development, and physical activities, both for infants and toddlers with disabilities and for those who are at-risk.

Frede, E., & Barnett, W. S. (1992). Developmentally appropriate public school preschool: A study of implementation of the High/Scope curriculum and its effects on disadvantaged children's skills at first grade. *Early Childhood Research Quarterly, 7*(4), 483–499.

Gamezy, N. (1991). Resiliency and vulnerability to adverse developmental outcomes associated with poverty. *American Behavioral Scientist 34*, 416–430.

Goldstein, S., & Goldstein, M. (1992). *Hyperactivity: Why won't my child pay attention?* New York: John Wiley.

Grossman, D., Degaetano, G., & Grossman, D. (1999). *Stop teaching our kids to kill: A call to action against TV, movie and video game violence.* New York: Random House.

Jackson, B. R. (1997, November). Creating a climate for healing in a violent society. *Young Children, 52*(7), 68–70.

Kagan, S. L. (1997, May). Support systems for children, youths, families, and schools in inner-city situations. *Education and Urban Society, 29*(3), 277–95.

Karweit, N. (1993). Effective preschool and kindergarten programs for students at-risk. In B. Spodek (Ed.), *Handbook of research on the education of young children* (pp. 385–411). New York: Macmillan.

Landau, S., & McAninch, C. (1997). Young children with attention deficits. In E. N. Junn & C. Boyatzis (Eds.), *Annual editions: Child growth and development 97/98* (4th ed.). New York: McGraw-Hill. (Original work published in *Young Children*, May 1993.)

Attention-deficit hyperactivity disorder (ADHD) is a frequently misunderstood, complex disorder. This review article describes ADHD, its possible causes, treatments, and the effects of the disorder for children in the classroom setting.

Levine, M. (1998). *See no evil: A guide to protecting our children from media violence.* New York: Jossey-Bass.

McAlister, B. G. (1997, Spring). Growing up in a violent world: The impact of family and community violence on young children and their families. *Topics in Early Childhood Special Education, 17*(1), 74–102.

McMath, J. S. (1997, March). Young children, national tragedy, and picture books. *Young Children, 52*(3), 82–84.

Noonan, M. J., & McCormick, L. (1993). *Early intervention in natural environments: Methods and procedures.* Needham Heights, MA: Brooks/Cole.

Offering readers a variety of empirically validated "best practices," Noonan and McCormick's book focuses on early intervention methods for infants, toddlers, preschoolers, and kindergartners who are developmentally delayed or at-risk.

Ramler, M., & Rice, S. (1997, Summer). Looking beyond chronic illness: Helping children be children. *Texas Child Care, 21*(1), 12–15.

Rief, S. F. (1993). *How to reach and teach ADD/ADHD children.* West Nyack, NY: The Center for Applied Research in Education.

Rubin, K. H., LeMare, L. J., & Lollis, S. (1990). Social withdrawal in childhood: Developmental pathways to peer rejection. In S. R. Asher & J. D. Coie (Eds.), *Peer rejection in childhood* (pp. 217–249). New York: Cambridge University Press.

Sroufe, L. A. (1996). *Child development: Its nature and course.* New York: McGraw-Hill.

This book has information on gender socialization and gender development; emotional development, prenatal effects of crack, AIDS, and AZT; genetic research; postnatal development, including information on how brain growth is influenced by experience; infant intelligence, assessment, bilingualism, early roots of morality, cross-cultural education; and mixed gender social relationships.

Stephens, K., et al. (1996, September–October). When children are difficult. Beginnings Workshop. *Child Care Information Exchange, 111,* 43–50, 55–62.

Swick, K. J. (1997, Spring). Strengthening homeless families and their young children. *Dimensions of Early Childhood, 25*(2), 29–34.

Turecki, Stanley. (1989). *The difficult child.* New York: Bantam Books.

Werner, E., & Smith, R. (1989). *Vulnerable but invincible: A longitudinal study of resilient children and youth.* New York: Adams, Bannister, & Cox.

Werner, E., & Smith, R. (1992). *Overcoming the odds: High-risk children from birth to adulthood.* New York: Cornell University Press.

Wodrich, D. L. (1994). *What every parent wants to know: Attention deficit hyperactivity disorder.* Baltimore: Paul H. Brookes Publishing Company.

HELPFUL WEB SITES

http://www.ccw.org/home/   Center for Child Care Workforce focuses on improving the quality of child care services by upgrading the wages, benefits, training opportunities, and working conditions for child care teachers and family child care providers.

http://www.naeyc.org/resources/default.asp   National Association for the Education of Young Children. This essential early childhood organization offers a wealth of resources for early childhood workers and parents seeking professional information about developmentally appropriate programs, career training, and accreditation.

http://institute.wheelock.edu/   Wheelock College Institute for Leadership and Career Development (formerly the Center for Career Development in Early Care and Education) provides professional development and child advocacy to support high-quality children's programs.

For additional information on positive child guidance, visit our Web site at
http://www.earlychilded.delmar.com

Chapter 4
Guidelines for Effective Guidance

OBJECTIVES

After reading this chapter, you should be able to:
- Develop specific strategies for effective guidance.
- Formulate guidelines for responding to inappropriate behaviors.
- Identify methods to shape positive behavior.
- Specify techniques for assertive redirection and follow-up.

Healthy, well-developing children are naturally lively and full of silliness.

IGNORE MILDLY ANNOYING BEHAVIOR THAT IS NEITHER HARMFUL NOR UNFAIR

Children are not helped by intrusive and overwhelming attempts to change too much of their behavior at one time. Adults do well to focus disciplinary actions on urgent priorities while overlooking mildly annoying behaviors that are neither harmful nor unfair to others. In dealing with a child who has behaved aggressively but who also bites her fingernails and rocks her chair back and forth, an adult should initially focus attention only on the aggression. A mental note could be made to address the other problems in a more subtle and indirect manner at a later time, well after the aggression has been resolved. We adults sometimes have a tendency to "unload all barrels," overwhelming children with too many demands, especially when we are angry and upset. If a child has an unusual number of behavior problems, a medical professional may be able to identify a common cause and recommend possible solutions.

FOCUS ATTENTION ELSEWHERE

When a child does something that is mildly annoying or embarrassing (but not unacceptable), the adult may resolve the problem simply by focusing the child's attention elsewhere. A baby who is banging a spoon on a metal high-chair tray in a restaurant may be distracted by a parent who plays peek-a-boo or dangles a softer, quieter toy. A thumb-sucking toddler may be distracted from the sucking by being given an interesting toy to explore. A curious preschooler may be distracted from handling items on shelves in the grocery store by being allowed to help push the grocery cart or to help arrange foods in the basket as they are selected.

DISCREETLY REDIRECT SLIGHTLY INAPPROPRIATE BEHAVIOR TO MORE POSITIVE SUBSTITUTE BEHAVIOR

Slightly annoying behaviors can also be redirected by involving the child in an activity that **replaces** (cannot be done simultaneously with) the undesirable behavior. For example, a child who is picking at her nose can be directed to use a tissue to blow her nose. Without ever even mentioning the nose-picking, the adult can explain how using a tissue, throwing away the tissue, and then washing hands may keep others from catching a cold.

In order to redirect slightly inappropriate behaviors, we can identify activities that involve the part, or parts, of the child's body currently being used in the undesirable action, then an alternative action involving those body parts can be substituted. For example, a child who is using her hands to feel the blossoms of a neighbor's delicate and expensive garden plants could be shown how to put her hands behind her back or in her pockets while she leans over to smell the wonderful fragrance of the gardenias. She could also be redirected to use her hands to gather interesting leaves and acorns from the ground.

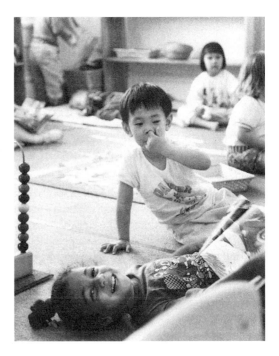

"Here is a tissue. After you blow your nose, I will help you wash your hands."

This helps the child know that it is okay to explore and enjoy nature, but not okay to damage another person's property. Snapping, "Don't touch those plants!," discourages curiosity, a key factor in the child's long-term ability to develop intellectually. Of course, standing by passively while one's child damages a neighbor's prized gardenias would be rude and disrespectful.

ASSIST THE CHILD IN RECOGNIZING THE GENERAL EFFECTS OF POSITIVE BEHAVIORS

Another method for gently redirecting minor misbehaviors involves focusing the child's attention on the positive outcome of more desirable behaviors. The adult gives information to the child. The adult might say, "If you put your glass of milk on the top corner of your place mat, it will be safely out of your way until you want to drink it." A teacher might say, "If you erase mistakes slowly and lightly, your paper will look very nice." A toddler can be told, "I like to hear 'thank you.' Oh, how nice! Brett remembered to say 'thank you.'"

TAKE TIME TO THINK BEFORE YOU RESPOND TO BITING

WHAT TO LOOK FOR

1. Does the biting seem to be a reflexive response rather an aggressive act?
Babies under one year have limited self-awareness and almost no conscious control over their behavior. A baby beginning to cut teeth may bite unexpectedly while breast-feeding. An older baby may bite when emotionally overwhelmed with discomfort, excitement, fatigue, or fright. In fact, an older baby involved in an overly exciting game of peek-a-boo may be laughing wildly one moment then suddenly bite anything or anyone who is handy the next moment.

2. What were the circumstances surrounding and just prior to the biting?
Toddlers in the second and third year of life have begun to gain some control over their behavior, but they have limited verbal skills and may feel powerless and overwhelmed when they are frustrated, angry, in pain, or frightened. It is almost inevitable that toddlers discover the sheer power of a bite:

WHAT TO DO

1. Be calm, firm, and consistent.
Establish eye contact at eye level, make gentle but firm physical contact with the child, and calmly but urgently say, "No biting. Biting hurts." Then immediately redirect the child's attention to a different activity. Gently stroke the bitten child or adult while soothingly saying, "Gentle . . . be gentle." If needed, carry the biter to a different location and engage her in a totally different activity. Trying to have a baby or young toddler sit in "Time out" makes absolutely no sense, but an abrupt change in location and activity will interrupt the behavior and reinforce a growing sense in the child that biting is not okay and will not be tolerated.

2. Prevention is the key.
Focus your energy on preventing that first bite by providing close supervision, and by removing sources of frustration and stress. Biting is contagious! A toddler who gets bitten is highly likely to try out this new

(continues)

TAKE TIME TO THINK BEFORE YOU RESPOND TO BITING *(continued)*

WHAT TO LOOK FOR

toddler teeth can make even a big strong grownup flinch and howl. No wonder it is so tempting for toddlers to latch onto this tactic for self-expression. Kicking and screaming may be ignored, but a bite is sure to get immediate attention from just about anyone.

Remember that babies and toddlers are just beginning to develop the ability to think about an action (biting) then consciously choose *not* to do it. Learning takes time, consistency, and patience. In the initial stages of learning, a baby or toddler may bite, then immediately look up, shake her head, and say, "No, no!"

3. Has the biting become chronic?
While most older babies and toddlers bite someone at some time or other, chronic biting is a different matter. A preschool-aged child who still bites is a source of serious concern. Biting is painful, it can be a source of infection, and adults and other children must be protected.

Ask yourself:

- Are there other indications that the child may be experiencing emotional or health problems?

- Are there reasons the child might be feeling overwhelmed and helpless?

- Is the child generally developing as expected for her age?

- Is the child being exposed to violence and aggression through television, movies, and games?

- Is the child being abused?

- Are the child's physical needs being met? Is she getting adequate sleep, nutrition, and health care?

- Does the child feel unconditionally loved and accepted by the adults in her life?

WHAT TO DO

tactic on others. Biting spreads in a toddler classroom faster than a runny nose in January. Diligent supervision and developmentally appropriate care will help adults prevent biting outbreaks. Be sure children are getting plenty of rest, a calm environment, and plenty of emotional nurturing.

Boredom is a major source of stress for babies and toddlers, so ensure a safe, accessible environment with interesting things to explore and challenge budding motor skills. Babies and toddlers need things to climb over, under, and around; things to empty, fill, and carry around; things to stack, knock down, and bang together; and safe substances for exploring unfamiliar sounds, sights, smells, tastes, and textures.

3. Convene a "summit meeting" of parents and caregivers.
Bring the adults together—not to blame anyone—but to brainstorm the problem and collaborate in problem-solving. There is usually not a single problem leading to chronic biting, but a cluster of irritants that are interfering with the child's ability to develop self-control.

Typically, child care staff blame the family, the family blame the child care staff, and everyone blames the child. Success is most likely, however, when the adults resist the temptation to point fingers, and all commit themselves to systematically identifying and removing possible causes of the misbehavior. The simple act of meeting regularly and cooperatively to discuss progress and strategies has an almost magical effect on chronic misbehavior. Medical experts and counselors who specialize in evaluating and treating developmental problems can be a tremendous asset to families and teachers. Don't hesitate to call on them.

IMMEDIATELY INTERRUPT BEHAVIOR THAT IS HARMFUL OR UNFAIR

Children rely on adults to enforce rules and protect individual rights. Children will be willing to "play by the rules" only if they come to believe that rules are meaningful. Consistency and fairness in the enforcement of rules help children learn to trust authority figures. Behaviors that are harmful or unfair must be interrupted immediately by a responsible adult.

Adults do not help children become cooperative and respectful by passively watching them fight, saying, "They'll just have to learn to stand up for themselves. When Jimmy has had enough of Gerald hitting him, he'll learn to hit back." We also fail to help children when we say, "Don't come tell me that someone hit you. I don't want to hear about it!" Children can be helped to resolve their own disagreements, but they must know that adults will reliably stop unacceptable, hurtful behavior.

INTERVENE AS FIRMLY AS NECESSARY BUT AS GENTLY AS POSSIBLE

When we find it necessary to stop an unacceptable behavior, we should always proceed as firmly as necessary to stop the unacceptable action, but as gently as possible to remind the child that he is accepted and respected as a person, even if his behavior must be ended.

Children will be willing to "play by the rules" only if they come to believe that rules are meaningful.

As Miss Melanie firmly pries a toddler's clenched fingers one-by-one out of another screaming toddler's hair, she says with a tone of urgent concern (not anger) in her voice, "Ouch! Pulling hurts. No pulling. Touch gently, please!" After the toddlers are safely separated, she softly strokes each toddler's hair saying, "Gentle, be gentle. Please touch hair gently." Miss Melanie has interrupted a harmful behavior as firmly as necessary but as gently as possible.

Roger grabs a little car from his friend Chris and runs away. Chris yells and starts to cry. Mr. Reese follows Roger (persistently but without chasing him), saying in a deeply concerned tone, "Stop, please. Roger, I need you to stop so we can talk about Chris' car." When Roger finally pauses for a second, Mr. Reese says, "Thank you for waiting. Let's sit down and talk about Chris' car. You like Chris' car, don't you? It's really a neat car, isn't it?"

Mr. Reese does not immediately attempt to snatch the car away from Roger. He patiently asks, "What should you do if you want to see someone else's toy? Should you ask, 'May I play with your car?'" Roger hungs his head and says, "But if I ask him, he might say no." Mr. Reese answers, "You're right. He might say yes or he might say no. Would you like for me to come with you so you can ask? If he says no, I will help you find a different toy to play with. Remember, taking things without asking is not allowed, so when you choose a toy, no one will be allowed to take your toy away without asking you first, right?"

Roger's unfair action has been stopped, firmly but gently, and Roger has had a chance to learn a very important lesson. Although rules sometimes stop him from doing what he wants to do, they also ensure that his own rights are protected.

Enforcing fair rules protects the rights of all children.

MAINTAIN OBJECTIVITY

Marilyn's three-year-old daughter, Stephanie, waited patiently (although she was becoming very bored) while her mother shopped for new towels in a department store. Stephanie caught sight of a little boy about her age shopping with his mother on the other side of a large pillow display. Stephanie peeked around the edge of the pile of pillows to get a better look at the little boy. He grinned at her. Embarrassed, she quickly scrambled back behind the pillow display. Unfortunately, in her haste, she dislodged the display, and an avalanche of pillows piled down on top of her.

Two salespersons rushed over (looking very annoyed), and several other shoppers stared at the mess. Marilyn was startled and horrified to see what Stephanie had done. She grabbed Stephanie by the arm and marched her off to the ladies' lounge to have a "few words." Marilyn did not manage to stay objective about her daughter's behavior. She took her own feelings of embarrassment out on Stephanie. She could have been more helpful to Stephanie if she had been able to maintain a more objective and less emotional perspective.

We can greatly assist the development of self-control in children by staying focused on the reality of a situation rather than on adult feelings that are not relevant to the child's problem, such as preconceived notions and biased attitudes that do not relate directly to what the child has done. Marilyn's guidance will be more effective if she can push aside her feelings of humiliation (and apprehension that complete strangers will think she is a bad mother). Marilyn should focus on the objective reality of the situation: Stephanie had been trying to wait patiently, she did not intentionally do anything wrong, and she was obviously feeling upset and embarrassed already.

Even a child who has misbehaved deserves reassurance that he is still loved.

Positive child guidance is a teaching process. As in any educational process, powerful emotions such as anger, disgust, or the threat of harm, damage rather than assist the process of learning. People, children included, are better able to concentrate and absorb information when they are reasonably calm and relaxed. A terrified child may remember vividly the look of daggers in a parent's eyes, but completely forget the whole point of the reprimand and not be able to recall what behavior caused the problem in the first place.

It is perfectly normal and healthy for us to feel waves of sheer fury now and again. Because of our size and power, however, it is appropriate for us to release most of those feelings of frustration and rage away from young children by jogging, punching and kneading bread dough, or by pounding out melodies on a piano. It is not fair or helpful to blow children away with powerful and scary expressions of anger. We can be honest without being overpowering.

REMOVE THE CHILD FROM A PROBLEM SITUATION

Removing a child from the scene of a conflict allows a cooling-off period for the adult and child, removes whatever temptation the child is having difficulty with (out of sight, out of mind), and ensures that a gawking or giggling audience is not watching and triggering further misbehavior. Although compromise should never be considered during the heat of a full-blown tantrum, compromise after the child has gained control may serve as an effective role model for the child to imitate as she learns to talk rather than scream to get what she wants.

Occasionally, adults have no choice but to pick up a young child who may be kicking and screaming and haul the child (as gently as possible but as firmly as necessary) away from the scene of a conflict. A preschooler who is having a tantrum in a grocery store because she cannot have the candy bar she wants should probably be escorted, or if necessary, picked up and carried out of the store. She can be helped to understand that she has two, and only two, choices: she can sit and cry for a long, long time in the car with her patient but assertive father, or she can return to the grocery store and continue the shopping trip, accepting the fact that there will be no candy bar.

If the father, through consistent verbal and nonverbal communication, convinces his daughter that he will not become angry or argumentative, but that he will also absolutely not back down, the little girl will soon recognize the futility of a long, dramatic, exhausting fit of crying. She will learn that that sort of thing simply does not work.

When she seems ready to throw in the towel, recognizing that she cannot bully or manipulate her father, she should be given an opportunity to "save face." At this point, restraint, tactfulness, empathy, and perhaps an appropriate compromise (letting her choose a nutritious snack to take home) would keep the situation from having a winner and a loser. The little girl's future cooperativeness will hinge on her feeling confident that she can be cooperative without losing her dignity and autonomy, and without having her past mistakes thrown in her face.

TAKE TIME TO THINK BEFORE YOU RESPOND TO INAPPROPRIATE SEXUAL ACTIVITY

WHAT TO LOOK FOR	*WHAT TO DO*
1. Does the behavior appear to be simple, child-like curiosity? Toddlers or preschoolers take a moment in the bathroom to compare, touch, explore, or talk about their genitals. A preschooler whose mother is breast-feeding pulls off	**1. Take care not to overreact.** These behaviors are perfectly normal expressions of healthy curiosity. Sometimes, it is appropriate to acknowledge the differences and take advantage of a "teachable moment." For example, say, "Yes, boys and

her shirt to "breast-feed" the doll in the housekeeping center.

2. Does the behavior appear to be cyclical self-stimulation?

Like thumb-sucking, nail-biting, and hair-twisting, masturbation may become a child's stress reduction habit. A young child rubs her genitals when extremely tired or upset, or simply as a falling asleep habit.

3. Does the behavior appear to be non-sensical silliness or intended to shock adults or entertain other children?

Preschoolers stuff bark mulch in their underwear and waddle around the playground giggling and chanting, "We got big butts!" Children taunt each other with bathroom insults like "I saw your wee-wee" or "You're a pooh-pooh diaper baby."

4. Does the behavior appear to be oddly unchild-like? Does it seem to be a childish imitation of adult sexual behavior?

You find two preschoolers hiding behind a bush with one on top of the other imitating adult sexual activity. A child playing dolls invents a pretend scenario that involves graphic sexual behavior or language.

girls have different bodies, but everybody's special. Girls grow up to be women and boys grow up to be men." If needed, the behavior can be gently and matter-of-factly redirected to a different activity.

2. Gently redirect the behavior.

If the child is an infant or toddler, there is little to do but ignore the behavior and focus your energy on removing sources of stress. Be sure the child is getting plenty of rest, a calm environment, and enough emotional nurturing. If the child is a preschooler, be more proactive in helping the child replace the habit with a more socially acceptable substitute behavior. For example, "Would you like to hold this teddy bear when you fall asleep to help you remember not to rub your bottom?" "You must go into the bathroom when you need to touch your bottom."

3. Be understanding, firm, and consistent.

Follow the basic guidelines for handling any misbehavior. For example, say, "Bark mulch is not for putting in your underwear." Taunting should always be stopped. Say, "Be kind, use kind words. Mean words hurt. If you feel angry, tell your friend *why* you feel angry. Tell him, 'I feel angry when you take my blocks.'" Remember that overly shocked reactions from adults or laughter from other children can tempt a child to repeat the behavior to get attention.

4. Take an honest look at the big picture.

Have you noticed any other warning signs that the child is being molested or sexually abused? Does it seem likely that the child has been exposed to pornography or sexual behavior at home, school, or by other children? Is the child significantly delayed in social and/or emotional development? Does the child appear to be unhappy and withdrawn much of the time? Is the child seriously aggressive or rebellious? If the answer to any of these questions is yes, immediately seek advice from a counselor, child protective service professional, or other expert.

ASSERTIVELY SHAPE POSITIVE BEHAVIOR

When a child must be subjected to an unpleasant occurrence, the situation should be discussed squarely and honestly to give the child a chance to cooperate voluntarily. The situation should not, however, be allowed to stall or become a stalemate if the child refuses to cooperate. When medicine must be applied to a scrape on an unwilling child's knee, the adult must quickly and matter-of-factly explain what must be done, then get the unpleasant task over. The longer discussion, whining, and arguing are tolerated, the more unpleasant and stressful the task of applying medicine will become.

Separation is a good example of a necessary but unpleasant occurrence in the lives of toddlers. Before a separation, parents must be given all the time they want to visit with their child and express affection. A parent should not be rushed but should clearly indicate to the caregiver when she is ready to leave (and willing to actually walk out the door). At this decisive moment of separation, a skilled caregiver will firmly but lovingly state, "Mommy needs to leave now. You may give mommy a hug and wave bye-bye through the window, or, if you need, I can hold you while mommy leaves." If the child is clearly not willing to hug mommy and wave good-bye, then the parent and caregiver can move quickly and assertively to get the separation over with, even if the child resists loudly and has to be held.

The caregiver can express empathy, "Yes, you love your mommy. You miss her when she leaves. Sometimes I miss my mommy too. Did you know I have a mommy? Let's go see the dolls. Would you like to feed a bottle to our baby doll? Which baby doll do you want?" One can shape positive behavior by making sure that it happens. Adults can often help children avoid situations in which they may experience failure by quickly and decisively making the right thing happen and then rapidly moving on to happier activities, all this without giving an appearance of frustration, anger, guilt, or disgust with the child's inability to actively cooperate or comply. Children's negative feelings should be acknowledged and accepted, but they do not necessarily need to be dwelled on for a lengthy period of time.

Infants and toddlers in child care need a calm, consistent routine for separating from parents in the morning—waving bye-bye, finding a favorite toy or activity, or being held and talked to by a caregiver.

Separating from parents may be especially frightening for some children, expecially those who have had little experience getting to know caring adults outside their family.

TEACH GROUND RULES

Children need to know exactly what is expected of them. Simple, consistently enforced guidelines help children learn to respect and abide by rules. Children, however, must have adult help to understand and remember ground rules. Following are several ways adults can actively teach children about rules.

ROLE PLAY

Give children a chance to "act out" or practice the correct following of rules. For preschoolers, switch roles so that the child can see and experience an appropriate response. Pretend to be the child and allow the child to pretend to be the adult, or pretend to be the child's troublesome friend, for example, "I will pretend to be Bert. Let's pretend I just pulled your hair. Can you point your finger at me, make a frown, and say, 'Don't pull my hair. That hurts!'?"

REPETITION

Children need many opportunities to hear a rule repeated before knowledge of that rule has fully reached the child's long-term memory bank. Any adult who has experienced an electrical power failure but mindlessly continued attempting to turn on appliances and lights knows that having knowledge of a thing does not necessarily bring about an immediate change in habitual behaviors. We have to remind ourselves over and over, "Oh, yes, I can't listen to the radio. . . . Oh, the electric can opener won't work. . . . Oh, the clock is not right." Children need and deserve patient reminders of rules and expectations so they will be encouraged to change their habit patterns.

DISCUSSION

Rules have a great deal more meaning for children when they really understand reasons for the rules. Adults should remove from their vocabulary that age-old phrase "because I said so," which so often has been used as a blanket explanation for all rules and regulations issued by adults. Positive guidance requires that adults explain things to children simply and honestly; for example, "You must use the blunt knife instead of the sharp knife. I don't want you to get cut." "You may not open the gate without permission because the street is busy and dangerous." "You must wash your hands with soap and water before you eat. Your hands are dirty and you could get sick from getting germs in your mouth."

CLARIFY EXPECTATIONS

If we want children to follow our instructions, we must make sure they really understand what we intend for them to do. Adults often speak in vague, general terms. They say things such as "Be good," "Be nice," "Act like a big girl." What children need are simple but specific statements of our expectations. For example, we might say such things as:

- "Sit down please. Make sure your bottom is in the chair and your feet are on the floor."

- "Please hold your milk with both hands."

- "Please wait at the bottom of the slide until the person in front of you has gone down the slide. Then, you may climb up and have your turn."

- "I need for you to use a soft, slow voice to talk to me about your sister. I don't like to hear whining and screaming."

Additionally, adults sometimes assume that children automatically know how objects are intended to be used. Instead, children over the age of three need to be told specifically what various objects are for. Babies and toddlers put bowls on their heads, try to eat decorative plastic fruit, and attempt to pull tee shirts on like underpants! (That's why they're so much fun to be around.) One can gently guide them toward the proper use of objects, but they need a great deal of freedom to explore safe objects thoroughly, using all their senses and muscles to discover their world. If a baby or toddler stands up in a chair that could fall, she should tactfully be redirected to a safer place to climb, or else the chair should simply be removed. A child past three, however, can be told, "Please remember, a chair is for your seat, not your feet."

"Be kind. Please remember to use words instead of hitting. Tell Andy you don't want him to push you off the slide anymore."

Children past three can be taught the difference between toys, tools, and weapons; for example, "A toy is something you can play with, a tool is something useful to help you, and a weapon is intended to hurt someone. At school we use toys and tools but not weapons." A ball can be used as a toy to play catch or it can be used as a tool to knock a kite out of a tree, but it must not be used as a weapon to hit someone in the face. A fork should only be used as a tool to pick up food, not as a toy to wave around or as a weapon to poke at another child. School-aged children are especially capable of comprehending and identifying categories of objects, and will spontaneously point out to one another, "That pencil is a tool. It's for writing. You mustn't use it like a toy or a weapon!"

MAINTAIN CONSISTENCY

In order for children to behave appropriately, there must be consistency, with a reasonable level of flexibility, in the adult's expectations and enforcement of rules. Discipline should not be enforced based on the adult's mood or coincidental circumstances. For example, it would be inconsistent to indicate to a young child (through our actions), "You can walk around the house eating and dropping crumbs, except when I am too tired and crabby to clean up after you or when we have company." There should either be a consistent rule that eating takes place at the table, or that eating at various places in the house is allowed as long as family members clean up after themselves.

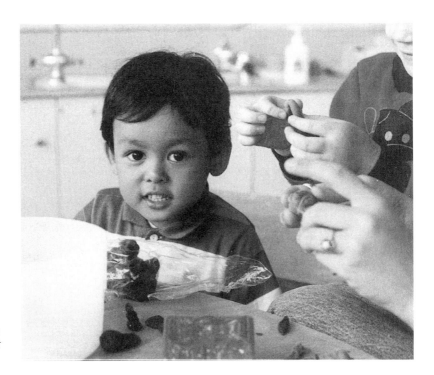

"Be safe. Play Doh is for molding, not for eating."

Older children, who have a clear understanding and acceptance of specific rules, can deal with occasional exceptions to those rules. They can understand that family members are expected to eat in the kitchen, even though breakfast in bed is a perfect Mother's Day surprise, and a pizza around the coffee table might be a perfect treat for a slumber party. Toddlers and young preschoolers, on the other hand, do not have a full grasp of rules. They view the world in very literal, black-and-white terms. An action either is or is not allowed. They become very frustrated and confused, and tend to ignore a rule altogether if it seems to them to be inconsistently enforced. For example, little ones should never be allowed, even once, to ride in a car without being properly buckled into an appropriate car seat. If they believe that there is absolutely no chance that the car will move until they are seat-belted, they will accept the car seat as a fact of life rather than something to be negotiated through whining and resisting.

In order to be consistent, adults should make very sure that a child's behavior is not laughed at on one occasion and reprimanded on another. Bathroom terms that brought giggles at home may not be nearly so funny at church or synagogue, or when announced loudly at a family gathering. The toddler with spaghetti in his hair may be adorable the first time, but if he receives a great deal of attention (laughter, photographs, calling the neighbors to come see), he may be inclined to repeat the behavior on a regular basis, which will not be nearly so entertaining to harried parents the second, third, or fourth times. In the early childhood setting, consistency, with reasonable flexibility, is essential.

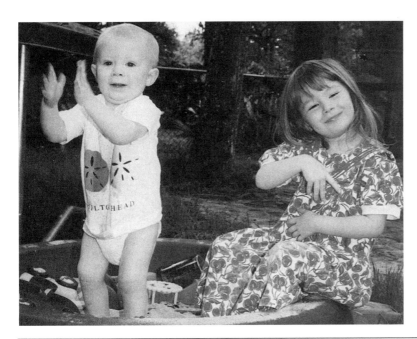

"Thank you for remembering to put all of the sand toys back in the sandbox."

Marty, a toddler teacher, tried to teach her 18-month-olds not to climb on the low, redwood picnic table on their playground. Toddlers who climbed on the foot-high plank table were removed and placed on a foot-high, redwood plank deck nearby for a "time-out." Marty knew that decks were to walk on and tables were not. To the toddlers, however, the rule about climbing seemed inconsistent. Both structures looked about the same. They were being removed from one and placed on the other as a negative consequence. Being on the second structure was intended to teach them not to get on the first structure. Of course, the toddlers were never able to make sense of Marty's rule, so, for the most part, they simply ignored it.

ADAPT OBJECTS, EVENTS, AND ATTITUDES TO REMOVE POSSIBLE CAUSES OF PROBLEM BEHAVIOR

There are many situations in which it is easier to change the circumstances surrounding the child than it is to change the child. Additionally, it is almost always more nurturing and less stressful for everyone involved if adults focus on setting the stage for proper behavior rather than on reprimanding children after they have behaved improperly. For example, if children are running in the classroom, it will be better and easier to change the room arrangement to make running difficult than to endlessly remind children to walk. If toddlers persist in spilling their milk, they can be given smaller cups with only an ounce of milk at a time. That way, if they do have a spill, very little milk is wasted and very little effort is needed to clean it up.

Rather than yelling to get the attention of rowdy children, an adult can use a dramatic whisper. Children will almost always pay more attention to a wide-eyed, dramatic whisper than to a rude, bellowing voice.

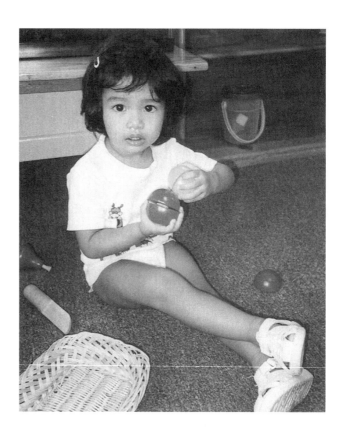

"Those are round and look a lot like our throwing balls don't they? But they are hard. They can hurt, so they're not for throwing. Let's be safe. I'll help you find a ball that is soft and good for throwing."

If children in a preschool program consistently become tired and irritable on field trips, then perhaps field trips can be rescheduled to a different time of day or to a shorter time period. Or perhaps trips can be made less often but to more carefully chosen locations. When confronted with troublesome behavior problems, we should ask ourselves, "Instead of trying to change the child, is there any way I can reasonably change the child's environmental surroundings or my own actions or attitudes to ease the problem?"

OFFER ASSISTANCE AND ENCOURAGEMENT

Children thrive on positive attention. They usually become very compliant when adults say, "How can I help you remember this rule?" "What can we do to make it easier for you to get to bed on time?" "Let's practice the words you should say when you feel angry." Positive guidance means that adults work very, very diligently to help children behave appropriately. Their goal is not just to punish children for behaving inappropriately.

GIVE UNDIVIDED ATTENTION

Children immediately recognize whether an adult is serious enough about what she is saying to stop and see that a request is followed. Even toddlers and preschoolers know that instructions do not mean much when they are given by an adult casually glancing back across her shoulder, making an offhanded comment across a room, "Come on now, put those toys away." In contrast, chil-

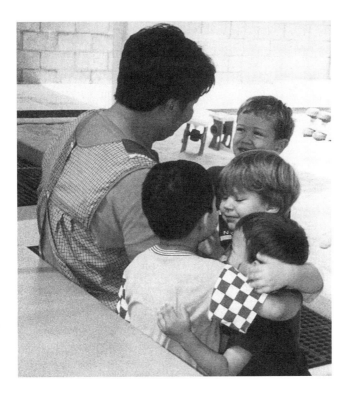

Physical touch can be very comforting.

dren sense that instructions mean a great deal when the adult stops what she is doing, walks to the child, bends down to eye level, gently touches the child's shoulder, and looking directly into the child's eyes, says in a gentle but firm tone, "Sherrie, I need you to stop now and put the blocks away." A half-hour of nagging and threatening from across the room will not have the impact of a gentle touch and one quiet statement made eye-to-eye using the child's name.

Undivided attention has a powerful effect on children. In positive child guidance, attention focused directly on children will be assertive, positive, and self-esteem building rather than negative, angry, and destructive of pride and confidence. The following four actions can be carried out in a positive way to show children that they have our undivided attention and that we really care about their behavior:

1. Eye Contact
Move close and try to establish eye contact. A shy child or a child who has experienced eye contact as part of threatening, angry interactions will feel compelled to look away. Do not force the child to look you in the eye, but rather attempt to win the child's trust by associating eye contact with positive, loving interactions. If the child does look you in the eye, sincerely commend him, "Thank you for listening so well."

2. Body Positioned at Child's Level
Bend down to the child's eye level. Staring down one's nose at a child tempts the child to look away. Being stared down on may also seem cold, threatening, or belittling to the child.

3. Appropriate Touch

Gently placing a hand on a child's shoulder or arm, or lightly holding one or both of the child's hands, helps focus attention. If the child is sitting on the floor, gently touching a foot or knee will obtain the child's attention and communicate caring concern. Appropriate touching is never grabby or forced. Follow the child's signals. Children usually make it very clear whether they find the adult's touch aversive or comforting

4. Use of Child's Name

Using a child's given name or accepted nickname is more personal and appropriate than general terms of endearment such as "sweety" or "honey." Adults in early care and education settings must learn every child's name very quickly in order to be effective. Sadly, some young children hear their names yelled so often as a reprimand that they fail to respond as we would expect when their name is used in a positive context. They do not recognize their name as a symbol for who they are, but only as a negative word that means they are in trouble.

REDIRECT INAPPROPRIATE BEHAVIOR FIRMLY AND RESPECTFULLY

When a child's inappropriate behavior must be stopped, cooperation can be gained and resentment avoided simply by offering the child an acceptable alternate activity. A child who is pouring milk back and forth from cup to bowl during a meal may be told, "You may not play with your food. After lunch (or after nap), I will show you a good place for pouring." The child could then be directed at an appropriate time to pour, squirt, dribble, and splash to her heart's content with dishes and toys at a sink, a bathtub, a commercial water table, an outdoor wading pool, or a plastic basin placed within her reach with an inch or two of water.

When children feel angry, they hit, kick, pinch, and scratch. These typical aggressive behaviors must be stopped. The child's anger should, however, be given an appropriate outlet. When a child is told, "Hitting hurts; no hitting is allowed," the adult should also add, "Use words. Tell Jessica you don't like it when she steps on your fingers. Show Jessica your fingers and tell her how much they hurt."

Common sense and knowledge of the basic principles of child development will guide the effective use of **redirection** (interrupting an inappropriate activity and involving the child in a more appropriate choice). The idea is to replace a misbehavior with a desired behavior so that the focus is on what the child should do rather than on what the child should not do. It is important, however, to ensure that the replacement activity does not become a "reward" for inappropriate behavior. **Operant conditioning** is the process of reinforcing or strengthening a behavior by rewarding it with a pleasurable response.

Miss Kimberly, a toddler caregiver in a child care center, was concerned about the biting that was happening on almost a daily basis in her room. She thought that perhaps the toddlers were biting because their gums were uncomfortable with teething and they needed strong oral stimulation. She decided to offer hard crackers for the toddlers to bite as a substitute for biting each other. Within a few days, she discovered, to her dismay, that the toddlers were attacking and biting each other whenever they felt hungry for crackers. They had become conditioned to expect crackers in response to biting.

CLEARLY EXPRESS APPROPRIATE FEELINGS

Although it is very appropriate for adults to be honest in their expression of feelings to children, an adult's expression of anger can be too overwhelming for a young child to handle. Rage has no place in positive child guidance. When confronted by a large, snarling, furious grown-up, a young child has two possibilities; recoil in fear and try to stay out of the grown-up's way, or fight back by being rebellious and insubordinate. Neither of those options help the child become a more confident, competent, and cooperative person. Children who are frequently shamed develop a general sense of guilt and unworthiness.

Rather than focus on feelings of anger, the adult can identify the underlying feelings that caused the anger. We can ask, "Am I feeling angry because I was startled, disappointed, worried, frightened, or frustrated?" Instead of saying, "I am furious with you," we can say, "I felt really frightened when I didn't know where you were. I was afraid you were hurt or lost. I was so upset I felt like crying." Following are several other examples of appropriate verbal expressions of adult feelings that give the child information but do not directly attack anyone.

- Surprise, Disbelief
  "I can't believe this beautiful plant has had its leaves torn off. Plants can die if their leaves are harmed."

- Sadness, Disappointment
  "I feel very sad when I find books with the pages torn out. Books are beautiful and fun to read, but they aren't of any use when they are ripped apart."

- Concern, Worry
  "I feel worried when I see you scratching your mosquito bite. Scratching may cause it to become infected and sore. Let's cover it with a bandage."

- Apprehension, Fear
  "I feel very frightened when I see you climbing on the top rail of the fort. You must stay off the rails or else choose a different place to play on the playground."

- Distress, Frustration
  "I feel very frustrated when I find the door has been left open. We can't keep our house warm and comfortable inside, when a door is left open. Please check the door each time you go out to make sure it's properly closed."

EXPLAIN THE POTENTIAL CONSEQUENCES OF UNACCEPTABLE BEHAVIOR

Children past the age of three are usually perfectly capable of mentally connecting the cause-and-effect relationship between their conscious actions and potential consequences. If simple, polite, assertive statements of rules and expectations do not bring about an appropriate response from children, then it is time to discuss potential consequences. Explaining potential consequences is not the same as bribing, intimidating, or giving idle threats. It is intended to inform the child, to give an honest, sincere warning of an impending consequence. It is not intended to manipulate, coerce, or trick the child into behaving a certain way, but rather to give the child honest, reasonable choices such as "If you do this, this will happen. If you do that, that will happen." We should only give children reasonable choices that we know we will be comfortable carrying out. It is not acceptable to say, for example, "If you don't come with me this instant, I will

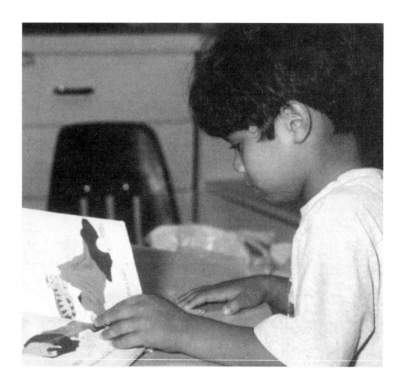

"Thank you for turning the pages so gently and carefully."

leave you here in the store by yourself." This is an idle and illegal threat that leaves parents and teachers only two options: lose credibility or neglect the child. Both of these are unacceptable.

The old cliché, "You can lead a horse to water, but you can't make him drink" fits children quite well. We can offer a well-balanced meal to a young child, but we cannot presume to force the child to eat it if she chooses not to. What we can do is say, "You may eat your vegetables and meat if you feel hungry. If you are not hungry enough to eat your dinner, then you may wait until breakfast to eat. I will put your plate in the refrigerator in case you change your mind." This statement is assertive, confident, and reasonable, but not threatening or punishing. It is merely a recognition that the child has choices about her own body, and the adult has choices and responsibilities about what foods are healthy and appropriate to offer.

PROVIDE PERSISTENT FOLLOW-UP, AND ENFORCE LOGICAL CONSEQUENCES FIRMLY AND RESPECTFULLY

A motto to be emblazoned in the memory of all adults who deal with children is, "Say what you mean, and mean what you say." There is no magic wand or bag-of-tricks in positive child guidance; only persistence, persistence, persistence! Adults who persevere in firm, assertive, respectful, and caring discipline will surely see positive results in the children they care for and teach. Children may be very persistent in their patterns of misbehavior. We, as adults, however, must be even more persistent in our supervision, follow-up, and enforcement of reasonable, logical consequences.

The nurturing adult resolves conflicts assertively but respectfully.

The consistency of small but persistent nudges toward appropriate behavior is far more effective than erratic and inconsistent explosions of anger, harsh punishments, or intimidating threats. The gentle, rippling stream etches deep patterns in solid rock. Pounding on rocks with sledge hammers changes the shape of the rocks but risks a lot of damage in the process.

EMPHASIZE UNCONDITIONAL CARING AND AFFECTION

Unconditional caring, the giving of affection without any strings attached, is the foundation on which good discipline is built. Unconditional caring lets children know that they do not have to perform or achieve or submit to be loved and respected. We may disagree with things they do and work hard to change them, but we will still love and care for the child. Adults should create an environment that tells children verbally and nonverbally (Clarke, 1978):

- "You have a right to be here. I'm glad you are who you are."

- "It is okay for you to have needs."

- "You don't have to be cute (sick, sad, mad, or scared) to get attention and approval."

- "It's okay to be smart, curious, and inventive and still get support and protection at the same time."

- "I'm glad you are growing up."

- "I'm not afraid of your anger."

- "You can express your feelings honestly, openly, and respectfully."

- "You can be independent and still have needs."

- "You can think before you make a rule your very own." "You can trust your feelings to help you know." "It's okay to disagree."

- "You don't have to suffer to get your needs met."

- "I love you."

MAINTAIN AND EXPRESS CONFIDENCE THAT A PROBLEM WILL BE RESOLVED

Guiding children can be frustrating and distressing at times. We look at our children and shake our heads, wondering if they will ever gain self-control and self-discipline. We must, however, firmly maintain and express confidence that specific problems will be resolved and our children will learn to behave appropriately, at least most of the time. Our confidence will strengthen children and convince them that control over their own behavior is a reachable goal.

PROTECT THE CHILD'S DIGNITY AND PRIVACY

When positive but assertive disciplinary measures are necessary, children should be afforded the dignity of being talked to in private. They are humiliated by being corrected in front of their friends, or even in front of other adults. Adults should refrain from discussing, in front of a child, all the careless, immature, and improper things the child might have done. Adults should refrain from talking and laughing about the child's past mistakes. And, most of all, adults should treat children the way they themselves like to be treated: with dignity and respect.

The nurturing adult listens and reflects the child's feelings, then helps her resolve her problems in a fair way. Children's negative feelings should be acknowledged but not dwelled upon.

BE WILLING TO START OVER TO FORGIVE AND FORGET

In positive child guidance, adults should do the best they know how to do and then never look back. Worrying about the past, carrying grudges, or keeping mental lists of past misdeeds all undermine positive child guidance. For young children, every day is a new day. No matter what happened yesterday, today can be a good day and a successful day. When children know that adults are willing to forgive and forget, they will be more compliant and more willing to admit it when they know they are wrong. Forgiveness encourages honesty in children and motivates them to try harder to meet adult expectations.

POINTS TO REMEMBER

- Consistency and fairness in the enforcement of rules help children learn to trust authority figures.

- Behaviors that are harmful or unfair must be interrupted immediately by a responsible adult.

- Children's negative feelings should be acknowledged and accepted, but not dwelled on.

- The enforcement of discipline should never hinge on the adult's mood or coincidental circumstances.

- It is usually easier to change the circumstances surrounding the child than it is to change the child.

- Attention focused directly on children should be assertive, positive, and self-esteem building.

- To show children they have our undivided attention, we give eye contact, position our body at the child's level, give appropriate touch, and use the child's name.

- Children are indeed full-fledged human beings and, as such, should be treated with the respect we give to and expect from other people we admire and care deeply about.

PRACTICAL APPLICATION

WILL AND THE CREAM CHEESE WON TON

Renee and Tom are loving and assertive parents. They have taught their children—Amy, who is ten, and Will, who is five—to respect the rights of others. They have consistently provided firm guidance tempered with unconditional love.

One evening, the entire household was aflutter with excitement because the children's grandparents had arrived for a short visit. Since Renee and Tom both worked, Renee had picked the children up from child care and Tom had picked up Chinese food for dinner from a favorite restaurant. Tom made sure to include an order of cream cheese won tons; the children were not too wild about Chinese food, but they both especially loved the restaurant's specialty: cream cheese won tons.

The children helped set the table with festive place mats and napkins, and even a candle. Everyone sat around the table chatting and enjoying dinner. Will perched on his knees in the big dining chair so he could see better. He listened attentively to every word of conversation as he slowly nibbled at the food on his plate.

As the family members finished eating, they pushed back their plates and continued to sit at the table, laughing and talking, catching up on family news and funny stories about the children and all their great adventures and escapades. When Tom had finished eating, he leaned back in his chair, stretched out his long legs, and draped an arm across the back of Will's chair. Tom really enjoyed these family get-togethers. As he laughed and talked, he happened to glance at Will's almost empty plate. He noticed one last cream cheese won ton pushed to the back of the plate. Absentmindedly, he picked up a fork, stabbed the won ton, and popped it into his mouth.

The instant Tom swallowed the won ton, he saw a stricken look fall across Will's face, and he knew he had made a big mistake. Will leaned close to his dad's ear and whispered intently, "Dad, we have to go to a lonely place and talk." Quietly, Tom got up from the table and followed Will to the bathroom. Tom sat down on the side of the bathtub while Will ceremoniously closed the bathroom door and then, with big tears sliding down his cheeks, said, "Dad, you're not supposed to take other people's things without asking. That was the only cream cheese won ton left, and I was saving it for last. You did a wrong thing."

Tom lifted Will into his lap and they hugged each other long and hard. Tom said, "You're right, son. I did do a wrong thing and I apologize."

Tom almost had tears in his own eyes, but his heart was filled with pride that his son had been able to stand up for his rights and also had made a special effort to spare his dad's dignity by asking to talk in a "lonely place."

DISCUSSION QUESTIONS

1. Why do you suppose Tom ate Will's won ton? Have you ever inadvertently hurt a child's feelings? How did the child respond?
2. How do you think Will learned to resolve problems the way he did? Why do you think he asked for a "lonely place" to talk with his father?
3. How would it make you feel if a child responded to you the way Will responded to his father? How do you imagine Will's father felt? What do you suppose he was thinking during his conversation with Will?

RELATED READINGS

HELPING CHILDREN COPE WITH ANGER

American Academy of Pediatrics (1995). *Caring for your school-age child: Ages 5–12.* New York: Bantam Books.

Brown, J. R., & Dunn, J. (1996). Continuities in emotion understanding from three to six years. *Child Development, 67*(3), 789–803.

Crockenberg, S. (1997). How children learn to resolve conflicts in families. In E. N. Junn & C. Boyatzis (Eds.), *Annual editions: Child growth and development 97/98* (4th ed.). New York: McGraw-Hill. (Original work published in *Zero to Three*, April 1992.)

Gives strategies for modeling conflict negotiation skills that include directives, explanations, and compromise. Acquiring these skills early should have many long-term benefits for children.

Cummings, E. (1987). Coping with background anger in early childhood. *Child Development, 58*(4), 976–984.

Fabes, R. A., & Eisenberg, N. (1992). Young children's coping with interpersonal anger. *Child Development, 63*(1), 116–128.

Flynn, C. (1996). Regional differences in spanking experiences and attitudes: A comparison of northeastern and southern college students. *Journal of Family Violence, 11*(1), 59–80.

Gallo, N. (1997). Why spanking takes the spunk out of kids. In E. N. Junn & C. Boyatzis (Eds.), *Annual editions: Child growth and development 97/98* (4th ed.). New York: McGraw-Hill. (Original work published in *Child*, March/April 1989.)

Hennessy, K. D., Rabideau, G. J., Cicchetti, D., & Cummings, E. M. (1994). Responses of physically abused and nonabused children to different forms on interadult anger. *Child Development, 65*(3), 815–828.

Hyman, I. A. (1997). *The case against spanking: How to discipline your child without hitting* (1st ed.). Hoboken, NJ: Jossey-Bass Psychology Series.

The author documents the long-term negative effects of spanking—how it brutalizes kids and creates violent adults—and gives common sense advice on alternative methods for dealing with such everyday situations as what to do when your toddler becomes fussy in the grocery store or how to react if your child runs into the street.

Jalongo, M. (1986). Using crisis-oriented books with young children. In J. B. McCracken (Ed.), *Reducing stress in young children's lives* (pp. 41–46). Washington, DC: NAEYC.

Ladd, R. E., (Ed.). (1996). *Children's rights re-visioned: Philosophical readings.* Belmont, CA: Wadsworth Publishing.

Leach, P. (1996, July 9). Spanking: A shortcut to nowhere. Available at: http://cnet.unb.ca/orgs/prevention_cruelty/spank.htm

Lewis, M., & Michalson, L. (1983). *Children's emotions and moods.* New York: Plenum.

Lewis, M., & Saarni, C. (1985). Culture and emotions. In M. Lewis & C. Saarni (Eds.), *The socialization of emotions* (pp. 1–17). New York: Plenum.

Miller, P., & Sperry, L. (1987). The socialization of anger and aggression. *Merrill-Palmer Quarterly, 33*(1), 1–31.

Ruben, D. (1996, September). Should you spank? *Parenting*, 136–141.

Russel, J. A. (1989). Culture, scripts, and children's understanding of emotion. In C. Saarni & P. L. Harris (Eds.), *Children's understanding of emotion* (pp. 293–318). Cambridge, UK: Cambridge University Press.

Saifer, S. (1996, Winter). Dealing with hitting and aggression in the classroom. *NHSA Journal, 15*(1), 37–39.

Samalin, N., & Whitney, C. (1995, May). What's wrong with spanking? *Parents, 70*(5), 35–36.

Straus, M. (1995). *Beating the devil out of them: Corporal punishment in American Families.* New York: Lexington Books.

Zeman, J., & Shipman, K. (1996). Children's expression of negative affect: Reasons and methods. *Development Psychology, 32*(5), 842–850.

HELPFUL WEB SITES

http://www.udel.edu/bateman/acei/ Association for Childhood Education provides information about the ACEI, its journal and book publications, conferences, and membership
information.

http://www.naeyc.org/ National Association for the Education of Young Children gives information on the organization, its publications, activities, and conferences. Contains a searchable
index to articles in the NAEYC publication *Young Children*.

For additional information on positive child guidance, visit our Web site at
http://www.earlychilded.delmar.com

Chapter 5
Planning the Prosocial Environment

OBJECTIVES

After reading this chapter, you should be able to:
- Define prosocial behavior.
- Identify components of the nurturing social environment.
- Recognize supportive and effective adult behaviors.
- Outline strategies for initiating positive behavior in children.

PROSOCIAL BEHAVIOR

Prosocial behavior is the opposite of antisocial behavior. Prosocial behavior benefits others and demonstrates the presence of a social conscience. **Antisocial behavior** harms others, and indicates a disregard for the rights and needs of others. The concept of prosocial behavior focuses on three critical elements of a child's beneficial or helping interactions with others:

Children are like little sponges, taking in everything they see, hear, touch, taste, and smell.

THREE KEY ELEMENTS OF PROSOCIAL BEHAVIOR

- Cooperation—working with others unselfishly toward a common goal

- Empathy—putting oneself into others' shoes, to feel what they feel, to have insight into their thoughts and actions

- Altruism—behaving generously, acting in a way that benefits others with no motive of personal gain.

Since patterns of natural human growth and development teach us that young children always begin life locked into **egocentrism** (or self-centeredness), we know that prosocial behavior is not an inborn trait, but a slowly learned way of acting that wins approval and affection from others.

Young children are not likely to postpone immediate gratification in order to work cooperatively with others toward a common goal. They do not start life with a capacity to recognize that others have feelings and needs similar to their own. And, of course, they do not come into the world equipped with the logical, cause-and-effect thinking skills necessary to understand that generously giving a valued object or favor today may bring affection and loyalty from a friend tomorrow (Peterson, 1983). Children adopt prosocial behaviors only after much experience and practice in an environment that demonstrates and nurtures positive social interaction.

SETTING THE STAGE FOR APPROPRIATE BEHAVIOR

We give subtle messages to children about how we expect them to behave by the surroundings we plan for them. We can prevent many behavior problems before they ever begin simply by careful planning, by understanding children's developmental needs, and by creating a perfect match between their needs and the settings around them.

HOW CAN THE PHYSICAL ENVIRONMENT SUPPORT PROSOCIAL BEHAVIOR?

Parents need to adapt home environments to make them safe, childproof, and interesting for children of various ages. Periodically, as children grow, parents must reexamine their children's bedrooms, playrooms, and play yards to see that the space matches the child's growing skills and interests. Children can gradually deal responsibly with and reliably use and put away more complicated equipment and furnishings.

Children tend to treat other children much the same way they have been treated by the important adults in their lives.

Adults planning living space for groups of children also have a challenging task facing them. The well-planned early childhood environment is orderly but not rigid, clean but not sterile, and interesting but not overstimulating. In other words, it is carefully balanced. The only way to be sure that it is properly balanced is to watch the children who live, play, and work there, to see if the environment seems overwhelming, boring, frustrating, or just right.

WHAT ARE INEFFECTIVE CHILD CARE ENVIRONMENTS LIKE?

Some early childhood settings have an atmosphere that seems halfway between a festival and a flea market. Almost every square inch of the walls is plastered with pictures, posters, signs, crafts, and notices. Things dangle from the ceiling like a swarm of butterflies, and furniture and toys form a wall-to-wall obstacle course on the floor. Walls and furniture are painted colors such as taxicab yellow or iridescent lime green. Special rugs are purchased with bright, busy, dizzying patterns of letters, numbers, and game boards to "stimulate learning."

This kind of environment invites loud, wild, unbridled activity. Children will probably feel comfortable running, leaping off tables, and bellowing across the room. Adults will probably have great difficulty guiding children into quiet concentration on a puzzle or book, teaching children to walk rather than run, and use soft "inside voices" rather than screaming and yelling. Children may initially have great fun in this environment but will likely become bored, tired, and overwhelmed eventually. Since the adults are likely to have difficulty coping with the children's level of intensity, they may become irritable and restrictive, falling into negative power struggles with the children.

Other early childhood settings have an atmosphere somewhat like a dentist's waiting room. They are stark white, or cool, pale pastel colors, and they smell strongly of disinfectant. The sparse furnishings have an eerie appearance as if they have never been touched by human hands. Insipid elevator music may be piped in softly, and any toys or books seem to be on display rather than intended for actual use (they may actually be arranged out of the children's reach). The adults seem most anxious that the children "don't mess anything up." Painting, water play, and messy clay are out of the question. Everything the children do may be regimented into rigidly controlled activities that the whole class does together.

Nothing about this environment invites children to explore or interact with the materials provided. They become passive recipients of the experiences adults provide, and they are pressured to "sit still, be quiet, and don't touch anything without permission." The children may at first be subdued, restrained, even intimidated by their surroundings, but eventually they will become bored, restless, and rebellious.

RECOGNIZING A DEVELOPMENTALLY APPROPRIATE ENVIRONMENT

Developmentally appropriate early childhood settings are warm and homey. There are focal points of interest at various places in the environment (displays of children's artwork, holiday decorations, or decorative touches), but they are not overwhelming. Ceilings, walls, and floors are muted, neutral tones so that the visual emphasis is on brightly colored toys, learning equipment, and the children's art "masterpieces."

The environment is well lighted with plenty of sunny windows. Acoustical ceiling tiles soften the sound level. Furniture and equipment are arranged to break the floor space into clearly defined learning centers in order to discourage running, to encourage focused attention on

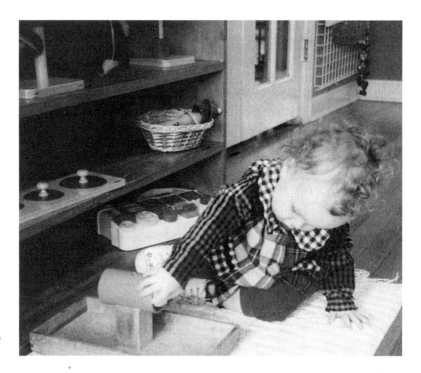

The well-planned environment is warm and homey.

learning materials such as books, puzzles, and blocks, and to allow easy supervision. Messy activities such as food preparation, clay, water play, and painting are regularly available for children three and older, and structured to be used successfully and independently.

> *The lessons are individual, and brevity must be one of the chief characteristics.*
> *Maria Montessori (Montessori & Hunt, 1989)*

In a developmentally appropriate preschool classroom, painting may be routinely set up with a day's supply of paper available to be clothespinned onto a child-sized easel. Just an ounce or two of fairly thick paint in a couple of nontip containers with short, fat paintbrushes makes the activity almost "goof-proof" for a young child wanting to paint "all by himself." A clothesline is ready nearby for hanging wet paintings to dry. There are classroom pets such as hamsters and fish, plants for the children to water and enjoy, and many opportunities for children to be involved in real-life activities such as preparing food and cleaning up.

Whether an environment is designed for infants, toddlers, preschoolers, or school-aged children, individual children's levels of development and interests are taken into consideration. Toddlers cannot function properly in environments that are arranged with hazardous and inappropriate furniture and toys, even though that same equipment may be perfectly suited to preschoolers. Infants and toddlers need unstructured toys and materials for sensory exploration and safe motor skill practice.

School-aged children will be bored and offended if they are placed in a room filled with preschool blocks, picture books, and baby dolls. They, too, need a space suited to their special needs and interests. In after-school care settings, children need a "clubhouse" environment with games, music, and quiet places to study. Outdoors, they need a soccer field, a basketball hoop, and elementary-sized swings and slides.

WHAT EFFECT DOES THE ENVIRONMENT HAVE ON CHILD GUIDANCE?

In developmentally appropriate environments, behavior problems are minimized simply because children are challenged and their needs are met. They are busy and excited about their accomplishments. At the beginning of the year, adults often have to simplify an environment to ensure that children can manage independently and successfully. Gradually, as the children develop new skills, adults add new materials and increase the complexity of the environment so that it continually challenges the children. Adults are constantly searching for materials that match children's skills perfectly, somewhere right in the middle, between materials that are so simple that they are boring and materials that are so complex they are overwhelming. Adults in the developmentally appropriate environment allow children to carry out play activities individually or in small groups of their own choosing rather than marching them all lockstep to do the same activities at the same time as a large group. Large group activities for preschoolers are limited to short periods of time for sharing, singing, and hearing stories read. Large group activities are avoided altogether for infants and toddlers.

The adult constantly looks for ways to increase the children's independence and mastery of their environment. He has taught the children how to spread their jackets on the floor, stand with feet near the collar or hood, stick hands in the arm holes, then flip the jackets over their

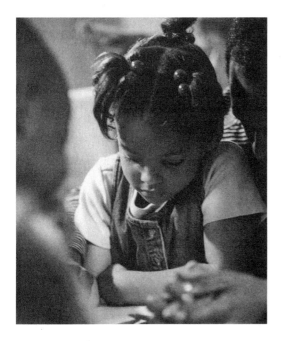

The well-planned environment is challenging but not overwhelming.

heads. Like magic, they know how to put their own coats on without help. He has used color-coding to help children know where things go. Everything in a yellow container goes in the art center; everything red goes in the science center. He has even taped pictures of toys and games on shelves to remind children where to put things away. Children are allowed to rearrange the playhouse furniture in the housekeeping center, as long as they remember to be good citizens and put it back when they are finished. They feel the environment is their space. They feel pride and self-confidence. They know the adult is their ally, not their enemy. The stage is set for positive child guidance.

HOW DO SCHEDULES SUPPORT POSITIVE BEHAVIOR?

Another critical concern in planning for positive child guidance relates to pacing or scheduling. Young children fiercely resist being hurried and they can barely tolerate being forced to wait. They have their own pace. Different children have different paces. By scheduling large blocks of time for **child-directed** (independent) activities, children feel freer to work and play at their own pace. One child may take only three seconds to paint a paper plate turkey to his satisfaction, while another child may want to spend twenty minutes painting it just the way he wants. Children appreciate a schedule that is consistent enough to give them the security of predictable patterns, but not so rigid that it cannot adapt to their individual needs.

If children are forced into a rigidly scheduled large group activity, the fast child will be bored and tempted to get into mischief as he waits for others to finish. The slow child will be forced to stop painting before he has fully benefited from the learning value of the activity. He may also feel frustrated and irritable because he did not have the opportunity to finish the project he obviously cared about. Individualized, self-paced, child-directed learning is not only developmentally appropriate, but it also strengthens self-esteem and supports positive guidance.

Parents also have to pay close attention to scheduling in order to set the stage for positive child guidance. Bill and Irene both work. They hate getting their three children up in the morning. Because evenings are so hectic, the children often do not get to bed until 9:30 or 10:00 P.M. Of course, they are cranky and out-of-sorts when their parents try to wake them at the crack of dawn. Bill and Irene are so rushed in the morning that they wait until the last possible moment to get the kids up. Then there is a mad rush to get them dressed and fed. Almost always, there is conflict with one or more of the balky, groggy children.

To plan for more successful behavior, Bill and Irene will have to reschedule their evenings to make sure they and the children have adequate rest. They will also have to get the children up in the morning as early as possible rather than as late as possible so the children have time to wake up, and plenty of time to eat and dress without being hassled. Rushing a sleepy child is an almost guaranteed way to create an unmanageable child.

THE NURTURING SOCIAL ENVIRONMENT

Adults who hope to stimulate prosocial behavior in young children must first establish a nurturing social environment, a setting in which children feel safe enough and comfortable enough to be cooperative, empathetic, and altruistic. Children who worry about being hurt, feel stressed to perform beyond their capability, or feel pushed into competition with playmates will probably have little interest in prosocial behavior. Children who are afraid that their own needs will not be met may not be able to be generous with others. A child may behave in a prosocial manner in one setting but not in another; day-to-day behavior depends to a great extent on the surroundings (Hartshorne & May, 1928).

HOW RELAXED, PLAYFUL ENVIRONMENTS ENCOURAGE PROSOCIAL BEHAVIOR

Early childhood is a special time in one's life. The young of other mammals (puppies, kittens, colts, and so on) frolic and play as they develop the skills they need to survive in adulthood. Adults of various species go about the serious work of providing food, shelter, and protection while the young chase around, pouncing on bugs, climbing trees, rolling in the grass, and having pretend fights. Their gleeful freedom enables them to coordinate muscles and practice skills.

Young human beings also need a protected period of childhood in which to play and explore. If children are forced into somber, little-adult behavior, they may turn sour and critical. Instead of taking pleasure in their friends' playful antics, they may feel compelled to report, or "tattle," to adults about even the most trivial misdeed of another child. Children should feel free to complain to adults when personal rights have been violated, and to report misbehavior to authorities (adults) when rules have been broken or hazardous behavior is taking place. That kind of "telling" is sincere and should never be labeled tattling. Frivolous or malicious telling, however, is a different matter. The child who obsessively tells, hoping to get peers in trouble, may expect adults to stamp out or punish every silly or childish behavior and to reward him for telling, for playing the role of "little Mr. Goody Goody." This behavior is inappropriate and should be addressed.

A child who persists in "telling" on others for no good reason will seem antisocial to playmates who have been "told on." The child who tattles, however, will probably have inferred from adult criticisms of childish behavior that it is not okay to be a child, to be "one of the gang." This child may feel aloof and apart from other children: he may actually view himself as a little adult. These feelings hinder the development of friendships that lead to wholesome cooperative play, and to

The nurturing social environment is relaxed and playful.

optimum social and emotional development, so we need to let the child know that it is definitely okay to be a "silly kid" sometimes. Children can be helped to refrain from "tattling" on other children when they are taught to help a friend who made a mistake. "Yes, Shelley, I see that James forgot to take his turn. How can we help him remember?"

A relaxed, playful atmosphere for babies and young children helps them develop tolerance and a sense of humor. Exposure to adults who are tolerant of others and do not take themselves too seriously greatly aids children in developing the ability to feel empathy for others. Adults sometimes forget to step into children's shoes to feel what they feel and see things from their perspective.

Adults consider sitting back, staring into space, and doing nothing an indulgent luxury. Children consider this sitting and doing nothing an aversive punishment. Adults have a slower, quieter rhythm or pace than children and may feel annoyed by children's squealing, wriggling, wrestling, and running. Intolerant adults force children to function within the adult's comfort zone for noise and movement. In contrast, when young children sense the generosity of adults who kindly tolerate and gently redirect the bustling chaos of active, noisy children, then the children in turn learn to demonstrate generosity and tolerance for others.

Instead of expressing exasperation, Allen, a young daddy, sits down and has a good laugh when his toddler walks in wearing underwear on his head rather than on his bottom. Mrs. Farrel, a long-time member of Weight Watchers, grins and takes it as a sincere compliment when little Jennifer says, "I think you're beautiful. You're the prettiest fat lady in the whole world." Miss Cindy laughs good-naturedly with her school-agers after the gruesome spider that has startled her turns out to be nothing more than a plastic Halloween party favor.

We might be tempted to take normal childish behaviors more seriously than necessary, or even become angry and punitive with the children described above. In a relaxed, playful atmosphere, however, children can learn discipline, but they can also learn that it is okay to be generous and forgiving (Mussen & Eisenberg-Berg, 1977). Children learn that it is okay to make mistakes, because parents, teachers, and caregivers are allies, not enemies. It is okay to be playful and silly at times because others can let down their barriers and share in a good laugh.

Clearly, there is a boundary between silliness and genuine misbehavior, between playfulness and antisocial activity. Playfulness is neither hurtful nor mean-spirited; maliciousness is both. Silly behavior that is not totally appropriate can be dealt with patiently and with a sense of humor, even though it may need to be firmly redirected at some point if it begins to interfere with necessary routines or to annoy others.

CREATING A COOPERATIVE SETTING

When adults say things like, "See if you can put your lunch box away before anyone else" or "Whoever is quietest can be first in line," children are encouraged to be competitive rather than cooperative. We are often tempted to use competitive challenges because they work so much more powerfully and effectively than nagging or threatening, and seem less negative. Remember, even if something works well to achieve short-term goals, it may not necessarily achieve the long-term goals we seek. In the long run, getting children's coats on quickly or getting trash picked up without a second reminder is not nearly as important as fostering cooperative and caring relationships among children who will someday be adult citizens.

By urging children to win at the expense of others, we may be establishing patterns of greediness and a lack of regard for the feelings of others. It is far more helpful to redirect children's natural competitive urges into competition with their own best records: "I wonder if you can build these blocks even higher than you did yesterday?" or "Deonicia, you are so quiet and still. You must be ready for lunch. Would you like to be our leader today?"

DEVELOPMENTALLY APPROPRIATE ACTIVITIES, MATERIALS, AND ROUTINES

Bored children become irritable and mischievous. Children who are pushed beyond their limits into irrelevant memorization or tedious busy work may become antagonistic and rebellious. Unhappy children are more likely to behave in antisocial ways. When adults hold unrealistic expectations for children, stressful, even angry, relations erupt. This friction becomes contagious and soon, interactions among the children themselves are tinged with irritability and annoyance. This is quite obviously not a productive situation for children to learn and to practice prosocial behavior.

The secret to a cooperative, caring, and generous atmosphere among young children lies in our meeting children's basic needs: social, emotional, physical, and intellectual. An overwhelming need of early childhood is the need for engrossing, entertaining, and rewarding activity. John Dewey, Maria Montessori, Jean Piaget, and other experts have shown us that children love to learn. These experts have made it clear that children learn easily through spontaneous as well as guided play experiences. Children find fulfillment in activities that are developmentally appropriate.

Children become deeply involved in their play and are amazingly relaxed and compliant when their need for fulfilling activity is met. This kind of productive, fulfilling activity is defined as being developmentally appropriate.

WHY CONSISTENCY IS SO IMPORTANT

Teachers, parents, and child care providers quite often are trapped by the idea that if something does not work the first time, then it will never work. Children eventually change a behavior when they finally comprehend and remember that the action will quickly and consistently be stopped or redirected. A caregiver who decides that preschoolers should learn to scrape their plates independently after lunch may feel exasperated when the children mistakenly throw their plates and utensils away on their first try. A kindergarten teacher may throw up his hands in frustration after disastrously introducing fingerpainting for the first time to rowdy five-year-olds who leave school looking like splotchy rainbows. And any adult who has ever dealt with toddlers knows that the point simply does not get across the first hundred times one-year-olds are told that sticks and leaves should not go in one's mouth.

Children learn positive ways of interacting with others when we can be consistent and persistent (not angry and impatient). We can avoid a great deal of irritation simply by recognizing that it takes time for children to absorb new skills and habits. Our task is to structure a consistent and predictable environment for children where they are allowed adequate periods of time to develop new skills introduced in tiny, bite-sized bits.

ACTIVITIES SHOULD BE . . .

- Relevant—match the child's capabilities and interests
- Active—encourage movement
- Sensorial—appeal to the five senses

TO SUPPORT POSITIVE BEHAVIOR . . .

- Get to know children personally, and respond to their individual capabilities, interests, and preferences.

- Plan room arrangements that minimize frustration, congestion, and confusion for children.

- Prepare and arrange interesting toys and activities that relate to all areas of children's development: social, emotional, and physical, as well as intellectual.

- Establish routines that allow uninterrupted blocks of time for spontaneous, self-directed play in a carefully planned environment.

- Make arrangements for hands-on exploration of real objects to be a natural and integral part of learning activities.

- Allow children to express their own individuality by making their own choices within clearly defined limits, by saying, for example, "Would you rather paint or play with clay?" "Would you rather have orange juice or milk?" "Would you rather wear a skirt or blue jeans?"

- Greatly limit situations in which children are forced to sit still, to wait for something to happen, or to stand in line (toddlers are especially unable to cope with these situations).

We adults are prone to set absurd goals. We focus our attention on children's behavior in fits and spurts. We ignore messiness for months or years, then suddenly insist on neatness: this minute! Three-year-old Fernando had always traipsed around the house after his bath in a big, soft bath towel. When he was ready to get dressed, he had a habit of dropping the damp towel in a heap on his bedroom floor. Freshly scrubbed little boys wrapped in towels are so endearing that his parents had always quietly tolerated his towel-dropping ritual. One day, however, his poor mom reached the end of her patience and yelled, "Fernando, get this wet towel into the bathroom, and I mean step on it!" After she cooled off a bit, she peeked into the bathroom to check on Fernando. There he stood in the middle of the bathroom, crying pitifully but standing obediently on the towel.

HOW CAN I SUPPORT COOPERATIVENESS?

We live in an instant society. When we feel a child is old enough to behave in a certain way, we want that behavior instantly. One popular paperback book confidently tells parents that children can be toilet trained in a day. In reality, children cannot master toilet training in a day, a week, or even a month. A two-year-old may go from diapers to dry pants literally overnight, but this only happens after the child has mastered hundreds of little prerequisite skills. The toddler must gradually learn how to recognize body sensations, communicate needs, inhibit sudden impulses, consciously manipulate the muscles that control elimination, and even balance on top of a big scary bowl of water, all this just to please grown-ups! Many children will be three or older before they have gained reliable control over bowel and bladder.

Consistent, Predictable Routines Help a Child Ease Comfortably into Learning New Skills
For months, toilet training may consist only of talking about the potty, looking at it, exploring it, and sitting for a second or two on it, just as a playful part of diaper-changing routine. It may

be months before the child's consistent, predictable routines expand to include actually using the potty. The important thing is that the child keeps moving in the right direction. Someday, nobody will remember or care how fast or slow the learning was.

Children are quite naturally inclined to resist when they are confronted with a sudden, unexpected demand that they change a long-standing behavior. Likewise, some of us adults put up quite a fuss when we were first told that we ought to wear seat belts in cars. We argued, "But it feels weird . . . but I'm not accustomed to it . . . but I don't want to change." A toddler who has never had a worry in the world about when or where to relieve himself might well feel those same feelings when we insist that he ought to keep his pants dry by urinating in a toilet. Consistency and predictability in our expectations for children help them accept and gradually adapt to our standards. Children do not instantly develop an ability to take turns or to resist greedily grabbing a toy. Slowly and persistently, however, we can nudge children into behaving in a more responsible and prosocial manner.

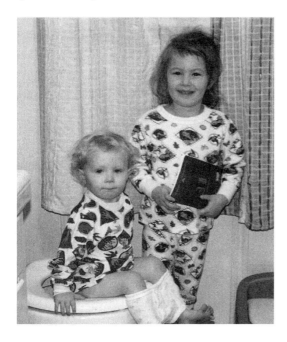

A great big toilet can be pretty intimidating to a very little person!

THE NURTURING ADULT

One might jump to the erroneous conclusion that a nurturing parent, teacher, or caregiver is one who is either a saint or a pushover. The word *nurture*, however, means to train, to educate, or to nourish. The truly nurturing adult is simply an honest, emotionally healthy person who has learned how to be both assertive and caring at the same time.

HOW CAN I BE MORE NURTURING AND PATIENT?

Teaching children in a way that nourishes them does not mean pointing out every flaw, criticizing every imperfection, and punishing every lapse in judgment. In fact, the first step toward shaping children's behavior positively is simply setting a good example; that is, modeling appropriate behavior. Unbeknownst to us, many of children's most upsetting misbehaviors are little more than instant replays of our own behavior in a context we do not expect. Take, for example, the classic irony of an adult saying, "If you don't stop hitting people, I'm going to spank you."

SPANKING

Positive child guidance never includes the practice of spanking children. In developmentally appropriate child care programs, spanking or any other kind of physical punishment is always strictly forbidden. Slapping, pinching, biting, and shaking children are dangerous and clearly unacceptable ways for adults to guide children in any situation. Unfortunately, in many homes and some schools, parents, teachers, and principals spank or paddle children to discipline them.

Most parents admit that at least on some occasion, they have spanked their own child. Sadly, the most frequently spanked children are toddlers and developmentally delayed or learning disabled children. For many parents who spank, it is probably more of an expression of their frustration and feelings of helplessness in trying to manage their child than a consciously planned guidance strategy. There are other adults, however, who sincerely believe that causing children to feel pain will make them behave more appropriately. Early educators do a great service to their communities by sharing information with parents on how to provide positive child guidance.

To learn more, read:

Straus, M. (1995). *Beating the devil out of them: Corporal punishment in American families.* New York: Lexington Books.

Couture, L. A. (2001). Corporal Punishment: Society's Remaining Acceptable Violence. Condensed essay based on unpublished Master's Thesis entitled, *Evidence against the Efficacy of Corporal Punishment.* Available online: http://www.childadvocate.org/AcceptableViolence.htm.

Dale, S. (1993, Winter). Spanking as an addiction, *Mothering, 69,* 31–35.

Flynn, C. (1996). Regional differences in spanking experiences and attitudes: A comparison of northeastern and southern college students. *Journal of Family Violence, 11*(1), 59–80.

Parents and Teachers against Violence in Education (PTAVE) (2002). Project NoSpank. Alamo, CA: PTAVE. Available online: http://www.nospank.net/toc.htm.

Slaby, R. G., Roedell, W. C., Arezzo, D., & Hendrix, K. (1995). *Early violence prevention: Tools for teachers of young children.* Washington, DC: NAEYC.

Straus, M. A., Sugarman, D. B., & Giles-Sims, J. (1997). Corporal punishment by parents and subsequent antisocial behavior in children. *Archives of Pediatrics and Adolescent Medicine, 155,* 761–67.

Straus, M. A., & Gelles, R. J. (Eds.). (1990) *Physical violence in American families: Risk factors and adaptations to violence in 8,145 families.* New Brunswick, NJ: Transactions.

Straus, M. A. (1994). *Beating the devil out of them: Corporal punishment in American families.* San Francisco: New Lexington Press.

Strassberg, Z., Dodge, K. A., Pettit, G. S., & Bates, J. E. (1994). Spanking in families and subsequent aggressive behavior toward peers by kindergarten students. *Development and Psychopathology, 6,* 445–461.

If a child is overly loud and boisterous, we may focus on being particularly soft-voiced and calm. If a child is angry and unyielding, we can model patience and forgiveness. If a child is aggressive and hurtful, we can demonstrate gentleness and kindness. Being nurturing must not be used as an excuse to ignore behaviors that must be stopped. Our own prosocial behavior will be a good example for the child as we assertively protect property and personal rights by interrupting and redirecting unacceptable behavior. Additionally, we can make a mental note to find future opportunities, after a conflict situation has been resolved, to continue modeling desired behaviors such as calmness, forgiveness, and gentleness. This focus on assertive but nonaggressive guidance is particularly noteworthy, since many adults rely on angry and aggressive methods of discipline. In the late 1960s, 94 percent of the U.S. adult population approved of spanking a child. More recent studies show a decrease to 68 percent in 1994 (Straus & Mathur, 1996). Studies over the past 20 to 30 years generally show 70 percent to 90 percent of parents believing it is sometimes "necessary to discipline children with a good, hard spanking." In terms of actual practice, studies generally show corporal punishment (especially spanking) to be widely used, with some 90 percent of parents (or children) reporting having used it at least once (Pitzer, 1997; Day, Peterson, & McCracken, 1998; Straus, 2001; Simons, Johnson, & Conger, 1994). Although **corporal** (physical) punishment tends to result in immediate child compliance, it also increases aggression, slows moral internalization, and risks mental health (Gershoff, 2002).

ASK THESE QUESTIONS ABOUT ANNOYING BEHAVIORS

- What specific aspects of the behavior are particularly annoying to me?
- Is there any way that I may have been inadvertently setting an example for that behavior?
- What positive behavior could be modeled and reinforced to replace the undesired behavior?
- How can I model appropriate behaviors so the child will be sure to notice and respond?

HOW DOES A NURTURING ADULT RESPOND TO AGGRESSION?

Mrs. Young cares for one-year-olds in a mothers-day-out program. When a toddler bites, she does whatever she has to—as firmly as necessary but as gently as possible—to stop the biting and to get the bitten child free from the biter. In a deeply concerned (but not angry) voice, she tells the biter assertively, "No biting, biting hurts." She then takes great pains to model touching the bitten child gently. Mrs. Young delicately strokes the bitten child's arm, saying in a soothing voice, "Gentle. Be gentle." Often, the biter will imitate her and touch the other child, then she responds, "That was so gentle. Thank you." Slowly, the toddlers begin to absorb the gentleness they see in Mrs. Young's actions every day.

When the children are older, Mrs. Young will begin emphasizing another concept: using words rather than aggression to express anger. Since she uses the word no very sparingly and only when she really intends for an action to stop, the children learn through observation that it is a powerful and important word. We will not hear Mrs. Young snapping at a child, "Don't you dare say no to me!" She allows children to express their thoughts and feelings verbally.

By being positive and assertive rather than negative and confrontational with children, Mrs. Young does not overuse the word no herself. Consequently, she does not hear the word no from toddlers very often. When she does, however, she acknowledges the balky child's feelings, even if the child cannot reasonably be allowed to have his own way. She says, "I know you don't want to wash your hands right now, but you must have clean hands in order to be allowed to eat." Furthermore, she actually coaches her toddlers in the skill of saying no. She prompts them, "Can you tell Marcus no? Say, 'No, Marcus. My cracker. Mine.'" In time, children learn by direct teaching as well as by imitation to use words rather than aggression to express their feelings of anger.

CAN CHILDREN LEARN APPROPRIATE BEHAVIOR THROUGH IMITATION?

Although babies and toddlers are only able to mimic bits and pieces of behaviors they observe, even these first attempts at **modeling** (imitating) are critically important to their development. Preschoolers imitate entire sequences of behavior. Preschoolers are in a particularly sensitive period of their lives for imitation. As they mime adult actions in their play, we get to see them reenact their world as they perceive it (Mussen & Eisenberg-Berg, 1977). These glimpses into their world range from the delightfully funny to the downright alarming. Children's imitative play discloses their innocent misconceptions of the adult world, as well as the fears and pains they sometimes feel.

School-aged children imitate, but they are more selective in choosing role models. They are constantly (but unconsciously) absorbing subtle behavior characteristics from those around them. But they are not likely to mimic the behaviors of adults or children they do not like. They will make conscious attempts, however, to talk, dress, and act like those they admire (Bandura, 1977). Adults can enhance positive imitative learning by becoming a respected and admired member of the child's immediate world rather than an aloof and distanced authority figure.

Rather than focus all our attention on correcting children's behavior, we must take a cold, hard look at ourselves and correct some of our own flaws.

(Illustration by Gregory Nemec. Reprinted with permission from Teachers College Reports, Columbia University, *Vol. 3, No. 1, Winter 2001.)*

Children are likely to be happy and cooperative when their needs are met.

Imitation is an important and logical tool for teaching prosocial behavior. Adults waste a great opportunity to have impact on children if they do not become particularly aware of their own actions and attitudes as well as those communicated by such cultural media as television (Aidman, 1997; Bandura, 1977; Cairns, 1979; Gerbner & Gross, 1980; Lefkowitz & Tesiny, 1980; Leland, 1997; Parke & Slaby, 1983). If children spend long periods of time watching television, they are bound to internalize the language and behavior they see there. The nurturing adult will closely monitor and limit programs to avoid overexposure to violent, irresponsible behaviors.

Rather than focus all our attention on correcting children's behaviors, we must take a cold, hard look at ourselves and correct some of our own flaws. Even if we are unsuccessful in weeding out all of our personal quirks and imperfections, we will certainly become more sensitive to the child's dilemma of truly wanting to stop an undesirable behavior but not being able to accomplish it. If our goal is to develop children's self-discipline and self-control, then we had best see how much of those admirable characteristics we are able to muster so we can show children (rather than just tell them) how people should behave.

AM I A POSITIVE ROLE MODEL?

- Can children easily observe cooperation, empathy, and altruism in my day-to-day actions?

- Are my values evidenced clearly in the environment I provide for children?

- What kinds of books do I read to them?

- What kinds of toys, movies, and television shows do I make available?

HOW CAN I BE MORE ATTENTIVE TO CHILDREN'S INDIVIDUAL NEEDS?

Nurturing adults respond to children's individual needs. Parents generally have no difficulty in seeing their own children as individuals. Family intimacy and shared history throughout a child's life make it likely that there is at least awareness of (if not respect for) individual differences. A key problem for parents may be accepting individual differences among their children and resisting the temptation to compare them to one another. A parent may say, "I'm sure that Ramona will love taking piano lessons just like her older brother did," while knowing full well that little Ramona would much rather do "wheelies" on a bicycle than learn to play the piano.

In a group setting, sadly, young children may be seen as tiny cogs in a very large machine. Babies' diapers may be changed not when they become wet or soiled, but at routinely scheduled times. Eating, playing, and sleeping may take place as scheduled for whole groups rather than in response to children's individual feelings of hunger, playfulness, or fatigue. A child may not be hungry for breakfast on a given day or may be really tired before naptime. It is easy for a child to feel very overlooked in a group. While routines are essential to "sanity and survival" for group caregivers, nurturing adults will find ways to be sensitive and make allowances for children's individual needs.

A nurturing adult will not be callous to children sleeping facedown on uncovered plastic mats in sweaty August heat, or make little ones nap with their shoes on simply because taking shoes off and putting them back on is too much bother. The nurturing adult would not be inclined to toss snack crackers unceremoniously onto a bare table without even the dignity of a napkin or paper plate. A nurturing adult will really care about the comfort and feelings of individual children. Even if every individual need cannot reasonably be met, the nurturing adult will express awareness of and concern for children's individual circumstances. Showing attentiveness to children's individual needs is an excellent way to demonstrate cooperative behavior for them.

Adults should become actively involved in the child's world so they will not be seen as cold, aloof authority figures.

HOW CAN I PROVIDE AFFIRMATION, AFFECTION, AND ACCEPTANCE?

Affirmation, affection, and acceptance assure a child that he is wanted and appreciated. Unconditional positive regard is the process through which affirmation, affection, and acceptance are conveyed. In contrast, conditional affection is attention given to a child only when he pleases the adult. Conditional affection carries the hidden message, "I will only love you if you are good." Unconditional positive regard lets children know they are liked simply for who they are, not for how they perform at any given time. Children absorb the message, "You are a loved, worthwhile individual even if you sometimes make mistakes." According to Clarke (1978), in order for children to develop healthy self-esteem, they must absorb the following clear messages from the words and actions of their caregivers:

AFFIRMATIONS FOR BEING

- "You have a right to be here."
- "I'm glad you are who you are."
- "It's okay for you to have needs."

AFFIRMATIONS FOR BECOMING INDEPENDENT

- "You don't have to do tricks (be cute, sick, sad, mad, or scared) to get attention."
- It's okay to be curious and try new things on your own."

AFFIRMATIONS FOR LEARNING TO THINK

- "You can stand up for the things you believe even if there is some risk involved."
- "You can own the consequences of your own actions; others don't have to rescue you."
- "It's okay to make mistakes as long as you accept responsibility for making amends."

AFFIRMATIONS FOR DEVELOPING AN INDIVIDUAL IDENTITY

- "You can express your own thoughts and feelings without fear of rejection."
- "It's okay to disagree."
- "You can trust your own judgment."

Sometimes, the preceding messages of affirmation can be verbally expressed to children. They can also be conveyed to children in day-to-day actions throughout children's lives. Affirmation is communicated to a baby by his caregiver's facial expression during such routines as diaper changing. If he looks up and sees disgust or annoyance in the caregiver's face, he will sense that it is not okay to be a baby and to need a dirty diaper changed. If he sees a relaxed smile, he will know that he is welcome and his needs are okay. If a preschooler accidentally tramples a flower

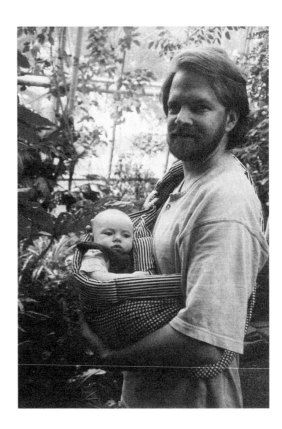

Nurturing adults care about children's comfort.

bed while trying to pull weeds like his daddy, he will sense affirmation as his dad patiently acknowledges the child's good intentions and teaches him how to weed the garden without trampling.

Nurturing adults are not afraid to show affection to children (Hoffman, 1979). Smiles, warm hugs, and sincere interest in a child's world let him know that he is the recipient of unconditional positive regard. Appropriate affection should never be intrusive, overwhelming, or one-sided, but rather respectful and reciprocal. A basic human need is for a sense of belonging. We human beings are essentially social creatures. We cannot really be happy or functional without a secure feeling that we have a place in the social order around us. The most desirable social position is one in which we feel admiration, acceptance, and approval from the important people around us.

If that situation cannot be found, people (children as well as grown-ups) may opt for negative substitute relationships to find recognition and acceptance. People assume leadership by becoming gang members, achieve recognition by defying rules, and hold others' attention by shocking, frightening, or angering them. The very last thing children (or anyone else) will settle for is being ignored and left out. Only the most emotionally disabled members of society retreat into and accept a life of total social isolation.

To stimulate prosocial behavior, the nurturing adult will be generous in making sure children know that they are accepted and approved. Instead of focusing only on children's unacceptable behaviors, the nurturing adult makes a point of noticing and commenting on positive behaviors,

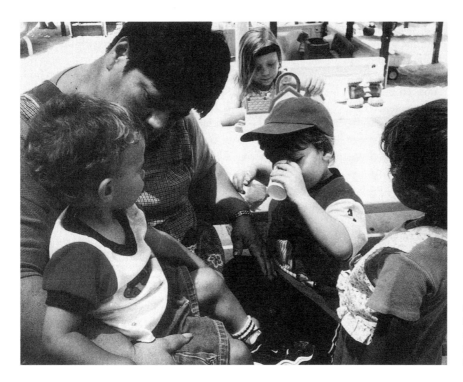

Nurturing adults who treat everyone with respect become role models of prosocial behavior.

thanking the child for remembering to wipe his feet, commenting on the lovely colors in his crayon drawing, and listening with interest to his excited but rambling account of a weekend camping trip. The nurturing adult is careful to separate clearly the difference between "bad" actions and "bad" people: "I don't like hitting, but I like you very much. You are a good person. You can learn to use words rather than hitting." In spite of inevitable disciplinary intervention from time to time, the nurtured child always knows he is a good and worthwhile human being.

HOW CAN I PROVIDE POSITIVE RECOGNITION AND ENCOURAGEMENT?

On special occasions, children want and deserve recognition and encouragement just as we do in our own personal and professional lives. An occasional, sincere pat on the back can trigger a surge of motivation in us (Mussen & Eisenberg-Berg, 1977). Too much praise, however, can be burdensome, causing us to feel pressured to live up to unrealistic standards. We either awkwardly stammer thank you, or worse, become addicted to praise, needing more and more every day to maintain our self-esteem. A suddenly famous guitar player was asked recently what he missed most about the formerly quiet life he led before he found fame. He quickly replied, "I miss just sitting down with people to talk about music. Everyone tells me how much they admire my work and how wonderful they think I am, but how can you answer that?"

Recognition and encouragement are more moderate alternatives to an overabundance of gushy or insincere praise. Often, we praise a child by stating a value judgment such as, "Oh, what a good boy you are!" Unfortunately, by implying that cleaning up makes him "good," we hint that if he does not continue the action in the future, he might become "bad." (Young children tend to think in simplistic terms: if you are not good, then you must be bad.)

Recognizing and encouraging are different from praising. To recognize and encourage a child, we might say, "I noticed that you wiped the table with a sponge. The table is clean and beautiful. Thanks!" The recognition is very specific (tells exactly what the child did) and encourages the child by letting him know that we appreciate the action. He is not labeled good or bad, just sincerely acknowledged for a job well done. The nurturing adult says thank you very frequently to children. When children do the right thing, it is not appropriate or helpful to dredge up old problems, saying, for example, "Why didn't you do this yesterday?" or "Well, now that you have done this, you can do everything else I've been telling you to do." Children who are overwhelmed with criticism become very defeatist. They think, "Why should I even try? Everything I do just gets me into more trouble." The child will feel more encouraged if he is allowed to "glow" in every little bit of success before tactfully being guided by a nurturing adult to complete other unfinished tasks.

Praise focuses a child's attention on gaining external rewards. Recognition and encouragement focus the child's attention on internal rewards, feelings of accomplishment, pride, and self-worth. Internal rewards build the child's capacity for self-control and self-direction.

AM I WILLING TO ENFORCE RULES EVEN IF IT WOULD BE EASIER TO LOOK THE OTHER WAY?

The nurturing adult is able to be both assertive and caring at the same time. Mr. Leone really enjoys children. He is tender-hearted and kind, but has trouble being assertive. When Jenny runs to him complaining, "Anna pulled my hair and broke my new crayons," Mr. Leone shrugs and says, "I'm sure it was just an accident." When children throw food during lunch, Mr. Leone pretends he does not notice but tries to distract the ringleaders by talking loudly about the weather, "Listen, I think I hear thunder. Do you hear that?" Mr. Leone is kind, but he is definitely not assertive. Lackadaisical permissiveness cultivates antisocial and aggressive behavior in children (Sears, Maccoby, & Lewin, 1957).

Children Want and Need Rules.

A truly nurturing adult earns children's respect by being firm and fair in a way that reminds children that a sturdy protective wall of reasonable limits surrounds them and keeps them safe. (They also need to know, of course, that this "wall" of rules can and will be broken in specific situations where it becomes a hindrance rather a help to the children.) What they do not need is anger and retaliation. Anger is frightening to people generally because it can cause them to lose control of their actions. Children especially feel vulnerable since they have not developed the self-control to stop themselves from going too far when they are angry and out of control. Children feel nurtured and safe when they know they can trust a strong adult to stop them before they behave aggressively or destructively. They also want to know with certainty that their safety and rights will be protected if someone else loses control. The nurturing adult is not hesitant to enforce appropriate rules fairly and firmly.

AM I WILLING TO PROTECT INDIVIDUAL RIGHTS?

Mary Beth is the mother of two young children, a five-year-old boy, Trey, and a three-year-old girl, Betsy. Betsy adores her big brother and attempts to follow every step he takes. Sometimes, when Trey is alone, he seems proud of Betsy's attention and plays with her for hours, but when he has friends his own age to play with, he chases Betsy away and tells her to leave him alone. One day, while Mary Beth is waxing the kitchen floor, she hears a loud altercation in the backyard. Betsy is crying because Trey and his chums will not let her play with them and are taunting her by chanting, "Betsy is a tag-along! Betsy is a tag-along!"

Since Mary Beth's mind is on the "waxy yellow buildup" problem in her kitchen, she is tempted for a moment to order Trey to entertain his little sister and stop the silly nonsense with his friends. Luckily, however, she stops to assess the individual rights of everyone involved in the situation. As a parent, she has a right to do her housework without interruption, but, of course, she also has an obligation to care for her children (she thinks children are considerably more important than waxy yellow buildup). Trey has an obligation to treat his sister with kindness and to help out by entertaining her from time to time, but he also has a right to lead his own life and to play with his own friends. Betsy has a right not to be called names but she also has an obligation to respect her brother's privacy and to learn to play alone sometimes.

After Mary Beth patiently listens to complaints from all sides, she says, "Trey, Betsy feels hurt when you call her names. You have a right to play with your friends, but name-calling can't be allowed. Let's make a compromise. Please push Betsy on the swing for a few minutes so that I can finish my work in the kitchen, then I will bring Betsy in the house, and you and your friends can have the backyard to yourselves until your friends go home. Betsy, you may play with Trey for a few minutes, then you and I will go inside and I will show you how to give your dolls a bath."

Because Mary Beth is a nurturing parent, she is able and willing to make an extra effort to see that everyone's rights are protected and that everyone behaves responsibly. She does not do only what seems expedient or convenient at the moment, but tries hard to create an environment of fairness and mutual respect for the rights of others.

POINTS TO REMEMBER

- Prosocial behavior is that which cooperates with, cares about, and helps others.

- To develop prosocial behavior, children must interact with peers in a nurturing social environment.

- Children who are afraid that their own needs will not be met will not be able to be generous with others.

- Encouraging children to compete with each other reduces cooperativeness.

- The nurturing adult is an honest, emotionally healthy person who is both assertive and caring.

- Imitation is an important and logical tool for teaching prosocial behavior.

- Affirmation, affection, and acceptance assure a child that she is wanted and appreciated.

- Unconditional positive regard is the process of conveying affirmation, affection, and acceptance.

- Recognition and encouragement are appropriate alternatives to an overabundance of gushy or insincere praise.

PRACTICAL APPLICATION

WILLIAM AND THE NATURE WALK

Brenda's three-year-olds were ready to go outside. Several days of heavy autumn rains had kept them indoors in the child care center, so today's clear sky and bright sun were a welcome invitation to break away from usual morning routines and release some pent-up energy.

Brenda and her assistant teacher, Theresa, decided that playing on the playground was out of the question since there were still big puddles in the sandbox and under the swings. "A nature walk," Theresa suggested, "would be perfect. There are lots of pretty fall leaves, and we could walk to the park to collect acorns and leaves for our science center."

The children excitedly prepared for their walk. Each child chose a "buddy" to hold hands with, and the pairs of young children danced and wriggled with anticipation as Brenda and Theresa helped them get into a straight line on the sidewalk.

"Remember," said Brenda, "we need to hold hands with our partners and walk very carefully on the sidewalk until we get to the park." Before they had gone even a few feet, however, William, who had just turned three, saw a bright yellow leaf and, dropping his partner's hand, bent down to pick it up. Louisa, the older three-year-old directly behind William, immediately tumbled on top of him.

Brenda helped William and Louisa up, then, kneeling at eye level to William and gently taking his hand, said politely but firmly, "Excuse me, William, you must wait until we get to the park, then you can look for leaves. Remember, be safe! Hold hands with your partner." She then gave William a little pat on the shoulder and a smile as she announced, "Okay, is this train ready to go again? Let's chug, chug, chug down the railroad track! Whooo, whoo! Ding, ding, ding!"

Within minutes, William was again distracted and stooped to pick up an irresistibly bright red leaf, and poor little Louisa was sprawled on top of him just like before. This time, however, she quickly scrambled to her feet, took William's hand and said in a confident voice, "Exsqueeze me, Weeyum! When you do dat, I faw down!" (Excuse me, William! When you do that, I fall down!)

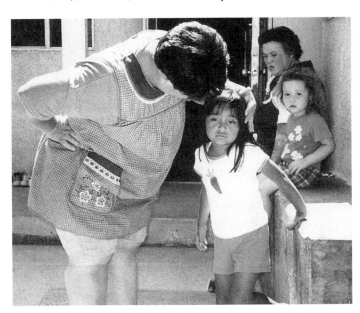

Children want and need reasonable limits.

DISCUSSION QUESTIONS

1. Why do you think Louisa was able to use words to express her frustration with William rather than biting or hitting him?
2. How should Brenda respond to the interaction between William and Louisa? Should she do anything further to correct William's behavior? Should she attempt to reinforce Louisa for remembering to use words?
3. What should Brenda and Theresa do if William continues to disrupt the nature walk? Can you think of anything preventive that could be done to stop the problem and avoid difficulty on future walks?
4. Are these children learning prosocial behavior? How?
5. Did Brenda and Theresa seem playful, consistent, assertive, and sensitive to the children's basic needs? Did it appear that developmentally appropriate activities and routines were being carried out?

RELATED READINGS

SUPPORTING PROSOCIAL BEHAVIOR

Asher, S. R., & Coie, J. D. (Eds.). (1990). *Peer rejection in childhood.* New York: Cambridge University Press.

Bredekamp, S., & Copple, C. (Eds.). (1997). *Developmentally appropriate practice in early childhood programs* (rev. ed). Washington, DC: National Association for the Education of Young Children.

Britton, L., & Turner J. S. (Illustrator). (1993). *Montessori play & learn: A parents' guide to purposeful play from two to six.* New York: Crown.

Adapts Montessori-based activities to home settings for parent use. Shows how, by physically adapting a home to encourage a young child to take part in family activities, parents can stimulate and direct the child's natural curiosity.

Burts, D. C., Hart, C. H., Charlesworth, R., & Kirk, L. (1990). A comparison of frequencies of stress behaviors observed in kindergarten children in classrooms with developmentally appropriate versus developmentally inappropriate instructional practices. *Early Childhood Research Quarterly, 5*(3), 407–423.

Burts, D. C., Hart, C. H., Charlesworth, R., DeWolf, D. M., Ray, J., Manuel, K., & Fleege, P. O. (1993). Developmental appropriateness of kindergarten programs and academic outcomes in first grade. *Journal of Research in Childhood Education, 8*(1), 23–31.

Chenfeld, M. B. (2000). Get the elephant out of the room! We're finished with the Es! *Young Children 55*(6), 20–22.

Offers tips for energizing the classroom by building curriculum on unexpected opportunities for learning and supporting children's self-motivation through spontaneous discovery learning.

Chung, A. (2000, July). *After-school programs: Keeping children safe and smart* (Free booklet from the U.S. Department of Education). This document was prepared under contract ED-00-PO-1711 to the U.S. Department of Education. Jessup, MD: Editorial Publications Center.

Discusses the importance of safe and enriching after-school learning opportunities for children and youth. This booklet explains what works in after-school programs, and provides resources and examples of communities with strong after-school programs. To access copies online, go to: www.ed.gov/pubs/edpubs.html. *To order paper copies, write to: ED Pubs, U.S. Department of Education, P.O. Box 1398 20794-1398. Fax request to: 301-470-1244. Send e-mail requests to: edpubs@inet.ed.gov. Or call toll-free: 1-877-433-7827 (1-877-4-ED-PUBS). To use a telecommunication device for the deaf (TDD) or (TTY), call 1-800-437-0833. This report is available in alternative formats (Braille, large print, audio tape, or computer diskette). Call the Alternate Format Center at 202-205-8113.*

Driscoll, A. (1995). *Cases in early childhood education: Stories of programs and practices.* Needham Heights, MA: Allyn & Bacon.

This book provides case studies showing developmentally appropriate practice and reflective teaching methods. It gives examples of a variety of practices seen in a range of settings. The "snapshots" provide examples of typical situations in early childhood settings and examples of developmentally appropriate practice with the day-to-day problems and issues that happen in "real classrooms."

Edwards, C. P., Gandini, L., & Forman, G. E. (Eds.). (1998). *The hundred languages of children: The Reggio Emilia approach—Advanced reflections,* (2nd ed.). Westport, CT: Ablex Publishing Corporation.

The Hundred Languages of Children gives a comprehensive overview of the schools of Reggio Emilia, Italy. Notable differences in the Reggio Emilia curriculum include the following: the curriculum is based on projects that grow out of the teachers' observations of students, collaborative relationships are emphasized, and documentation provides a foundation for evaluation and planning.

Gestwicki, C. (1999). *Developmentally appropriate practice.* (2nd ed.) Clifton Park, NY: Delmar Learning.

This book is designed to assist teachers in implementing the widely recognized philosophy of developmentally appropriate practice. The text is organized into "environments" for each developmental stage to help focus on specific appropriate responses and to nurture overall development.

Gordon, A., & Browne, K. W. (2004). *Beginnings and beyond* (6th ed.). Clifton Park, NY: Delmar Learning.

Comprehensive approaches to the curriculum, education, developmentally appropriate practice, and other hot topics in early education.

Gronlund, G. (2001). Rigorous academics in preschool and kindergarten? Yes! Let me tell you how. *Young Children 56*(2), 42–43.

By understanding the nature of early learning, teachers integrate traditional academic goals and objectives into spontaneous play activities to help children create learning geared to their own interests and abilities.

Hewitt, K. (2001). Blocks as a tool for learning: A historical and contemporary perspective. *Young Children 56*(1), 6–13.

Reviews the importance of block play and construction to the historical context of early childhood philosophies in Europe and the U.S. including Friedrich Froebel, Maria Montessori, Caroline Pratt, and Patty Smith Hill.

Hirsh-Pasek, K., Hyson, M., & Rescorla, L. (1990). Academic environments in preschool: Do they pressure or challenge young children? *Early Education and Development, 1*(6), 401–423.

Honig, A., & Wittmer, D. (1992). *Prosocial development in children: Caring, sharing, and cooperation: A bibliographic resource guide.* New York: Garland.

Honig, A. S., & Wittmer, D. S. (1997). Helping children become more prosocial: Ideas for classrooms. In K. M. Paciorek & J. H. Munro (Eds.), *Annual editions: Early childhood education 97/98* (18th ed.). New York: McGraw-Hill. (Original work published in *Young Children*, January 1996.)

Teachers can promote positive social development by emphasizing cooperation and conflict resolution as they guide behavior. Families should be involved in programming to encourage social interaction with special needs children.

Howell, J., & Corbey-Scullen, L. (1997). Out of the housekeeping corner and onto the stage-extending dramatic play. *Young Children 52*(6), 82–88.

Describes methods for extending dramatic play into a classroom play project to better support children's development.

Hurwitz, S. C. (2001). The teacher who would be Vivian. *Young Children 56*(5), 89–91.

Reviews Vivian Paley's ideas on children's language practice, writing, and problem-solving through play, storytelling, and playacting, and emphasizes the importance of teachers' having effective listening skills.

Hyson, M. C., Hirsh-Pasek, K., & Rescorla, L. (1990). The classroom practices inventory: An observation instrument based on NAEYC's guidelines for developmentally appropriate practices for 4- and 5-year-old children. *Early Childhood Research Quarterly, 5*(4), 475–94.

Jensen, B. J., & Bullard, J. A. (2002). The mud center: Recapturing childhood. *Young Children, 57*(3): 16–19.

Describes an inexpensive, child-friendly outdoor mud "kitchen" stocked with cooking utensils, measuring implements, found items, and buckets of dirt and water to create an engaging dramatic play area that promotes children's cooperation, communication, responsibility, and learning.

Katz, L. G. (1999, December). *Curriculum disputes in early childhood education.* ERIC digest. Champaign, IL: ERIC Clearinghouse on Elementary and Early Childhood Education. (ERIC Document No. ED436298.)

This article compares instructivist and constructivist approaches to early childhood education, and suggests that attention to children's intellectual development may inadvertently be overlooked by both sides.

Katz, L. G., McClellan, D. E., Fuller, J. O., & Walz, G. R. (1995). *Building social competence in children: A practical handbook for counselors, psychologists and teachers.* Greensboro, NC: ERIC Clearinghouse on Counseling and Student Services.

Kilpatrick, W. (1997). The moral power of good stories. In E. N. Junn & C. Boyatzis (Eds.), *Annual editions: Child growth and development 97/98* (4th ed.). New York: McGraw-Hill. (Original work published in *American Educator*, Summer 1993.)

Stories help to make sense of our lives, claims William Kilpatrick, and they offer children vivid examples of morals and good values. This essay urges educators and parents to use stories as a powerful means of communicating about character and virtue to children.

Lawhon, T., & Lawhon, D. C. (2000, Winter). Promoting social skills in young children. *Early Childhood Education Journal, 28*(2), 105–110.

Points out how social relationships can be improved through the child's efforts and those of supportive teachers, parents, and caregivers. Presents two observation checklists: one for children's behaviors and another for adult self-assessments.

Leong, D., & Bodrova, E. (1996). *Tools of the mind: A Vygotskian approach to early childhood education.* Upper Saddle River, NJ: Merrill Education/Prentice Hall.

Lewin, K., Lippitt, R., & White, R. (1939). Patterns of aggressive behavior in experimentally created social climates. *Journal of Social Psychology*, 271–299.

Three leadership styles—authoritarian, democratic, and laissez-faire (permissive)—were studied and typical outcomes identified. Findings support the value of democratic child guidance in lieu of authoritarian or permissive styles.

Lillard P. P. (1988). *Montessori: A modern approach* (reissue ed.). New York: Schocken Books.

A classic overview of the Montessori method.

Mahany, B. (1997). Mrs. Paley's lessons. In K. M. Paciorek & J. H. Munro (Eds.), *Annual editions: Early childhood education 97/98* (18th ed.). New York: McGraw-Hill. (Original work published in *Chicago Tribune*, June 25, 1995.)

Vivian Paley was a kindergarten teacher at the University of Chicago Lab School for 24 years. She has deep respect for young children and considers the kindergarten classroom an important place for social development. Paley regards teaching as a moral act.

Montessori, M., & Chattin-McNichols, J. (1995). *The absorbent mind* (reprint ed.). New York: Henry Holt.

Dr. Montessori gives an in-depth look at the workings of young children's minds. She describes how spontaneous activities of children are often misunderstood by adults as mischief or needless "fooling around" when the actions are actually "the work" of being children. She argues that young children are driven to explore and learn about their world.

Moran, M. J., & Jarvis, J. (2001). Helping young children develop higher order thinking. *Young Children 56*(5), 31–35.

Strategies for supporting the process of learning, helping children build confidence, social skills, and problem-solving.

NAEYC. (1996). Using NAEYC's code of ethics. Why don't you teach the basics? *Young Children 51*(5), 48–49.

Responses to a conflict between teachers who are trying to implement a new curriculum based on developmentally appropriate practice, and parents who believe the basics are not being taught and that the moral values they teach at home are being undermined.

Ramsey, P. G. (1991). *Making friends in school: Promoting peer relationships in early childhood.* New York: Teacher's College Press.

Ratcliff, N. (2001). Use the environment to prevent discipline problems and support learning. *Young Children 56*(5), 84–88.

Explores strategies for planning an effective classroom environment to minimize crowding, deal with inadequate space, monitor problem areas, create calm, structure appropriate activities, establish routines, and plan transitions.

Stork, S., & Engel, S. (1999, Winter). So, what is constructivist teaching? A rubric for teacher evaluation. *Dimensions of early childhood, 27*(1), 20–27.

Gives an overview of constructivist theory and practice, along with an assessment tool to help teachers broaden their teaching skills.

Yen, S., & Ispa, J. M. (2000, March). Children's temperament and behavior in Montessori and constructivist early childhood programs. *Early Education and Development, 11*(2), 171–86.

This study indicates that very active boys are slightly more likely to be perceived as behavior problems in Montessori than in Constructivist settings. No similar trends were revealed for female students.

HELPFUL WEB SITES

http://www.childrensmusic.org/   Children's Music Web offers links to children's music sites, a discussion forum, and a music magazine with activities for children.

http://www.childrenssoftware.com/   Children's Software Review offers software information and reviews, and tips on how to evaluate software for children.

http://www.theideabox.com/   Idea Box—Early Childhood Education and Activity Resources is a commercial site that offers activities, games, songs, crafts, and recipes. Each segment shows time required, suggested age level, and degree of difficulty. Also offers a bulletin board where teachers and parents can exchange ideas and hints.

http://www.wellesley.edu/WCW/CRW/SAC   National Institute on Out-of-School Time, Wellesley College Center for Research on Women.

http://www.nncc.org/   National Network for Child Care offers links to child care resources such as curriculum, child development, disability, diversity, licensing, and business management.

http://ericeece.org/reggio.html   Reggio Emilia offers Web sites and documents related to the approach to early childhood education developed in the preschools of Reggio Emilia, Italy. (List compiled by the ERIC Clearinghouse on Elementary and Early Childhood Education.)

http://www.ed.gov/index.jsp   U.S. Department of Education, Partnership for Family Involvement in Education.

For additional information on positive child guidance, visit our Web site at
http://www.earlychilded.delmar.com

Chapter 6
Positive Communication

Effective guidance depends on positive communication.

OBJECTIVES

After reading this chapter, you should be able to:
- Identify effective listening strategies.
- Address feelings and emotions underlying communication.
- Recognize the rationale for positive statements of instruction.
- List the characteristics of assertive communication.
- List the characteristics of nonproductive communication.
- Discuss strategies for positive confrontation.

BUILDING A FOUNDATION FOR POSITIVE COMMUNICATION

Positive communication is like a dance filled with expressive and responsive give and take. Children begin this interactive dance early in life but effective communication skills are acquired gradually over many years. Children can best learn to communicate effectively by imitating and interacting with adults who model well, setting an example for and participating with children in both conversational roles, speaking and listening, and leading and following.

WHEN DOES COMMUNICATION BEGIN?

The development of communication begins before birth when the fetus hears the muffled tones of her mother's voice. The **auditory physiology** (all those little body parts in and around the ears) of infants is relatively well developed at birth. Immediately after birth, the infant may turn toward or startle at sounds, and may even be able to distinguish the mother's voice from that of another female (DeCasper & Fifer, 1980). Although newborns have not yet developed any concept of language, they respond attentively to the sounds of speech (Begley, 1997a; Eisenberg, 1976; Kuhl, 1981; White, 1995).

One-day-old infants move their bodies in rhythm to the sounds of a caregiver's speech (Condon & Sander, 1974). One-month-olds are able to discriminate between certain vowel sounds (Trehub, 1973). In time, babies learn to mimic bits and pieces of adult communication such as inflection, intonation, facial expression, and timing, as well as the give and take of dialogue.

HOW ADULTS CAN ASSIST THE DEVELOPMENT OF EARLY COMMUNICATION SKILLS IN INFANTS

From the time children are infants, adults should both lead and follow in communication with them. An adult may lead by talking to an infant in a way that is sensitive to the baby's mood and attention span. An infant will participate in this interaction by watching and responding as the adult speaks, and then, when the interaction becomes too intense and tiring, by looking away, grimacing, or yawning to signal fatigue and the need for a time out (Brazelton, Koslowski, & Main, 1974; Field, 1982; Shore, 1997; Stern, 1974; White, 1995).

A sensitive adult will follow the baby's lead by being quiet until after the baby rests for a few seconds, then look back indicating that she is ready to interact again. The adult may also follow the infant by waiting for the infant to make some sound, then repeat the baby's gurgling, cooing, or babbling. This form of baby talk (or "parentese"), in which the baby leads, is very useful for helping babies get a sense of conversational give and take long before they are able to say or understand any words (Bruner, 1978a, 1978b).

When adults pace their interactions with infants so that a specific infant behavior elicits a predictable adult response, infants begin to learn that their environment is controllable and predictable, which increases their motivation for involvement in surroundings and stimulates learning. Infants who sense they are powerless over interactions may become distressed, irritable, or passive and withdrawn (Watson, 1973).

The beginnings of communication take place in infancy.

Older babies learn to look back and forth between an object and a caregiver, grunting, point-ing, or reaching to indicate a desire for the object (Harding & Golinkoff, 1979). This effort to communicate reflects the child's dawning ability to bring about a desired action by communi-cating with adults. Well developing toddlers grasp the essential elements of conversation: mean-ingful words, intonation, inflection, facial expression, gesture, and give and take. It may be impossible, however, to make much sense of what the toddler is trying to say. An adult who is tactful will find ways to avoid repeated requests that toddler repeat herself.

A positive and supportive response to children's early attempts at speech will encourage con-tinued effort (Hess & Shipman, 1967). Excessive correcting or prodding discourages further practice. Even after two-year-olds have mastered many of the words and phrases of the language, they will need a bit of gentle prompting to carry on a dialogue. Adults can help by asking sim-ple questions (for example, "Is this your big teddy bear? What is your teddy bear's name?") to maintain the child's active participation in a conversation (Honig & Wittmer, 1997; Kaye, 1982).

WHAT ARE TYPICAL CHARACTERISTICS OF EARLY SPEECH?

Usually, toddlers seem oblivious to the notion that one should speak only when a listener is pres-ent. One- and two-year-olds sometimes carry on animated self-talk while engaging in solitary play (Weiss & Lillywhite, 1976). In fact, toddlers may stare blankly and silently when urged to talk, then jabber freely later when alone or with a very trusted caregiver. Toddlers who are new to a group care setting may attend for weeks or months before trying to communicate verbally with a nursery school teacher, even though parents report they talk a great deal at home with family members.

Three- and four-year-olds gain the vocabulary needed to understand and express many ideas and feelings, and they become more concerned that there is an audience present for conversa-tions. A preschooler who thinks an adult is not listening may move directly into the adult's line of vision or may even try to hold the adult's face to keep that person from looking away. It is not uncommon, however, for two preschoolers to be looking straight at each other, chatting excitedly at the same time without either of them seeming to notice that neither is listening. Preschoolers also talk to inanimate objects such as stuffed animals and television characters without seeming to be bothered that these objects are not very responsive listeners.

School-aged children become more refined in their communication. They finally recognize that communicators must take turns listening and speaking in order for anyone to be heard. Their growing vocabulary and maturity increase their capacity. Toddlers and younger preschool-ers tend to be physical in their expression of feelings. Anger may be expressed by biting or hit-ting and affection by bear hugs and moist kisses. In contrast, school-agers use words more expertly to express affection or to lash out when they feel angry. They tend to use insults, threats, or name-calling to express anger and verbal promises of friendship to show affection. Although school-agers are no longer as sensitive to imitation as younger children, who seem to absorb everything they see, school-agers are still likely to emulate, and thus be influenced by, adults and children they admire (Bandura, 1977).

WHY POSITIVE, MUTUAL COMMUNICATION IS IMPORTANT FOR CHILD GUIDANCE

As children develop and their communication style changes from stage to stage, adults must rec-ognize and adapt to the various limitations of children in order to guide them toward effective communication. The achievement of effective child guidance really hinges on the achievement of mutual communication. The ultimate goal of positive discipline is not just to control or manipulate children externally but rather to stimulate inner control based on responsibility and respect for the rights of others. This inner control depends on an understanding of the needs and expectations of oneself and others gained through open, honest dialogue.

Preparing children to function as adults in a democratic political system requires that children become competent communicators. In an autocracy, citizens can blindly and ignorantly follow leaders without ever discussing or questioning commands. For a democracy to work, citizens must accept responsibility to grasp, understand, and take a stand on various issues. These goals are achieved by communication: listening, reading, discussing, and so forth.

The most effective tools for children to learn communication skills are modeling and practicing. Children learn effective skills as they watch, listen to, and interact with consistent adults who set a good example. Children are able to make those skills a part of their repertoire by practicing again and again the words and interactions they have observed. Therefore, adults who care for and teach children need well-developed communication skills. These skills help them to:

- understand and interpret children's needs accurately.

- clearly express expectations to children.

- teach effective communication to children by modeling.

Adults often complain that children do not listen. The view presented here proposes that children be taught effective communication skills through exposure to capable models and by participation in appropriate interactions.

Through daily experience and practice, children learn to listen to others and to express their own feelings and ideas.

EFFECTIVE LISTENING

Randall pulls his chair up to the table close to his teacher, and spreads out a large sheet of drawing paper and an assortment of crayons. He says, "Hi, Miss Katie. I'm gonna color me a big picture." Miss Katie glances at him and smiles briefly, saying, "Umm humm, that's nice." Miss Katie's attention is focused on a group of children playing across the room. She does not seem to notice Randall as he repeats, "Look, Miss Katie, look here!"

Finally, Randall tugs at her sleeve and says, "Look at this. I'm drawing great big mountains. My daddy took me camping and I found lots of rocks. Wanna see my real mountain rocks?"

Randall jumps up from his chair and begins emptying his pockets onto the drawing paper. Miss Katie suddenly sees his small pile of rocks and pebbles. She says in a stern voice, "Randall! What is all this? Get these dirty rocks off here. Go throw them in the trash. You can't color with rocks all over your paper."

Randall stammers "but, but . . ." as tears fill his eyes. Miss Katie insists, "Randall, would you quit making such a fuss and just do what I said."

Randall hangs his head and drags his feet as he slowly shuffles across the room to the trash can. One by one he ceremoniously drops his pebbles, his "real mountain rocks," into the trash. Miss Katie did not listen.

HOW ATTENTIVE LISTENING CAN NURTURE THE CHILD'S DEVELOPING SENSE OF SELF

The greatest need children have is for attention, recognition, and a sense of belonging. If a child is routinely ignored, she may begin to feel invisible. Much that is called misbehavior is simply an attempt by a child to become visible one way or another. A child who does not feel a sense of belonging may gradually become alienated, rebellious, or withdrawn.

The surer a child is that she is an accepted member of a group, the more confident and co-operative that child will be. Adults can indicate their recognition and acceptance of a child by listening well. Attentive listening includes:

- maintaining eye contact

- giving relevant nonverbal gestures such as nodding, smiling, and appropriate touch

- giving relevant verbal responses to draw out and encourage the child to continue

- waiting patiently for the child to complete what she is saying, without rushing the child or trying to finish the child's sentences

This polite, attentive listening not only gives children the confident feeling that what they have to say is important enough for the adult to listen, but also teaches children by modeling how they should listen to others. Also, careful listening will help the adult hear, interpret, and respond accurately to children's needs.

THREE BASIC HUMAN NEEDS UNDERLYING REQUESTS FOR HELP

Gazda et al. (1990) define three needs that are at the heart of communications indicating a desire for some kind of response or help. Adults and children have the same basic human urge to get their social, emotional, intellectual, and physical needs met. Young children (and sometimes older children and adults) function at an unconscious level in which they react to a vague feeling of need without recognizing or understanding that need. There are an infinite number of complicated ways that people of all ages approach others to get help, but at the bottom of all that complexity are three simple human needs. These three needs are expressed as requests for:

- action or information (Please do . . ., or Please tell me . . .)

- understanding and attention (Please listen and show concern for me . . .)

- inappropriate interaction (Please let me cling, whine, complain, undermine, and so on . . .)

Time, effort, and practice are required if one is to become skilled at recognizing the underlying needs hidden in everyday communications. A question such as "Where is my mommy?" may be a simple request for information, or it may be an emotion-packed request for understanding and attention by a child who knows very well where mommy is. A major source of miscommunication is the tendency of persons in the helping role to jump to the wrong conclusion and respond in a way that does not meet the real need of the person requesting help. Listening carefully and waiting attentively for the child to find words to express herself encourage the child to practice speaking. Impatience can discourage the child and delay language development.

ARE THESE LISTENING AND HELPING STRATEGIES ONLY APPROPRIATE FOR USE WITH YOUNG CHILDREN?

The following sections will give strategies for identifying and responding to expressed needs. These strategies are not intended as gimmicks or as a bag-of-tricks to manipulate children's behavior, but as a respectful and effective way of communicating with children and adults. As has been previously stressed, children learn by modeling. Children will quickly recognize an adult who is snide and sarcastic with other adults but artificially sweet or patronizing with children. Parents and early childhood professionals set the emotional tone for children's interactions and personal relationships. The communication method presented here can be most effective only if it is applied to adult to adult, adult to child, and child to child interactions. We can't say, "Do as I say and not as I do."

The phrase "children are people, too" has become such a cliché that the significance of its meaning has been lost. But children really are people who deserve the same dignity and human rights as anyone else. Children's perceptions are different, their logic and experience are limited, and their needs, roles, and responsibilities are not the same as those of adults, but they can definitely feel the sting of humiliation and the pain of rejection. Most adults can remember in vivid detail some painful experience that occurred early in their childhoods. Yet we often act as if children's feelings do not really merit much consideration. Every baby or child is, in fact, the very same person who will someday be a teacher, senator, artist, or carpenter. The events of that person's early childhood will be an integral part of her character and personality, whether these events are consciously remembered or not.

Children learn as if by **osmosis** (absorbed through one's skin). They soak in information simply by living day to day in an environment. Effective listening is not only a learning objective for chil-

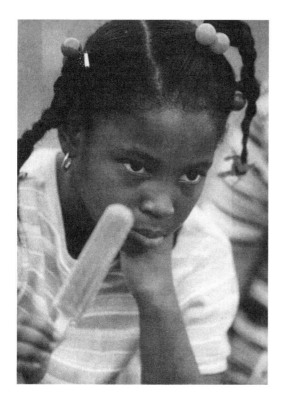

"No one will listen to me!"

dren but also a necessary component of children's daily lives, to be used directly with children as well as among the various adults who interact with children. For example, an ancient proverb says: "Tell me and I forget; show me and I remember; let me experience for myself and I understand."

Children learn to listen well by experiencing respectful listening as a regular part of daily life. Simply telling children to listen is not enough.

APPROPRIATE RESPONSES TO REQUESTS FOR ACTION OR INFORMATION

Joey, an 18-month-old, sits on a small stool, rocking and crying, "Beah, beah, ma beah." Miss Rosario squats beside him and gently coaxes him to show her what he wants. Joey quickly leads her to the bathroom. He stretches his arm toward a high shelf where diaper bags are kept. Urgently, he opens and closes his hand pleading, "Beah, beah!"

Miss Rosario takes his diaper bag from the shelf. Immediately she sees that Joey's fuzzy white teddy bear is inside. She says, "Oh, you want your bear. Is that right, Joey, bear?"

Joey nods and says, "Ma beah." He hugs his bear and toddles away dragging it by one leg.

Learning to communicate effectively is an important part of daily life.

Even though Miss Rosario could not understand Joey's words, she recognized that Joey was requesting action from her. People who work with young children spend a great deal of time responding to requests for action or information. Some requests are straightforward and simple to understand: "Is it time for snack yet?" or "Tie my shoe, please." Other requests, like Joey's request for his bear, are difficult to interpret.

Requests may also be hidden or masked. What sounds like a simple statement may really be intended as a request for action. "I can't sleep," may really mean, "Come sit by me and read me a story." A comment may really mask a request for information. "Latecia's mama is too fat" may really mean, "Latecia told me there is a baby in her mama's tummy, and I am very frightened and confused." Since children do not have fully developed communication skills, adults must accept additional responsibility for keeping the channels of communication open and clear.

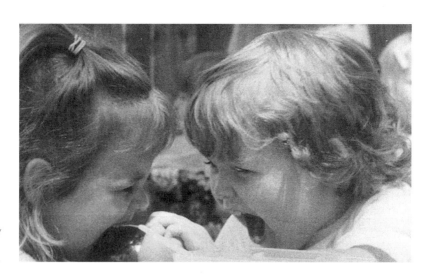

Very young children must gradually learn to express their angry feelings in words rather than action.

> *Five-year-old Malika is standing on the playground beside her teacher, Mrs. Johnson. She sees a caterpillar crawling toward her and starts to shriek. Mrs. Johnson bends down and gently allows the fuzzy caterpillar to crawl onto a leaf she is holding. Malika screams, "It's gonna kill you! Is it gonna kill you?"*
>
> *Mrs. Johnson says, "No, Malika. This little caterpillar has a very tiny mouth and no teeth and no poison. He likes to eat leaves. When he gets very fat, he will wrap himself in a cocoon that is like a little blanket. While he is inside, he will change into a beautiful butterfly. Then, after a long time, that beautiful butterfly will come out of the cocoon and fly away." Mrs. Johnson helps Malika make a suitable home for the caterpillar in a large jar. Later, at circle time, she reads a book called* The Very Hungry Caterpillar.

Mrs. Johnson has redirected Malika's fear of bugs to curiosity about science and nature. Mrs. Johnson recognized that underneath Malika's shrieking and screaming was a need for information. Mrs. Johnson responded to a hidden request for information.

> *After a birthday party, four-year-old Seth sees that his mother is wrapping leftover cake. He says, "Mommy, I want more cake, please." His mother says, "No, Seth. No more cake." Seth begs, "Please, I'm hungry. I want more cake."*
>
> *Seth's mother bends down to Seth's eye level and takes his hand gently. In a sympathetic voice, she says, "Seth, I understand that you really want more cake. That cake tasted great, didn't it? But a lot of cake is not good for you. I love you and I want you to have a healthy body and healthy teeth, so I have to say no. No more cake."*
>
> *Seth pulls his hand away, bouncing up and down, whining and flapping his arms like an angry old hen (the preschooler's dance of frustration and impending tantrum). Seth's mother does not flinch a muscle. In a very calm tone she says, "It's okay to feel angry. Sometimes I feel angry, too. Sometimes I get so angry I feel like crying. Sometimes I feel so bad that I just need a hug."*
>
> *Without looking at her face, Seth climbs into his mother's arms and gets a long hug. Suddenly, he brightens and says, "How 'bout apples. They make you get strong teeth like Superman." His mom smiles and replies, "You know, Seth, that sounds like a great idea." Seth's mother clearly understood her son's request for action, but she also knew that providing what he wanted was not in his best interest.*

Seth's mother loved him enough to say no to his request and enough to accept an appropriate compromise. Adults are ultimately responsible for the health, safety, and welfare of children in their care. Complying with potentially harmful or unfair requests hurts children and, eventually, damages adult–child trust and respect. Sometimes, adults are tempted to comply with questionable requests to avoid conflict or in a misguided attempt to win the child's affection. Not only has Seth's mother stood firm in making the decision that is in Seth's best interest but also has taught a very valuable lesson.

Her gentle strength has shown Seth an example of self-discipline, doing the right thing even though it would be easier to give in and avoid a fuss. Through her calm, patient persistence, even when he threatened a tantrum, she serves as a positive role model for Seth. Seth can learn positive coping skills, to stay calm, and persist in finding a solution when he feels upset. (Some adults inadvertently reinforce children's tantrums by pitching tantrums of their own.) And, most importantly, her sensitive understanding of his feelings helps him know that he is loved and respected, even while a limit is being enforced.

APPROPRIATE RESPONSES TO REQUESTS FOR UNDERSTANDING AND ATTENTION

Some requests may appear on the surface to be requests for action or information, but they are not. The real need at the core of this type of communication is for someone to listen and show interest.

> *Mr. Wilke watches as his kindergartners work and play in various learning centers. Angelica, a shy five-year-old, is alone in the art center. As Mr. Wilke walks past, she calls out, "Mr. Wilke, I need some help." He smiles and perches his tall frame onto the little chair beside her. Angelica hands him her paper and plastic scissors and says, "Help me cut, I don't know how to."*
>
> *Mr. Wilke has always made careful observations and kept records of his students' levels of skill with learning center materials. He feels sure that Angelica does know how to use scissors. He looks at the situation and mentally rules out possibilities such as broken scissors or thick paper that is too difficult. He decides that Angelica may not really be seeking action (cutting for her) or information (teaching her how to cut), but instead, seeking understanding and attention.*
>
> *Mr. Wilke knows it will not help Angelica to embarrass her by confronting her in a harsh way. He also knows that he does not want to reinforce her perception that she can get the attention she needs by feigning incompetence. He says, "Sometimes cutting seems really hard, doesn't it?" He gently pats her shoulder and adds, "Would you like for me to sit beside you while you try cutting this yellow paper?" Angelica eagerly cuts her jagged paper while Mr. Wilke watches attentively. After a few minutes, as he gets up to leave, he says, "Angelica, you must really feel proud that you cut that out all by yourself."*
>
> *Mr. Wilke was correct in his assumption that Angelica was really requesting understanding and attention. Seeking attention is not a perverse behavior that must always be extinguished in children. Human beings are primarily social beings; we all need attention from others in order to thrive. The goal with young children is not to stop attention-getting behaviors but to teach children how to get an appropriate amount of attention in a socially acceptable manner. If Mr. Wilke observed that Angelica continued in a pattern of pretending ineptness to get attention (see "How Should Caregivers Respond to Requests for Dependency or Inappropriate Interaction?" pg.000), it might become necessary for Mr. Wilke, privately and tactfully, to confront her behavior by saying, "Angelica, you seem to need some attention. It's okay to need attention. Please say, 'Mr. Wilke, I feel lonely. I need some attention.' That will help me know exactly what you need."*

In an environment in which needs are respected, children come to know that it is okay to have needs and feelings. Sometimes, adults inadvertently give children the impression that their needs or emotions make adults angry. This problem often occurs when the adults are having a difficult time getting their own emotional needs met.

A particularly helpful strategy for dealing with feelings and needs honestly and respectfully is through a technique called **active listening** (sometimes referred to as reflective listening, empathetic listening, or responsive listening). In active listening, the listener refrains from lecturing, advising, or informing. She simply listens and reflects the feelings she perceives from seeing and hearing the other person. This gives the listener plenty of time to really hear the other person, to let the other person know her feelings and needs are important and respected, and to think of ways to help the person resolve the problem.

> *Jenny, who directs an infant/toddler child care program, treats the teaching and caring staff with the same respect and dignity she expects them to extend to the babies. She knows that even infants and toddlers are unconsciously absorbing the behaviors around them. She also knows that caring for little ones can sometimes be incredibly stressful.*
>
> *Fred, a four-month-old whose mother has just returned to work from her maternity leave, is crying. He has attended the child care program for only a few days and he has cried most of the time. Kate, his primary caregiver, has tried everything she knows to calm him. She has walked him, patted him, rocked him, and is at the end of her patience.*
>
> *Kate storms into the director's office and demands, "What is that child's problem? Nothing I do works. What am I supposed to do?" Luckily, Jenny realizes that Kate is not really seeking action or information. What Kate needs most is understanding, so Jenny offers her a chair and closes the door for privacy. Instead of focusing on solving baby Fred's problem, Jenny focuses on hearing and understanding Kate's feelings. In a caring voice, Jenny says, "Kate, you seem really frustrated."*
>
> *"You bet I am," replies Kate, "I don't think I can deal with his crying another minute. I don't even know if I ought to work with children. I am really at my wit's end."*

Sometimes all that is needed is a little understanding and attention.

Wisely, Jenny refrains from making judgments, giving information, or taking action. Gazda et al. (1990) notes that rushing to give a helpee a quick solution is "cheap and dirty" advice, since the helper has not had a chance to learn all the facts. If one's problems were so easy to solve that an "off the top of the head" solution were adequate, one would wonder why the person suffering the problem had not already thought of it.

Instead of rushing to tell Kate why she has a problem or how to solve it, Jenny simply mirrors to Kate (through active listening) what she hears Kate saying. She responds with nonjudgmental active (or reflective) listening statements that begin with phrases such as:

- what I'm hearing you say is . . .
- in other words, you are saying that . . .
- it sounds as if you feel . . .

> Jenny says, "Kate, it sounds like what you're saying is that you're feeling so frustrated that you're afraid you've lost your patience. You seem to be wondering if you're really cut out to work with children." A calmness settles over Kate as she realizes that she is not being judged or told what to do, but that her director is really listening and understanding what she is saying. She thinks for a moment and says, "I guess I'm just having a bad day. I really do love working with babies. It's just that Fred keeps screaming no matter what I do." Jenny leans close and touches Kate's arm. "You know, it sounds like you feel inadequate because you can't stop Fred's crying. I think Fred is lucky to have someone like you to care so much and try so hard to comfort him."
>
> Streams of tears spill down Kate's face. She feels enough trust to let go of her feelings and let everything out that has been bottled inside her. Now that her own needs for understanding and attention have been met, she can return to her nursery classroom and try again to meet Fred's needs for understanding and attention.

Even though Fred did not see or hear the adult interaction (and would have been too young to make sense of it if he had), he undoubtedly sensed the tension and frustration in Kate's voice and body language when she was upset. He will feel and benefit from the calmer, more accepting attitude Kate will have when she returns to care for him. By sensing the patience and understanding of his caregiver, Fred will begin learning the coping skills he will need to develop confidence and self-esteem as he grows older.

HOW SHOULD CAREGIVERS RESPOND TO REQUESTS FOR DEPENDENCY OR INAPPROPRIATE INTERACTION?

Adults who care for young children often have difficulty knowing where understanding ends and dependency begins. A child begs, "Hold me," "Put my coat on for me," or "Help me finish my puzzle." Many adults struggle to know what is right for the child. Is holding, helping, and nurturing meeting the child's needs or reinforcing a pattern of dependency?

Under usual circumstances, as soon as children are able, they spontaneously break away from various levels of dependence on adults. Toddlers stubbornly resist the hovering care that was necessary to their survival as infants. Adolescents rebel against the close parental attachment that protected them in early childhood. For most children, achieving independence is the motivating force behind the process of growing up. But this force does not always move steadily forward. Even highly competent, well-developing children regress from time to time and need the security of someone big to depend on. A bit of babying, on infrequent occasions, does little harm to well-developing children. This regression only seems to recharge their energy and desire for independence. But for chronically dependent children, coddling undermines self-esteem and destroys initiative.

In certain situations, children learn to be helpless (Altenor, Kay, & Richter, 1977; Finkelstein & Ramey, 1977). Some adults have difficulty accepting change and may fail to recognize a child's emerging capabilities. Other adults may inadvertently interfere with children's efforts at learning to function independently because they may simply not understand the process and importance of the development of autonomy.

Children's first efforts to do things by themselves are often messy and fraught with mistakes. Babies learning to feed themselves splatter, smear, and spill food. Toddlers learning to dress themselves put both feet in the same leg hole of their training pants. Preschoolers learning to tie their own shoes create nightmarish knots in their shoelaces. And school-agers learning gardening walk on the seedlings they have just planted. Little mishaps such as these are a necessary part of learning by experience. In a demanding, perfectionist, or punitive atmosphere where a child begins to fear making mistakes, she may learn to avoid risk by becoming passive, by not attempting anything that requires initiative or involves the chance of failure.

Children who have learned to be helpless and dependent (learned helplessness) need special guidance and support to break away from patterns of dependency. Children sometimes express requests for dependency through such actions as persistent whining, clinging, or regularly demanding special favors such as being first in line, sitting in the teacher's lap, or being carried. Indulging these inappropriate requests is not helpful for children.

Solicitations for dependence should be redirected in a way that encourages more appropriate behavior. An infant who whines for help after one half-hearted attempt at reaching a toy needs to be encouraged to try again rather than simply be given the toy. A preschooler who whines, feigns exhaustion, and begs for help putting blocks away may respond to a game such as "I'll close

Even highly competent, well-developing children regress from time to time.

my eyes. You tell me when to open them, and I'll count how many blocks are on the shelf." Or a kindergartner who follows the teacher, clinging and asking for help, may need to be given some important responsibility such as helping a younger child.

In some cases, redirection is not enough. It may be necessary to clearly communicate unwillingness to participate in interactions that indulge or solicit inappropriate dependency, spread gossip, reinforce inordinate complaining, or involve actions that turn adults or children against one another. Gazda et al. (1990) state that, "If you encourage inappropriate behaviors, even by silence, you may lose your opportunity to help, and you could unwittingly become a model for negative or hurtful behavior."

Gazda further adds that this rule is easier to preach than to practice because it is necessary to end the inappropriate interaction without offending the person initiating it. Offending a child or other adult damages trust, closes off communication, and projects an image of haughtiness. The recommended response is a polite but firm refusal to be part of the inappropriateness accompanied by a straightforward, warm, and respectful indication of caring about the person as an individual (Gazda et al. 1990).

Tactfulness, fairness, and warmth ease the sting of a refusal to participate in an inappropriate interaction. For example, Mr. Hernandez arrives one afternoon and prepares to teach his after-school gymnastics class. Sarah and Cynthia, twin third graders, eagerly volunteer to help spread mats. As Sarah and Cynthia help, they confide to Mr. Hernandez how much they dislike James, one of the least popular boys in the gymnastics class.

Sarah says, "Ugh! We can't stand James. He's fatter than an elephant." Cynthia chimes in, "Have you ever listened when he laughs? He sort of snorts and makes some weird sound." They giggle uproariously.

Mr. Hernandez values the positive relationship he has with Sarah and Cynthia and does not wish to embarrass them, but he also knows that to smile and say nothing would be tacit approval of their remarks about James. That would be hurtful to James and fails to guide Sarah and Cynthia toward more appropriate behavior.

Mr. Hernandez carefully chooses his words then bends down, touching each girl lightly on the shoulder. He says gently, "I don't feel good talking about James." Then his tone brightens and he deftly changes the subject, "But, you know what, I surely do like all this great help. How about this balance beam, girls. Do you think you both can get at that end and help me move it? Thanks."

Mr. Hernandez has not been judgmental or critical. He has simply and politely declined to participate by focusing on his own feelings. The girls probably felt a moment of embarrassment, but they also knew their teacher accepted and cared about them. As a result of this encounter, the girls may become more thoughtful about ridiculing others, not because of an external fear of punishment or chastisement, but from a growing internal sense of right and wrong bolstered by a strong and admired role model in the person of Mr. Hernandez.

ARE LISTENING AND HELPING STRATEGIES RELEVANT TO THE CARE OF BABIES AND TODDLERS?

The complexity of words and sentences must always be adjusted to the level of maturity of one's listener. However, the integrity and content of one's message need not be diluted. Physical actions, facial expression, intonation, and gestures convey a sense of one's message, even to an infant.

Mrs. Wang, who cares for infants in her church's mother's-day-out program, hears 11-month-old Kyle crying. He is banging on a low cabinet door that is locked with a child-guard latch. Mrs. Wang perceives the baby's cry is a request for action. Kyle wants the cabinet door opened. Mrs. Wang tries to distract him with several toys, but he continues to cry and pull at the door.

Mrs. Wang picks Kyle up, kicking and screaming, and carries him to her big rocking chair. She rocks and pats Kyle as she says in a caring voice, "I really understand that you want to explore that cabinet, but the things in there could hurt you. I can't let you play there because I like you and I want to keep you safe." As Kyle begins to calm down, Mrs. Wang carries him around the nursery showing him alternative areas to explore and continues to talk to him.

Kyle does not understand her words but he definitely can sense her warmth and empathy, and he can sense the firmness of the limit she has set. He may test the limit many more times, but Mrs. Wang's warmth will communicate to him that he is still accepted as a person. Her consistency will communicate to him that limits are sometimes a part of life. She recognizes that babies explore limits because they have a limited capacity to understand or remember rules and because they learn through trial and error. She will refuse Kyle's demands that she open the locked cabinet, but his actions will not change her feelings about him.

Additionally, by talking to Kyle, Mrs. Wang is able to focus her own thoughts and feelings on the situation. She, as well as Kyle, needs to hear the words she has said. By expressing in words the reasons she is doing what she is doing, she feels reassured that she is doing the right thing. Also, by putting her feelings into words, she is able to make sure her facial expression and body language are consistent with the message she wants to convey to Kyle.

Mrs. Wang, knowing that Kyle could not really understand her words, might have said instead, "Listen, I'm tired of fooling with you. Are you just trying to bug me?" However, it is nearly impossible to say these words in a sincere, warm, and caring way. Mrs. Wang's face and tone would probably have conveyed sarcasm, impatience, and blaming to Kyle. In an unconscious way, he would have absorbed these negative feelings and reflected them in his behavior. Also, words like *brat*, *fooling*, and *bug* are ambiguous cliché words that do not help Kyle learn language. Luckily for Kyle, Mrs. Wang would not think of behaving rudely to him any more than she would be rude to anyone else she respected and liked as a person.

ADDRESSING UNDERLYING FEELINGS

Most people who work with children would agree that child care and early childhood education are emotionally draining occupations. Young children ride an emotional roller coaster. They can go from laughter to tears in the blink of an eye. Responsive adults who are closely involved in the lives of young children are pulled along in the wave of emotions from the elation of a new discovery to the heartbreak of a best friend who says, "I hate you."

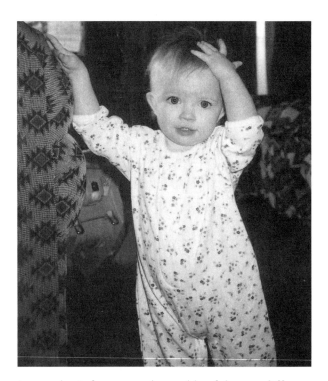

Babies and toddlers pay close attention to an adult's face and tone of voice, even if they do not understand the words that are spoken.

Children's emotions are real. Before six months, infants are only capable of three undifferentiated emotions: pleasure, wariness, and rage. By nine months, the baby has a dramatically increased range of emotional responses. By age three, children have virtually the entire panorama of human emotions (Sroufe, 1979).

An important part of early childhood learning is the child's gradually developing awareness of feelings and the child's growing ability to express those feelings. Very young children react unconsciously. A toddler may whine and act out in an aggressive way without realizing that she is feeling hunger, discomfort, fatigue, and so on. Adults play an important role in identifying, labeling, and explaining children's feelings to them. Adults also give children important feedback about certain behaviors by expressing relevant adult feelings.

WHEN AND HOW SHOULD ADULTS EXPRESS THEIR FEELINGS TO CHILDREN?

Discretion must be used in expressing adult feelings. Young children can be overwhelmed if adults unload too much on them or if the expression is too intense. Simple, clear statements of feelings limited to relevant situations are most helpful. Following is a fill-in-the-blank statement called an "I message" that is very helpful for stating feelings appropriately and in a nonthreatening way (Gordon, 1970):

When _____ happens, I feel _____ because _____ .

This statement does not contain the word you. Statements such as "You make me angry," or "You are hurting my ears with your yelling," may induce an unnecessary feeling of guilt in the child by suggesting blame. Positive discipline should bring about responsibility rather than guilt. It is more helpful to say simply and sincerely, "When there is loud screaming, I feel uncomfortable because the noise hurts my ears. I need for you to use a soft voice." "Biting makes me feel really upset because biting hurts and biting is dangerous. It is okay to bite crackers and apples, but it is never okay to bite people."

If adults consistently use assertive yet controlled words to express strong feelings, then children will eventually imitate by using words instead of physical attacks to express their own anger and frustration. A child will also feel more compliant when the adult's anger is focused on the action rather than on the child.

Additionally, adults can clarify and express positive feelings using the same sample sentence. For example, "When I see you share a special toy, I feel proud because I know you are learning how to get along." (In positive contexts, the word "you" does not suggest blame.) "When the sun is shining, I feel elated because we can go outside and enjoy the grass and trees." "When I discovered that you had put every single block away all by yourself, I felt like jumping up and down because I was so happy and proud."

Positive and negative expressions of feelings can have a powerful impact on a child's behavior, but only when the person expressing those feelings is admired and liked by the child. Neither adults nor children are particularly concerned about the feelings of someone who is not liked or respected. In fact, knowing that a disliked adult's ears hurt with loud noise would stimulate screaming from some children who may purposely intend to inflict pain or to manipulate attention from the adult.

Attempting to identify the child's feelings focuses our attention on the underlying causes of misbehavior.

HOW CAN CHILDREN BE HELPED TO UNDERSTAND THEIR FEELINGS?

In the previous section on requests for understanding and attention, nonjudgmental active (or reflective) listening was described. This kind of listening and responding can assist children in identifying, labeling, and understanding their feelings. A major difference here is that often, the child's feelings must be inferred from her behavior.

> *Carolyn is a child care professional teaching and caring for a group of four-year-olds. As her children come inside for a snack from the playground, she says, "Ummm, I feel hungry. Do you feel hungry, Clay?" Clay agrees and the children expand on Carolyn's expression of hunger: "I am as hungry as a tiger." "I'm so hungry I could eat this whole building." "I'm so hungry I could eat the whole world!"*
>
> *The children giggle about eating the whole world as they find their seats at the table. Clay rushes to sit by his best friend Misha, but Ellen has already taken the chair. Clay stamps his foot and complains loudly as he shakes the back of the chair he wants. The child in the chair stubbornly holds on.*
>
> *Carolyn quickly comes to intervene in the brewing fight. She kneels down at eye level to Clay and says, "You feel angry because someone took the chair you wanted. Can you use words to tell Ellen how you feel?"*
>
> *Clay shouts, "I want that chair. Gimme it, now!" Ellen grips the chair tighter and ignores him. Carolyn turns to Ellen and says, "Ellen, can you tell Clay how you feel?" Ellen looks at the floor and shakes her head no. Carolyn asks her, "Would you like me to tell Clay how you feel?" Ellen vigorously nods yes.*
>
> *Carolyn says, "Clay, Ellen is feeling very upset because you are shaking her chair and yelling at her. She got here first and she doesn't want you to take her chair away." Clay begins to shake the chair again, so Carolyn firmly removes his hands from the chair. Then, restraining his hands, but with concern and empathy in her voice, Carolyn says, "Clay, I know you feel really frustrated, but you have two choices. You may choose another chair and have a snack, or you may come out in the hall and talk with me until you feel better. What do you choose?"*
>
> *From experience, Clay knows Carolyn is gentle and caring, but he also knows that she always means what she says. He does not relish the idea of throwing a tantrum that will only succeed in delaying his snack.*
>
> *Carolyn sees a look of indecision on his face and quickly says, "Look, Clay. There is an empty chair right at the end of the table by Joey. Would you like to sit there?" Clay decides that Joey would not be so bad to sit by after all and shuffles along to take a seat.*
>
> *Carolyn smiles and pats his shoulder.*

HOW CAN CHILDREN BE HELPED TO CONFRONT TROUBLESOME FEELINGS?

Adlerian psychologists focus on exploring the motives for negative behavior. Dreikurs and Cassel (1974) list four goals of misbehaviors that are based on children's mistaken logic:

1. Children who are deprived of opportunities to gain status through useful contributions often seek attention by acting helpless, silly, bratty, artificially charming, lazy, inept, or obnoxious.

2. Children who do not feel they are accepted members of their family or social groups may seek power by acting bossy, rebellious, stubborn, vengeful, or disobedient.

3. Children who feel so beaten down that they no longer care about struggling for power retaliate by seeking revenge by hurting others the way they feel they have been hurt. They may injure peers, destroy property, express contempt, distrust others, and defy authority.

4. Children who become trapped in passive, destructive forms of attention getting by being overly criticized may eventually become so discouraged they give up all hope and expect only failure and defeat. They seek only to be left alone. They may be passive, withdrawn, and depressed, paralyzed by feelings of inadequacy and hopelessness.

Dreikurs recommends that older children be confronted in a friendly, noncritical way at a relaxed time rather than during a time of conflict. The child can be engaged in conversation exploring the motives for her typical behaviors, then tactfully asked the following questions:

- Could it be that you want attention?

- Could it be that you want your own way and hope to be boss?

- Could it be that you want to hurt others as much as you feel hurt by them?

- Could it be that you want to be left alone?

Although these questions are not appropriate to ask infants and very young children, adults may find it helpful mentally to run through the list of questions to gain insight into possible unconscious causes of misbehavior in children under three. For children of any age, identifying the underlying feelings that motivate behavior make it possible to respond to children's emotional well-being rather than only chasing and eliminating symptomatic misbehaviors.

Once the motive for behavior is diagnosed, adults can better respond to the misbehavior. If attention is the goal of the misbehavior, it can be removed as a response for inappropriate behaviors and given abundantly instead for appropriate or constructive behaviors. If bullying is the goal, adults can remove themselves from power struggles and focus on allowing children to feel they are respected and responsible group members. If revenge is the goal, adults can assist children in making friends and experiencing successful accomplishments. If solitude is the goal, adults can offer encouragement, persist in including the child, and find ways to make the child feel worthwhile.

By seeking understanding of behavior rather than blame for it, adults have an opportunity to open new doors of communication with children. As children mature and develop self-awareness, open lines of communication will help them assume greater responsibility for their own actions and choices. By the time children reach adolescence, it is especially important that they have developed some conscious awareness of their own motives and goals. It is essential that open, honest communication has become an accepted and routine part of every child's daily life.

POSITIVE INSTRUCTIONS VERSUS NEGATIVE COMMANDS

A key factor in positive communication is focusing on identifying and stating desired behaviors rather than focusing on inappropriate behaviors. Children and adults tend to respond more cooperatively to positive requests than negative admonitions. For example, a parent would probably feel more responsive to a request from a child care worker worded, "Please check to see that Kelly has enough diapers for the day," rather than, "You never bring enough diapers for Kelly." The difference in children's responses to negative and positive commands is stark.

Additionally, toddlers are so limited in their comprehension of language that they only tend to hear and respond to key words in sentences. If an adult tells a toddler, "I do not want you to touch this cake," the toddler may actually hear, "Do . . . want . . . touch . . . cake." And, of course, since the toddler wants to touch the cake, she probably will. The adult could bring about better communication by designating a desired activity to replace touching the cake. The adult could provide paper and crayons at a location away from the cake and say, "Please color on this big piece of paper," which the toddler may accurately interpret as, "Color . . . big . . . paper."

Toddlers and young preschoolers have difficulty hearing and interpreting every word of sentences, and also have difficulty thinking about a behavior, then inhibiting that behavior. Thinking and doing are almost inseparable at this stage of development. For example, if an adult says firmly, "No spitting," to a young child who has not even yet thought of spitting, she may comprehend both words but, as she thinks about not spitting, it is almost inevitable that the child will act out the spitting. The statement "Don't wet your pants" causes the child to have a mental image of wetting pants, which may trigger urination. The statement "It is time to use the potty" evokes a mental image of sitting on the toilet, which is desired.

Following is a list of typical negative commands and alternate positive commands.

NEGATIVE COMMANDS	POSITIVE REQUESTS
Don't run in the hall.	Walk slowly, please.
Don't spill your milk.	Use both hands, please.
Quit poking at Jimmy.	Hands in your lap now.
Shut up.	Please listen quietly.
Stop interrupting me.	It is my turn to talk now.
Don't talk with a full mouth.	Swallow first, then talk.
Quit shoving in line.	Walk carefully, please.
Stop yelling my name.	Say my name softly.

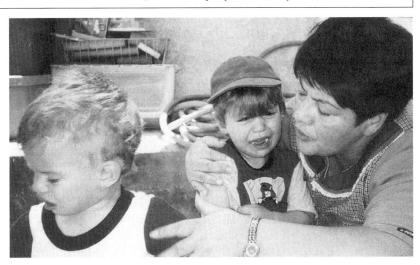

Effective caregivers are assertive and caring at the same time.

Negative commands are strongly entrenched as habit patterns for many of us. Time, commitment, motivation, and persistence are needed to break any habit pattern, and communication habits are no exception. Many adults find that as they try to improve their communication style, they first begin to hear themselves using ineffective phrases but cannot seem to stop using them. A toddler, standing in a puddle with an innocent and surprised look saying, "Go potty," is taking the first tentative step toward changing a habit pattern. An adult who feels guilty about yelling "shut up" to a child may be taking the first step toward consciously controlling and changing an ineffective communication strategy.

CHARACTERISTICS OF ASSERTIVE COMMUNICATION

Communication is always intended to convey a message, just as a radio transmitter is intended to transmit a radio program. In order for the music of a radio program to be heard, the waves sent from the transmitter have to match the receiver equipment in one's radio. The communication transmitted from an adult must match the mental and emotional equipment of the child or the message will simply not be received.

Children, and adults as well, will close off communication that is incomprehensible, threatening, vague, or rude like tuning out or turning off a radio with unpleasant static noise. Although one may sometimes feel justified in lecturing or lashing out, there is no value in conveying a message if the message is rejected. Our goal is to have messages accepted and acted upon.

KEY FACTORS IN ASSERTIVE COMMUNICATION

Simplicity Is the First Rule for Assertive Communication

While babies, toddlers, and young children need plenty of opportunities to hear the rhythm and flow of complex adult language, assertive statements need to be short and to the point. Decide what needs to be said and say it in as few words as possible. Verbal clutter gets in the way of stating a desired action.

The younger the child, the more essential simplicity becomes. Toddlers need simple two- or three-word sentences such as, "Sit, please," or (if a child has already bitten), "No biting. Biting hurts." Preschoolers need only slightly longer sentences such as "Apples are for eating, not for throwing," "Please hold your glass with two hands," or "A chair is for your seat, not your feet."

Honesty Is Essential for Assertive Communication

Children quickly identify adults who do not really mean what they say. Empty threats are counterproductive. They only teach children that adults cannot be relied on to do what they say, no matter how many times they insist that "this time I really mean it!" It is never acceptable to lie to children or to trick them into compliance. They should be told honestly when a parent is leaving, even if that causes tears. Feeling sad is a natural and healthy response; feeling tricked is not.

Directness Helps Communicators Get Right to the Point

Rambling, hinting, and insinuating are of little value to adult listeners and are totally lost on children. Instead of saying, "The art area is getting pretty sloppy, children," say, "Please pick up all of the scrap paper and put it in the trash can. Thank you. Now get a sponge and wipe the table." Instead of saying, "Let's keep it down now," say, "Please walk softly and speak quietly." Words used with children should be literal words with clearly definable meanings. A phrase such as "You two cut it out now" should mean that scissors and paper are involved.

Tact Keeps Channels of Communication Open

Gushing sweetness is usually not any more palatable to young children than it is to adults, but tactfulness and sincerity are greatly appreciated. It is tactful to say, "Your glass may tip off the table. Please push it back away from the edge. Thank you." It is not tactful to say, "Stop being so careless with your glass of milk." It is overly patronizing to say, "Here, sweetheart, let's push our little glass back so we don't spill it, okay honey?" Children can be given affection and kindness without being drowned in cloying sweetness.

Concreteness Makes Communication Clear

Abstractions like good and bad can be very confusing to children. The statement that lying is bad, for example, may cause a child to think she is a bad person. It is more concrete to say, "If you lie, other people may not trust you. They may learn not to believe things you say." With younger children, concreteness is expressed through actions. It is not concrete to tell a toddler, "Be nice to your friends." A toddler has no real concept of the word nice. It is a vague, value-laden term for which no two adults would have exactly the same definition. A toddler would not know precisely what one does to be nice. It is concrete to repeat, "Touch softly," while demonstrating stroking the friend's arm gently. The toddler can see and comprehend exactly what action is expected.

Respect Is an Integral Part of Assertive Communication

It is impossible to have open, honest communication with someone for whom one has disgust and disdain. In a democracy, one should have as much respect for the person who is a garbage collector as for the president, even though each has distinctly different roles and responsibilities. One should have as much respect for the person and human rights of a newborn as for any other member of society. Respect for children is expressed by recognizing and protecting their dignity and rights. A police officer may stop a citizen and issue a penalty that makes the citizen feel very unhappy, but the officer has no right to hurt, humiliate, or threaten the citizen. Respectful adults assertively enforce fair rules without name-calling, teasing, embarrassing, hurting, or bullying. A respectful adult confronts children privately and focuses on improving behaviors rather than on punishing children.

Optimism Boosts Cooperation by Sharing Hope

A child trying to cope with an assertive adult needs to know that the adult really believes she can succeed. Confrontation is softened and made more acceptable by reassurance that problems can indeed be solved. After confronting Jennifer, one might say, "Jennifer, everyone makes mistakes. Our mistakes help us learn. Perhaps tomorrow, you can help by reminding the younger children how important it is not to run out of the gate without permission."

Flexibility Is Necessary to Distinguish Assertiveness from Stubbornness

No matter how firmly one intends to carry out a plan of action, the possibility always exists that additional information could indicate the need for a change in plans. Young children need consistency to make sense of what is expected of them, but that need is not contradictory with their need for flexibility. (The trick is finding the right balance.) Effective, assertive, guidance requires that adults provide as much consistency as possible but also as much flexibility as needed to make discipline humane and reasonable.

Adults must constantly seek a balance between firm, predictable limits and the flexibility to listen, adapt, and compromise appropriately. For example, an adult might firmly refuse to talk about or compromise a stated rule while a child is pitching a tantrum and behaving very inappropriately. Later, however, when the child is calm and able to explain logically her problem with the rule, the adult might decide that justice is best served by bending or eliminating the rule. With a very young child, the adult may rely on direct observations rather than verbal discussions to determine if a rule is fair and reasonable.

Confidence Strengthens Assertive Communication by Projecting Assurance that What Is Being Said Is Really Meant

Children are especially sensitive to nonverbal signals or cues from facial expression, intonation, body positioning, and the use of hands and feet. Adults who do not really believe children will do what is asked of them project an air of uncertainty and weakness. A clear-eyed look of confidence greatly increases the probability of compliance from children as well as from listeners of any other age. Fidgeting, speaking in a weak or shrill voice, and avoiding eye contact hint to the child that compliance is not really expected.

When adults say sarcastic things such as, "Well, let's see if you can keep from being a little monster, as usual, running around and tearing everything up while we wait for the doctor," children know immediately that they are expected to behave badly. In contrast, a confident adult might say firmly but caringly, "Here is a book to look at quietly while we wait. We must sit very still. People are not allowed to be rowdy and noisy in a doctor's office." This indicates assurance that the adult believes the child can and will behave appropriately.

Persistence Makes Assertive Communication Work

Punishing, threatening, and intimidating get quick results on the surface but undermine discipline in the long run. Assertive communication does not always bring about an immediate solution, but persistence over time makes it an effective and lasting technique for solving problems. Adults are sometimes tempted to surrender to children's demands when first efforts at communication do not bring about an immediate resolution. However, a generous amount of persistence will reap

When we truly understand a child's feelings, we can more accurately identify possible reasons for her inappropriate behavior.

important benefits by letting children know that we really mean what we say. A child may stubbornly reject a rule on a whim, but if we persist in letting her know we expect the rule to be followed, she will almost surely comply eventually. As with the tortoise and the hare in their fabled contest, slow and steady wins the race.

Empathy May Seem out of Context with Assertiveness, but Instead It Is Absolutely Essential

Sympathy means feeling sorry for others; empathy means walking in their shoes, feeling what they feel. Assertiveness without empathy is hollow and insincere. Assertiveness with empathy is strength and love rolled into one. A little person with grimy hands, a runny nose, and a knack for creating havoc does not always trigger feelings of warmth and empathy in parents and caregivers. Nonetheless, effective communication requires sincere understanding and caring. Empathy is expressed to listeners, from infancy to adulthood, primarily through the eyes and face, but all other verbal and nonverbal cues can also express empathy (or the lack of it).

For example, adults can begin reprimands by making an initial positive statement of some kind to show empathy. An adult might take a child by the hand and say, "I know you just want to play with the kitty, but chasing him and pulling his tail really frightens him. Would you like to feed him to show him you're his friend?"

CHARACTERISTICS OF NONPRODUCTIVE COMMUNICATION

Adults use many different communication styles. Of course, some styles are more effective than others. The least effective styles usually deal only superficially with the content of the communication and fail completely to address the feelings or emotions of the persons sharing in the communication. It is most important that adults avoid the communication pitfalls that inhibit dialogue and alienate children (or others of any age).

Gazda et al. (1990) lists nine common stereotypes of ineffective communication styles.

1. Florist—avoids issues through flowery euphemisms
2. Detective—skirts issues by persistently prying with questions
3. Magician—vaporizes problems with the wave of a wand
4. Drill sergeant—avoids conflict by barking orders
5. Foreman—clouds issues by the use of compulsive busyness
6. Hangman—induces guilt to avoid confronting problems
7. Guru—covers over issues by giving a cliché for every occasion
8. Swami—smoke screens issues by predicting dismal outcomes
9. Sign painter—dismisses problems by tacking labels on them

While two-dimensional stereotypes do not reflect the complex facets of real people, they are helpful for identifying characteristics real people display from time to time. One stereotype may be the predominant way an individual responds, but others might recognize a little bit of each stereotype in their behavior occasionally. The purpose of these stereotypes is not to label children or adults but to better recognize and understand ineffective communication styles.

HOW DO PEOPLE BEHAVING LIKE THESE STEREOTYPES RESPOND TO PROBLEM SITUATIONS INVOLVING CHILDREN AND ADULTS?

Florists simply do not see any problems. If a child communicates that she has been hurt by another child, the florist ever so sweetly croons, "Why Suzy, I'm sure he didn't mean to hurt you!" If a tearful child sobs, "I hate my mommy," the florist teacher just smiles knowingly and says, "Of course you don't hate your mommy. Children don't hate their mommies." The florist loses many opportunities to communicate by tossing garlands of optimism rather than confronting and exploring problems.

Detectives want answers: "Why did you do that?" "Who did it first?" "Did I tell you not to do that?" "What do you think you're going to do now?" The listener is not only dazed by the battery of questions but also tempted to lie or to give whatever answers the detective seems to want.

Magicians dismiss issues conveniently. If a child says, "Someone pushed me off the swing," the magician says with flourish, "Yes, but playtime is over now so it really doesn't matter does it?" If a father expresses concern that his baby's pacifier is lost, the magician responds, "That's okay. Sarah really doesn't need a pacifier. She'll scream for an hour or two then forget all about it."

Drill sergeants do not have time to communicate; they are too busy barking orders. The drill sergeant nursery school teacher hears a heated argument in the block center. Instead of encouraging communication, she says, "Get these blocks picked up off the floor. Kaleb, tuck in your shirt. Samantha, you wouldn't have these problems if you'd pay attention and mind your own business."

The *foreman* keeps everyone so busy they cannot think about problems. A mother confides to her child's kindergarten teacher that her husband has left her and she has lost her job. She is worried that her son, Joshua, is being affected by her stress and depression. The foreman teacher responds, "You need to get out of the house and stop feeling sorry for yourself. Take an art class. Volunteer at the hospital. Throw a party." The mother leaves feeling even more guilty and overwhelmed.

The *hangman* dishes out blame. The hangman's favorite phrase is, "Well, I'm not surprised. You know, it's your own fault." When Jamey asks his hangman preschool teacher, Miss Judy, for help printing his name, she says, "If you had paid attention last week, you would already know how to do this." When the director asks Miss Judy for help with a new child who is crying for his mother, Miss Judy says, "Of course he's crying. What do you expect? Did you see the way his mother let him manipulate her? She's to blame for this."

The *guru* has a mental storehouse of meaningless clichés to scatter like rose petals over problems. A mother asks her toddler's nursery teacher if she thinks speech therapy is needed for the child. The guru teacher answers brightly, "Well, a stitch in time saves nine!" A nine-year-old boy asks his guru dad why countries have scary things like nuclear bombs and is told, "An ounce of prevention is worth a pound of cure." A four-year-old cries, "Nobody likes me. I don't have any friends." Her guru teacher responds, "Well, you have to be a friend to have a friend." The guru's pat answers end dialogue rather than stimulate insight and understanding of problems.

The *swami* is not exactly a comfort in time of need. She is always prepared to predict all the terrible and hopeless things that will probably happen as a result of the listener's actions. When a three-year-old runs into the house crying because she has a splinter in her finger, her swami mother says, "I told you not to play on that seesaw. Now you're going to get an infection and I'm going to be stuck with a big doctor bill. Look at this, your fingernail will probably turn black and fall off." Of course, there is the classic swami response, "Johnny, when you fall out of that tree and break both your legs, don't come running to me."

Sign painters make quick work of problems by assigning labels. A nursery school teacher complains to her coworker that she is having difficulty with one of her toddlers having temper tantrums. The sign painter coworker shrugs his shoulders and says, "I don't know of anything you can do about terrible twos. They're just that way." In a parent conference with child care staff, a single mother asks, "What is happening to my son? He seems to be trying to hurt everyone and everything around him." A sign painter teacher pats her on the shoulder and says, "Hey, all hyperactive kids do that." Meaningful communication is hindered by sign painters. There hardly seems to be any reason to discuss a problem after a label has been stamped on it with such finality.

IF THESE STEREOTYPICAL COMMUNICATION STYLES ARE INEFFECTIVE, WHAT WILL WORK?

In each of the above stereotypes, the communicator avoids, dismisses, evades, or thwarts feelings. An effective, assertive communicator addresses feelings with kindness, respect, and honesty. Often, it seems easiest to do whatever is expedient to stop a child's crying, end a dispute, or make a parent or coworker feel better. Unfortunately, when feelings are pushed under the rug, they can fester into even more unmanageable feelings.

MANAGING THE POSITIVE CONFRONTATION

When confronting a problem issue, one should first use active listening to allow the child or adult to identify, explore, and express feelings related to the situation. "Cheap and dirty" advice should not be tossed out lightly. Instead, persons being helped can be guided to recognize the choices they have and the possible outcomes of those choices. Only then can a person be assisted in solving her problem. Adults must assume responsibility for solving their own problems before real help can be given. Imposing unwanted help on another adult is almost always counterproductive. Helping children is another matter. If a child does not show motivation to solve a problem, parents and caregivers must assume that responsibility for the child. The child should be assisted as firmly as necessary but as gently as possible in confronting and solving problems.

WHEN IS CONFRONTATION APPROPRIATE?

Albert is waiting excitedly for his dad to pick him up from his child care center. He and his buddy, Joshua, have been planning to ask if they can spend the night together. As they dig in the sand, they giggle and scheme about the fun they will have watching television and eating grape popsicles.

Finally, Albert sees his dad. Both boys run to the gate and watch as Albert's dad parks his car. Before his dad is even inside the gate, Albert is talking so fast that his dad cannot understand him. Albert's dad hoists him into the air saying, "How's my big boy?" Albert excitedly says, "Daddy, can Joshua spend the night? Can he? Huh? Can he?"

Albert's dad takes both boys by the hand and as they walk up the sidewalk, he says quietly, "No, son, I have some paperwork I need to do tonight. This is not a good day. I will be happy to call Joshua's parents, though, and arrange for him to stay over one night next week."

Albert pulls his hand away and starts to cry. His dad bends down and says, "You really had your heart set on having Joshua spend the night, didn't you?" Albert nods yes through his tears. His dad continues, "You feel sad and angry because next week seems a long time away." Albert nods again.

His dad hugs him and says, "It's okay to cry. Even grown people cry sometimes. I bet Joshua feels pretty bad, too." Albert stops rubbing his eyes and looks at Joshua. Albert throws his arms around his dad's neck for one last round of begging, "Pleeeeease, daddy, I promise we won't bother you." His dad's expression remains calm and empathetic. He says, "Albert, it is okay to ask, and it is okay to cry and feel sad, but the answer won't change. Joshua can't spend the night tonight."

Albert's next tactic is pouting, but his dad remains calm and firm as he gathers Albert's belongings and prepares to leave. As his dad buckles him into his seat belt, Albert plants a wet kiss on his cheek and says, "I love you, daddy." His dad grins and says, "I love you, too, son."

Albert's dad successfully avoided the stereotypes described previously. He did not delay confrontation by saying, "We'll talk about it later." He did not avoid confrontation by giving in to something he knew he would regret. He did not squelch confrontation by saying, "I don't want to hear another word about this. Hush right now or I won't let Joshua stay with you next week either." He did not try to force Albert to like the decision by arguing with him, and he did not try to make Albert agree with him and stop being mad.

Instead, Albert's father confronted Albert simply, directly, and immediately but with a great deal of empathy and respect. He listened, made what he believed was a fair decision, allowed Albert to express his feelings, and then recognized and reflected those feelings. In the end, Albert probably felt very secure in knowing his dad was a strong authority figure to be relied on rather than a weakling to be manipulated or a tyrant to be dreaded.

HOW CONFRONTATIONS WITH CHILDREN CAN BE MADE POSITIVE AND ASSERTIVE

Anger undermines assertive confrontation. An adult who becomes enraged with a child should do only what is necessary to protect the child's safety and well-being on an immediate basis. She could ask for assistance from another adult who is calm, leave the baby screaming in the crib and do deep breathing and relaxation exercises, or say to an older child, "I feel angry now. I will talk to you when I feel calm."

Confrontation should be delayed until the adult feels in control and is able to muster some level of empathy. Hurtful confrontations attack children in an angry, punitive way. Effective, assertive confrontations guide, protect, and nurture children; they do not intimidate them.

An angry adult may find it helpful to think about and answer the following questions:

- Why do I feel the way I feel?

- What did I feel before I felt anger? Was it frustration? Fear? Embarrassment?

- Am I simply afraid to say no to this child?

- Am I tired, hungry, not feeling well?

- How would I feel right now if I were the child?

- Are my expectations reasonable?

Adults who lack assertiveness are usually afraid to use the following three phrases in their daily speech: "I want . . .," "I need . . .," and "I feel. . . ." Parents and other caregivers often try so hard to keep children happy that they suppress their own wants, needs, and feelings. Then, instead of being appreciated as long-suffering martyrs, they are taken advantage of, and eventually they explode in anger and resentment. They are rarely appreciated. The more they try to give, the more children and other adults expect of them. As they learn to take an assertive stand, they discover that they are less angry, more appreciated, and a great deal happier.

HOW ATTENTION CAN BE KEPT FOCUSED ON CONFRONTING THE ISSUES AT HAND

The stereotypical communication styles previously presented were described as adult characteristics; however, these same evasion tactics are often used by children. (Remember, children learn by modeling.) Children who have imitated parents and caregivers with poor or manipulative communication styles are especially prone to using those styles to evade issues.

Children evade confrontations by persistently asking questions, by issuing bossy little commands, and by giving cliché responses such as "Everyone else's mother lets them stay up as long as they want." Children not only learn roles directly by imitating them, but also create roles as mirror-image opposites of those to which they are exposed. The child of a drill sergeant parent may learn to behave as a magician: "Get that trash picked up off the floor!" "What trash? I don't see any trash. Where? That's not trash. That's my cans I'm saving."

The more adept adults become in direct, assertive communication, the more successful they will be in keeping children's attention focused on confronting and resolving problem issues. Children will not need to evade issues when they trust adults to confront issues in a gentle but firm and fair manner. For many children and adults, the thought of a confrontation triggers terror, since their primary experiences with confrontation have been frightening interactions filled with rage, their own rage as well as the rage of powerful, threatening adults.

Confrontation, without anger, is an essential and healthy part of social interaction.

HOW CHILDREN CAN BE TAUGHT RESPONSIBILITY

Responsibility cannot be taught through lectures. Responsibility can be shown through example, it can be nurtured and reinforced, and, most importantly, it can be learned first hand by dealing with the consequences of one's own actions. Adults often feel compelled to prevent children from experiencing consequences: "You have to eat this! You might get hungry later." They rescue children: "You were careless and left your doll in the rain. Now I'll have to buy you another." The child feels only the adult's annoyance. She is not allowed to feel the natural consequences of behaviors.

It is better for the child to have support and warmth from adults as she feels and owns the sting of unpleasant consequences from poor decisions. Adults must prevent dangerous or damaging consequences. A child cannot learn firsthand the consequences of such things as running out into a busy street or never brushing teeth. However, exploring and discussing possible consequences should be a part of confrontations.

We can tell a great deal from body posture and facial expressions. What do you suppose these two children may be feeling?

Rather than lecturing children about consequences, adults should make simple statements ("If you throw food, you will have to leave the table.") and ask simple questions ("What do you think could happen if you stood on the edge of the balcony?"). Children can be encouraged on a regular basis to explore potential consequences. Children who have a habit of considering and weighing consequences are well on their way to becoming responsible and self-directed.

POINTS TO REMEMBER

- Adults influence children by setting a good example for them and by encouraging them to practice appropriate communication skills.

- Responsive, active listening is essential to child guidance, but dependency and inappropriate interaction must be firmly and respectfully redirected.

- Feelings and emotions must be considered in order to provide appropriate responses to behaviors.

- Adults can assist children in developing responsibility by encouraging children to talk about and think about the potential consequences of their behavior.

PRACTICAL APPLICATION

"I'LL LEAVE YOU HERE FOREVER"

Marlene pauses in the shopping mall waiting for her two-year-old to catch up with her. Her four-month-old, who is asleep on her shoulder, is beginning to feel very heavy. "Crystal," she calls to her two-year-old, "Please come on. We need to get home."

Crystal stalls as she climbs on and off benches and stops to look at other shoppers. Her mother loses patience, "Crystal! You come here now or you're going to be sorry." Crystal ignores her.

Marlene walks quickly back to Crystal, and taking her firmly by the wrist says, "Let's go." Crystal responds with the rubbery-legs strategy toddlers use when they rebel. Her legs go limp as she slumps to the floor, dangling from the wrist her mother is clutching and whining, "Don't want go home."

Marlene realizes that she cannot safely carry her baby and Crystal both out of the shopping mall. In exasperation, she snaps, "That's it, I'm leaving. If you won't come, then I'll just leave you here forever. Good-bye!"

She turns and begins to walk briskly out of the mall. She hears Crystal howling and running to catch up with her.

DISCUSSION QUESTIONS

1. What would you have done in Marlene's place? Why?
2. What has Crystal really learned from the interaction?
3. Could anything have been done to prevent Marlene's predicament?
4. Role-play the scene using positive, assertive communication and confrontation, then compare possible outcomes.

RELATED READINGS
EFFECTIVE COMMUNICATION

Covey, S. R. (1998). *The 7 habits of highly effective families: Building a beautiful family culture in a turbulent world.* New York: St. Martin's Press.

   Sharing insightful experiences from his own life and from the lives of other families, Covey gives practical advice on solving common family dilemmas.

Devine, M., & Olmstead, P. J. (1991). *Babytalk: The art of communicating with infants and toddlers.* Cambridge, MA: Perseus Publishing.

Diffily, D., & Morrison, K. (1996). *Family-friendly communication for early childhood programs.* Washington, DC: National Association for the Education of Young Children.

Edwards, C., Gandini, L., & Forman, G. (1993). *The hundred languages of children.* Norwood, NJ: Ablex.

French, L. (1996, January). "I told you all about it, so don't tell me you don't know": Two-year-olds and learning through language. *Young Children, 51*(2), 17–20.

Friedman, E. H. (1990). *Friedman's fables.* New York: Guilford.

   Teaching by parable has an old and honorable tradition. Ed Friedman, rabbi and family therapist, writes stories that are funny, but also profound, even shocking, as they present lessons of family life in a slyly modern, hard-nosed reevaluation of the wisdom of the ages. Dr. Friedman presents stories to show that neither insight, nor encouragement, nor intimidation can in themselves motivate an unmotivated person to change. These provocative tales playfully demonstrate that new ideas, new questions, and imagination, more than accepted wisdom, provide each of us with the keys to overcoming stubborn emotional barriers and facilitating real change, both in ourselves and others.

Mahoney, G., & Neville-Smith, A. (1996, Summer). The effects of directive communications on children's interactive engagement: Implications for language intervention. Topics in *Early Childhood Special Education, 16*(2), 236–50.

Marschark, M. (1997). *Raising and educating a deaf child.* New York: Oxford University Press.

Swick, K. J., et al. (1997, Summer). On board early: Building strong family-school relations. *Early Childhood Education Journal, 24*(4), 269–73.

Turnbull, A. P., & Turnbull, H. R. (1997). *Families, professionals and exceptionality: A special partnership* (3rd ed.). Upper Saddle River, NJ: Merrill Education/Prentice-Hall.

Collaboration means sharing resources and creating a context that empowers families and professionals alike. The book presents comprehensive, data-based, and conceptually consistent approaches for families and professionals to collaborate for empowerment.

White, M. (2002). Teachers on Teaching. A lesson on listening. *Young Children 57*(3), 43.

Argues that young children be allowed to mull over ideas and construct theories of their own. By listening to the children and following their lead, teachers can encourage investigation and support learning.

HELPFUL WEB SITES

www.talkingwithkids.org   Talking with Kids about Tough Issues is a national initiative by Children Now and the Kaiser Family Foundation to encourage parents to talk with their children earlier and more often about tough issues like sex, HIV/AIDS, violence, alcohol, and drug abuse.

www.mediafamily.org   National Institute on Media and the Family is a national resource for research, education, and information about the impact of media on children and families. Based in Minneapolis, Minnesota, the National Institute on Media and the Family was created to provide information to parents and other adults about media products and their likely impact on children so they can make informed choices. The National Institute on Media and the Family was founded by David Walsh, Ph.D., in 1996.

INTERNET STARTING POINTS FOR PARENTS AND CAREGIVERS

CYE-L@cunyvms1.gc.cuny.edu
Children, Youth, and Environment
email: ssi@cunyvms1.gc.cuny.edu

CYFERNET
http://www.cyfernet.mes.umn.edu/
Children, youth, and family information:
    includes ADOTINFO, FATHERNET,
    and PAVNET (Partnerships Against
    Violence)

ECENET-L@postoffice.cso.uiuc.edu
Young children, birth to age 8
email: ericeece@uiuc.edu

ECEOL-L@postoffice.cso.uiuc.edu
Early childhood educators online
email: bonnieb@maine.bitnet

ECPOLICY-L@postoffice.cso.uiuc.edu
Early childhood policy issues
email: ericeece@uiuc.edu

FAMILY WORLD
http://family.disney.com/
Electronic magazine from Parent Publications
    of America, Inc.

MCHNet
Information on health and young children
http://www.ichp.edu/distance/

MULTIAGE@Services.dese.state.mo.us
Mixed-age grouping
email: catchley@mail.coin.missouri.edu

NCCIC
National Child Care Information Center
  publications and directories
  http://nccic.org/NPIN
Information for parents and educators
http://npin.org/

PARENTING-L@postoffice.cso.uiuc.edu
Parenting of children from infancy through
  adolescence
ericeece@uiuc.edu

REGGIO-L@postoffice.cso.uiuc.edu
The Reggio Emilia (Italy) approach to early
  education
ericeece@uiuc.edu

SAC-L@postoffice.cso.uiuc.edu
School-age care
email: ericeece@uiuc.edu

U.S. Department of Education
gopher://gopher.ed.gov
U.S. Department of Education publications
  and announcements
http://www.ed.gov

U.S. Department of Health and Human
  Services
U.S. Department of Health and Human
  Services Publications, program description,
  and services
http://www.acf.dhhs.gov

ERIC/EECE. (1995). A to Z: The Early
  Childhood Educator's Guide to the
  Internet. ERIC Clearinghouse on
  Elementary and Early Childhood
  Education. University of Illinois at
  Urbana-Champaign, Children's Research
  Center, 51 Gerty Drive, Champaign, IL
  61820-7469.

For additional information on positive child guidance, visit our Web sit at
http://www.earlychilded.delmar.com

Chapter 7
Positive Action

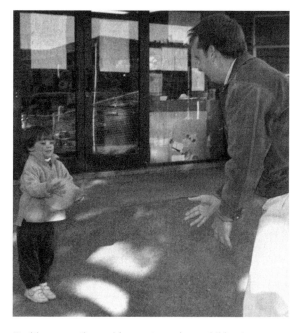

Positive, assertive guidance strengthens children's confidence and self-esteem.

OBJECTIVES

After reading this chapter, you should be able to:

- Create a setting that is supportive to positive child guidance.
- Focus on the role of nonverbal communication and body language in assisting positive behavior.
- Define logical and natural consequences, and understand their importance in guidance.
- Identify reasonable and effective circumstances for the use of external reinforcement.

NONVERBAL CUES AND BODY LANGUAGE

The environment gives messages to children about what we expect from them, and our own physical postures, movements, and gestures communicate a great deal of information to them. We may not even be aware of the body language signals we are sending out which the children are receiving and to which they are reacting.

WHAT IS THE SIGNIFICANCE OF NONVERBAL CUES FOR YOUNG CHILDREN?

Before verbal language is well developed, young children rely heavily on our **nonverbal communication** (body language such as gestures, facial expressions, and tone of voice) in their interactions with others. Infants pay attention to the touch, facial expressions, and sounds of their caregivers to interpret the adults' moods and expectations. Even a six-month-old baby can recognize clear differences between the meanings of a frowning parent with his hands firmly on his hips and a smiling parent with his arms stretched toward the baby. Rather than interpreting the meaning of a caregiver's words or sentences, very young children focus all their attention on sense perception. They pay attention to things they can actually see, hear, feel, taste, or smell.

As children reach preschool age, they gradually pay more attention to the actual words in adults' speech, but they are still very sensitive to nonverbal cues. (Drumming my fingers on the table may be my cue, or signal, that I am feeling annoyed.)

WHY SHOULD NONVERBAL CUES BE CONSISTENT WITH VERBAL COMMUNICATION?

Adults must take nonverbal expressions into consideration whenever they attempt to communicate with children. A typical situation in which children receive conflicting messages between verbal and nonverbal cues occurs when children are brought to an early childhood setting for the first time. Typically, a parent will say, "You'll have a lot of fun playing with other children, and I will be back later to pick you up. It's okay now, go ahead with your teacher." The words are full of confidence and optimism. The adult, who focuses only on the words, may not notice that she is tense, strained, and anxious in appearance.

Children pay close attention to the nonverbal signals adults give as part of their communication.

The adult's facial expression is one of uncertainty, her voice sounds uncharacteristically high, and her hands are wringing and twisting nervously. Instead of leaving quickly, she hangs near the child while insisting that the child "act like a big boy and go play." The parent says she is going, but she looks as if she is staying.

Of course, the child pays more attention to the nonverbal cues than to the spoken words. He will sense that his parent is frightened and unsure about leaving him, so he will probably feel frightened and unsure about being left. He will probably resist being left with a great deal of volume and energy. If, on the other hand, he senses that his parent is confident and optimistic, he may feel a bit uncomfortable at first, but he is likely to adjust more quickly and easily to the separation. He absorbs the confidence of his parent as she smiles and says in a relaxed tone of voice, "I know you will have a great time today," then leaves.

> *Elena, a preschool teacher in a child care center, took her youngsters outside to play early one summer morning to avoid the midday heat and humidity. As the children played happily, Elena looked up and noticed swarms of hungry mosquitoes circling in clusters near the eaves of the building.*
>
> *She stood silently with her arms tightly folded across her chest, staring at the buzzing dive bombers and wondering what she should do. Should she take the children back inside? Should she spray the children with repellent? She felt a tug at her skirt. Willie, a three-year-old who had been riding around Elena on a tricycle and watching her carefully, blurted out in a sad voice, "Miss Elena, how come you're mad at me?" Willie read Elena's body language and sensed tension and frustration. Since he was a normally developing preoperational child, he naturally (and egocentrically) assumed that he was the cause of Elena's unhappiness.*
>
> *Elena had not realized the effect her nonverbal body language could have on the children around her. Since the vocabulary and language comprehension skills of young children are so limited, their understanding of their environment hinges on their ability to be very alert to nonverbal cues from those around them.*

FOCUS ATTENTION AT THE CHILD'S EYE LEVEL

If an adult stands across the room from a child and casually looks over a shoulder, saying, "Letecia, don't touch those scissors; you'll cut yourself," Letecia will probably interpret that the adult is not too concerned about the danger of the scissors and will probably not enforce the command. It is likely that Letecia will continue to touch the scissors while watching the adult carefully for stronger or more direct cues about the scissors.

If the adult stops what he is doing and bends down to the child's eye level, holding out a hand for the scissors and says, "Please give me the scissors. These are too sharp. They could cut you. We'll find you a plastic pair," the adult's assertive nonverbal communication matches his verbal communication. Letecia is likely to perceive that the adult "means business" and is willing to follow through to see that the sharp scissors are removed.

As Letecia decides whether to comply with the command she has been given, she will read the adult's facial expression (is there a playful twinkle in the eye or a look of concerned resolve?), tone of voice (is there a weak tone of uncertainty or a tone of absolute confidence?), and hand gestures (are hand motions assertive or physically threatening?). If the adult's nonverbal cues are too playful or casual, Letecia will assume that she really does not have to comply. If they are too threatening and intrusive, Letecia will be likely to bristle and resist the command. If they are assertive, caring, confident, and no-nonsense, Letecia may decide that it is a good idea to comply quickly and willingly.

HELPING CHILDREN RESOLVE PROBLEMS INDEPENDENTLY

A primary goal for early childhood development is the growth of personal responsibility and independence in children. Learning how to behave appropriately requires self-control, which is closely related to responsibility and independence. In order to become socially competent, children need to learn to **negotiate** (settle disputes through discussion) so they can successfully resolve at least some of their own problems.

Children often come to adults begging to be rescued from various unhappy situations. Sometimes, the child's grievance is legitimate. Children have a right to call on someone bigger, stronger, and with more authority when their rights have been violated, just as I have a right to request legal help if my own rights have been violated.

If I call a police officer for help because my purse has been stolen, I will feel very resentful if the officer responds by saying things like:

- "Don't tattle!"

- "Don't be so stingy. The thief probably needed the money worse than you do anyway."

- "You got what you deserved. You shouldn't have been carrying a purse that would tempt people anyway."

- "Well, did you tell the purse-snatcher you didn't like that?"

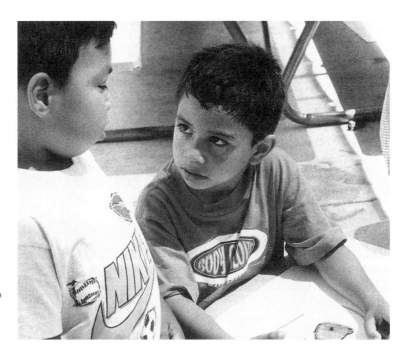

Children have a right to ask for adult help when their rights are infringed upon.

We are a tiny bit embarrassed by some of our most frequently used expressions when we step back and compare them with what we expect from others.

Nevertheless, there are occasions when the child should not be rescued by an adult. In order to foster independence, children should be helped to do as much for themselves as they can reasonably be expected to handle successfully. Common sense will tell us that there are times we need to firmly nudge children into assuming responsibility for resolving problems they encounter.

WHAT IS BIBLIOTHERAPY?

Bibliotherapy is the process of using books to help children think about, understand, and work through social and emotional concerns. Reading with children can be therapeutic. While some children experience events that are life changing and traumatic, all children experience events that worry or confuse them. Adults can use reading to help children come to grips with issues that create emotional turmoil for them. Reading can also be used to raise awareness about the rights and needs of others, and can be very effective in preventing and resolving behavior problems.

Choose books that are appropriate—Books should match children's ability level, capture their imagination, and be relevant to their cultural experiences.

Create an emotionally supportive environment—Children need to feel completely safe to ask questions and express thoughts freely, even if the topic is a sensitive one. Sometimes, reading a story about someone else makes it possible for a child to talk about painful or frightening concerns.

Encourage creative problem-solving—Adults should encourage children to talk about how the characters in the book might be feeling and how they deal with their experiences. Ask children things like, "What would you do if you were that little girl?" "How would you solve her problem?" "What are some different things she could have done?" "What lesson did she learn?"

*For a list of children's books that address values and feelings, see Appendix A.

To learn more, read:
Burnett, J. (1997). *Opening the world to children: Using books to develop problem-solving strategies.* Portland, OR: Annual International Conference of the Association for Childhood Education.
Mohr, K. A. (1993). Metamessages and problem-solving perspectives in children's literature. *Reading Horizons, 33*(4), 341–346.
Riecken, T. J., & Miller, M. R. (1990). Introducing children to problem solving and decision making by using children's literature. *Social Studies, 81*(2), 59–64.

HELP CHILDREN LEARN TO USE WORDS TO EXPRESS THEMSELVES TO EACH OTHER

Toddlers scream, hit, shove, and bite primarily because they lack the verbal ability to express themselves otherwise. They are transparent and physical in letting another child or adult know they feel angry. We may regret the onset of name-calling in children past three, but we are very likely to see a decrease in physical aggression as verbal communication skills are mastered.

Preschoolers discover they can cause a peer to dissolve in tears just by calling her a "weenie baby" or by tauntingly chanting nonsense words such as "Nanny, nanny, boo, boo! Nanny, nanny, boo, boo!"

In positive child guidance, children are taught ways to communicate feelings honestly and assertively without having to resort to verbal aggression. Following is a list of adult statements that facilitate child-to-child communication:

- "Jarrod, please say, 'Excuse me, Christie, I need to get past.' Christie doesn't like to be shoved."

- "Alva, use words. Tell Erin you feel very angry when he grabs your crayons without asking. Would you like for me to help you tell him?"

- "Erin, Alva feels really mad when you grab her crayons. Can you ask for a crayon? Can you say, 'Please, may I have a crayon?'"

- "Jerusha, thank you for saying, 'Excuse me, this chair is mine.'"

- "Adam and Beth, you need to sit here on the step and talk until you both feel better."

- "Beth, your friend Adam says you scratched his face. Adam, Beth says you wadded up her drawing and threw it in the wastebasket. Adam, you're upset because your face really hurts."

- "Beth, you're sad because you really wanted to take that picture home to your mother."

- "Can either of you think of some way to make your friend feel better?"

- "That's a great idea, Adam, you could get the drawing out of the trash can and try to smooth it out."

- "Yes, Beth, I think Adam would really like a wet paper towel to hold on his scratched cheek."

By giving children help in knowing exactly what to say to playmates when trouble breaks out, we encourage them to use appropriate words rather than inappropriate physical or verbal aggression. It is okay (even desirable) for children to express strong emotions. We should never push children into being so "nice" that they hold their emotions inside. Our goal is to channel their emotional expression into words that inform rather than words that hurt.

SHOULD WE FORCE CHILDREN TO APOLOGIZE?

It seems very odd that we tell children, "Be honest. Always tell the truth," then proceed to order them to "tell so-and-so you're sorry" (never even wondering if they actually feel sorry). No child should be encouraged to say he feels something that he really does not feel. It is more appropriate to simply point out how the other child feels. He may spontaneously give some indication of remorse or regret if he really feels it.

If a child appears to be sorry for something he has done, it may be helpful to say, "Would you like to tell Ricky that you're sorry about what happened?" "Would you like me to tell him for you?" It is even more important for us to find some way to help the child make amends to Ricky. He will feel good about himself if he has a chance to make things right. We discourage children terribly when we imply to them, "You have made such a mess of things that there is no way you can undo what you've done."

WAYS CHILDREN CAN MAKE AMENDS

- Say "I'm sorry."

- Get a damp paper towel for a friend to place on his bumped knee.

- Bring the friend a bandage.

- Share a toy.

- Give a hug.

- Pick up the blocks that were knocked over.

- Ask if the friend would like sit at your table.

- Draw a picture.

- Make a homemade card that says "Be my friend."

- Sit by the friend until he feels better.

- Ask, "What can I do to make amends?"

HOW CAN WE ENCOURAGE VOLUNTARY SHARING?

Sharing should also be voluntary. If my friend picked up a book I was reading and walked off with it, I would think him very rude. Strangely, when one child is looking at a book and a peer takes the book without asking, we are tempted to say, "You need to share. Look, there are lots of books. Just choose a different book. Don't be so stingy with the books."

I have a right to my own property and possessions. I can offer someone the use of my scissors, but that person really should not barge in and take them, especially if I am using them at the moment. I expect guests in my house to be respectful of my personal possessions, yet parents often allow visiting children to barge into their own child's room and play with any toy they want. If their own child puts up a fuss, we hear them say, "You have to share."

We all want children to be generous and polite, but we can encourage generosity most by protecting a child's property rights so he feels it is safe to invite others to share. The more vulnerable the child feels about losing his possessions, the more tightly and greedily he will guard them.

Graciela quietly moved from cot to cot in the darkened child care room as restless four-year-olds settled in for naptime. Several of the children could always be counted on to fall sound asleep almost before she got the light off. Most took ten or fifteen minutes to wind down and fall asleep. Then, of course, there were the really challenging three who squirmed and fidgeted, and tried everything in the book to keep themselves awake! Graciela never knew if she would eventually get them to sleep or not. She especially worried about Brett, because his parents had complained that he was so exhausted when they picked him up from child care that they were not able to spend enough quality time with him in the evenings.

> *Brett was lying on his stomach with his chin resting on one hand and the other hand twisting a loose thread hanging from his blanket. Graciela moved quietly to his side. She sat down cross-legged on the floor beside him and gently stroked his back. She bent close to him and whispered, "Brett, thanks for being so quiet and still. You were so quiet, I couldn't hear a single sound."*
>
> *Brett grinned and felt very good about himself.*

HOW CAN WE RECOGNIZE AND ENCOURAGE INTERNAL CONTROL?

Nurturing adults should always be alert to opportunities for recognizing and reinforcing little indications that a child is making progress in controlling impulses and resisting tempting but inappropriate behaviors.

LOGICAL AND NATURAL CONSEQUENCES

Children learn skills and information through active involvement in their day-to-day environment. They learn by watching others, by being told things, and most importantly, by experiencing life. In life, actions are often followed by logical or natural consequences. If I forget to water my potted plant, it will probably die (a natural consequence). If I am regularly late to work, I may lose my job (a logical consequence). No one is trying to hurt or annoy me. These consequences are merely the way the world works. Through them, I learn that I must behave in certain ways if I want to avoid undesired results and achieve desired goals.

SHOULD CHILDREN BE RESCUED FROM THE CONSEQUENCES OF THEIR ACTIONS?

Sometimes, when we see a child feeling disappointed or sad, we may be tempted to interfere and rescue him from the consequences of his own actions. It is not, however, a useful practice for us to rescue children from the logical and natural results of their actions and choices so long as the consequences are reasonable and safe! We would never risk a child being run over as a natural consequence of running into the street or allow a child to go hungry as a logical consequence of spilling food.

> *Tina arrived home after a family outing to a downtown movie theater and suddenly yelled, "Oh, no! I left my purse in the theater." Her dad fumed and sputtered, "Tina, why are you so careless? It'll take me a half hour to drive back downtown, and by then the purse will probably have been stolen. You'd lose your head if it wasn't tied down."*
>
> *After yelling at Tina for twenty minutes while she sniffled and made excuses for her behavior, he called the theater and drove back downtown alone to search for the purse.*

Even though Tina's dad reprimanded her loudly and angrily, in actuality he **rescued** her from any responsibility for her forgetfulness. (He absorbed the consequences for her.) He was the one who made the telephone calls, drove all the way back to the theater, and did the searching. Tina had nothing to do but feel miserable and stupid. Tina's dad would have used natural consequences if he had said:

Tina, I'm sure you feel awful about losing your purse. Can you think of anything we could do to find it? Would you like for me to help you look up the telephone number of the theater? Would you like for me to drive you back to the theater so you can look for it? I don't know if we'll find it or not. Purses left in public places often get stolen.

Tina's dad would have used logical consequences if he had said:

Tina, it isn't fair for me to have to drive all the way back to town. Next time we go to the theater, you will have to leave your purse at home. When you're a little older, you can try again. Perhaps by then it won't be so hard for you to remember your things.

By helping Tina find ways to solve her problem (rather than solving it for her), Tina's father guides her to focus on her forgetfulness as the problem, not her father's anger. She realizes that her discomfort results from the natural or logical consequences of her forgetfulness, not from someone trying to punish or embarrass her. She will become responsible when she learns to remember her possessions simply because it is frustrating and inconvenient to lose them, not just to please her father. If Tina learns to behave appropriately only to please her father, she may be tempted to behave inappropriately just to annoy him when she is angry with him or feeling rebellious.

WHAT IS THE DIFFERENCE BETWEEN PUNISHMENT AND GUIDANCE?

Punishment is negative. It is intended to hurt, humiliate, or pay a child back for something he has done. The purpose of guidance, in contrast, is to teach children (assertively and respectfully) to behave appropriately. Discipline is a part of positive child guidance; punishment is not. Following are examples of punishment versus discipline as used with a preschooler.

PUNISHMENT

"Don't you dare touch that cake. Get away from here and go play. If I catch you fooling around with it, you're really gonna get it!"

"I saw you touch that cake. Get in the time-out chair and stay until I say you can get up. Everyone's going to see you sitting in the 'naughty' chair and know that you were being bad."

"I'd better not see you get up! If I see you try to get up I'll make you stay twice as long."

Punishment is used to bully or coerce children into behaving the way we want them to behave. Some of the ways adults punish children are by:

- spanking, slapping, arm-yanking, and shaking.
- biting, hair-pulling, or pinching (so he will know how it feels).
- withdrawing affection, ignoring, avoiding eye contact, and not speaking.
- humiliating the child, putting him in a position to be ridiculed.

- endlessly lecturing, nagging, or harping on problems that are past history (they are done, the child cannot undo them).

- forcing the child to sit or stay somewhere for a set period of time, regardless of whether the child is sincerely remorseful and ready to make amends.

- arbitrarily taking away privileges, and forbidding activities that the child particularly enjoys (especially privileges that are totally unrelated to the child's offense).

DISCIPLINE/POSITIVE GUIDANCE

"This is Stephen's birthday cake. No one is allowed to touch it. It isn't fair to mess up Stephen's beautiful cake. You may look at it but only if you keep your hands in your pockets."

"You seem to be having a hard time remembering to keep your hands in your pockets while you look at the cake. You need to come sit on the time-out chair until you feel sure you can re- member our rule about not touching the cake. Come and tell me when you are sure you can look at the cake without touching."

"I like the way you are keeping your hands in your pockets while you look at Stephen's cake. Stephen will be so happy when he sees his beautiful birthday cake. Ummm, it smells good, doesn't it?"

Positive guidance is used to nurture and shape children's behavior. Following are some of the ways adults discipline children using positive guidance.

- Changing the surroundings to remove the likelihood or temptation for misbehavior

- Focusing the child's attention on logical and natural consequences that will, or may, follow a specific behavior

- Expressing concern for the child's feelings, but refusing to rescue the child from reasonable and safe consequences that are natural or logical results of his behavior

- Carefully supervising the child to prompt or cue appropriate behavior and remind the child of rules

- Firmly but respectfully redirecting the child's behavior away from inappropriate actions and substituting more appropriate activities

- Decisively stopping or interrupting any behavior that is clearly dangerous or unfairly re- sponding as firmly but as gently as possible

- Physically removing a very young child from a conflict or during a tantrum (even if the child is kicking and screaming) when it is necessary to protect the child and the environment

- Letting an older child know that you refuse to join him in her tantrum, but that you will be glad to talk when he is ready to speak calmly and respectfully

- Assuring the child that he is loved and valued; letting him know that you accept and respect his negative feelings, even if you must stop his negative action (it is okay to feel angry but not okay to hurt others)

There is a very fine line, sometimes, between punishing and guiding. A controversial concern for many early childhood educators is whether to use something called "time-out" as a consequence for inappropriate behavior. In their efforts to avoid overtly negative punishments, many early childhood professionals have for years responded to misbehavior by having children sit in time-out, by "the thinking wall," or in "the thinking chair." More negative versions have banished children to the "bad chair," the "baby chair," or the "naughty corner." Several early childhood experts have cautioned that children should not be required to sit any longer than three minutes for every year of the child's age; for example, nine minutes for a three-year-old, fifteen minutes for a five-year-old. In reality, it is not uncommon for children in some settings to be forced to sit many times that length of time.

Today, some experts say that time-out is a viable and positive method of guiding behavior while other experts insist that time-out just allows children uninterrupted time to plot their revenge. The real issue, however, is not whether a time-out chair is used or not used (or whether a penalty is imposed or a privilege is denied). The concern lies in how the adult goes about his enforcement and why he does what he does. Following are several ways to tell the difference between punishment and guidance.

PUNISHMENT . . .

lowers self-esteem	embarrasses
humiliates	discourages
degrades	belittles
hurts (physically or emotionally)	socially isolates
angers	emotionally abandons
frustrates	denies affection
thwarts efforts	

GUIDANCE . . .

builds self-esteem	gives confidence
strengthens character	encourages
respects	enhances self-image
heals	facilitates trust
gives hope	gives emotional support
models coping skills	is loving and caring
enables efforts	

At this point, one might respond by saying, "Those lists are lovely, but when little Elroy draws on my freshly painted walls with his crayon, I'm furious. I don't care about enhancing his self-image, I just want to wring his little neck!" Actually, Elroy's infuriating behavior gives us an excellent opportunity to put our preaching into practice. We can show Elroy, through our own behavior, that feeling angry is natural and normal, but hurting, humiliating, or belittling others

Sitting in time-out can feel lonely and embarrassing.

is simply not okay. Socially accepted rules for appropriate behavior do not apply only to children; they apply to all of us.

Having Elroy tediously scrub the crayon marks off the wall and taking the crayons away until he can be more carefully supervised are both assertive and effective disciplinary methods. They are a part of positive child guidance, but only if the adult's attitude is optimistic and assertive rather than mean-spirited and punitive. Our attitude toward Elroy should be one of helping him succeed in behaving more appropriately in the future, not making him miserable by punishing him for his bad deed.

> *These children, to be well trained and educated, should never hear from their teacher an angry word, or see a cross or threatening expression of countenance.*
>
> *Robert Owen (1958)*

HOW CAN I BE FIRM WITHOUT SEEMING ANGRY?

In order to be firm and fair in guiding children, deeds must be seen as separate from the person who did them. In other words, what a child has done may have been dishonest, but that does not mean the child is now a dishonest person. Since children are prone to become what we tell them they are (remember that prophecies are often self-fulfilling), we must be very careful about what we tell children they are. It is helpful to tell a child, "Pouring water on a cat is a thoughtless and unkind thing to do. You are a kind and thoughtful boy, but even kind, thoughtful boys make mistakes. The important thing is to do better next time."

Following are some helpful and some not-so-helpful phrases.

HELPFUL

"Spitting at people is not allowed!"

"Why do you feel angry with your brother?"

"What will happen if you spill the paint?"

"After your room is clean, then you may watch TV."

NOT HELPFUL

"You are a naughty boy!"

"Why are you so bad?"

"Don't act like a dummy."

"You lazy thing! Look at your messy room."

"I am still a good person even if I sometimes break a rule."

Phrases that are not helpful do little more than stereotype children in negative roles (naughty, bad, stupid, lazy). Helpful phrases give children very specific information about what is expected, without labeling the child in a negative way. Children always appreciate being reminded, "I'm very upset with what you did, but I'm not angry with you. I still love you a whole lot, even when you make mistakes."

AVOID OVERINDULGING AND OVERPROTECTING CHILDREN

Caring adults know how to say no. The idea of positive child guidance is sometimes interpreted to mean that adults are slaves to children, that adults must somehow keep things happy, glowing, and idyllic for children at all times. This could not be further from the truth. We have an obligation to be fair, caring, and available, but we are not responsible to make sure that children are completely happy at every moment of their lives.

Caring for and guiding children is physically demanding, emotionally draining, and intellectually taxing work, and growing up is not an easy task for the children either. Adults and children will sometimes be at cross purposes, so there are bound to be conflicts. Overindulgence and overprotection (sometimes referred to as spoiling) are not a part of positive child guidance. Not being firm enough is just as damaging as being too firm.

One mother says, "But I have to give Lindy ice cream while I'm preparing dinner. If I don't, she screams and holds her breath until she turns blue. I have no choice!" Of course, Lindy's mother does have a choice. She is the only one tall enough to reach the freezer!

Lindy's mother needs reassurance that it is perfectly okay for Lindy to cry. Lindy feels frustrated and crying is her way of expressing herself. When Lindy was a helpless newborn, her mother needed to respond quickly to her cries of hunger to instill in her a sense of trust. Now Lindy is older. She can **delay gratification** (wait a few minutes) for her needs to be met. In fact, she must learn how to delay gratification if she is ever to develop responsibility and self-control.

Her mother needs to feel more relaxed about Lindy's breath-holding. Babies and toddlers often forget to breathe for a few seconds when they are very stunned or hurt. Parents often hear the loud thump of their toddler falling, then a moment of silence, then finally loud, howling cries. The toddler isn't holding her breath to be manipulative; that's just how her body works. If, however, a great deal of attention is paid to that pause in her breathing, the child might eventually learn to hold her breath just for dramatic effect. Unless Lindy is suffering from a disorder such as **apnea** (a breathing disorder characterized by brief interruptions of breathing during sleep), the worst that will happen is that Lindy will succeed in causing herself to faint, at which time breathing will automatically resume.

The most effective way for Lindy's mother to deal with the child's behavior is to assertively and caringly acknowledge that wanting ice cream is okay, but that no ice cream will be served until after dinner. The mother could tell Lindy, "I know you wish you could have ice cream. It's all right to cry. Sometimes I cry when I'm mad or upset. You may cry as long as you need to. If you need to cry for a long, long time, then you must cry in your room so that you don't hurt other people's ears."

After Lindy has finished crying (remember, no child ever cried forever), her mother can redirect Lindy's hunger (present a compromise) by offering peanut-butter crackers or apple slices. Or, if she senses that even bringing up the subject of hunger would cause another scene, she may wait and offer a nutritious treat the next time she anticipates a problem, before Lindy even has a chance to mention ice cream. She can also choose not to purchase ice cream for a while to reduce Lindy's temptation (as well as her own temptation to give in). Whatever she does, she must not give in to Lindy's tantrum and reinforce her inappropriate behavior by rewarding it with ice cream.

Giving in to Lindy's demand—while, at the same time, yelling, complaining, or making her feel guilty—is inappropriately overindulgent and very confusing. Lindy may not learn that the word no really means no, or she may come to view herself as an unlovable and spoiled brat, thinking badly of herself but not really knowing how to behave differently.

HELP CHILDREN LEARN TO MAKE CHOICES WITHIN LIMITS

Children need freedom within clear limits. Freedom without limits is not really freedom. Instead, it is chaotic and dangerous. Jesse's parents have tried to give him complete freedom.

> *Jesse rules the family with the total abandon of a dictator. Whatever is being served for breakfast is not what he wants. Even if he is asked in advance for his breakfast order, he goes through several changes of mind. His parents meekly pour out bowls of cereal and make waffles or throw away waffles and make oatmeal.*
>
> *Whatever clothes Jesse's mother has chosen for him to wear are almost never to his liking either. He stamps down the hall like a little emperor and ceremoniously stuffs the clean clothing into the laundry hamper. His mother meekly offers alternate selections of clothes she hopes he will like. Sometimes, Jesse goes to school wearing clothes that are totally inappropriate for the weather or the setting.*
>
> *His parents wonder why he is so demanding. They are so proud of their beautiful little boy, and they want so much for him to love them that they fail to use good judgment. They also hate to confront him and risk an ugly scene. They do not realize it, but what Jesse really wants and needs are strong, loving parents who are willing and able to help him grow up. Secretly, Jesse realizes he is acting like a baby.*
>
> *Jesse did not become a dictator overnight, and he will not be able to change into a reasonable and polite person overnight. With time and patience, however, Jesse can learn to make choices within clearly defined, reasonable limits. Jesse can be given a choice between eggs and cereal, between the red shirt and the blue shirt, and he can be allowed to deal with the natural and logical consequences of refusing to accept the limits he has been given.*
>
> *His parents can explain, "Jesse, if you're not hungry enough to eat the corn flakes you asked for, then you're obviously not very hungry for breakfast." "You may take ten minutes to choose what you want to wear from these clothes. If you are not able to choose, then I will choose for you. If you are not dressed and ready for school on time, you will be tardy. I will not write a note to your teacher excusing your lateness." "If you stuff clean clothes in the laundry hamper, you will have to help with the extra laundry by sorting and folding clothes instead of watching television."*

In order to enforce freedom of choice within reasonable limits, Jesse's parents will have to make a commitment to confront Jesse with love and persistence. Of course, in the long run, Jesse will be a happier, friendlier, more likable person.

EXTERNAL REINFORCEMENT

Developing children's inner control and motivation for behaving acceptably have been addressed throughout this text. Previous sections have emphasized the concept that children must want to behave well, that they must assume responsibility for their actions. Positive child guidance is not a gimmicky strategy to manipulate children into behaving according to our specifications, but instead a process of guiding children to become competent, confident, and cooperative human beings who behave well, not to win favors but because behaving well is the right thing to do.

Now, however, it is time to look at the opposite side of the coin: techniques for refining external control. Some behaviors do not come from internal motivation. They are unconscious habits that are very resistant to even the most sincere desire for change. We know from our own experiences that wanting to quit smoking, lose weight, or exercise regularly is not always enough to make those things happen. I can want desperately to lose weight, but if I am unconsciously conditioned to open the refrigerator every time I pass it, I may be my own worst enemy.

Jeremy tells his mother that he does not want to practice the piano each day (as his piano teacher has asked him to do). Consequently, his mother delves into Jeremy's inner motivations. She talks with him about his hope to become a famous musician and his feelings of pride when he masters difficult pieces of music. If Jeremy really has an inner desire to play the piano, and the lack of practicing is simply a matter of establishing new habits, then giving him a cute little sticker as a reward each day that he practices may work wonders. If he does not practice because he lacks inner motivation, then stickers will be a waste of time. In fact, they may be worse than a waste of time. Jeremy may make his decision not to practice based on the fact that he is only giving up a little sticker that really is not very valuable anyway. Also, if Jeremy is coerced into practicing to get a reward, he may respond to future reminders of things he is supposed to do by saying, "What will you give me if I do it?"

In contrast, when Jeremy decides to train his pet chicken to "play the piano" for a county fair, he does not waste any time telling the hen how proud she will feel; he just drops a pellet of corn into her dish each time she inadvertently steps on the keyboard of the toy piano he has placed on the floor of her cage. Before long, Jeremy's chicken clucks loudly and pounds on the piano keyboard every time she sees him.

My placing coins in a candy vending machine every day may be every bit as mindless as the chicken's stepping on the toy piano keyboard to get pellets of corn. I may need to change my external surroundings to break my habit cycle. Perhaps I could walk a different route so that I do not pass the vending machines, think of a reward to give myself if I resist candy bars for a whole week, or even bring nutritious, low-calorie snacks with me as a substitute when I am tempted to eat candy. We can assist children in breaking undesirable habits in exactly this same way.

EXTERNAL CONDITIONS THAT SUPPORT APPROPRIATE BEHAVIOR

Stephanie runs up to her mother when her mother arrives to pick her up from her child care center. Stephanie has a handful of drawings, and she is dancing around her mother squealing, "Mommy, look what I made! Look what I made!" Stephanie's mother is busy chatting with other mothers, so she ignores Stephanie. Finally, Stephanie throws the drawings down on the ground and yells, "I hate you, mommy!" Instantly, her mother bends down and says (with a tone of disgust), "Stephanie, what do you want?"

Stephanie has learned a lesson that her mother did not intend to teach her: "When you want your mother's attention, be hateful and destructive because you will get attention faster than by just asking for attention."

Children generally do whatever they need to do to get their needs met. Many unconscious habits are formed simply because they work. We need to analyze our daily procedures very carefully to identify how children get the things they want and need in the environment.

Does the child who pushes and shoves the hardest always get to be first in line? Does whining and arguing always succeed in extending bedtime or television viewing time? Does pitching a fit mean the child does not have to buckle his seat belt? Does the child who misbehaves the most during story time get almost all of the adult's eye contact, verbal contact, physical contact, and name recognition? Remember, even negative attention is preferable to being ignored.

We also need to consider the powerful effect of **intermittent** (occasional) **reinforcers**. People who gamble do not need to get a reward every time they put money in a slot machine. They will keep feeding money to "one-armed bandits" for hours just to get a chance at one really big payoff. Children, likewise, can pester for hours on the chance that a disgusted adult will finally give in and reward their inappropriate behavior with the desired privilege or response. Without realizing it, we may be reinforcing and rewarding dysfunctional and annoying behaviors on a daily basis. By consciously looking at what a child gets out of various behaviors and changing our own behaviors, we may take big steps in preventing or resolving many frustrating misbehavior patterns.

WHAT IS BEHAVIOR MODIFICATION AND HOW SHOULD IT BE USED?

Behavior modification is a specific method for changing a child's behavior by following a highly structured process. In this process, the adult:

- observes a child's present behavior.

- identifies a desired future behavior.

- breaks the distance between the two behaviors into tiny steps.

- systematically reinforces each small step as the child moves closer to the desired behavior.

Behaviorists see learning as a process of piecing together a chain, one link at a time. The process is external to the child, since the adult chooses the skill to be learned and then rewards that behavior in the child.

Elinor is a beautiful little girl who is a victim of autism. She cannot speak and she constantly flutters around the room flapping her arms and making small grunting sounds. Pleading with her to stop these behaviors would only confuse her, making her so anxious that the behaviors would probably increase. Using behavior modification, however, would be an effective and caring way to shape her behavior into more socially accepted patterns.

Elinor's teacher, Thomas, simply ignores the flapping and watches carefully for the instant that Elinor stops to look at something. Immediately, Thomas gives Elinor a tiny paper cup of Cheerios®, her favorite cereal, and says, "Good girl, Elinor." Over a period of months, very quietly and unobtrusively, Thomas has conditioned Elinor to focus more of her attention on the toys and books in the classroom and to spend a great deal less time flapping and grunting. Very important, Thomas ignored Elinor's undesirable behavior but he never ignored or withdrew affection from Elinor herself.

Thomas' next task is to gradually wean Elinor off of the cereal and replace that reinforcement with shiny plastic coins he calls tokens. Eventually, he hopes that Elinor will comprehend that if she collects a certain number of tokens, she can trade them in for a special treat, privilege, or snack.

Children with developmental delays, learning deficits, and language disabilities may lack the ability to discuss or reflect on their inner motivations. Behavior modification may truly be a godsend for guiding these children.

Behavior modification can be used very successfully with well developing, even gifted, children. It is, however, essential to enlist the bright child's voluntary and active cooperation. Adults and children who are capable of examining their own and the motives of others will feel betrayed or coerced if they realize that their behavior has been manipulated without their knowledge. If I, for example, suddenly realize that someone has rigged the candy vending machine to steal my quarters (so I will stop buying candy), I will feel furious. I may stubbornly eat even more candy just to assert my own autonomy.

Behavior modification works most effectively with bright children when adults are straightforward about their plan. An adult might say, "Ginger, let's make a little booklet to help you remember to go to the bathroom on time. I will set the timer for one hour, and each time it rings, if your pants are still dry, you may paste a special sticker in your book. Do you think that would help you remember? Would you like to try it?"

Obviously, the sticker booklet will only help if Ginger is wetting her pants simply because she has a habit of delaying visits to the bathroom. A young toddler will not suddenly be able to master toilet training just to get stickers. The strategy also will not work if Ginger has inner motivation problems (such as needing to be a baby to compete for attention with a new baby in her family). If, however, Ginger really wants to stop wetting her pants and she just needs a little boost to break a bad habit, she is likely to cooperate fully and feel very proud of herself when she succeeds.

WHY BEHAVIOR MODIFICATION DOES NOT WORK ALL THE TIME

Behavior modification is a powerful tool when used appropriately. A primary concern, however, is that ignoring inappropriate behavior may become an excuse to give up responsibility for children's unacceptable behavior. Tactfully overlooking certain inappropriate behaviors may be helpful in some situations and reinforcement has tremendous impact on habit patterns. There is a risk, however, that if used inappropriately, behaviorist tactics can become manipulative and aloof. Ignoring can become punitive and hurtful when the adult is working *on* the child rather than *with* the child.

As adults, we have a responsibility not to stand by passively while a child is labeled as bad or wild, but to actively involve ourselves in making it easy for children to behave properly, and very,

very difficult for them to behave improperly. We may not always succeed but we can give our most persistent and energetic effort! Then, at least, a child with behavioral problems will know we care very much about him and that we will not give up on him, no matter what he does.

Parents and educators are becoming more and more aware that punishment and threats are not effective. Punishment, even if it is disguised as "consequences," often triggers immediate compliance, but tends to increase aggression and damage the crucial bond between adult and child. In their efforts to avoid punishments, teachers and parents turn to the use of stickers and stars, As, praise, awards, and privileges to induce children to master skills and obey adults (Kohn, 1990, 1993, 1994; Fantuzzo, et al., 1991). Rewards can gain temporary compliance from children, but are no more effective than punishments at helping children to become self-directed learners or caring, cooperative, responsible people (DeVries & Zan, 1994).

> In short, good values have to be grown from the inside out. Attempts to short-circuit this process by dangling rewards in front of children are at best ineffective, and at worst counterproductive. Children are likely to become enthusiastic, lifelong learners as a result of being provided with an engaging curriculum; a safe, caring community in which to discover and create; and a significant degree of choice about what (and how and why) they are learning. Rewards—like punishments—are unnecessary when these things are present, and are ultimately destructive in any case (Kohn 1994).

Child guidance programs and commercial classroom management "kits" that rely on rewards and consequences should be avoided by any early educator or parent who value moral development more than mindless obedience, and want children to become responsible for their own behavior. Moral reasoning develops best in a caring environment where children learn by relying on problem-solving, collaboration, and cooperation to resolve social predicaments (DeVries & Zan, 1994; Solomon et al., 1992).

POINTS TO REMEMBER

- We can prevent many behavior problems before they ever begin simply by careful planning, by understanding children's developmental needs, and by creating a match between their needs and the environment.

- Our physical postures, movements, and gestures communicate a great deal of information to children.

- If nonverbal cues are too threatening and intrusive, children bristle and resist commands.

- If requests are assertive, caring, confident, and respectful, children are more likely to comply quickly and willingly.

- Toddlers behave aggressively because they lack the verbal ability to express themselves otherwise.

- Insisting that children apologize, whether or not they feel regret, is neither an honest nor effective way to guide them.

- Punishment is intended to hurt, humiliate, or pay a child back for something he has done.

- Guidance is intended to teach appropriate behavior.

PRACTICAL APPLICATION

THE BIG BOYS AND THE VERY MUDDY DAY

Mrs. Belk taught first graders in a neighborhood public school for several years. She already had her undergraduate degree in early childhood education but had decided to upgrade her skills by taking a graduate course in psychology at a nearby university. She had only been enrolled in the class for a few weeks, but the professor had already lectured on various methods for reinforcing positive behaviors rather than focusing only on inappropriate behaviors. What a great idea, she thought: ignore the negative and reinforce the positive.

Mrs. Belk was eager to try some new disciplinary techniques on several of her more difficult children, especially Chad, a six-year-old who tended to be her group's ringleader for inappropriate behavior. Chad was tall for his age and wiry. He appeared to be a thin child, but he was surprisingly muscular. His calf muscles were rock-hard and bulged conspicuously on his skinny legs. Mrs. Belk thought that he probably worked off every ounce of fat by being in a constant state of motion.

For two years, he had been taking daily prescription doses of a medication for **hyperactivity** (which his doctor referred to as hyperkinesis or attention deficit disorder). His parents and teachers agreed that the medication helped him to function at home and at school, but he still had a difficult time dealing with the limits that adults set, and adults had a difficult time coping with his frenetic level of activity and wildly impulsive behavior.

The past week had been particularly stressful for Mrs. Belk. Chad had been even more out of control than usual. It had rained for so much of the week that the children had not gotten to play outside a single time. Mrs. Belk was beginning to feel as if the classroom were shrinking and the children multiplying.

She looked out the window. The sun had come out and the only problem with the playground was that there were still some very large mud puddles here and there. Mrs. Belk flipped the light switch on and off several times to signal the children that it was time to put away their work and gather on the rug for storytime. When the room was clean and the children were all sitting around on the floor in a big circle, Mrs. Belk said, "How would you like to go outside to the playground?"

To their gleeful shouts of, "Yes, yes, yes!" Mrs. Belk answered, "We can go outside on one condition. Everyone has to agree only to play on the dry areas. There are mud puddles and you will have to remember to walk around them." The children eagerly agreed to stay on dry land. Chad and his buddies were so excited that they could hardly contain themselves, but they promised Mrs. Belk that they would not forget about the mud puddles.

Mrs. Belk opened the door and was stampeded by squealing, laughing children. As Mrs. Belk walked out into the bright sunlight, she took a deep breath of fresh air and felt a great sense of relief to be outside the stuffy classroom.

After only a few seconds, she saw Chad running backward to catch a ball, and splat, he stepped right into the mud. Mrs. Belk stood with her hands on her hips, glaring at Chad and thinking about whether to have him sit on the bench for ten minutes for breaking a class rule.

She knew that it was a real effort to keep Chad sitting for ten minutes. Mrs. Belk dreaded a confrontation and decided that she just did not have the energy to deal with Chad at the moment.

She started thinking about what her professor had said about it being helpful to ignore inappropriate behavior—and besides, she thought, maybe his stepping in the mud was really an accident—so she looked the other way and decided to ignore Chad. Within seconds, several children were pulling at her shirt sleeves saying, "Mrs. Belk, Mrs. Belk, look, Chad is in the mud!" Mrs. Belk told them, "Go play and don't pay any attention to Chad."

Within minutes, two of Chad's favorite cohorts, Eddie and John, also six, were hollering as Chad stamped his foot in the mud, splattering mud on them. They found it necessary, of course (after they nervously looked back to make sure Mrs. Belk's back was still turned), to stamp their feet in the mud, splattering Chad from head to toe. The chase was on with half the class frantically telling Mrs. Belk, "Look, look at Chad!" and the other half squealing and laughing as the three boys chased and slid in the mud.

Mrs. Belk saw that her strategy was not working. With the look of daggers in her eyes she shouted, "Okay, everybody line up at the door to go inside." All of the children (except Chad, Eddie, and John) hurried to the door and made a straight line. In a loud voice, Mrs. Belk stared straight at the three boys and said, "I'm waiting. Not everyone is ready to go inside." She thought, "There is no way I am going to chase those three around in this mud. They are just doing this to get attention. They'll come as soon as they think we are really going inside."

Mrs. Belk opened the door and said, "Everyone walk quietly in the hall, please." While the group of children were being led inside, they nervously glanced back and forth at Mrs. Belk and the three boys running around outside. They knew the three boys were in a lot of trouble, and they knew Mrs. Belk was angry. The three boys chased and played in the mud, pretending not to notice that the others were going inside and trying to look tough and macho. By this time, their shoes and clothes were caked with mud and they were beginning to feel very uncomfortable.

As soon as Mrs. Belk had ushered her line of children inside, she asked another teacher to watch her class while she stood behind the door where the boys could not see her and watched them through the glass. The other teacher's mouth dropped open as she saw the mud-covered boys. Mrs. Belk said, "They're just doing this for attention, so the best thing is to ignore it. I'm sure they'll get tired of it in a few minutes when they realize they don't have an audience, and then they'll beg to come inside."

Within five minutes, a teacher, whose room overlooked the playground, ran down the hall and said, "Mrs. Belk, you've got to get those boys inside! They've taken off all their clothes and they are on top of the fort throwing mud balls at the building and at cars."

The playground was a mess. The building and cars were a mess, and the boys were a mess. The situation was no longer salvageable. The boys had to be forcibly brought inside. The principal called their horrified parents to come and get them. There was no easy way for the boys to make amends for their behavior or to save face in front of their peers, parents, and teachers. They had taken part in an open rebellion, a serious and scary step for a child and a damaging precedent for future behavior.

DISCUSSION QUESTIONS

1. What are some possible reasons for Mrs. Belk's ignoring the muddy boys? Evaluate those reasons.
2. List some ways that you think these problems could have been avoided.
3. What could Mrs. Belk have done that might have prevented or stopped the inappropriate behavior?
4. What do you think the muddy boys were thinking and feeling throughout this episode?
5. What do you think the rest of the children were thinking and feeling?
6. How would you have responded if you were the principal? The parents? Another teacher in the building?
7. If you were Mrs. Belk, what would you say or do when the boys came back to school the next day?

RELATED READINGS

HELPING CHILDREN DEVELOP SELF-CONTROL

Buzzelli, C. A. (1992). Research in review. Young children's moral understanding: learning about right and wrong. *Young Children 47*(6), 47–53.

Addresses processes of moral development in young children.

Caulfield, R. (1996, Fall). Social and emotional development in the first two years. *Early Childhood Education Journal, 24*(1), 55–58.

Crockenberg, S. (1997). How children learn to resolve conflicts in families. In E. N. Junn & C. Boyatzis (Eds.), *Annual editions: Child growth and development 97/98* (4th ed.). New York: McGraw-Hill. (Original work published in *Zero to Three*, April 1992.)

According to Susan Crockenberg, children learn how to settle conflicts from early experiences in the home. When faced with a child's behavior problem or conflict, parents can model and provide their young children with practice in conflict negotiation skills by using strategies that include directives, explanations, and compromise. Acquiring these skills early should have many long-term benefits.

Crosser, S. (1997, March–April). Helping children to develop character. *Early Childhood News, 9*(2), 20–24.

Davis, J. (2001). Caregivers' Corner. The day Pork Chop died (almost). *Young Children 56*(3), 85.

Describes how the impending death of a pet helped a group or preschoolers learn coping and grieving skills.

Dowrick, N. (1997, October). "You can't shout at them because they just cry": Student teachers with nursery children. *International Journal of Early Years Education, 5*(3), 255–261.

Eaton, M. (1997, September). Positive discipline: Fostering the self-esteem of young children. *Young Children, 52*(6), 43–46.

Gartrell, D. (1997, September). Beyond discipline to guidance. *Young Children, 52*(6), 34–42.

Grossman, S. (1996, September–October). Passing Vickie's test: Building self-esteem and trust by following through with rules. *Early Childhood News, 8*(5), 6–12.

Honig, A. S. (1996). *Behavior guidance for infants and toddlers.* Little Rock, AR: SECA.

Honig, A. S., & Wittmer, D. S. (1996). Helping children become more prosocial: Ideas for classrooms, families, schools, and communities. *Young Children, 51*(2), 62–70.

Hunter, T. (2000). Modeling possibilities. *Young Children 55*(5), 40.

Presents strategies for indirect teaching through modeling to encourage discovery learning and problem-solving.

Kilpatrick, W. (1997). The moral power of good stories. In E. N. Junn & C. Boyatzis (Eds.), *Annual editions: Child growth and development 97/98* (4th ed.). New York: McGraw-Hill. (Original work published in *American Educator*, summer 1993.)

Stories help children make sense of their lives, offer children concrete examples of morals and values, and stimulate discussion in the classroom and at home.

Krogh, S. L., & Lamme, L. L. (1985). "But what about sharing?" Children's literature and moral development. *Young Children 40*(4), 48–51.

Explains how children's books can be used to help children discuss moral issues. Reviews past views of moral understanding, and examines how changes in children's cognitive, social, and emotional abilities, as well as changes in their family relationships, influence their development of moral understanding.

Vander Wilt, J. (1996, Winter). Beyond stickers and popcorn parties. *Dimensions of Early Childhood, 24*(1), 17–20.

Wallace, E. (1997, May–June). Do you recognize this parent? *Early Childhood News, 9*(3), 32–33.

HELPFUL WEB SITES

http://www. uca/gary.ca/~dkbrown/index.html   Children's Literature Web Guide presents information on award-winning children's' books and authors, resource lists, book reviews, and discussion forums. http://www.ucal

http://www.ala.org/parentspage/greatsites/   Great Sites! From the American Library Association, this site gives librarians' book recommendations.

http://www.med.jhu.edu/peds/neonatology/protect   Protect Your Child on the Internet. Information and resources provided by the Johns Hopkins University Department of Pediatrics' "Pediatric Points of Interest."

For additional information on positive child guidance, visit our Web site at
http://www.earlychilded.delmar.com

Chapter 8
Addressing Persistent, Unproductive Patterns of Behavior

OBJECTIVES

After reading this chapter, you should be able to:
- Identify persistent patterns of dysfunctional behaviors.
- Categorize problem behaviors in terms of their misguided purpose.
- Define the typical characteristics of problem behaviors.
- Recognize various hidden reasons for children's misbehavior.
- List steps to resolve conflicts between adults and children.
- Define strategies for meeting special needs.
- Identify appropriate resources for problem-solving.

Feelings of self-worth make it possible for a child to learn acceptable behavior.

REACTING TO NEEDS— MASLOW'S HIERARCHY

Human beings—children and adults—behave in many complicated ways in order to get their emotional needs met. At the heart of almost any behavior lies the desire to acquire something, whether an object, an experience, or a feeling. Although some behaviors may be directed toward frivolous whims, many behaviors focus on basic human needs. Maslow (1943) developed a theory of human motivation. He proposed that basic needs are arranged in a hierarchy, a pyramid in which each overriding level of need has to be met before successive levels of need can be addressed. Following is Maslow's list of emotional needs that motivate behavior. People need:

- freedom from discomfort—to have food, water, shelter, and so on.

- physical safety—to feel secure from danger.

- a sense of belonging—to feel loved.

- self-esteem—to feel valued and self-sufficient.

- to stretch intellectually—to know and understand.

In other words, a child who is starving will be distracted from playing and learning. Her primary concern will be food. A child who is frightened and insecure will show little interest in making friends or building castles with blocks. A child who feels unloved will not be able to function independently and confidently. In fact, very young children will tend to do whatever seems to work to get their needs met, no matter how annoying or uncivilized their behavior seems to the adults around them, since they have not yet developed the ability to inhibit their impulses. Only after their basic emotional needs have been met can we expect them to be calm, cooperative, and curious learners (Brewer, 1998; Bullock, 1997; Feeney, Christensen, & Moravcik, 1996; Gibbs, 1997; Kagan, 1997; McAlister, 1997).

WHAT IS THE ROLE OF SELF-ESTEEM IN REPEATED MISBEHAVIOR?

Unmet needs are a hidden cause of repeated patterns of dysfunctional behavior in children. In order to behave well, children must have a strong sense of self-esteem. Many behavior-disordered children seem to be walking around with a big, black hole inside them where their self-esteem ought to be. Self-esteem has become more and more emphasized over the past few decades as a characteristic that seems closely tied to school success and social adjustment (Kokenes, 1974; Wittner & Honig, 1997). Early childhood educators have especially focused on activities intended to foster self-esteem. Children, unfortunately, do not suddenly develop a sense

A sense of belonging is essential to the development of positive self-esteem.

If others consistently see a child as lovable, capable, and worthwhile, she will probably feel high self-esteem. Exposure to racism and bigotry devastate self-esteem and sow the seeds of hatred.

of self-worth simply because we sing a cute song about being special and color in between the lines on a workbook sheet that says, "I am special."

HOW CAN I SUPPORT THE CHILD'S DEVELOPMENT OF SELF-ESTEEM?

The perception of "value" children place on themselves reflects the "value" important others place on them (Coopersmith, 1967; Randy, Hoover, & Kindsvatter, 1997; Roberts, 1997). If parents and caregivers see a child as lovable, capable, and worthwhile, then the child will probably have a high level of self-esteem. Children begin to develop self-esteem from birth, but only if their needs are met by attentive caregivers, they feel safe and loved, and they are consistently treated with respect (even while they are being disciplined). Although it may be possible to rebuild damaged self-esteem, it is more effective to support the development of a positive self-concept from the very beginning.

If a child's early experiences have been damaging to her sense of self, it is essential to begin fostering self-esteem and to teach her appropriate ways to get her needs met. With a great deal of support and patience, children can unlearn old, inappropriate behaviors that may have been the only way they knew to get their needs met in a confusing or unsupportive environment. Repeated cycles of inappropriate behavior are difficult to handle, and adults easily fall into behaviors that are as inappropriate as that of the children they are trying to help. Verbal abuse, yelling, sarcasm, ridicule, and shoving are all inappropriate adult behaviors.

A key to success in dealing with children who have developed habit patterns of inappropriate behavior is for the adult to persistently pull the child up to a more acceptable level of behavior rather than allowing the child to pull the adult down to the child's level of immature and inappropriate interaction, advice that is easy to give but never easy to put into practice.

> *There is nothing so strong as gentleness, nothing so gentle as real strength.*
> St. Francis de Sales (de Sales & Ryan, 1972)

THE NO-LOSE METHOD OF CONFLICT RESOLUTION

Often, children and adults become locked in a struggle over who will be in control. These power struggles become win-lose situations in which the only way the adults get their needs met is for children to submit to control, and the only way for children to get their needs met is for adults to submit to control. This tug-of-war pits adults and children against each other. Typically, this results in misbehavior patterns becoming well established. Antagonism between adults and children can also begin to interfere with the pleasurable, nurturing interactions that strengthen self-esteem and are a critical part of daily life for children. Adults find themselves chronically annoyed with children, and children become more and more resistant and noncompliant.

The no-lose method of conflict resolution is a strategy for avoiding power struggles, and for adults and children working together to solve problems positively and cooperatively. Following are six steps to use in resolving conflicts (Dinkmeyer & McKay, 1982; Gordon, 1970).

CONFLICT RESOLUTION

Step 1—Use reflective listening to clarify feelings.
Teacher: "Michonda, are you feeling angry because Amy pulled on your swing?"
Michonda: "Yes. She keeps pulling on me and she won't leave me alone."

Step 2—Generate possible solutions by brainstorming.
Teacher: "What are some things you could do to solve this problem?"
Michonda: "I could run away from her."

Step 3—Evaluate the probable consequences of possible solutions.
Teacher: "Do you think that will work?"
Michonda: "I don't think so. She would probably just start chasing me."
Teacher: "Hmmm . . . what if you ask Amy why she's bothering you?"

Step 4—Choose the best possible solution.
Michonda: "Okay, but what if she won't listen to me?"
Teacher: "Would you like for me to come with you?"
Michonda: "Yes."

Step 5—Carry out the solution.
Michonda: "Why are you being so mean to me and making me mad?"
Amy: "Because you won't play with me. You just keep swinging all the time. I don't like swinging anymore."
Michonda: "Well, I don't want to dig in the sandbox all the time."
Amy: "Will you play with me if we play like we're dinosaurs in the jungle?"
Michonda: "Okay . . . but can I be Tyrannosaurus Rex this time?"
Amy: "Sure! I'll be a flying dinosaur with big sharp claws . . . okay?"

Step 6—Evaluate how well the solution worked.
> Teacher: "Michonda and Amy, I'm happy to see you playing and having fun together. You must feel proud that you were able to solve your problem all by yourselves."

Please note that the teacher gently guided Michonda and Amy through the process of resolving their problem, but did not solve the problem for them. The girls not only find a way to get along better on this particular day, but also experience the process of peaceful resolution and practice appropriate conflict resolution skills.

DREIKURS' MISTAKEN GOALS

Taking steps to involve a child in conflict resolution is important, but in order to break a persistent cycle of inappropriate behavior, steps must also be taken simultaneously to see that the child's emotional needs have been met. Adler (1931), a colleague of Freud, theorized that inappropriate behavior stemmed from inadequate early guidance. He believed that some children were kept from developing a sense of competence and self-worth by doting or dominating parents who saddled them with an inferiority complex, causing them to adopt inappropriate ways to exert control and feel competent.

Dreikurs (Dreikurs & Cassel, 1974) further developed this idea for teachers and parents by proposing four mistaken goals that he hypothesized to be the root of long-standing, habitual patterns of inappropriate behavior. He theorized that children behave inappropriately because of their overwhelming urge to:

1. get attention from others.
2. gain a sense of control.
3. get revenge for their own perceived hurts.
4. remove themselves from frightening or painful situations.

Each of the mistaken goals is directed toward getting an emotional need met: the need for recognition, the need for a sense of control over one's life, the need for fairness, and the need to avoid stressful and frightening situations. Unfortunately, each behavior listed above may seem to make the child feel a little better temporarily, but it actually compounds and worsens her problem in the long run. There is a snowball effect in which the child's inappropriate responses increase the negativity and hostility in her environment, which in turn increases her emotional neediness and the likelihood of her behaving more and more inappropriately in the future.

Typically, we respond in a way that is precisely opposite to the response actually needed by the child. For example, we are tempted to ignore the child who is acting out to get attention, but that will cause her to have even more need to act out. We are tempted to get into a stern power struggle with the controlling child, "to show her who's boss," but this makes her feel even more powerless and out of control. We are sorely tempted to inflict pain on the aggressive child who bites or hurts another child, but angry aggression on our part can make the child even more resolved to get revenge. Additionally, we are tempted to shrug our shoulders and give up altogether on the withdrawn child who hides under a table, twisting her hair or bumping her head on the wall, but our abandonment only allows her to sink deeper and deeper into isolation.

In order to bring about real change, we must cure (or at least relieve) the problems that cause persistent patterns of inappropriate behavior, and retrain children in appropriate methods to get

Sometimes children need to learn new ways to get their emotional needs met.

their emotional needs met. It is not effective to tackle inappropriate behaviors as if they existed in a vacuum. When behavior is often not appropriate, the child's misbehaviors can be thought of as symptoms and the child's emotional neediness as an underlying disease. Suppressing behavioral symptoms without paying attention to the emotional well-being of the child may only result in the eruption of new or different symptoms, just as treating the fever of an infection without giving an antibiotic to kill the bacteria that caused it will probably mean a return of the fever.

Healing can take place only when the child feels she is an accepted and worthwhile group member, she has some sense of control over her life, she is treated fairly and respectfully, and she feels optimism that she can succeed in whatever is expected of her. If these feelings blossom in the child, then we can say that she has self-esteem and the four key reasons for persistent misbehavior no longer exist. The child will no longer need to rely on misbehavior for emotional survival, and can begin to break habit patterns and learn more effective ways to get along with others.

Feelings of positive self-esteem blossom in young children as they live and play in a nurturing environment.

ATTENTION-SEEKING BEHAVIOR

CLINGING, FEIGNING INEPTNESS

Human babies are born helpless and vulnerable. It makes sense that they become emotionally attached to caregivers, and that they are most comfortable and secure when they can feel, see, or hear the caregiver's closeness. In a more primitive society, an infant's very survival could depend on staying close to a caring adult. As soon as infants are able to identify and distinguish among family members, caregivers, and strangers, they generally show signs of stranger anxiety and separation anxiety. A baby who has always cooed, gurgled, and smiled for anyone will suddenly cry when a stranger leans close to admire her and tickle her chin. A one-year-old who usually toddles around the house getting into everything may become subdued and clingy while a visitor is in the house.

This **bonding** (becoming emotionally attached to a caregiver) is a healthy and normal phase of development. Attachment to a dependable caregiver is an essential factor in the development of trust. We do no favor to babies and toddlers when we push them too early to break away from the adults who care for them. Babies who are allowed to develop secure, loving bonds with responsive caregivers become friendlier, more independent, and more successful preschoolers later (Bretherton & Waters, 1985; Lamb, Thompson, Gardner, & Charnov, 1985). Close attachment in infancy does not, as parents often worry, cause children to become spoiled, clingy, attention-seekers.

Clingy children who pretend they cannot do anything without help suffer from poor self-esteem. They have not been "loved" too much, although they may well have been overindulged and overprotected in ways that stunted their long-term development of healthy confidence and independence. Overindulgence and overprotection are poor excuses for real love, which is respectful and matched to a child's needs, rather than being intrusive or overwhelming. In many cases, clingy children may have been given too little attention and attachment. Their need to bond may have never been fully satisfied so they cling to baby behaviors. Clingy children only feel comfortable and loved when they are being fussed over and cared for. They long for the adult to cuddle them and to rescue them from their responsibilities.

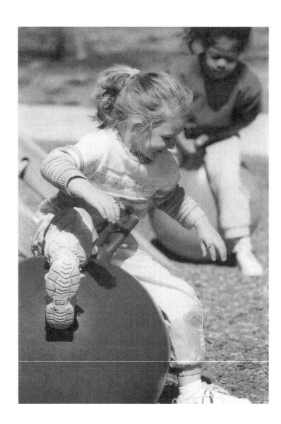

Children who feel good about themselves feel comfortable behaving in a natural and spontaneous way, but they also are able to accept reasonable limits.

ARTIFICIAL CHARM, COMPETITIVENESS

Children who are insecure in their sense of belonging often adopt an artificial charm. Younger children learn how to play the role of the adorable and irresistible child, while older children gush with insincere compliments. This niceness may vanish instantly, however, whenever the child feels threatened by attention directed toward someone else. The child may swing from absolute charmer to cold competitor in seconds. We need to focus on developing the child's sense of security and self-esteem by giving sincere affection and encouragement at appropriate times. We also need to set firm limits and help the child know that she is loved for herself, not for her fake charm.

CLOWNING, ACTING OUT, SILLINESS

Children use clowning, acting out, and silliness to get attention not only from adults, but also from other children. Some children only seem to feel sure that they are loved and appreciated when they are at the center of attention with everyone looking at them, and either laughing or chiding. Children may be especially likely to get silly when they feel embarrassed or pushed into a corner. For some children, being a clown is a way of saving face and protecting damaged self-esteem.

We need to take care to allow clowning children to save their dignity. They should be corrected privately and respectfully when their acting out is unacceptable. It is also essential that they be given opportunities for responsibility and leadership in positive settings as well as

Adults can help children become aware of the feelings of others.

chances to entertain others in appropriate ways. For example, a child might be encouraged to plan a skit for classmates, chosen to pass out napkins or refreshments during a celebration, or allowed to sing, dance, or act out a story at group time.

LAZINESS, COMPULSIVENESS, OBNOXIOUSNESS

Lazy, compulsive, or obnoxious behaviors may be a child's unconscious way of forcing adults to pay attention. They also signal a lack of self-esteem in the child. The child labeled as lazy may receive negative attention when adults nag, take over the child's responsibilities, or insist that other children help or do the child's work for her. Children who overeat, bite their nails, tease, or purposely disgust other children and adults are also giving strong indications that they do not feel good about themselves.

Persistent, assertive, and loving guidance will build the child's respect for herself by helping her know that the adult cares deeply enough to become actively involved in redirecting her inappropriate behaviors. For example, a child who persists in running around the playground terrifying other children with bugs and worms could be firmly redirected from poking the creatures in others' faces to constructing a terrarium for the science center out of an old aquarium, some rocks and dirt, and a few little plants. There, the insects and earthworms could be displayed in a socially acceptable manner that does not frighten or disgust others.

CONTROLLING BEHAVIOR

MANIPULATIVENESS, VENGEFULNESS

Manipulative means trying to trick someone into doing something that she really does not want to do. Adults often set an example for this behavior in their attempts to gain control over the child's behavior. We tell children things such as, "Eat your bread crusts because they will make your hair curly" or "Bend over, this shot won't hurt a bit!" We should not be surprised to hear a kindergartner say, "Give me your candy bar and I'll be your best friend forever."

Sometimes, manipulativeness can become excessive and vengeful as children struggle to gain control of the children and adults around them. Adults need to define clear limits and help children become aware of the feelings and reactions of those around them. Adults can recognize and verbalize feelings. For example, "Sallie, I know you really want Alvie's doll, but the doll belongs to Alvie. Alvie doesn't like to play with you when you try to take her doll. You may choose a different toy, or you may play by yourself."

POUTING, STUBBORNNESS

Children who want control but fail to get their way with others may react by pouting, stubbornly refusing to participate or "causing a scene." The toddler who wants (but does not get) ice cream for dinner, for example, may push her plate off the high-chair tray, kick her feet, scream, shake her head, and generally refuse to have anything to do with carrots and roast beef.

It is most important for the child to discover that she is loved and respected.

Parents and early educators do no favor either by giving in to the toddler (and thus encouraging her controlling behavior) or by forcing nutritious food on her against her will. They can, however, avoid a power struggle by simply removing the toddler from the high chair and allowing her to express her anger. The adults can express sincere empathy, but allow the child to be stubborn without showing a great deal of attention or concern.

For example, the adult may say, "It's okay to cry. When you feel better, your dinner is right here waiting for you." When she has finished screaming, she may or may not want dinner. Either way, she will not starve before the next meal. The child's need for a sense of control can be met by allowing her to choose when she is ready to eat, not by letting her succeed in demanding things that are not in her best interest. Between the lines, the adult is saying, "You may make your own choices—within reasonable limits—but you must also deal with the consequences of your choices."

COPING TECHNIQUES

Caring for an unhappy child can be stressful and overwhelming. Early childhood educators need to have a plan to help them get through difficult times. Keep these tips in mind.

- Remember not to take the crying personally. Babies and young children are coping the best they know how at the moment.

- Take deep breaths. Try to relax as much as possible. A screaming child can be very frustrating. You will need to stay calm to figure out the best way to resolve the problem.

- Your first concern should be to make sure the child is safe and secure. An out-of-control child may harm herself or others. If necessary to protect the child or others, restrain the child as gently as possible but as firmly as necessary.

- Softly and calmly repeat reassuring statements such as, "I know you're feeling angry now," "When you feel better, we'll talk," and "It's okay to cry. Sometimes I cry when I'm feeling angry, too." This will remind the child (and yourself) that you are not angry.

- Take turns with the child if another appropriate adult is available. Amazingly, having a calm, uninvolved adult take over in the middle of a tantrum may break the cycle and help the child gain control.

- Make it a point to talk later about stressful situations. Identify early childhood professionals who seem to have developed effective coping skills themselves. They may be able to give helpful suggestions.

- Don't be afraid to accept or ask for help from experts. Seek out expertise in books, Web sites, college early childhood departments, and medical resources.

BULLYING, REBELLING

Some children, when failing to gain control by other means, resort to bullying or rebelling. They gain control over smaller children by overwhelming them physically with their size and strength. Grown-ups are not usually so easy for a small child to bully. A child, consequently, might be tempted to control adults by being so rebellious, so out of control, that adults feel totally helpless.

It is important, however, that adults not allow themselves to lapse into feelings of inadequacy. The child needs strong, reliable adult support in order to give up inappropriate behaviors and form new habits.

It is also essential for adults to avoid power struggles with the bullying or rebelling child. Head-to-head confrontation will trigger an increase in angry rebellion and will not solve the problem. Aggressive, bullying behavior on the part of adults further establishes the role model for this undesirable behavior. Instead, adults must find ways to build a positive relationship with the child and to help the child feel a sense of belonging. Clear limits are essential, as well as logical consequences, but the most important step is for the child to discover that she is loved, respected, and appreciated. Then she will be able to relax and relinquish her tight-fisted attempt to control those around her.

PREVENT BULLYING

Create a Positive, Calm Environment
A well-planned, orderly, developmentally appropriate environment sets the stage for calm behavior. Additionally, calm, supportive adults provide excellent role models for children. Strictly limit books, television, and movies to age-appropriate materials featuring positive behavior.

Provide Positive Role Models
Most important, be a positive role model for caring, respectful behavior. Don't say things like, "Do what I said because I said so." "Do what I say or you'll be sorry." Don't angrily grab the child, shove her, or yank her arm. Harsh, controlling adults set an example for bullying. Stay calm and think before acting. Count to ten backward. Regularly take steps to reduce your own stress: exercise, listen to music, laugh with friends, or whatever works for you. Seek information or help to cultivate more effective anger management skills. Consciously practice positive conflict resolution every day. Force yourself to try it even if it feels awkward at first.

Provide Nurturing Peer Relationships
Never allow children to be abusive or cruel to each other. Help children learn that teasing is "good teasing" only if everyone is laughing and having fun. Hurtful teasing is bullying and will not be tolerated ever. Celebrate diversity. Help children learn to value individual differences. Teach them to be caring and compassionate. All people have feelings and deserve respect, regardless of their gender, race, religion, size, or special needs.

Help Children Recognize and Understand Their Own and Others' Emotions
Regularly talk about feelings. Identify and label feelings for children: angry, sad, happy, frustrated, excited, worried, and so on. Encourage them to identify emotions in picture books. Encourage children to describe how they think friends or story characters might be feeling. Use reflective listening to get children to talk and think about their own feelings.

Help Children Learn to Accurately Perceive Social Situations so They Can Respond Appropriately
Stimulate children's thinking by asking questions and encouraging discussions about social situations. For example, while reading stories, ask questions like, "What does the boy see?" "What do you think is happening?" "How do you think the boy feels about that?" "What do you think he will do next?" "What do you think he should do?" "Why?" After disagreements or

problems have occurred, encourage the children to discuss the incident objectively. Help them analyze why the disagreement might have taken place, what emotions they think each were feeling, and other ways they might have responded that would have been more positive.

Help Children Learn to Predict the Consequences of Their Actions, Particularly Those Involving Aggression

Start early with babies and toddlers, helping them learn to predict simple cause-and-effect sequences in everyday activities. Playfully pretend to put your adult foot into the toddler's shoe. If the toddler is able to comprehend that the shoe will not fit, she will be delighted and want to repeat the game. "What will happen if I eat the banana without taking the peeling off?" Continue to talk about consequences as the child matures. "What do you think will happen if you throw the blocks?" "How will your friend feel if you scream at her and push her?" "How would you feel if someone called you a hurtful name?"

Help Children Learn How to Use Group Processes to Resolve Social Problems

Preschoolers and schoolagers can learn to talk about problems as a group. Have a class meeting or a family meeting to talk through a problem together, to brainstorm possible solutions, and to decide on a plan. Children can be selected to role-play problem behaviors to help the group explore what is happening, why it's happening, and what can be done to prevent it or resolve it.

To learn more, read:

Banks, R. (1997). Bullying in schools. *ERIC Digest*. Champaign, IL: ERIC Clearinghouse on Elementary and Early Childhood Education. Document # ED 407 154. Available online: http://www.ed.gov/databases/ERIC_Digests/ed407154.html.

Bloch, D. (1993). *Positive self-talk for children: Teaching self-esteem through affirmations*. New York: Bantam Books.

Freedman, J. S. (Ed.). (1999, July 10). Easing the teasing. *ERIC Digest*. Champaign, IL: ERIC Clearinghouse on Elementary and Early Childhood Education. Document # ED431555. Available online: http://www.ed.gov/databases/ERIC_Digests/ed431555.html.

Freedman, J. S. (1999). Preventing violence by elementary school children. *ERIC/CUE Digest*, 149. New York: ERIC Clearinghouse on Urban Education, Institute for Urban and Minority Education, Teachers College. Document # ED431555. Available online: http://www.ed.gov/databases/ERIC_Digests/ed436602.html.

Noddings, N. (1996). Learning to care and to be cared for. In A. M. Hoffman (Ed.), *Schools, violence, and society* (pp. 185–98). Westport, CT: Praeger.

Slaby, R. G., Roedell, W. C., Arezzo, D., & Kendrix, K. (1995). *Early violence prevention: Tools for teachers of young children*. Washington, DC: National Association for the Education of Young Children.

Sullivan, K. (2000). *The anti-bullying handbook* (1st ed.). Oxford, UK: Oxford University Press.

U.S. Department of Education, Office of Civil Rights. (1999). *Protecting students from harassment and hate crime: A guide for schools*. Washington, DC: U.S. Department of Education.

Wallach, L. B. (1994). Violence and young children's development. *ERIC Digest*. Champaign, IL: ERIC Clearinghouse on Elementary and Early Childhood Education. Document # ED369578. Available online: http://www.ed.gov/databases/ERIC_Digests/ed369578.html.

(continues)

PREVENT BULLYING *(continued)*

CHILDREN'S BOOKS ADDRESSING AGGRESSIVE BEHAVIOR

Carlson, N. (1985). *Loudmouth George and the sixth-grade bully.* New York: Puffin Books.
Walker, A. (1991). *Finding the green stone.* San Diego: Harcourt Brace Jovanovich.
Bosch, C. W. (1988). *Bully on the bus.* Seattle, WA: Parenting Press.
Naylor, P. R. (1992). *Reluctantly Alice.* New York: Dell.
Cohen-Posey, K. (1995). *How to handle bullies, teasers, and other meanies: A book that takes
    the nuisance out of name calling and other nonsense.* Highland City, FL: Rainbow Books.
Stoltz, M. (1985). *The bully of Barkham Street.* New York: Harper & Row.

DISRUPTIVE BEHAVIOR
DESTRUCTIVENESS, AGGRESSIVENESS

Children whose self-esteem is lacking may deteriorate into disruptive habit patterns of destruc-
tiveness and aggression. These behaviors tell us that the child feels a sense of hopelessness. She
may believe that she has already been rejected by others so that it really does not matter what
she does: nobody will like her no matter how she behaves. These feelings discourage her from
developing self-control over her impulses.

The destructive or aggressive child must know that she will be stopped and that others' rights
will be protected. In an extreme situation, a parent or early educator may have no choice but to
restrain a child to prevent her from harming herself or others. A caregiver in a child care facility
who feels helpless and intimidated by a child does great harm to that child by allowing her to

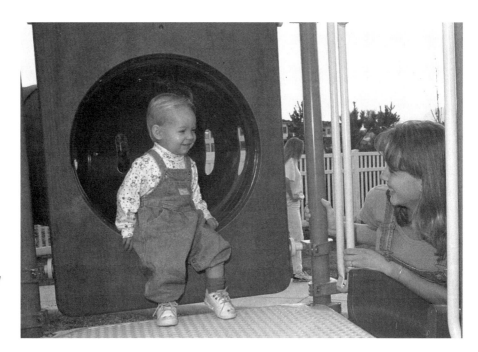

*Healthy emotional
development
hinges on the
development of
basic trust.*

bite, kick, shove, pinch, scratch other children, and destroy shared toys. The caregiver must believe that she has two responsibilities:

1. To befriend the child during noncrisis times and rebuild her feelings of self-esteem
2. To take steps to interrupt outbursts of aggression, and protect other children and the physical environment

The caregiver may need to ask for help from another staff member or administrator, or from the parents. However tempting it may be for adults to make excuses (no one will help me, I'm a single parent, my director is too busy, there is nowhere else for the child to be, psychologists are too expensive), the adult must not stop until she finds the support that is needed. Although it will probably not be necessary to call in local law enforcement for help with a fifty-pound child who is throwing rocks, the caregiver must have confidence that if one strategy for stopping the child from hurting others does not work, then other strategies will be tried until something does work! Although it is rarely appropriate in early childhood settings, the adult must be willing, in a crisis situation, to physically restrain the child as firmly as necessary but as gently as possible.

In dealing with a very difficult child, behavior modification may be an essential and effective tool for regaining a manageable relationship with the child. A reinforcer (token reward) must be selected that is meaningful and desirable to the child; the specific desired behavior goal must be identified in concrete terms; and a schedule of when, how, and under what circumstances the reinforcement will be given should be planned with the child. Reinforcement must always be immediate. As the child makes little steps of progress toward the desired behavior, she is instantly reinforced with a reward (such as a sticker, a plastic disk, or checks on a chart) that can be exchanged at a predetermined number for special privileges or treats.

Behavior modification will be most successful (especially with an older child) if she has enthusiastically agreed to participate in the plan. If the child likes and respects the adult and really wants to change some behaviors and habits she knows are unacceptable, she may be surprisingly willing to participate in a voluntary behavior modification plan, at least during the brief periods in which she is calm and logical. During the entire process of behavior modification, the child must be helped toward the eventual weaning from external control to internal control. She can be told from the very beginning, "Changing bad habits is very, very hard for anyone! These little prizes will help you remember to use words instead of hitting. After a while though, you won't need little prizes anymore. You'll remember to use words so people will like you and want to play with you."

CONTEMPT, MISTRUST

Contempt and mistrust in children sadden and dismay us. The child filled with contempt has so much mistrust of others that she seems to despise everyone. We may find it necessary to backtrack and work on the basic development of trust. Just as a first grader who lacked visual discrimination and vocabulary would need remedial work before she could learn to read, the child who feels contempt must relearn the essential lesson of infancy—to trust others, to believe that adults are reliable, predictable, and accepting—before she can learn to behave appropriately.

A child who feels that she has received a great deal of hurt and unfair treatment in her life will not easily place her trust in adults. Adults will have to earn that trust through consistent fairness and sincere interest in the child's well-being. Adults can facilitate the development of trust in the child by modeling trust. They can find opportunities to place trust in the mistrustful child

Children learn socially acceptable ways to express negative feelings.

in situations in which the child is very likely to succeed and in which a failure to live up to the adult's trust can safely be overlooked.

FITS OF ANGER, TANTRUMS, DEFIANCE

Children who regularly indulge in fits of anger, tantrums, and defiance need to know that the adults who care for them are not cowed by these behaviors, but they also need to know that adults will not explode into their own fits of anger. Angry, defiant behaviors may unconsciously be intended to strike back at adults who are perceived to be enemies. Adults, consequently, must take steps to build a cooperative relationship with the defiant child, to become the child's ally and friend while refusing to participate in inappropriate interactions with the child.

We can help children let go of explosive behaviors by responding matter-of-factly but steadfastly to the child's eruptions. An adult may be forced to remove or restrain the child in extreme circumstances, but the adult can be very sure the child recognizes that there is no anger or punitiveness in those actions; just firmness and resolve. Also, the adult can avoid overreacting to expressions of defiance such as vulgar language or spitting.

No adult wants to be spit at or to see a child spit on others, but our own angry or violent outburst will make the child's problem worse, not better. Instead, a patient but very firm adult might say, "If you need to spit, you may spit in the sink. Spitting in the sink is fine. Spitting on people is not allowed, though. It makes them angry and it could get germs on them. If you spit, you can't play. You'll need to sit here by me until you are sure you are through spitting."

The child needs to learn that defiant tantrums are really a waste of time since they have no effect on the adult. The tantrums will not bring about special favors and they will not succeed in "driving the adult up the wall." Since persistently disruptive behavior is unconsciously intended to hurt others as the child feels she has been hurt, the child may delight in seeing adults frustrated, angry, and helpless.

WITHDRAWN, PASSIVE BEHAVIOR

CYCLICAL SELF-STIMULATION

When a child is overwhelmed by fear, stress, and anxiety, she may withdraw into her own little world. Although most children do things to make themselves feel better from time to time, the withdrawn child may sink into constant self-stimulation. This pattern is referred to as cyclical, since the child repeats the behavior cycle over and over. The cycle may consist of excessive thumb-sucking, nail-biting, hair-twisting, overeating, head-banging, masturbating, or any number of other self-stimulating actions.

Adults frequently find these behaviors very embarrassing and may focus on forcing the child to end the behavior without addressing the cause of the behavior at all. These behaviors tell us the child is feeling too stressed and overwhelmed to participate in usual activities. By focusing on reducing stress in the child's life and drawing the child out into pleasurable, nonthreatening activities, the child may be eased into more active involvement with things and people around her.

REJECTION OF SOCIAL INTERCHANGE

The severely withdrawn child may avoid eye contact, refuse to talk or play, and stay apart from others most of the time. Adults may mistakenly focus all of their guidance efforts on children whose inappropriate behaviors are active and annoying. Teachers, parents, and caregivers may view the child who is a loner as a good child who never bothers anyone. In reality, the child who is a loner may be more at risk emotionally than the difficult, loud, aggressive child. Self-esteem, trust, and a sense of belonging are all essential to building contact with the child who seems to have no interest in others.

INTERNALIZATION OF STRESS

Inhibited children sometimes turn all their bad feelings inward. Fear, anger, and frustration are not expressed; they are just held inside, and they may chip away at the child's sense of competence and self-worth. These children need opportunities to learn that they do not have to be perfect, it is okay to disagree, and they have a right to be who they are. As they develop stronger self-esteem, they will feel more comfortable expressing their feelings and actively standing up for themselves.

Children need opportunities to learn socially acceptable ways to express negative feelings. They need assertive role models and the freedom to say what they feel honestly (but respectfully). Adults should avoid telling children that their feelings are not real or valid by saying such things as, "That scratch doesn't hurt," "There's nothing to cry about," or "You have no reason to be mad!" Children must be allowed to feel what they feel, even though they must also learn to express negative feelings without hurting, harassing, or humiliating others. When children know an acceptable way to express themselves, they are likely to feel much freer about exposing their inner feelings.

DISPLAY OF INEPTNESS AND HOPELESSNESS

Feelings of depression are not the exclusive territory of adolescents and adults. Even very young children can show signs of depression. Overwhelming disruption in the child's daily life may contribute to her listlessness and display of ineptness and hopelessness. These children do not involve themselves in spontaneous play or creative expression. They seem to have no energy. They may sleep too much or too little. They are clearly at risk and need special guidance to rebuild self-esteem and give them the spark of hope that fuels healthy curiosity, spontaneous play, and active involvement with others.

SCREENING FOR DEVELOPMENTAL "RED FLAGS"

All children behave very inappropriately from time to time, no matter how well they seem to be developing and how cooperative, competent, and confident they are generally. Some children, however, behave inappropriately often enough to cause us serious concern. It is essential that we consider the possibility of physical causes for severe, persistent misbehavior. Various cues or signals could be taken as "red flags," or warning indicators, that something may be awry. Parents, teachers, and caregivers should never attempt to diagnose physical ailments or developmental delays. They should, however, watch carefully for indications that a child needs further evaluation by a physician or other expert to rule out or confirm physiological or psychological problems. (See Appendix G for additional resources.)

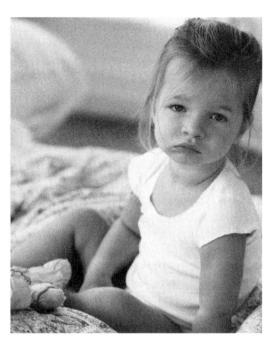

Partial hearing loss can be surprisingly difficult to notice.

CAN HEARING PROBLEMS AFFECT BEHAVIOR?

The ability to hear properly has an important influence on a child's ability to comply with adult instructions. A child who suffers from frequent nasal congestion, ear infections, and sinus drainage is a prime candidate for hearing difficulty. A young child may have occasional bouts of partial hearing loss or long, persistent periods of hearing difficulty due to these upper respiratory problems. Partial hearing loss can be surprisingly difficult for parents, teachers, and caregivers to notice. Since children pay close attention to body language and nonverbal gestures, they may appear to hear and understand more than they really do.

There are, of course, many other possible causes for partial or full loss of hearing as well. Medical evaluation and treatment may, in some cases, restore the child's hearing completely or at least make adults aware that a communication problem exists. Red flags signaling the possibility of a hearing problem include such things as:

- pulling, tugging, poking at, or rubbing the ears.

- slowness in learning to speak compared to age-mates.

- muffled or garbled pronunciation of words.

- consistent failure to follow even simple instructions.

- appearance of being socially isolated in group settings.

- unresponsiveness to group activities such as story reading.

OTHER PHYSICAL CONDITIONS THAT AFFECT BEHAVIOR

Since irritability and discomfort are both likely causes for misbehavior, there are any number of physical illnesses or conditions that could result in behavior changes. Muscular disabilities could hamper a child's ability to carry out tasks that might be expected, or developmental delays could make it impossible for a child to live up to typical adult expectations. Parents, teachers, and caregivers can assist medical personnel in evaluating a child who seems to be displaying signs of difficulty by observing and keeping records of behaviors on a daily basis that seem unusual for a child at a given age.

CAN THE PRESENCE OF BEHAVIORAL PROBLEMS SIGNAL THE POSSIBILITY OF CHILD ABUSE OR NEGLECT?

A very serious potential cause of developmental and behavioral problems can be the presence of abuse or neglect in a child's life. Although virtually any normally developing child can experience a rare incident of inappropriate treatment, children who lead lives filled with abuse and neglect are profoundly affected by that experience, even if they are not maimed or killed. Every aspect of their development is affected: intellectual, physical, social, and emotional (Dean, Malik, Richards, & Stringer, 1986; Finkelhor & Dziuba-Leatherman, 1997; Heineman, 1998; Hoffman-Plotkin & Twentyman, 1984; Ingrassia & McCormick, 1997; Kempe & Kempe, 1978; Lamb, Gaensbauer, Malkin, & Schultz, 1985; National Committee to Prevent Child Abuse, 1998; Wallach, 1997; Wang & Daro, 1998). (See Appendix B for additional resources.)

IS THE NUMBER OF CHILD FATALITIES INCREASING?

In the United States, more than three children die each day as a result of abuse and neglect (Wang & Daro, 1998). The U.S. Advisory Board on Child Abuse and Neglect reported the number of confirmed child abuse fatalities had increased 39 percent between 1985 and 1995 (U.S. Department of Health and Human Services, 1995). According to the National Committee to Prevent Child Abuse (Wang & Daro, 1998), the total number of child abuse and neglect reports has increased nationwide more than 49 percent since 1984. Young children are at the highest risk for abuse. Research suggests most fatalities occur to children under the age of five, with almost half under the age of one. Child abuse ranks as the second leading cause of death, after accidents, for children between one and five years of age (Wang & Daro, 1998).

Wang, C. T., & Daro, D. (1998). *Current trends in child abuse reporting and fatalities: The results of the 1997 Annual Fifty State Survey.* Chicago: National Committee to Prevent Child Abuse.

U.S. Department of Health and Human Services (1995, April). *A nation's shame: Fatal child abuse and neglect in the United States.* Washington, DC: A report of the U.S. advisory board on child abuse and neglect.

HOW AND WHY DO THESE FATALITIES OCCUR?

Between 1993 and 1995, 37% of all fatalities attributed to child maltreatment were the result of neglect, 48% from abuse, and 15% as a result of both forms of maltreatment. Surrounding circumstances related to these fatalities seem to present themselves year after year. According to a 1995 report by Wang and Daro (1998), states reported that substance abuse, by the abuser, was involved in anywhere from 4% to 65% of all substantiated cases. Additionally, 46% of children who died between 1993 and 1995 had prior or recent contact with child protective service (CPS) agencies. Children who have been reported to CPS agencies on more than one occasion should be watched very carefully for indications of recurring abuse (National Committee to Prevent Child Abuse, 1998).

HOW CAN MORE CHILD ABUSE FATALITIES BE PREVENTED?

Communities can help prevent child abuse deaths by fully supporting their child protective service agencies and ensuring the availability of treatment services for potential abusers. Additionally, alcohol and drug treatment services need to be expanded and made more accessible to pregnant and parenting women. Public agencies, however, cannot prevent all fatalities single-handedly. Other formal institutions such as schools, child care centers, hospitals, and all other members of the community must also play an active role in identifying and getting help for families at risk of abusive or neglectful behavior.

Child abuse is against the law. Every state has a designated agency that is mandated by federal law to receive and to investigate reports of suspected child abuse and neglect. Remember, reporting is a means of getting help for a child or family, not just a way to punish abusers. You do not have to prove that child abuse has occurred. That is up to the investigator to determine. To report a suspected case of child abuse, you should notify the designated agency in the state where the child lives. The agency is listed in the telephone directory, usually in the Government Blue Pages under Rehabilitative Services or Children and Family Services. In some areas, it may also be listed in the Yellow Pages. If you have difficulty finding the agency in your community, call your local police department or call the Childhelp USA/IOF Foresters National Child Abuse Hotline, (800) 422-4453 (4-A-CHILD). Childhelp USA/IOF Foresters keeps listings of child protective service agencies across the country.

Abused and neglected children's behaviors tend toward extremes: there seems to be no happy middle ground for these children. They may be diagnosed as learning disabled or they may be compulsive overachievers. They may be hyperactive or lethargic. They may be physically inept weaklings or street-smart, death-defying daredevils. They may either cling relentlessly to others or shun all social interaction. They may appear either dirty and unkempt or rigidly and spotlessly scrubbed, starched, and pressed. They may either defy authority altogether or compulsively try to please everyone at all times in all ways. They may always play the role of victim or brutally victimize others. The one characteristic that is shared by all abused and neglected children is their lacking or stunted sense of self. They do not have that essential component of all fully functional human beings, which is the positive feeling of self-worth that comes with self-esteem.

LOCATING COMMUNITY RESOURCES

Adults caring for children who have persistent misbehavior problems need help. Once possible causes for behavior problems have been identified, a search for appropriate community resources should take place. Families, schools, and child care facilities all have the potential to serve as resources for each other, to share ideas and methods, and to give each other emotional support and encouragement. Parents can learn a great deal from teachers and caregivers, and teachers and caregivers can learn a great deal from parents. Additionally, almost any community setting offers a wealth of potential resources such as the following (see listings at the end of this chapter for organizations, Internet addresses, and telephone numbers):

- The medical community—physicians, psychologists, and other therapists
- Governmental agencies—child protective service workers, child care licensing specialists, health departments, social workers, Head Start, and other publicly funded programs
- Religious entities—churches, synagogues, priests, ministers, counselors, congregational support groups
- Nonprofit organizations—self-help groups, associations focused on specific problems such as diabetes or hyperactivity, and parenting classes or seminars
- Treatment centers—special schools, testing clinics, or therapy facilities such as schools for the blind or physical therapy facilities for such diseases as cerebral palsy
- Public school systems—educational programs for exceptional children, early intervention programs for children at risk, school psychologists, and counselors
- World Wide Web connections—in ever chapter of this text you will find Internet starting points for early childhood development care and education

Parents often need help in overcoming feelings of pain and denial when they discover that their child has developmental, physical, or behavioral problems. They may hold an idealized image of their child and resist the notion that their child is, in fact, human and imperfect, having both strengths and weaknesses. They may need to be reminded that there is no shame in having a special need or an imperfection. There is only shame in not dealing with reality and not taking steps to help the child function as well as possible. Many potentially disabling conditions can be prevented or alleviated if they are identified and treated during infancy or earliest childhood, so early screening for developmental problems has special importance. Resource lists in the appendices offer many sources of free or inexpensive help for parents, teachers, and caregivers.

MEETING ADULT NEEDS

Children definitely have needs, but adults have needs, too. Caring for children is demanding, exhilarating, frustrating, and rewarding, but it is also exhausting. We can best care for children if our own social, emotional, physical, and intellectual needs have been met. We must set aside time for our own rest and recreation, and we must be able to admit to ourselves at times that we are not able to deal with children in a positive and productive manner. If children are dealt with in a caring and respectful manner most of the time, they will be likely to cope well and respect our own need when we say, "I'm too frustrated and angry to talk about this right now. I just want to be alone for a few minutes."

> *Ever tried?*
> *Ever failed?*
> *No matter.*
> *Try again.*
> *Fail again.*
> *Fail better.*
>
> Samuel Beckett (Knowlson, 1996)

We can be patient and reasonable with ourselves, recognizing that we, too, are imperfect. It is easy to sit down and think carefully about an ideal response to a misbehaving child, but it is not so easy to respond perfectly when the response is instantaneous and in the heat of conflict with that child. It is important for adults to be supportive, calm, respectful, and consistent, but it is most important for them to do something! Children must know that adults care enough to do something, even if it is not the best possible thing to do.

When we attempt to change our ways of dealing with children, we go through the same stages of learning that children go through when they learn new behaviors. For example, a toddler who has no concept of toileting will simply show no awareness when she makes a puddle on the floor. When she has developed a recognition of the desired behavior but lacks practice carrying it out, she will make a puddle, look down, smile sweetly, and say, "Go potty!" Of course, it will be too late to go to the potty then. Finally, when she has fully developed both the awareness and the skill to carry out the new behavior, she will notice the sensation of a full bladder and do what needs to be done to successfully use the toilet.

Adult caregivers have emotional needs, too. A strong, caring support structure among coworkers helps each individual cope with stress and fatigue that can lead to emotional burnout.

We go through that same process. At first, we may be totally unaware of the negative, destructive, and hurtful things we say or do with youngsters in the name of disciplining them. As we discover more productive and effective ways to guide them, we begin, for the first time, to hear ourselves saying or doing negative things. We feel frustration because we only seem to become aware of these actions after we have done them. We become aware of our inappropriate actions, but only after it is too late. Gradually, however, with persistence and practice, we are able to anticipate and respond more skillfully and appropriately. Eventually, our new behaviors become so natural to us that we can behave as we wish with almost no thought or effort.

Positive child guidance is a tool that can be used to help mature, caring adults teach young children the skills they need to lead productive, happy lives.

> *Treat people as if they are what they ought to be, and you help them to become what they are capable of being.*
> *Johann Wolfgang von Goethe, German poet, 1749–1832 (von Goethe, 1995)*

POINTS TO REMEMBER

- At the heart of almost any behavior lies the desire to acquire something to meet some need.

- Dreikurs proposed that mistaken goals cause children to misbehave to get attention, gain control, get revenge, or remove themselves.

- Seeing children as lovable, capable, and worthwhile supports the growth of self-esteem.

- The no-lose method of conflict resolution is a strategy for avoiding power struggles between adults and children.

- The destructive or aggressive child must know that she will be stopped and that others' rights will be protected.

- Children who regularly indulge in fits of anger, tantrums, and defiance need to know that the adults who care for them will not explode into their own fits of anger.

- Adults must recognize their own needs and imperfections in order to be effective in child guidance.

PRACTICAL APPLICATION

"THANK HEAVEN FOR SARAH"

Sarah taught and cared for a small group of children in her own home. She felt strong commitment to her work and believed that she made a difference in children's lives. She took great pride in operating her home-based child care program in a professional and responsible manner. She bristled at the term *baby-sitter*, so she referred to herself as a teacher, because that is what she believed she was with the babies, toddlers, and preschoolers in her care.

Robert was three. Sarah had been caring for him for several months and had become very concerned about his behavior. He always seemed to be in conflict with the other children, and he never seemed to listen or follow even the simplest of Sarah's directions. Sarah began to wonder if Robert had some problem that was causing him to misbehave. She watched him carefully and wrote down her observations about when, where, and why he seemed to get into trouble.

Sarah began to suspect that Robert could not hear as well as he should. She noticed that while all the other children ran to the window each morning when they heard the garbage truck, Robert either did not respond at all or was the last to look up and run to the window. One day,

Within every child is an adult in the making—and within every adult is a child who has just gotten older.

Sarah stood quietly behind Robert and said very softly, "Robert, it's time for lunch." Although other children quickly responded, Robert never even looked up from his puzzle.

Sarah approached Robert's parents about the problem on several occasions. She said, "I'm not an expert in hearing problems, but I'm wondering if Robert could have a hearing problem. Has his pediatrician ever tested his hearing?" Robert's father said, "That's ridiculous. He hears whatever he wants to hear. He just chooses to ignore grown-ups most of the time." Robert's mother said, "His doctor hasn't ever mentioned a problem and I don't see any reason to think anything is wrong."

Sarah continued caring for and working with Robert, but she still had a nagging feeling that his behavior was just not up to par for a child who seemed very bright in other ways. She noticed that his relationship with his parents had deteriorated and that he was almost constantly in trouble with adults or other children. Finally, she set an appointment to sit down privately to talk with Robert's parents.

Sarah, with kindness and respect in her voice, said "I know that you have to do whatever you think is right for Robert, but I have to do what is right for me and for the other children in my care. I have become very attached to Robert. He is so full of creative energy. However, much of the time, his behavior is out of control and I don't know if I am doing the right thing for him. I worry that he may not be able to hear, and I wonder if that is part of the problem. I just don't feel comfortable caring for him without some kind of screening to at least rule out the possibility of a hearing problem."

Robert's father blurted out, "Fine! We'll just find someone else to care for him. We are not about to set out on some wild goose chase, looking for problems that don't exist." Sarah responded, "I understand. You have every right to do only what you believe is the best thing for your child. I'm sure that I would do the same myself. I need you to understand, though, that I am having real difficulty with Robert's behavior, and I just don't feel comfortable caring for him if I'm not sure I'm doing the right thing for him and for the other children. I am willing to accept your decision, and I'll do anything I can to help with the transition to a different child care situation. The important thing is for each of us to feel comfortable with what we do."

Robert's mother was not eager to find new child care for Robert. She really liked the way Sarah cared for the children. Robert's mother had several long discussions with her child's doctor and with her husband, and finally convinced her husband that Robert should have his hearing tested in a medical clinic that specialized in that kind of thing.

A few weeks later, Robert's father stopped by to talk to Sarah. He said, "You know, I was so sure that nothing was wrong with Robert's hearing that I really resented you insisting on a hearing test. I can't believe it, but the doctor says he has a seventy-five percent hearing loss in one ear and a slight loss in the other. I just didn't know."

Sarah responded, "I could have been right or I could have been wrong. I'm no expert on hearing, but I do appreciate knowing more about why he may have been having such a hard time behaving. Thank you for being so tolerant of my questions and concerns. I think we can all work together now much more effectively to help Robert get his act together."

As Robert's father turned to leave, he patted Robert's head and said softly, "Thank heaven for Sarah."

DISCUSSION QUESTIONS

1. Do you think Sarah's actions were within her role as a caregiver?
2. Do you think Sarah went too far in insisting that Robert's hearing be checked?

3. How do you think this story would have ended if nothing had been wrong with Robert's hearing?
4. Specifically, what things did Sarah say or do that made her assertiveness more tolerable to Robert's parents?
5. What would you have done?

RELATED READINGS

American Academy of Pediatrics. (1995). *Caring for your school-age child: Ages 5–12.* New York: Bantam Books.

American Association for Protecting Children (AAPC). (1988). *Highlights of official child neglect and abuse reporting,* (1986). Denver, CO: American Humane Association.

Anderson, M. P. (2001). ACT against violence. *Young Children 56*(4), 60–61.

NAEYC initiated a national campaign—ACT Against Violence—using public service announcements on radio and television to advocate the message that adults model and teach what children know about violence. Information is provided in brochures and community-based training programs.Conte, J, R. (1986). A look at child sexual abuse. Chicago: National Committee to Prevent Child Abuse (NCPCA).

Bakley, S. (2001). Through the lens of sensory integration: A different way of analyzing challenging behavior. Young *Children 56*(6), 70–76.

Explains normal sensory integration processes and lists possible signs of sensory integration disorder. Provides techniques for teachers to use in working with children with sensory integration problems who feel out of control or overwhelmed.

Brophy, J. (1996). *Teaching problem students.* New York: Guilford.

Bullock, J. R. (1997). Children without friends. In E. N. Junn, & C. Boyatzis (Eds.), *Annual editions: Child growth and development 97/98* (4th ed.). New York: McGraw-Hill. (Original work published in *Childhood Education,* winter 1992.).

Describes the sociometric status of different kinds of children—the popular, rejected, and neglected—and the implications of not having friends. Suggestions are given for teachers to identify and help children without friends.

Conte, J. R. (1986). *A look at child sexual abuse.* Chicago: National Committee to Prevent Child Abuse (NCPCA).

Douglas, H. (1991). Assessing violent couples. *Families in Society 72*(9), 525–535.

Elkind, D. (1987, September). From our president: Children who bite. *Young Children, 42*(6), 2.

This article suggests ways to identify children who might bite and how to work with parents to prevent biting.

Finkelhor, D. (1986). *A sourcebook on child sexual abuse.* Beverly Hills, CA: Sage.

Finkelhor, D. (1994). Answers to important questions about the scope and nature of child sexual abuse. *Future of Children, 4*(2). Los Altos, CA: David and Lucille Packard Foundation.

Finkelhor, D., & Dziuba-Leatherman, J. (1997). Victimization of children. In E. N. Junn, & C. Boyatzis (Eds.), *Annual editions: Child growth and development 97/98* (4th Ed.). New York: McGraw-Hill. (Original work published in *American Psychologist*, March 1994.)

This article gives statistics showing that children are more often victimized than are adults. Victimology of childhood falls into three broad categories: pandemic victimization (e.g., assault by siblings, parents, peers), acute victimization (e.g., physical abuse), and extraordinary victimization (e.g., homicide). The authors call for more research and theory on childhood victimology using a developmental perspective.

Finkelhor, D., & Williams, L. (1988). *Nursery crimes: Sexual abuse in day care.* Newbury Park, CA: Sage.

Flynn, C. (1996). Regional differences in spanking experiences and attitudes: A comparison of northeastern and southern college students. *Journal of Family Violence, 11*(1), 59–80.

Fredriksen, K. I., & Scharlach, A. E. (1999, April). Employee family care responsibilities. *Family Relations, 48*(2), 189–196.

Explores family care responsibilities for children, and for ill and disabled adults.

Gallo, N. (1997). Why spanking takes the spunk out of kids. In E. N. Junn & C. Boyatzis (Eds.), *Annual editions: Child growth and development 97/98* (4th ed.). New York: McGraw-Hill. (Original work published in *Child*, March/April 1989.)

Spanking is a very common form of discipline, but is it effective? Perhaps more important, does it do short-term or lasting psychological harm? Nick Gallo addresses these issues and offers alternative techniques to help people realize that discipline does not mean spanking, but it does mean instilling self-control in the child.

Goodman, G., & Rosenberg, M. (1987). The child witness to family violence: Clinical and legal considerations. In D. Sonkin (Ed.), *Domestic violence on trial: Psychological and legal dimensions of family violence.* New York: Springer.

Gronlund, G. (1992). Coping with ninja turtle play in my classroom. *Young Children, 48*(1), 21–25.

Suggests ways adults can help children construct their own understanding of violence and aggression related to superhero play.

Heineman, R. V. (1998). *The abused child psychodynamic: Understanding and treatment.* New York: Guilford.

The book traces the interplay of neurobiological and psychological facets of behavior to show how abuse derails normal development and how psychodynamic psychotherapy can reestablish emotional connections. Chapters highlight issues involved when working with children who have been physically, sexually, and emotionally abused, exploring memory and disclosure, dissociation and externalization, and the relationship between action and spoken language.

Hilton, N. Z. (1992). Battered women's concerns about their children witnessing wife assault. *Journal of Interpersonal Violence, 7*, 77–86.

Ingersoll, B. D. (1997). *Daredevils and daydreamers: New perspectives on attention-deficit/ hyperactivity disorder.* New York: Doubleday.

Ingrassia, M., & McCormick, J. (1997). Why leave children with bad parents? In E. N. Junn, & C. Boyatzis (Eds.), *Annual editions: Child growth and development 97/98* (4th ed.). New York: McGraw-Hill. (Original work published *in Newsweek*, April 25, 1994.)

> *In 1993 alone, there were one million confirmed cases of child neglect and abuse in the United States. Yet, in many states, the child welfare system often strives to keep families intact rather than put children in the care of foster parents (who came into greater demand in the late 1980s when crack use increased dramatically). The authors raise difficult issues about America's care for children at risk.*

Jaffe, P., Wolfe, D., & Wilson, S. (1990). *Children of battered women.* Newbury Park, CA: Sage.

Kostelnik, M. J., Whiren, A. P., & Stein, L. C. (1986). Living with he-man. Managing superhero fantasy play. *Young Children, 41*(4), 3–9.

> *Explores reasons for superhero play (a kind of dramatic play) and discusses how such activity relates to children's development. Gives suggestions for teachers to redirect this play.*

Ladd, R. E. (Ed.). (1996). *Children's rights re-visioned: Philosophical readings.* Belmont, CA: Wadsworth.

> *This anthology helps students gain philosophical understanding as they pursue some provocative issues surrounding children's rights in our society.*

Landau, S., & McAninch, C. (1997). Young children with attention deficits. In E. N. Junn, & C. Boyatzis (Eds.), *Annual editions: Child growth and development 97/98* (4th ed.). New York: McGraw-Hill. (Original work published in *Young Children*, May 1993.)

> *Attention-deficit hyperactivity disorder (ADHD) is a frequently misunderstood, complex disorder. This review article describes ADHD, its possible causes, treatments, and the effects of the disorder for children in the classroom setting.*

Leach, P. (1996, July 9). Spanking: A shortcut to nowhere [www document]. http://cnet.unb.ca/orgs/prevention_cruelty/spank.html.NoSpankingPage.http://wwwocci.net/~rcox/nospan.html.

Lung, C. T., & Daro, D. (1996). *Current trends in child abuse reporting and fatalities: The results of the 1995 annual fifty state survey.* Chicago: National Committee to Prevent Child Abuse.

McCurdy, K., & Daro, D. (1995). *Current trends in child abuse reporting and fatalities: The results of the 1994 annual fifty state survey.* Chicago: National Committee to Prevent Child Abuse.

NAEYC. (1998). What would you do? Real-life ethical problems early childhood professionals face. "How do you know if you should suspect child Aabuse?" *Young Children 53*(4), 52–54.

> *Uses NAEYC's Code of Ethical Conduct to answer the question: "How do you know if you should suspect child abuse?"*

National Committee to Prevent Child Abuse. (1993). *Think you know something about child abuse?* Chicago: Author.

National Committee to Prevent Child Abuse. (1998). *Child abuse and neglect statistics.* Chicago: Author.

Nunnelley, J. C., & Fields, T. (1999). Anger, dismay, guilt, anxiety-the realities and roles in reporting child abuse. *Young Children 54*(5), 74–79.

Calls on early childhood professionals to take seriously their need to be active and knowledgeable about child protection. The authors urge ongoing staff training on legal responsibilities, school policies, signs of abuse, and strategies for coping.

Oyemade, U. J., & Washington, V. (1989). Drug abuse prevention begins in early childhood (and is much more than a matter of instructing young children about drugs). *Young Children 44*(5), 6–12.

Presents the underlying causes of drug abuse, and in contrast, the long-term positive social consequences of good programs for young children.

Rief, S. F. (1993). *How to reach and teach ADD/ADHD children.* West Nyack, NY: The Center for Applied Research in Education.

Rice, K. F., & Sanoff, M. K. (1998). Growing strong together: Helping mothers and their children affected by substance abuse. *Young Children 53*(1), 28–33.

Presents issues related to mothers who are substance abusers (addiction, recovery, impact on children, and how to provide support). Includes a short bibliography of children's books on substance abuse.

Roach, M. A., Orsmond, G. I., & Barratt, M. S. (1999, September). Mothers and fathers of children with Down syndrome: Parental stress and involvement in childcare. *American Journal on Mental Retardation, 104*(5), 422–436.

Parents of children with Down syndrome encounter special difficulties finding child care, meeting their exceptional child's needs (distractibility, inappropriate behavior), and meeting their own needs (depression, health problems, role-restriction).

Ruben, D. (1996, September). Should you spank? *Parenting*, 136–141.

Rubin, K. H., LeMare, L. J., & Lollis, S. (1990). Social withdrawal in childhood: Developmental pathways to peer rejection. In S. R. Asher, & J. D. Coie (Eds.), *Peer rejection in childhood* (pp. 217–249). New York: Cambridge University Press.

Samalin, N., & Whitney, C. (1995, May). What's wrong with spanking? *Parents, 70*(5), 35–36.

Salovitz, B., & Keys, D. (1988). Is child protective service still a service? *Protecting Children, 5*(2), 17–23.

Sedlak, A. (1996). *Early findings from the third national incidence study of child abuse and neglect: 1988.* Rockville, MD: Westat, Inc.

Straus, M. (1995). *Beating the devil out of them: Corporal punishment in American families.* New York: Lexington Books.

Straus, M. A., & Gelles, R. (1990). *Physical violence in American families.* New Brunswick, NJ: Transaction.

Stephens, K., Miller, K., Marsh, M., Buffin, L., & Duffy, R. (1996, September–October). When children are difficult. Beginnings workshop. *Child Care Information Exchange, 111*, 43–50, 55–62.

Thompson, S. H. (1998). Working with children of substance-abusing parents. *Young Children 53*(1), 34–37.

Explains the effect a parent's substance abuse has on children and how early child professionals can help the children.

Thoringer, D., Krivackska, J., Laye-McDonough, M., Jarrison, L., Vincent, O., & Hedlund, A. (1988). Prevention of child sexual abuse: An analysis of issues, educational programs and research findings. *School Psychology Review, 17*(4), 614–636.

Turecki, S. (1989). *The difficult child.* New York: Bantam Books.

U.S. Department of Health and Human Services, Children's Bureau. (1997). *National study of protective, preventive and reunification services delivered to children and their families.* Washington, DC: U.S. Government Printing Office.

Wang, C. T., & Daro, D. (1998). *Current trends in child abuse reporting and fatalities: The results of the 1997 annual fifty state survey.* Chicago: National Committee to Prevent Child Abuse.

Wodrich, D. L. (1994). *What every parent wants to know: Attention deficit hyperactivity disorder.* Baltimore: Paul H. Brookes Publishing Company.

HELPFUL WEB SITES

http://www.childabuse.org   Prevent Child Abuse America , an early leader in using computer networking to support child abuse prevention.

http://child.cornell.edu/army/army.html   Army Family Advocacy Programs. Major innovator in using prevention as an institutional focus in child abuse prevention. Called on Cornell University to build resources for marketing the prevention agenda.

http://www.americanhumane.org/cpmain.html   American Humane Association. Through its Children's Division, has worked for over a century to help improve and enhance public child welfare systems and private child-focused agencies in their responses to the plight of abused and neglected children.

http://www.ncac-hsv.org/   National Children's Advocacy Center. Focused on prevention and treatment options for physically and sexually abused children and their families. Uses a child-centered, family-focused approach.

http://child-abuse.com/   Child Abuse Prevention Network. A national collaborative project, with special private access services for members.

http://child.cornell.edu/   Child Abuse Prevention Network. Child abuse information and resources provided by the Family Life Development Center at Cornell University.

http://www.ag.uiuc.edu/~disaster/teacher/teacher.html   Children, Stress, and Natural Disasters: A Guide for Teachers covers what children may be experiencing, their responses to disasters, implications for teachers, and school activities and precautions related to disasters.

http://www.calib.com/nccanch/   National Clearinghouse on Child Abuse and Neglect Information. Information on child abuse and neglect in the United States. The Clearinghouse is a national resource for professionals seeking information on the prevention, identification, and treatment of child abuse and neglect, and related child welfare issues.

http://www.ndacan.cornell.edu   National Data Archive on Child Abuse and Neglect. The central data archive for researchers in child abuse and neglect in the United States. Our partners in providing Internet working skills for child abuse prevention.

http://www.childcarelaw.com   Child Care Law Center Administration for Children and Families.

http://www.familysupportamerica.org/content/home.htm   Family Support America promotes family support to strengthen families by identifying and connecting individuals and organizations that have contact with families by providing technical assistance, training and education, conferences, and publications, and by promoting the voice of families.

http://www.abanet.org/child   American Bar Association Center on Children and the Law. Key collaborators with Cornell's Child Abuse Prevention Network in building special Internet resources for legal problems in the field of child maltreatment.

http://www.activeparenting.com/   Active Parenting is a publishing company producing videos and materials for professionals in parent education, parent involvement, teacher-in-service, loss, and self-esteem for children.

 http://chadd.org/   Child Attention Deficit Hyperactivity Disorder (C.H.A.D.D.) support organization for families coping with ADD/ADHD.

For additional information on positive child guidance, visit our Web site at
http://www.earlychilded.delmar.com

Chapter 9
Taking a New Look at Children

OBJECTIVES

After reading this chapter, you should be able to:

- Identify personal biases that affect guidance.
- Recognize the difference between objective and subjective observations.
- List effective observation strategies.
- Use observations for prescriptive guidance.
- Identify components of the observation sequence.

To guide children effectively, we must become skillful observers.

IDENTIFYING PERSONAL BIASES

Gilda is a bright, gregarious ball of energy. When she was in kindergarten, she popped out of bed every morning before the sun was up because she loved going to school each day. Her teacher, Mr. Costa, seemed to really like her. He often invited her to help with classroom chores like feeding the goldfish or passing out napkins for snack. Since she learned concepts very quickly, he encouraged her to help other children, a responsibility she took very seriously. Gilda liked pretending that she was a teacher, and the younger children thrived on her persistent tutoring. Whenever anyone asked her what she wanted to be when she grew up, she always answered quickly, "A schoolteacher just like Mr. Costa!"

During Gilda's first day of first grade, she eagerly tried to get the attention of her new teacher, Mrs. Redwing, and jumped up to help pass out papers. Mrs. Redwing reprimanded Gilda for getting up out of her desk without asking and said, "Please stop asking me questions and just sit quietly and listen." Mrs. Redwing thought, "Oh, no, another hyperactive kid. That's all I need."

Over a period of time, Gilda has become impatient and unhappy. She cries in the morning and tells her father that she does not want to go to school anymore. Mrs. Redwing is upset, too. She is becoming more and more frustrated with Gilda's behavior, which eventually has become disruptive, and at times, even defiant. Mrs. Redwing has become especially exasperated with Gilda's attempts to help other children do their work whenever they have trouble, an action Mrs. Redwing considers a kind of "cheating."

One day, Mr. Costa and Mrs. Redwing are sitting in the teacher's lounge drinking coffee. Mr. Costa says, "How is Gilda doing this year? I really miss her . . . what a terrific little girl she is." Mrs. Redwing chokes on her coffee and sputters, "Gilda? You've got to be kidding! She drives me absolutely up the wall."

How is it possible for two people to see the same child's behavior so differently? We see children differently because we are different. Everything that we perceive with our senses (eyes, ears, and so on) is filtered through layers on layers of our own personal views. Our **biases** are these sets of beliefs, values, and assumptions that develop from our upbringing, our past experiences, and our personal philosophy of life.

Mr. Costa responds favorably to Gilda's energy and spontaneity because she reminds him of himself when he was younger. He values creativity so he is delighted by Gilda's bright mind. In contrast, because of her very strict upbringing, Mrs. Redwing learned early in life to suppress any fidgety impulses she had, so she finds it particularly annoying to deal with Gilda's chattering and bounciness, behaviors her parents would never have tolerated. These behaviors strike Mrs. Redwing as rude and reckless, even though she can remember resenting her parents' rigidity toward her when she was a child.

RESPONDING MORE OBJECTIVELY TO INDIVIDUAL CHILDREN

It is inevitable that some children will be more appealing than others to any given adult. Gender, culture, age, experiences, and temperament all affect our biases and shape our perceptions. Our own personality and style cannot be perfectly matched to the needs of every child; however, we can at least be honest about our bias and respectful in our treatment of children, regardless of their differences. Within families, parents sometimes admit that one of their own children seems easier to understand and manage while another child's behavior seems totally incomprehensible. In group settings, an adult may have difficulty admitting that he or she feels more comfortable with children who are small or large, male or female, black or white, rich or poor.

In order to respond more effectively to children's behaviors, we must focus on our own areas of bias. What preconceived notions do I have about children? Do I expect certain behaviors or motivations from children based on ethnic, gender, or appearance differences? How can I focus on who an individual child really is rather than on the stereotypes I associate with generalized groups or categories of people? Do I tend to have favorite and least favorite children? How do I respond differently to them? How can I be more objective?

One way to increase objectivity is to consciously separate facts from opinions. What do I actually **perceive** (through looking, listening, touching, tasting, and smelling), and what do I interpret intuitively based on my knowledge, experience, and/or bias? By sorting through our own thinking processes to separate facts from opinions, we can more accurately focus on actual child behaviors and scrutinize our interpretations of the meaning of those actions.

If Mrs. Redwing had separated the facts from the opinions in her own observations, she might have seen Gilda differently. For example:

Objective Observations (Mr. Costa and Mrs. Redwing both agree that these are accurate facts): Gilda talks frequently; begins tasks quickly; completes work before others in class; is active and quick in physical movements; expresses interest in the progress of classmates.

Mr. Costa's Interpretations: Gilda is very capable in verbal communications; she is a competent, bright student; she is enthusiastic about her schoolwork; she has leadership potential; she cares intensely about others.

Mrs. Redwing's Interpretations: Gilda ignores the teacher and class rules about talking; she rushes through her work because she does not take it seriously enough; she is overactive; she worries about the affairs of other children when that is none of her business.

When one's opinions are stated separately from observable facts and those opinions are clearly labeled as "subjective interpretation," then it is much easier to recognize and deal with personal bias. If we trick ourselves into believing that our opinions are objective facts, then we lose an opportunity to see children as they really are. We can consciously learn to be more objective in our thinking.

For example, the following observation is filled with opinions: "Erik angrily stomped into the kitchen trying to pick a fight with someone. He taunted his sister and hurt her feelings just to see her cry. He hoped she would hit him so he would have an excuse to get her in trouble." These statements are pure fantasy. We cannot see into Erik's head to look at his intentions or hear his thoughts.

What we can actually see and hear is that Erik "stomped into the kitchen. He looked around with a frown on his face. He pointed to his sister's sandwich and said, 'Yuk, are you going to eat that gooey mess?' His sister began to cry and threatened to hit Erik. Erik said, 'If you hit me, I'll tell mom.'" What we may interpret is that Erik seemed irritable, unhappy, and in a mood to agitate his sister.

To be objective, we must focus on the things we actually see and hear.

The first opinionated description tempts us to punish Erik for his obnoxious behavior because we assume we know why he behaved the way he did. The second, more objective way of reporting Erik's behavior, reminds us that we do not know everything that is going on in Erik's mind and heart. Objective observation encourages us to look further for reasons for actions and to better understand troublesome behavior.

THE OBSERVATION SEQUENCE

To be effective in working with children, we must become skilled observers so that we can constantly improve the quality of the care and education we provide. Our ongoing observations should result in concrete plans and changes in the curriculum and environment. Child guidance is much more an art than a science.

There is no clear-cut recipe for handling children that works for all children in all circumstances, but with careful observation, the adult can gather the information needed to make intelligent decisions and to select appropriate methods to prevent or respond to various problems. Later, the adult can observe to evaluate how effective the chosen guidance technique has been in solving the problem.

HOW OBSERVATION SUPPORTS POSITIVE GUIDANCE

In order for any effort at resolving a behavior problem to be effective, it must be well matched to the child's ability and frame of mind as well as to the circumstances surrounding the behavior. Does the child appear to be feeling angry and destructive or just bored and silly? Is the behavior habitual or a rare event? Is the child capable of benefiting from verbal reminders or is direct physical redirection required? What actually is the problem? When, where, and why does it occur? These are all questions that should be answered through careful observation.

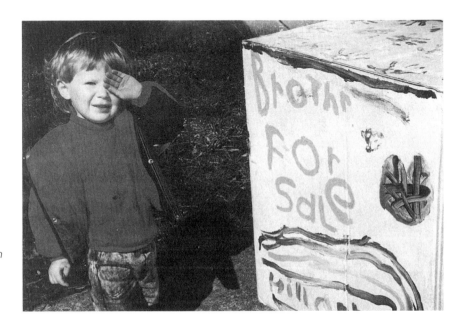

What observations can you make from this picture? (Hint: His big sister painted the box and he is not happy.)

WHAT DO I NEED TO GET STARTED?

There are many excellent checklists, kits, and observational instruments (tests) available commercially to assist early childhood professionals in observing children. For most parents, caregivers, and preschool teachers, however, the most useful record-keeping tool (and definitely the least expensive) is a simple pocket-sized spiral notepad and a pencil. If paper and pencil are available whenever something interesting occurs, it will be a great deal easier to get something written down. No record-keeping instrument of any kind is of value if it stays in a desk drawer or a file cabinet.

With a little pocket notepad, an anecdote can be described before the details are forgotten, tidbits can be added regularly to a running account, or some type of sampling checklist can be maintained. It is easy for us to think, "I don't need to write this down. I'm sure I'll remember it." But then, of course, we forget whatever it was that we were so sure we would remember.

HOW WILL I USE MY OBSERVATIONS?

Observations can be just for fun. Parents love observing their children, telling grandparents hilarious stories about the things the toddler has done or clever things the preschooler has said. Many families treasure photographs showing their children's changes in size and appearance over the years. Educators can enrich families' lives by providing information, photographs, anecdotes, and child-made keepsakes showing children's friendships, accomplishments, field trips, and interests. Many early educators (especially those caring for infants and toddlers) collect anecdotes, pictures, and other items throughout the year, then present each individual child's family with a scrapbook that will help the child and family remember the events and activities of that year. Scrapbooks are a terrific way for adults to support the development of children's self-esteem. Photographs and mementos remind the child how much he is valued by parents and educators who care for him.

Observations should routinely be used by parents and educators to determine developmentally appropriate activities for children. Is the child eagerly engaged in the toy, book, or activity? Or is he looking bored? The activity may not offer a challenge anymore. Does he seem frustrated? The game may be too complicated for his developmental level. Is the group of preschoolers fidgeting and misbehaving during story time? The story may be too long or not lively enough to hold their interest at that age.

Most important for the purposes of this book, observations must be used to lead early educators and parents through the daily process of positive child guidance. Positive child guidance is a problem-solving method. Adults observe how children are behaving at a given moment, figure out why they are behaving that way, and determine supportive methods to help the child become more responsible and self-disciplined. **Positive child guidance cannot succeed without effective and ongoing child observations.** It takes concentrated effort and practice to develop keen observation skills.

Interpreting observations is the process of **inferring meaning** from what has actually been sensed (seen, heard, touched, tasted, or smelled). In order to interpret what has been observed, one has to rely on a knowledge of child development in general as well as of the unique development of an individual child. Additionally, one can rely on firsthand experience with other children as well as with the individual child in question. All of this means we should take what we sense at the present time and mull it over using all of our past knowledge and experience to create new ideas about why the child may need to behave as he does.

Looking back over observation notes can be surprisingly enlightening. Children grow and change so quickly that we may be startled to look back at our notes about little Bronwyn and see that only three months ago, she cried and clung to us when other children were around. Now, she confidently approaches others to initiate play. By seeing a child's progress over time, we can make better sense of the child's immediate behavior, and know what help and guidance the child needs in order to behave more appropriately.

Personal bias must be kept in check while interpreting one's observations. Observation records, particularly objective checklists, may provide convincing evidence that our intuitive assumptions about a particular child have simply been wrong. Interpreting observations also gives us an opportunity to see things from the child's point of view. We may be annoyed with a child for interrupting our conversations, but after observing him carefully, realize that he really deserves to be included more in adult interactions and just needs to be taught how to join a conversation politely.

HOW DOES MY OBSERVATION BECOME A PLAN?

In a doctor's office, a patient is seen and observation records are written into a chart. The observations of the physician are then carefully interpreted (diagnosed): what is the meaning of the rash? . . . of the fever? . . . of the pain in the left foot? Then, most important, a plan is formulated (a prescription) to remedy the problem. The doctor prescribes bedrest or an antibiotic. We prescribe five minutes away from an activity, an understanding, heart-to-heart talk about hurting people's feelings, or a change in our own behavior toward the child by giving more positive attention or more developmentally appropriate activities.

WHAT IF MY PLAN DOES NOT WORK?

After a plan is formulated, the next step is action. Some adults take a fatalistic attitude toward children's misbehavior. They think children will not change and consequently do not bother doing anything other than complain about their inappropriate or immature behaviors. Young children are avid learners. They learn new habits much more easily than older children or adults. They just need time, effort, encouragement, and a great deal of practice to master the social skills and control of impulses they need to be responsible, cooperative group members.

Sometimes, even if the action we attempt does not really work very well, the simple fact that we are focused on the child's problem (and care enough to try to resolve it) may stimulate the child's own awareness of the problem and commitment to correct it. It will be very therapeutic for the child to see evidence from our actions that "I care about you. I am willing to make a real effort to help you learn to use words rather than fists to express your feelings. I won't give up on you."

As long as the action is positive and respectful of the child, it is far more important for us to formulate a plan and do something than to worry about being right every time. Perfectionists are often so paralyzed by their fear of making mistakes that they never get around to doing anything. Children can learn valuable lessons from our handling of our own mistakes. They can learn that everyone makes mistakes from time to time and that admitting mistakes is nothing to be ashamed of. We could set a good example by saying, "Joshua, I asked you to hold my hand on our walk to help you remember to stay on the sidewalk where it's safe. I made a mistake. I didn't think about how that might make you feel like a baby. Let's think of a different way to help you be safe."

HOW CAN I BE SURE MY PLAN IS WORKING?

Is what we are doing effective? In the evaluation phase, we make a complete circle and come back to observing. The only way we can be sure if we were on target in our first observation, interpretation, plan, and resulting action is to observe again and look for indications that our plan is or is not working. If it is working, we can relax and go on to the next problem. If it is not, we return to square one, collect more information through observation, and develop a new and improved plan of action. This cycle repeats until we successfully hit a plan that works (or the child outgrows the behavior, becomes the responsibility of the next teacher, or gets married and moves to another town).

OBSERVATION STRATEGIES

Researchers use carefully orchestrated strategies to collect objective data. Adults who care for young children rarely need such formal methodology; they simply need a workable plan for finding out the "what, when, where, and why" of children's problem behaviors so that they can respond effectively and appropriately. The following sections describe some useful methods for keeping track and making sense of puzzling or upsetting behaviors (Barko, 1997; Bentzen, 1997; Billman & Sherman, 1997; Bredekamp & Copple, 1997; Green & Stafford, 1997; Harms & Clifford, 1998; McLean, Bailey, & Wolery, 1997; Mindes, Ireton, & Mardell-Czudnowski, 1996).

WHAT IS AN ANECDOTAL RECORD?

An anecdotal record is an attempt to record in detail a specific episode that is of particular interest or concern. A specific event takes place that catches the attention of the adult. As soon as possible, the adult writes a narrative account; he tells the story of the event. He describes all of the pertinent details that he can recall such as what he actually saw, heard, or otherwise perceived with his senses. He will include verbatim quotes whenever possible to further clarify the interaction. Any personal opinions or interpretations will be set apart and clearly identified as observer's comments by such phrases as "It appeared to me that . . ." or "Therefore, it was my impression that. . . ."

Following is an example of an anecdotal record of a toddler biting incident:

Observations: Ricky wandered slowly around the room, whining and shaking his head. After about five minutes, he abruptly dropped to the floor and began to cry. Periodically, he stopped crying to sit up, suck his thumb, and twist a tuft of his hair while he looked around, then he would close his eyes, drop back on the floor, and begin sobbing again.

I picked up a handful of picture books and sat down on the floor beside him. I said, "Ricky, would you like to read a book? Look, it's a book about kitty cats." At first he ignored me, but finally he crawled into my lap and laid his head on my chest as he continued to suck his thumb and make the jerky little sniffing sounds that follow a bout of hard crying. I began to read the story about kittens.

After only a few minutes, Katherine toddled over and plopped into my lap practically on top of Ricky. Before I had even a second to respond, Ricky had grabbed Katherine's face and hair, and had sunk his teeth into her cheek.

Comments/Interpretations: Ricky was probably frightened and anxious because he has not been away from his mother very often. He seems to be showing evidence of a great deal of separation anxiety. He may have felt threatened by Katherine's presence since he has no sisters or brothers, and may not be accustomed to sharing adult attention with others. I will have to watch Ricky very carefully so that I can help him find ways to cope with his feelings, and I can anticipate and intervene better in situations where he might hurt another child.

WHAT IS A RUNNING ACCOUNT?

In a running account, a specific type of behavior is noted each time it occurs. A mother who worries that her child is not eating properly may keep a running account for a period of time, keeping track of when, where, and what her child eats during and between meals each day. After a few days or weeks, she could begin to see if specific eating patterns emerge. Does the child pick at meals but consume high-calorie junk food during frequent snacks? Does the child eat a well-balanced lunch and afternoon snack but often refuse supper? Does the child eat whatever is offered at home but get into power struggles over food with a caregiver in the child care center?

Following is an example of a running account of a four-year-old girl's incidences of nail-biting:

What observations can you make from this picture? (Hint: Look at the child's facial expression and body posture.)

> **Observations:**
>
> Monday, 8:00 A.M.—Celia bit her nails while watching cartoons on television; she had a very tense facial expression.
>
> Monday, 3:30 P.M.—Celia and her best friend Joel had an argument; after he told her he wouldn't play with her anymore, she sat by herself on the steps for a long time, biting her nails; again, she appeared very tense.
>
> Tuesday, 11:30 A.M.—Celia bit her nails while she waited for lunch; she appeared more bored than tense.
>
> Tuesday, 4:30 P.M.—Celia bit her nails the whole time she watched a television cartoon; her whole body appeared to be tense as she sat on the edge of her chair and strained toward the TV.
>
> Comments/Interpretations: Tension (and possibly boredom) seems to be triggering Celia's nail-biting. She was not seen biting her nails when she was coloring, playing dolls, or putting together puzzles. It may be helpful to redirect Celia to more active play and to discourage her watching television cartoons on a regular basis.

WHAT IS TIME SAMPLING?

The purpose of time sampling is to determine the patterns of occurrence and general frequency of specific behaviors either in an individual or in the entire group. In time sampling, a particular interval of time is selected: five minutes, thirty minutes, an hour, and so on. Then, at the designated time intervals, a checklist is marked to show whether the chosen behavior is or is not occurring at that moment. For example, an individual child could be watched at intervals to determine whether he is spending more time actively engaged in play or passively watching others. An entire class could be watched to see how often the reading center is used as compared to the block center. This procedure can give factual evidence to back up or refute an adult's intuitive impressions about the occurrence of various patterns of behavior.

Following is a time sampling checklist used by a preschool teacher to help her study her students' patterns of being "on task" (involved in productive skill development or learning activity) rather than misbehaving, wandering aimlessly, or just watching:

CLASSROOM OBSERVATIONS

Time	Misbehaving	Wandering	Watching
8:15 A.M.	James, Jill	Suzette, Amy, Tyler	Ben, Ann
8:30 A.M.	James	Amy	Suzette
8:45 A.M.	Amy, Suzette	—	—

(continues)

CLASSROOM OBSERVATIONS *(continued)*

9:00 A.M.	Tyler	—	—
9:15 A.M..	—	—	—
9:30 A.M.	—	Suzette	—
9:45 A.M.	Amy, Ben	Jill, Tyler	Suzette
10:00 A.M.	Suzette, Ann	Tyler	Jill, Amy
10:15 A.M.	Suzette	Ann, Tyler, Ben	Amy

Comments/Interpretations: This group of children have more difficulty staying on task at the beginning and the end of the morning. Their most productive time is between 8:45 and 9:30. Suzette, Amy, and Tyler may need special attention to help them focus on productive activity. James seemed able to avoid misbehavior after he settled into productive activity.

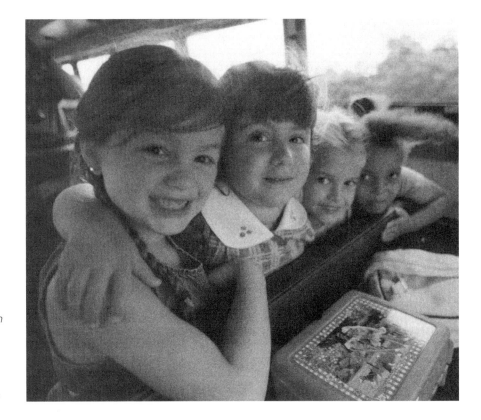

What observations can you make from this picture? What can you tell about their relationships with each other? What can you tell about their mood?

WHAT IS EVENT SAMPLING?

The purpose of event sampling is to determine the precise number of times a specific behavior occurs within a set period of time as well as the pattern of occurrence. Individual children can be observed for occurrences of a specific behavior, or an entire group can be watched, and a total number of occurrences of a behavior (such as aggression) can be recorded and tallied. In event sampling, a specific action (or actions) is designated for observation. When the behavior occurs, a checklist is marked so that after a given period of time, the adult can tally the exact number of times the behavior took place.

Following is an event sampling checklist used by a child care worker to determine the individual daily progress of several toddlers in their toilet training (each accident has been recorded as an x):

TOILETING ACCIDENTS

Names	Monday	Tuesday	Wednesday	Thursday	Friday
Reily	xxx	xxx	xxx	x	
Joseph	xx				
Mariette	xxx	xx	x	x	
Ella	xxxx	xxxxx	xxxx	xxxx	xxxx
Prichart			x	xx	
Bethany	xx		x		

Comments/Interpretations: Ella may not really be ready for toilet training at this time. It may be helpful to observe Mariette more closely to determine if she is having difficulty at a specific time of day or under specific circumstances. Reily had difficulty early in the week but managed to stay dry most of the day Thursday and all day Friday. He should probably be watched further to see what happens the following week.

WHICH METHOD OF RECORDING OBSERVATIONS WORKS BEST?

Checklists and narrative accounts can be used as tools for gathering information in many different situations. The particular advantage of narrative accounts is that they create word pictures that may provide insight into a child's behavior far beyond that originally anticipated when the event was recorded.

The adult can look back over several anecdotal records and discover new, previously overlooked relationships or details each time. The biggest drawback to narratives is, of course, that they are very time consuming and so can only be relied on for recording occasional rather than routine occurrences. Narratives collect qualitative information while checklists collect quantitative information. Qualitative information is focused on the descriptive qualities or characteristics of behaviors. Quantitative information is focused on numerical and statistical calculations that tell how often or to what degree behaviors occur.

Checklists leave out all of the details surrounding behaviors and focus only on the frequencies and distributions of occurrences. They are especially useful for making comparisons, not only of one child's behaviors to that of other children, but also to the child's own behaviors at other times of day, in other settings, or at an earlier age. The major advantage of checklists is the ease with which they can be used. The major drawback is that a great deal of important information about the extenuating background circumstances of a behavior are not recorded.

The checklist examples provided earlier gave a great deal more factual information about many more children than the anecdotal record and the running account; however, you probably feel that you know much more about what Ricky and Celia (described in the narrative accounts) are really like than any of the children listed on the checklists.

POINTS TO REMEMBER

- Everything that we perceive with our senses (eyes, ears, and so on) is filtered through layers upon layers of our own personal point of view (our bias).

- One way to increase objectivity is to make a conscious effort to separate facts from opinions.

- Observations help us evaluate how effective a chosen guidance technique has been in solving a problem.

PRACTICAL APPLICATION
THE MYSTERIOUS CASE OF THE SPINNING PEG

Felicia, an afternoon assistant in an infant/toddler child care center, is sitting on the floor and pulling the string of a "See and Say" toy. Lisa is laughing. Felicia asks, "Where are the fish? Can you see the fish? There they are, seven of them." She laughs and tickles Lisa's tummy. Other toddlers push close to Felicia as they laugh and interact with her. They watch every move that Felicia makes.

Lisa, who is 18-months-old, wanders away from them toward me as I sit on the vinyl padded tunnel. Lisa accidentally drops a large plastic peg she is carrying. When it hits the wooden stair by her, it spins for about five seconds. She stares at it with a look of wonder. She carefully picks it up and with great concentration, drops it on the step again, but this time it does not spin. She stares at it, squats beside the stairs, then proceeds to drop it again and again on the carpet.

It does not spin. She stands up and throws it down on the carpet. It does not spin! She bites it hard, throws it two more times, but still it does not spin. She leaves the peg lying on the floor and walks away. Felicia picks it up and puts it away.

Lisa comes over to me, looks at my writing and at my face. She pats my tablet and then pulls at the pages. She looks very seriously at my eyes. She then walks away. I hear her whine as she walks over to the play sink. She stops abruptly, looks at a plastic fruit, then with great interest she watches it as she drops it to the floor. It does not spin.

She sucks her finger and starts to cry. Felicia picks her up, comforts her, then walks away saying, "You're getting a little fussy. I wonder if you're hungry. Let me see if you get an afternoon bottle."

DISCUSSION QUESTIONS

1. What are the objective observations you could have actually seen, heard, and so on if you had been observing this interaction?
2. What are your own personal interpretations of the interaction?
3. Why do you think Lisa started to cry?
4. What can you tell about the relationship between Lisa and her caregiver, Felicia?

RELATED READINGS

DEVELOPMENTALLY APPROPRIATE ASSESSMENT

Barko, N. (1997). Labeled for life? In K. M. Paciorek and J. H. Munro (Eds.), *Annual editions: Early childhood education 97/98* (18th ed.). New York: McGraw-Hill. (Original work published in *Parents*, September 1996.)

Addresses pragmatic reasons for children being labeling as "exceptional," but also looks at how this labeling may cause difficulties for these same children if the diagnosis is wrong or the child's ability level changes significantly over time.

Benjamin, A. C. (1994). Observations in early childhood classrooms: Advice from the field. *Young Children, 49*(6), 14–20.

Bentzen, W. R. (1997). *Seeing young children: A guide to observing and recording behavior* (3rd ed.). Clifton Park, NY: Delmar Learning.

Seeing Young Children is designed to provide essential background information on many aspects of child development and recording techniques. These two bodies of information then form the basis for the individual to observe and record young children's behavior in child care centers, early childhood classrooms, homes, public schools, and various other kinds of settings.

Billman, J., & Sherman, J. A. (1997). *Observation and participation in early childhood settings: A practicum guide, birth through age five.* Needham Heights, MA: Allyn & Bacon.

Feinburg, S. G., & Mindess, M. (1994). *Designing and evaluating developmentally based programs for young children.* Needham Heights, MA: Brooks/Cole.

This book describes what makes a quality early childhood program, and explains the procedures through which quality programs can be developed, nurtured, and maintained. The authors discuss the process of designing and maintaining excellent programs that develop children's full potential throughout the curriculum and offer a guide for an ongoing process of evaluation.

Gaustad, J. (1996). Assessment and evaluation in the multiage classroom [Special issue]. *OSSC Bulletin, 39*(3–4).

Hannon, J. (2000). Learning to like Matthew. *Young Children, 55*(6), 24–28.

Addresses strategies for authentic, holistic assessment practices in observation and note-taking to better understand children, to effectively share information about the child's growth and learning with his family, and to continually improve one's own teaching methods.

Hills, T. W. (1992). Reaching potentials through appropriate assessment. In S. Bredekamp and T. Rosegrant (Eds.), *Reaching potentials: Appropriate curriculum and assessment for young children.* Washington, DC: National Association for the Education of Young Children.

Hills, T. W. (1993). Assessment in context—Teachers and children at work. *Young Children, 48*(5), 20–28.

To be developmentally appropriate and to best serve children's needs, assessment should be included as an integrated part of an overall program. It is most effective when it contributes positively to children's self-esteem and developmental process, recognizes children's individuality, and respects their family and community backgrounds.

Katz, L. G. (1995). *Talks with teachers of young children: A collection.* Norwood, NJ: Ablex.

Katz, L. G., & Chard, S. C. (1996). The contribution of documentation to the quality of early childhood education. *ERIC Digest.* Urbana, IL: ERIC Clearinghouse on Elementary and Early Childhood Education.

McLean, M. E., Bailey, D. B., Jr., & Wolery, M. (1997). *Assessing infants and preschoolers with special needs* (2d ed.). Upper Saddle River, NJ: Merrill Education/Prentice-Hall.

A text written for early childhood special educators and other professionals who work with infants and preschoolers, focusing on assessment for the purpose of planning effective intervention programs.

National Association for the Education of Young Children. (1991). Guidelines for appropriate curriculum content and assessment in programs serving children ages 3 through 8. *Young Children, 46*(3), 21–38.

Shepard, L. A. (1994). The challenges of assessing young children appropriately. *Phi Delta Kappan, 76*(3), 206–212.

Southern Association on Children Under Six. (1990). Developmentally appropriate assessment. Little Rock, AR: Author.

HELPFUL WEB SITES

http://www.ume.maine.edu/ECEOL-L/   Early Childhood Education On Line provides an early childhood education online listserv as well as links to many other Web sites. Addresses observation, assessment, curriculum, environment design, developmental guidelines, and professional development.

http://pedsexam.mc.duke.edu/   Assessment of Normal Child Development
- Development from birth to two years is assessed along the major developmental lines of gross motor, language, fine motor, and social. Reflexes are included in Newborn exams.
- To illustrate Normal Development, a single child was videotaped over two years at each routine exam recommended by the American Academy of Pediatrics.
- Video clips of each test are included, along with the entire assessment for each age.
- The tests shown are derived from the Denver II and other developmental assessment tools.
Video & Web site produced by Beatriz B. Morris, MD, Assistant Clinical Professor, Department of Pediatrics, Duke University School of Medicine.

http://www.nncc.org/Evaluation/evaluation.page.html   National Network for Child Care

- Information—an Internet source of over 1,000 publications and resources related to child care. Publications are research-based and reviewed.
- Kidcare—an e-mail listserve provides a way to communicate nationally and internationally with others who care about children and child care.
- Person-to-person—support and assistance from experts in child care and child development. Extension staff at each state's land grant university who are working in the area of children and youth are identified.
- Connections newsletters—issued four times a year for family child care, center-based care, and school-age child care.

National Network for Child Care is supported by the Cooperative State Research, Education and Extension Service, U.S. Department of Agriculture, and CYFERNet—the Cooperative Extension System's Children, Youth, and Family Network. E-mail: nncc@iastate.edu

For additional information on positive child guidance, visit our Web site at
http://www.earlychilded.delmar.com

Chapter 10
Serving Diverse Children and Families

OBJECTIVES

After reading this chapter, you should be able to:
- Recognize historical events related to beliefs about children.
- Outline the child's role in society.
- Identify the role of child guidance in a democracy.
- List changes in disciplinary strategies over time.
- Outline tenets of various folk ideologies of child guidance.
- Recognize cultural differences that affect child-rearing.
- Identify behaviorist approaches to guidance.
- Identify maturationist approaches to guidance.
- Identify developmental interactionist approaches to guidance.

HISTORICAL PERSPECTIVES AND GUIDANCE THEORIES

Child care and guidance practices have changed drastically through the years. Many child care traditions from the past would seem strange, even cruel, to modern parents. For example, swaddling, the snug wrapping of infants in strips of cloth or blankets, is an ancient custom that has persisted for centuries in many parts of the world. While snugly wrapping newborns in blankets is considered to be a very appropriate tradition in most modern cultures, the old practice of swaddling was intended to control the baby's movement and routinely continued until the child was old enough to walk. John Locke (1699) described the customary child care of his day:

> . . . rolled and swathed, ten or a dozen times round; then blanket upon blanket, mantle upon that; its little neck pinned down to one posture; its head more than it frequently

We celebrate our cultural and physical differences, and remember that underneath the skin, we are all very much the same.

needs, triplecrowned like a young page, with covering upon covering; its legs and arms as if to prevent that kindly stretching which we rather ought to promote . . . the former bundled up, the latter pinned down; and how the poor thing lies on the nurse's lap, a miserable little pinioned captive (cited in Cunnington & Buck, 1965, p. 103).

In western Europe during the first half of the 18th century, infants were seen not only as somehow less human than older people, but also as somewhat expendable. A wealthy mother usually sent her newborn infant to the care of a hired wet nurse who was expected to breastfeed and care for the child, often at the expense of the life of the wet nurse's own infant. Infant mortality rates reportedly reached as high as 80 percent in some areas as wetnurse mothers, in order to ensure their livelihood, gave birth to stimulate the production of breast milk, then sent their own infants to poorly maintained foundling homes (Weiser, 1982).

The writings of Rousseau toward the end of the 18th century both influenced and reflected a change in the cultural perception of childhood. He insisted that "everything is good as it comes from the hands of the Author of Nature" (Rousseau, 1893, p. 1). He argued that rather than being an evil creature who must have sin beaten out of him, the young child is born good and innocent. He believed that the harsh discipline techniques of that day, which were intended to provide the child salvation from original sin, tainted the child rather than provided healthy, normal growth. Rousseau's prescription for child care included breastfeeding by the natural mother, fresh air, loose clothing, and a minimum of interference from adults. Certain tribes of Native Americans in the 1900s particularly valued physical toughness in their children. To build up the child's resistance, newborns were plunged into cold water several times at birth, regardless of the weather. Their version of swaddling was to fasten the baby securely onto a cradleboard that could be conveniently hung inside the lodge, from a tree branch, from a saddlebow, or wherever family members were clustered. Babies were not released from the confines of cradleboards until they were able to walk (Weiser, 1982).

American mothers of European descent sent their infants and young children to the neighborhood widow or spinster for care and teaching. In these "dame schools," a baby might nap on a quilt in a corner of the kitchen while older children practiced reading from the New Testament (Weiser, 1982). Farm and slave children were valued as a source of free labor. Toddlers barely able to walk were assigned chores and held accountable for them. By the early 1900s, momentum had begun to build promoting the scientific study of the development of children and the dissemination of pertinent information to parents. Some of the writings of that day foretold future trends in thinking about young children. For example, a book produced by The Institute of Child Welfare at the University of Minnesota in 1930 warned parents that children's personal characteristics were not necessarily inborn:

As a matter of fact, the modern study of young children is indicating that such traits are in large part due to the manner in which the child is treated by adults and other children, rather than to inheritance. The parent who has the ideal of complete and unquestioning obedience, and who is forceful and consistent enough to obtain it, is likely to have a child who, when he goes to school, distresses a good teacher and delights a poor one by always doing what he is told and furthermore by always waiting to be told what to do. His whole attitude is that of finding out what authority requires and then complying, an attitude which, if maintained, is apt to result in incompetence, inefficiency, and unhappiness in adulthood (Faegre & Anderson, 1930, pp. 45).

The early 1900s brought changes in people's beliefs about childhood, and their expectations for children.

HOW THE MODERN WORLD HAS INFLUENCED THINKING ABOUT CHILD GUIDANCE

During the 20th century, ideas about children have been influenced by two world wars, alternating periods of economic depression and prosperity, and by growing scientific interest in child development research. At the end of World War II, Maria Montessori wrote such books as *Peace and Education* (1971) and *Reconstruction in Education* (1968) to express her view that the hope for world peace lay in a new education for young children. Montessori (1971) wrote:

> Certainly we cannot achieve [peace] by attempting to unite all these people who are so different, but it can be achieved if we begin with the child. When the child is born he has no special language, he has no special religion, he has not any national or racial prejudice. It is men [sic] who have acquired all these things (p. 6).

In the late 1940s and into the 1950s, researchers began to unlock some of the mysteries of early learning. The common belief that experiences of the first years of life were inconsequential to later development was pushed aside by more complex theories explaining the development of intelligence and personality. These new theories placed greater emphasis on early social interaction and exploration of the physical environment (Erikson, 1963; Harlow & Zimmerman, 1959; Piaget, 1952, 1962, 1963, 1968, 1970; Skinner, 1953; Wolff, 1963). In the 1960s, research into the learning processes of children from birth to school age flourished, and an estimated 23 million books on child-rearing were sold during the mid-1970s (Clarke-Stewart, 1978). Since the 1970s, there has been a mushrooming of parental as well as scientific interest in the processes of child growth and development (Elkind, 1997; Petersen, 1996).

Over the years, the educators, philosophers, and scientists have profoundly influenced our view on child guidance.

ALFRED ADLER

Adler developed a social constructivist view of human behavior based on value-oriented psychology. He believed human beings were capable of working cooperatively, living together peacefully, and striving for self-improvement, self-fulfillment, and to contribute to the common welfare of the community. He believed that people were not passive victims of heredity or environment but actively constructed their beings through their social interactions, experiences, and developing perceptions of the world. He saw human beings as constantly striving to compensate for their feelings of inferiority.

Adler's ideas are similar to those of **Abraham Maslow** who envisioned individuals as striving toward self-actualization, toward the full realization of their potential (Maslow 1970). Adler, like **Sigmund Freud**, believed that a person's personality was largely developed in the first five years of life. Adler's guidelines for the guidance of young children include the following concepts:

- Mutual respect based on a belief that equality is the inalienable right of all human beings.

- Reward and punishment are outdated and less effective than logical consequences.

- Acting instead of talking in heated conflict situations avoids arguments and resolves problems quicker.

- It is appropriate to withdraw from provocation but not to withdraw emotionally from the child.

- Teaching and training take time and patience.

- Adults should never do for a child what she can do for herself.

- It is critical to recognize and understand a misbehaving child's goal.

To learn more, read:

Adler, A. (1998). *Understanding human nature* (reprint ed.). Center City, MN: Hazelden Information Education.

Adler, A., Ansbacher, H. L. (Ed.), & Ansbacher, R. R. (Ed.). (1989). *Individual psychology of Alfred Adler: A systematic presentation in selections from his writings.* New York: Harper Collins.

Adler, A. (1963). *The problem child: The life style of the difficult child as analyzed in specific cases.* Oakville, Ontario: Capricorn Books.

Mosak, H. H., & Maniacci, M. (1999). *A primer of Adlerian psychology: The analytic-behavioral-cognitive psychology of Alfred Adler.* New York: Brunner-Routledge.

CARL ROGERS

Rogers' theory of personality evolved out of his work as a clinical psychologist and his deep respect for the dignity of all human beings. The clinical methods he developed focused specifically on the humane and ethical treatment of persons. He believed that human beings have an underlying "actualizing tendency" that motivates them to achieve their potential.

The idea of "self" is central to his theory. He believed that the self is constructed through interactions with others. One's self-concept is strongly influenced by the perceptions of those around her. Thus, valuing children and treating them with dignity and respect would help them construct a strong, positive self-concept. Disrespectful, humiliating, and dehumanizing treatment would damage the child's development of self-esteem. Rogers' argued that to reach their full potential, human beings must have positive regard from others that eventually leads to the development of positive self-regard.

Rogers' focus on psychological therapy differentiates him from Maslow, although their ideas are very similar. While his person-centered approach was developed for use in therapy, it has been adopted by educators to manage conflict resolution.

ROBERT R. CARDHUFF

Carhuff took the abstract theories of Carl Rogers and developed a systematic set of guidelines for effective interpersonal skills. The impact of his work has been dramatic. Numerous existing programs teaching appropriate interpersonal skills have been derived from this original source.

GEORGE MICHAEL GAZDA

Gazda took the work of Carkhuff and modified it further to create an effective system for teachers to use specifically to solve classroom management problems and to motivate children to change their inappropriate behaviors. His work focuses on effective strategies for perceiving

(continues)

GEORGE MICHAEL GAZDA *(continued)*

and responding, ineffective communication styles, nonverbal behaviors, confrontation, and anger. Gazda defined strategies for teachers that not only correct behavior problems but also strengthen children's self-concept and self-esteem at the same time.

To learn more, read:

Gazda, G. M. (Ed.), & Asbury, F. R. (1998). *Human relations development: A manual for educators* (6th ed.). Boston: Allyn & Bacon.

Rogers, C. R. (1961). *On becoming a person.* Boston: Houghton Mifflin.

Krebs, D., & Blackman, R. (1988). *Psychology: A first encounter.* Toronto: Harcourt Brace Jovanovich.

JEAN PIAGET

Piaget studied the development of intelligence in children and proposed a theory based on four predetermined stages of mental growth. His studies have had a major impact on the fields of psychology and education. Piaget spent much of his professional life listening to children, watching children, and studying research reports from other cognitive psychologists. He concluded that children's learning was progressively constructed by the children themselves through their interaction with their environment. He believed that children's logic for thinking and problem-solving was initially very different from the logic they would use later as they grew stage by stage toward adulthood. Children simply don't think like adults.

Piaget believed that children are little "scientists" who constantly create and test their own theories of the world. Children are not empty vessels to be filled with knowledge (as had been believed) but active builders of their own knowledge. Like **John Dewey** and **Maria Montessori**, Piaget took child learning very seriously. Montessori and Dewey set out to reform education, but Piaget only tried to understand and explain how children think and learn. Piaget, nonetheless, has had a profound effect on education throughout the world.

To learn more, read:

DeVries, R., & Zan, B. (1994). *Moral classrooms, Moral children: Creating a constructivist atmosphere in early education.* New York: Teachers College press.

DeVries, R., & Kohlberg, L. (1987). *Constructivist early education: Overview and comparison with other programs.* Washington DC: Nation Association for the Education of Young Children.

Duckworth, E., Easly, J., Hawkings, D., & Henriques, A. (1990). *Science education: A minds-on approach for the early elementary years.* Hillsdale, NJ: Lawrence Erlbaum Associates.

Furth, H. G. (1970). *Piaget for teachers.* Engelwood Cliffs, NJ: Prentice Hall.

Gruber, H. E., & Vonèche, J. (1995). *The essential Piaget.* Northvale, NJ: Aronson.

Lourenco, O., & Machado, A. (1996). In defense of Piaget's theory: A reply to 10 common criticisms. *Psychological Review, 103*(1), 143–164.

Piaget, J. (1985). *Equilibration of cognitive structures.* Chicago, IL: University of Chicago Press.

Piaget, J., & Inhelder, B. (1969). *The psychology of the child.* New York: Basic Books.

LEV VYGOTSKY

Vygotsky is remembered primarily for identifying what he called the "zone of proximal educational development" (sometimes referred to as the ZPD, ZoPED, or simply "the Zone"). He believed that children develop by exposure to skills, words, concepts, and tasks that are just beyond their ability but within a "zone" of possible achievement. He believed that adults played an important coaching role in helping the child grasp this new knowledge or ability during these teachable moments.

Vygotsky believed that children developed from their interaction primarily with adults but also with other children. This is a collectivist view of psychological growth, as opposed to the individualism of behaviorism and predetermined growth stages of Piaget. Vygotsky believed that child learning was inseparable from human history and culture. He believed that psychological development was the process of children learning how to use the ideas and tools developed by people throughout history such as language, number concepts, music, art, and so forth. He emphasized that language was the most important of the cognitive tools passed down through the centuries. Without language, children cannot fully develop self-awareness. Without self-awareness, children cannot think about, evaluate, anticipate, and control their behavior. Words become the framework through which we think, perceive, experience, and act.

To learn more, read:
Bruner, J. (1996). *The culture of education.* Cambridge: Harvard University Press.
Mooney, C. G. (2000). *Theories of childhood: An introduction to Dewey, Montessori, Erickson, Piaget & Vygotsky.* Saint Paul, MN: Redleaf Press.
Van der Veer, R., & Valsner, J. (1991). *Understanding Vygotsky: A quest for synthesis.* Cambridge, MA: Blackwell.
Wertsch J. V. (1988). *Vygotsky and the social formation of mind.* Boston, MA: Harvard University Press.
Wertsch J. V. (1985). *Vygotsky and the social formation of mind.* Cambridge, MA: Harvard University Press.

THE CHILD IN SOCIETY

Children occupy a very special niche in our society (Cowan & Cowan, 1992; Gutek, 1997; Hoffman & Manis, 1979). They are dressed in fancy clothing, photographed, given many colorful objects made especially for children (toys), fed special foods from tiny glass jars, and equipped with elaborate contraptions designed for sitting, swinging, strolling, eating, and crawling. Compared to previous cultures, children today are pampered and indulged. A bright-eyed baby decked out in several yards of lace, scented leakproof disposable diapers, and a huge bonnet will bring oohs and ahhs from shoppers in a supermarket and comments such as, "Oh, isn't it adorable! Look at its little shoes and its tiny earrings!"

The practice of referring to infants (and sometimes toddlers) with impersonal pronouns such as *it* tells us a lot about our perception of babies. The use of such descriptors as "it" and "thing" in reference to children gives a subtle indication that babies are not perceived as real persons. Several centuries ago, impersonal references to children were even more pervasive than they are

A contemporary baby finds himself the center of attention.

today. Children were commonly referred to as "it" well into early childhood: "in this age [birth to seven years] it cannot talk well or form its words perfectly, for its teeth are not yet well arranged or firmly implanted" (*Le Grand Proprietaire*, cited in Aries, 1962, p. 21). At the present time, in spite of indications that infants may generally be seen as somewhat less than fully human, we place a great deal more emphasis on the value and importance of individual children's lives than was evident in the past.

Parents may refer to a fetus as an "it" before the child's birth, but one almost never hears parents refer to their own baby as "it" afterward, especially after they have come to know and love her. Strangers are always more likely to refer impersonally to a baby or child. For example, a newspaper account of an alleged brutal child abuse murder quoted a district attorney explaining to shocked citizens why the murder victim, a two-year-old boy, had been given back to his natural mother after having been removed since early infancy for neglect: "Most reasonable people . . . might say the decision to put it [the child] back was probably a bad call. . . ." (Krupinski & Weikel, 1986). When asked about the use of impersonal references for babies, people often explain that "it" is used because the baby's sex may not be known. Interestingly, in discussing older children and adults, even if that person's gender is not known, it would be considered highly inappropriate to refer to that person (a salesperson, a mail carrier, or an acquaintance's teenager) as an "it." Only after an older child or adult dies is that person's body referred to as an "it."

HOW LIFE IS DIFFERENT FOR CONTEMPORARY CHILDREN IN TODAY'S CHANGING WORLD

Children today are not only valued but also are usually thought to have a fairly carefree existence, in contrast to earlier generations' use of child labor. In past years, young children have generally been allowed to spend a good portion of their days playing, fooling around, romping in the sunshine, and generally occupying themselves (sometimes in front of a television set). Child care has brought new levels of structure to many children's lives. In many early childhood programs, this

A young child is a full-fledged human being with personal rights and needs.

structure has enriched children's lives and assisted in their development of healthy and productive habits. In other child care settings, children spend a considerable amount of time sitting, waiting, being berated, standing in line, and taking part in activities that are initiated and controlled by adults and are carried out by lockstep groups of children (Werner, 1987).

Since many affluent parents are having fewer children and waiting until their professional careers are well established before having them, there is new pressure on some children to live up to the "fast lane" expectations of their parents. In the push for superbabies and superior children, many youngsters may be given gymnastics, music lessons, dance lessons, tutoring, and yoga before they ever start kindergarten. Their lives may become so full of "enrichment" activities that they run out of time to lie in the clover and experience wonder as they watch clouds go by. In an era when parents feel pressured to create a "superchild," they may inadvertently destroy some of the wonder and magic of early childhood.

The young child's role in contemporary society sometimes approaches that of a pet or a possession rather than a person deserving respect and dignity. From time to time, that role may mean that the child is indulged, pampered, forgotten, rushed, herded, and pushed (Kantrowitz & Wingert, 1997; Ladd, 1996; Silvers, 1997; Stengel, 1997). She may be expected to be perfect at all times, or be coerced to perform cute tricks on cue to entertain or impress adults. Our growing knowledge of and emphasis on early childhood has put youngsters on a pedestal. But, of course, being on a pedestal has distinct disadvantages as well as advantages. Being on a pedestal means that every move one makes is watched, judged, and managed. Early childhood experts have growing concerns that children are not being allowed the freedom to "just be children."

PREPARATION FOR PARTICIPATION IN A DEMOCRACY

Settings where young children live, work, and play (whether in a home or a child care facility) function as their small version of the world. As has been previously discussed, interaction in familial, educational, and caregiving communities helps children learn how to participate later in adult community life. Child guidance is the process by which adults help children learn appropriate ways to function as part of a group. In an **autocracy**, people would only need to learn blind obedience in order to function appropriately. People are dominated by a dictator who demands submission. In an **anarchy**, one could follow one's own desires and interests. Chaos prevails because no one governs. In a **democracy**, however, educated, responsible citizens are needed to provide effective self-governance through active participation.

The guidance practices carried out by adults can help children learn how to participate in a democracy by developing the necessary skills.

CRITICAL SKILLS FOR GOOD CITIZENSHIP

- Concept of citizenship—being cooperative, having a sense of fair play, and respecting the rights of others

- Initiative and self-reliance—being a self-starter, a lifelong learner, and a creative problem-solver

- Responsible work habits—having established habits of promptness, effort, and pride

- Sense of loyalty—recognizing that sometimes one's own immediate interests and desires must be pushed aside for the good of the whole community

---

HOW EARLY INFLUENCES AFFECT CHILDREN'S GROWTH AND DEVELOPMENT IN TERMS OF THEIR LEARNING APPROPRIATE BEHAVIOR

Modern researchers only recently, during the 1970s and 1980s, began studying how various approaches in early childhood programs affect children's development of characteristics, attitudes, and values. However, some educators have been focusing on personal development and citizenship as a part of early learning and guidance for more than a hundred years. John Dewey wrote dozens of books describing his theories of learning as a part of daily living. His world-famous school, which included preschool and kindergarten, was specifically designed to foster the characteristics that are essential for living in a democracy. His school opened in 1894 (Dewey, 1966).

It is essential for those parents, caregivers, and teachers who supervise young children to recognize that guidance is not just a process for getting children to behave appropriately today, but rather a process for helping children learn to live happy, productive lives. Guidance strategies cannot be judged only by how expedient they are at the moment but also by how effective they are in instilling functional living skills that relate to the "real" world.

Disciplinary tactics are aimed at controlling children's behaviors, often by the use of punishment. Guidance procedures are focused on the development of children's self-control and self-discipline. They rely on authentic experiences, logical consequences, and intrinsic rewards. Positive guidance is not a "bag of tricks" for coaxing or coercing children to do what we want them to do.

In a democracy, people have rights. If I break a law by driving in excess of a speed limit, I still have rights. A police officer is authorized to use only as much force as is appropriate and necessary to stop me. She is forbidden to hurt me, harass me, or humiliate me as a punishment, or to "get me back" for what I did. In fact, many police officers patiently persist with recalcitrant "perpetrators" by politely but firmly insisting, "I know you don't like being pulled over, sir, but you were exceeding the speed limit. May I see your license?"

If officers of the law behaved the way some adults do in handling misbehaving children, we would be shocked. Imagine an officer yanking a driver out of the car, angrily shaking the driver while yelling at her, and snapping, "If you ever do this again, I'll use a paddle on you and you won't be able to sit down for a week!" We would probably feel very angry and misused. Children feel that same way, too. It takes time and practice for children to grasp rules, but they can learn to be good citizens by the same technique that our judicial system is supposed to use: consistent persistence, and guiding as firmly as necessary but as respectfully as possible.

THE STRAIN OF CHANGING DISCIPLINARY TRADITIONS

Changing one's methods of dealing with misbehaving children is not easy. During our own childhoods, we absorbed a great deal of unconscious information about how adults and children are expected to interact. It is as if we had mental videotapes of disciplinary interactions stored unconsciously but ready for instant replay at any time. Without thinking, we sometimes hear the voices of our parents and teachers as we scold the young children in our care. However, the disciplinary methods that were appropriate and functional generations ago may be inappropriate and nonfunctional in preparing today's children for life in the next century (deMelendez & Ostertag, 1997; Hildebrand, Phenice, Gray, & Hines, 1996; Thorne, 1997).

The world is changing at an astonishing rate. As it changes, children need different kinds of experiences to prepare them for the future. A hundred years ago, children were not expected to prepare for a technological world where adaptability and flexibility were more valued than

A hundred years ago, a strong back and a willing attitude were generally considered to be all one needed to make a living—success in today's world requires a complicated set of skills and attitudes.

adherence to set routines. Minorities and females were not expected to prepare for the likelihood that they would be competing ambitiously in the business world. And females were not expected to prepare for the distinct possibility that they would, at some time or other, function as head of household and sole breadwinner.

Once we recognize the necessity for updating strategies for guiding and teaching children, it can be difficult to change our old habits. Unfortunately, we adults experience confusion and stress when the methods for dealing with children that begin to seem logical and right intellectually do not match the methods we experienced and lived in our own childhoods. Beliefs cannot be turned on and off like a light switch. Instead, they must be studied and practiced for years.

> Beliefs are altered primarily by experience, learning over a long period of time, and confidence in the authority of someone considered more knowledgeable (Costley & Todd, 1987).

Human beings, adults and children alike, are influenced by life experiences. But as human beings, we also have the ability to make choices, to take control of our lives, and even to make unexpected changes in our life journey. We are not merely leaves floating in the stream of life. Instead, we are fish, strongly influenced by currents and tides, but free to swim upstream if we have the strength and motivation. We can choose to break old habits and establish new ones, but it is not easy. It requires stamina, determination, and a great deal of persistent practice over time.

CULTURAL INFLUENCES ON CHILD GUIDANCE

The ideas that we take for granted about the nature of infancy and childhood are different from those held by others in different places in the world and at different times in history. Current views on early childhood are not universal and have not always existed. By carefully examining our own beliefs and assumptions about children, we can recognize and put into perspective biases that interfere with effective child guidance.

Child care practices have been strikingly different over time for various social classes. A long period of protected childhood has largely been a luxury of the middle and upper classes, and views of infancy have fluctuated according to cultural and class settings (Bremner, 1974; Cole, 1950; Froebel, 1887; Glubok, 1969; McGraw, 1941; Osborn, 1980; Rousseau, 1893; Ulich, 1954). Much of what is written about child-rearing, infant care, and early child care curriculum is intended to present a generic model for quality care. That assumes, of course, that all parents hold a similar idea about what kind of care is good and right for babies and young children. To the contrary, there is growing evidence that strategies for guiding young children hold significant cultural importance to parents from different backgrounds, and parents have very diverse ideas about what is and is not appropriate for guiding and disciplining children.

People from different cultural and economic backgrounds often hold starkly contrasting views about what proper child care really is. Methods of caring for and educating young children routinely expected by families in one community may shock and repel families in another community, and vice versa. A mother in one cultural setting may be astonished that a mother in another setting still allows her two-year-old to nurse at the breast, while the nursing mother may be horrified that the first mother allows her two-year-old to eat candy and drink soda. In some settings, people expect infants to be taken everywhere the parents go. They think that is good for babies. In other settings, people expect infants to be left safely at home in their cribs with a "baby-sitter." They think that is best for babies.

Routines considered very desirable by one parent may be seen as inane by another. Guidance strategies believed by some early childhood educators to be essential to healthy growth may be considered inhumane or manipulative by others. Some people believe misbehaving children should be spanked. Some people believe children should be made to sit in a chair for a few minutes for punishment. Some people do not like either of those two ideas. Practices can vary dramatically within a single family. Parents may be very protective and controlling with a first child, but relaxed and indulgent with the fourth. Hence, we see some typical personality patterns develop in children based on their birth order. Firstborn children tend to be more highly motivated and success-oriented than later-born children, possibly because of the increased attention and pressure they received from parents. Later-born children tend to be more interested in pleasing peers than pleasing authority figures.

What some consider to be essential experiences for effective early learning others consider utter nonsense. Some people think infants can be made to learn at an accelerated pace by being shown flashcards of letters and numbers. Others think no child of any age should be subjected to flashcards. Social workers, early educators, and child care professionals have often felt the tension among these opposing views, and have sometimes been snagged unknowingly by their own culturally biased assumptions.

Cultural perceptions of desirable and appropriate care for children reflect the perceptions and beliefs of a person at a given time and place in history. The socialization of a new generation reflects the goals, philosophies, and values of the parent generation related to their specific social and economic circumstances. In other words, culture plays a key role in defining acceptable methods for dealing with children. Cultural bias is inescapable. In order to create a supportive and **pluralistic cultural** environment, however, cultural differences must be understood, accepted, and respected. And they must also sometimes be compromised when strong evidence emerges, indicating that a culturally based tradition is harmful or ineffective in reaching desired goals.

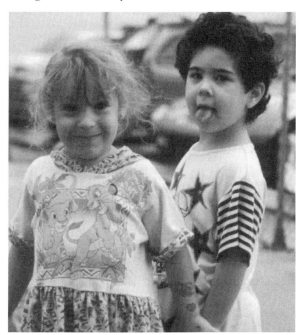

Training and experience are not the only factors that shape our views on child guidance. Our cultural values profoundly influence our perceptions about what guidance practices are most appropriate for children.

> *If the only tool you have is a hammer, you tend to treat everything as if it were a nail.*
> *Abraham Maslow (1993)*

Forming effective helping relationships between families and early childhood professionals hinges on recognizing and working through differences in backgrounds, personality characteristics, child-rearing perspectives, cultural beliefs, and role expectations (Bruns & Corso, 2001; Kochanek & Buka, 1998; Dinnebeil & Rule, 1994; Kalyanpor & Harry, 1999; Lynch & Hanson, 1998). Families are more likely to develop effective working relationships with professionals they trust (Dinnebeil & Rule, 1994). Of course, trust is essential to cooperative, effective collaboration between families and educators as they strive to provide positive guidance.

Cultural sensitivity does not include relying on stereotypes about what different groups like and dislike. Intragroup differences can be as great as intergroup differences (Lynch & Hanson, 1998). Every person should be seen and related to as a unique individual. Some people expect a formal relationship with early education professionals (Schwartz, 1995). Others expect an informal, friendly relationship (Gonzalez-Alvarez, 1998). If early educators dominate interactions, the family may feel uncomfortable, and may not be willing to talk about their needs and concerns (Dennis & Giangreco, 1996; Gudykunst, Ting-toome, & Nishida, 1996). Domineering teacher styles may be particularly offensive to families from traditional Hispanic, Native American, and Asian backgrounds (Gonzalez-Alvarez, 1998; Joe & Malach, 1998; Schwarz, 1995; Bruns & Caroso, 2001). Resourcefulness in finding community resources and skill in using interpreters are becoming more and more important for early education professionals. Communicating successfully with diverse families often requires finding community volunteers, family members, or professionals fluent in the families' primary language to answer questions and resolve problems (Ohtake, Santos, & Fowler, 2000).

PREPARING CHILDREN FOR THE REALITIES OF AN ADULT WORLD

From earliest childhood, children take in information about the roles and relationships of people and things in their environment. Consciously or unconsciously, adults are teaching children indirect lessons as a part of every interaction they have with children.

For example, a frustrated father at a gas station vending machine has explained to his toddler patiently over and over that the machine is broken, and he has no more money so he cannot get candies for her. After the little girl falls on the floor kicking and screaming for the candies, the father finds an attendant and insists that the machine be opened so his daughter can have the candy she wants. The tiny girl has learned two important lessons: one, sometimes authority figures do not tell the whole truth, and, two, if you make enough fuss, people sometimes find a way to get you what you want.

On one hand, we adults could rationalize any kind of harsh or careless behavior with children by explaining that we are simply preparing children for the "real" world. On the other hand, we could attempt to prepare children for what we believe would be a better world. Research into a phenomenon called self-fulfilling prophecy indicates that the expectation that something will occur actually increases the chances that it will occur (Rosenthal & Jacobson, 1968).

If children, therefore, grow up expecting to be treated with respect and fairness, they may actually behave in a way that evokes that treatment. If children grow up expecting to be treated harshly and unfairly, their behavior may trigger that response from others. The self-fulfilling prophesy may also occur because we are attracted to people and situations that match those of our childhoods. An abused child may feel familiar and comfortable with the idea that someone who says she loves you can also beat and hurt you "for your own good." That child may consequently grow up and marry an abusing spouse. People tend to be drawn toward that which is familiar and repelled from that which seems strange and unfamiliar.

We can best prepare children for life in the "real world" by modeling and teaching caring respectful behavior. By using developmentally appropriate practices to guide children, we help them develop the skills and knowledge they need for future success in a diverse global society.

HOW DO YOUNG CHILDREN LEARN ABOUT THEIR ROLE IN THE WORLD?

From birth to school age, children develop basic assumptions about how the world works and what their role is in that world. Children glean different sets of perceptions from different settings.

> *If a child's early childhood environment is rigid and children are herded through the day with no allowance for individual choice, they learn that the world is impassive and individual needs and interests do not matter.*

For example, children are all required to sit down at a long table. They are told and shown exactly how to glue precut pieces of a Santa Claus face onto a paper plate. If a child does this differently than the adult intends, the adult makes the child do it over or the adult does it herself and puts the child's name on it.

> *If, on the other hand, the environment is flexible and geared to individual needs, choices, and responsibilities, children learn that the world is malleable, and that with persistence and effort, they can have impact on the world around them.*

For example, winter holiday craft materials such as paper plates, glue, glitter, cotton balls, and bits of colored construction paper are made available in the art center. Children are not shown an adult model to copy, but rather are encouraged to use their own imaginations to create Christmas, Hanukkah, or other seasonal decorations. The children each responsibly clean up the materials they have used when they are finished. Unique differences in the finished products are recognized and honored, and all are displayed with pride.

> *If early authority figures are aloof from the children and control them by issuing steady streams of imperative commands ("Be quiet," "Sit up straight,. "Stand in line," "Don't talk"), children develop a perception of authority figures as omnipotent powers to be obeyed without question, enemies to be rebelled against, obstacles to be avoided, or irrelevant annoyances to be ignored.*

For example, the adult attempts to maintain total control by having children do everything in unison—they must all sit and wait passively while the adult has children come up to the front of the class one by one to point out letters of the alphabet or say numbers. Children must all line up to wash hands and use the toilet at the same time. Even if their food becomes stone cold, no child is allowed to eat lunch until all are given the signal to begin together. Children may even be required to stand in straight lines on the playground and do calisthenics for exercise (rather than running and playing freely). The adult imagines that no learning is taking place unless she is in charge and the children are quiet, controlled, and attentive.

> *If caring adults are warm, responsive, and assertive, children develop a perception of authority figures as dependable and resourceful allies to rely on for protection and help.*

For example, the adult structures the environment and the schedule to encourage children to function independently and individually as well as part of a cohesive group. Children choose learning materials from learning centers and work at their own pace during large, uninterrupted periods of time. They generally use the restroom according to their own body needs rather than group routines. Transitions from one activity to the next are flexible rather than abrupt. If a child finishes lunch earlier than others, she can throw away her trash, sponge off her area of the table, and then curl up and look at picture books until it is time for nap.

> *If adults treat children as underlings with few rights, and are careless, degrading, or threatening in their treatment of children, children learn to treat others with rudeness and aggression, and fail to develop self-respect.*

For example, adults often talk to each other as if the children weren't even present, sometimes laughing at or making fun of individual children. Adults order children around without saying please or thank you. Punishment is meted out according to the adults' moods and whims rather than based on fair and consistent rules. The adults act as if they are above rules.

Cultural pluralism means accepting, honoring, and valuing cultural differences.

> *If adults treat children with respect and concern for their comfort, dignity, and basic human rights, then children learn to expect politeness and civility in their dealings with others, and they learn to function with confidence and self-esteem.*

For example, adults behave as if children are the focal point of the environment and adults are facilitators or helpers. Adults are careful not to talk about children in a critical or humiliating way. Adults maintain a role of clear adult leadership while treating children with dignity and respect. All discipline is based on fair, consistent rules, and adults also show respect for class rules. If children are not allowed to eat, adults do not walk around in front of them drinking coffee and eating a doughnut. If an adult has to stand in a chair to change a light bulb, she explains why it was necessary for her to break a class rule about standing on furniture.

> *If an early childhood environment offers prepackaged curriculum kits, ditto sheets, and rote memorization as learning, children come to see learning as something irrelevant and external that is imposed by authority figures.*

For example, the adult stands over children, telling them exactly what to do and what will result from each action. Adults see "free play" as recess, fun but a waste of valuable time. Adults believe that children have little capacity for or interest in learning and so must be taught directly through adult-controlled and educationally preplanned initiatives.

> *If early curriculum is individualized, discovery-oriented, and based on developmentally appropriate practice, children come to see learning as something actively sought after and knowledge as something one can create. Their learning is spurred by intrinsic curiosity rather than by pressure from parents and teachers.*

For example, adults point out to children the possibilities of various materials and how to use them safely and appropriately, but they allow children to explore freely and to make spontaneous discoveries on their own. Adults trust children's ability to learn on their own as well as with adult assistance and direction.

> *If early role models limit their verbal communication to clipped criticism and commands, children, who are in the most formative period for language development of their lives may be discouraged in the development of a level of vocabulary, grammar, and expression that is necessary for school success later.*

For example, adults use worn out clichés, sarcastic overstatements, and meaningless threats. They say things like, "Move, or you're really going to get it!" "Shut up and sit down!" "Hush, I don't want to hear your voice!" "Everybody freeze this instant." "You'd better straighten up and get your act together." These imperative commands do not require any thinking, only blind obedience.

> *If early role models are articulate, accurate, and expressive in their verbal communication with children, and if they are responsive and supportive of children's attempts to express themselves, children can blossom in their development of linguistically elaborate communication skills, which form the basis for all later academic learning.*

For example, adults use meaningful statements of cause and effect, descriptions of actual events or consequences, and expressions of honest feelings. The adult's words are relevant to the actual situation. Children are expected to think, understand, predict, and evaluate actions and reactions. Children are exposed to a descriptive and elaborate vocabulary through the adult expressions. Adults say things such as, "If you stand up at the top of the slide, you may fall down." "If you hurt Genevieve, she may not want to play with you next time." "People have to wash their hands after they use the toilet to keep from spreading germs." "You must walk slowly and quietly here in the library because other people are trying to read." "I feel really sad when I see all the blooms pulled off our pretty petunia."

> *If early caregivers stereotype children by gender, ethnicity, or other characteristics, children build false assumptions about their limitations in the world.*

For example, adults may only select boys to act out the role of the fire marshal in a song or skit, totally ignoring girls who have their hands raised. Picture books are used that only show one ethnic, cultural, regional, or economic background. Adults take it for granted that all children celebrate Christmas and Easter. A particularly tall three-year-old is expected to behave more responsibly than a particularly tiny five-year-old. Children are singled out and treated differently according to how they look, how they dress, or what their parents do for a living.

> *If early caregivers see all children as unique individuals who can be helped to reach their own special potential, the children develop high expectations for themselves and the self-esteem needed to master challenges they set for themselves.*

For example, children are all seen as unique and valuable individuals. Books, puppets, and dolls are multicultural. Children are helped to appreciate various cultures through food, music, and holiday celebrations that expose them to many perspectives. Adults respect and help the children learn about religious and ethnic differences in children and their families. Girls and boys are expected to participate fully in all activities, and girls are especially encouraged to be competent and confident.

WHEN DOES CULTURAL LEARNING BEGIN?

Learning is important and possible for human beings at all stages from birth to death. However, during the earliest years of life, people are in a particularly fertile period for learning (Baillargeon, 1997; Begley, 1997a; Berk, 1997; Berndt, 1997; Boyatzis, 1997; Bruner, 1978a, 1978b; French, 1996; Hildebrand, 1997; Leong & Bodrova, 1996). In the first half-dozen years of children's lives, they absorb the cultural beliefs and values of their parents and early caregivers. As they

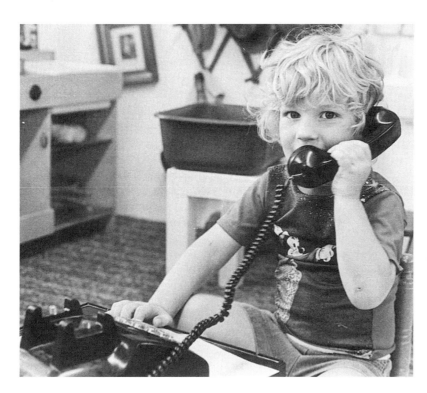

Children not only imitate what we do, but also how we do it.

grow older, they begin to take in cultural perceptions more and more from external sources such as other children, books, television, movies, records, role models, and folk heroes. Because child care by caregivers other than parents plays an important role in the development of most children today, we must look carefully at the kind of social and emotional nurturance child care settings provide children.

PARENT EXPECTATIONS RELATED TO SOCIAL AND ECONOMIC SETTINGS

A basic survival mechanism for the species is the process through which adults recreate for children miniature communities that reflect and represent the adults' perceptions of the larger adult community. For example, if parents perceive that their own successful participation in the society hinges on being obedient and taking orders or taking control and giving orders, then they will expect their children to be exposed to imperative commands. If, on the other hand, parents perceive that giving and taking orders are inappropriate in their own adult dealings, then they will probably feel more comfortable with their children being allowed to negotiate and make compromises rather than being told what to do (Miller, 1986).

Parents who endure long hours of crushing boredom in repetitive jobs may see nothing wrong with their children being pressured early in life to sit still for long periods without complaining or resisting. These adults may also be very tolerant of rowdy "cutting loose" behavior when it is the children's free-play time, since work and play are totally separate and unrelated in the adults' lives. If extreme financial limitations in a community cause parents to depend for their very survival on cohesion, cooperation, and frequent help from their relatives and neighbors, then it is likely that they will expect their children at an early age to accept major responsibility for chores like tending farm animals, cooking, cleaning, or taking caring of younger children. If these parents are expected in their jobs to follow set procedures and are not encouraged to think or evaluate, then it is natural that they will expect rote memorization rather than creative thinking as the core to their children's learning. If parents perceive that the world is full of hard knocks, unfair practices, and personal insults, then they may unconsciously toughen their children for survival by exposing them early to a world that is harsh and not always fair or logical. The children learn early that they will not always get whatever they want when they want it (Cook-Gumperz, 1973).

At the opposite extreme, parents with abundant financial resources and stimulating jobs live in a very different world and thus expect a very different environment for their children. Their work may be creative and self-directed. Their hobbies may also be creative and self-directed, and require as much concentration and effort as their work, so there is not a clear distinction between work and play for them. These parents probably expect a creative environment for their children in which children can initiate their own self-fulfilling activities through innovative thinking and active involvement. Children are expected to master challenges simply for the fun of it.

Since comfort and individuality are priorities in this cultural viewpoint, a young child would probably not be expected to care for younger siblings; that would be someone else's responsibility. Parents may expect their children's desires to be met quickly and fully. Parents would unconsciously condition children to be prepared for a world in which they will expect to be treated fairly and respectfully (perhaps even preferentially), and to get what they want much of the time. Our culture includes many variations of adult life other than the two extremes described here. Parents, caregivers, and teachers approach their work with children from many different cultural perspectives. One cultural perspective is not necessarily any better than any other. However, it is clear that early experiences prepare children to fit into existing cultural settings (Beaty, 1997; Cárdenas, 1995; Clark, DeWolf, & Clark, 1992; Denby, 1997; Derman-Sparks & the A.B.C. Task Force, 1989; Flynn, 1996; Gaetano, Williams, & Volk, 1998; Gonzales-Mena, 1998; Gordon & Browne, 1996b; Krogh, 1995; National Association for the Education of Young Children, 1993; Phillips, 1988).

Unfortunately, preparation for one cultural setting may make it difficult for a child to function in a totally different cultural setting (Lubeck, 1985). The child conditioned to obedience and rote memorization may be very confused and overwhelmed if she, as an adult, finds herself in a situation that requires initiative, innovation, and creative problem-solving. And a child who has been conditioned to a pliable world where she always has her needs met immediately may be cruelly unprepared for adversity in a tough, unfair "real world" situation. Ideally, all children from all settings could have enough multicultural exposure to various perceptions of the world that they could learn the skills to function in whatever setting they choose or find themselves in, and not be limited to functioning in only one strata in the diverse cultural rainbow available. The day is long gone when children could be reared to stay in the community of their birth, to live their entire lives and to die without ever venturing out into the larger world and dealing with people whose perceptions are quite different (Gough, 1993; Harrison, Wilson, Pine, Chan, & Buriel, 1990; Howard, 1993; Majors & Billson, 1992; McLoyd, 1990; Stevenson, Chen, & Uttal, 1990). Children can be helped to appreciate differences by learning more about how all people are the *same*, regardless of color, clothes, language, size, food preferences, or special needs.

RESPECTING FAMILIES' RELIGIOUS BELIEFS AND CUSTOMS

Public early childhood programs are required by law to provide an environment free from harassment or intimidation directed at any person's race, color, religion, national origin, sex, age, or disability. Any form of harassment or intimidation is not tolerated. Most private facilities also strive to prevent discrimination simply because it is the right thing to do, as well as an effective and professional business practice. Failure to prevent discrimination could result in a devastating lawsuit, a lost reputation, and a failed business. It can also damage children's self-esteem and impair their ability to function well in a diverse society.

Unless parents are informed that a program is religious in nature, teachers should focus on supporting multicultural learning by offering diverse learning experiences in an environment of tolerance and respect. Teachers, however, should allow children to express their own beliefs and traditions. There is a stark difference between children freely expressing their own beliefs and teachers instructing children in one particular set of beliefs without parents' prior knowledge and consent. Allowing children the freedom to pray, for example, is very appropriate. Instructing children how to pray without parental knowledge or approval would not be appropriate, and might be construed as a form of discrimination or disrespect.

Developmentally appropriate programs teach tolerance and respect for individual beliefs and customs. Every family's individual religious and cultural perspectives are to be respected. Some cultures prohibit foods common in other cultures, some religions forbid the celebration of birthdays, and some Native American families are offended by Thanksgiving because it commemorates the coming of European people to North America (which they believe harmed their culture and their people). Every family is unique, and as far as the developmentally appropriate early childhood program is concerned, every family's beliefs and customs are special to that family. By internalizing tolerance and respect for others, children learn an important life skill. They develop the ability to see things from someone else's point-of-view, a crucial social and cognitive developmental milestone.

In recent years, even Halloween has become a point of controversy for early childhood professionals. Parents can hold strong opinions about Halloween for a number of reasons. They may love Halloween, object to it for religious reasons, see gruesome costumes as offensive, fear dangers associated with trick-or-treating, or simply dislike commercialism directed at children. Teachers worry about managing behavior in classrooms filled with children focused on candy and costumes, and they may worry because toddlers and younger preschoolers are sometimes terrified by masks or costumes because they can't distinguish between real and pretend.

Developmentally appropriate programs can provide neutral alternatives to celebrations that concern some parents. For example, the traditional Halloween party in a classroom could be replaced by a fall costume event geared to the cognitive and social skills developed through role-playing. Teachers can further support children's creative expression by allowing the children to create their own costumes with grocery sacks, construction paper, tape, and markers; and their own masks with face-painting. Children express their individual cultural ideas and traditions within established ground rules.

(continues)

RESPECTING FAMILIES' RELIGIOUS BELIEFS AND CUSTOMS *(continued)*

Whenever possible, appropriate materials and activities can be brought into the classroom to help the children explore diverse cultural traditions. Developmentally appropriate programs avoid endorsing traditions tied to religious beliefs without prior knowledge and consent of the parents. Teachers trust parents to decide what cultural traditions and religious beliefs are right for their child. Teachers stay focused on "ground rules" that are based on the core values of democracy: be safe (don't unreasonably cause harm to oneself or others), be kind (respect the rights, beliefs, and possessions of others), and be neat (don't unreasonably damage shared property or the natural environment).

UNDERSTANDING CULTURAL DIFFERENCES

Cultural differences affect the way a person perceives or thinks about things. Almost every aspect of human existence is affected by culture to some extent. Culture defines for us what is right and what is wrong, our values, our day-to-day behavior, our relationships with others, and our perception of our own worth. Religion, ethnic customs, political affiliations, gender roles, social rituals, food preparation, literature, art, and music all express cultural uniqueness and serve to pass cultural traditions from one generation to the next. **Cultural pluralism** is a term used to describe the process of accepting and honoring cultural differences. If the concept of cultural pluralism is made an integral part of the first years of children's lives, they may be better able, as they grow up, to avoid being pulled into struggles with racial hatred, prejudice, or the stereotyping of individuals based on gender, religion, ethnic origin, age, or handicapping conditions.

Honoring cultural differences involves recognition and **respect**. While few people openly admit to prejudice, most of us consciously or unconsciously lump people together to some extent: boys are aggressive, the French are romantic, and overweight people are jolly and good-hearted. Some generalizations are patently untrue, while others revolve around some kernel of truth, but all generalizations have exceptions. There are boys who are gentle and nonaggressive, French lovers who are clods, and overweight people who are crabby and mean.

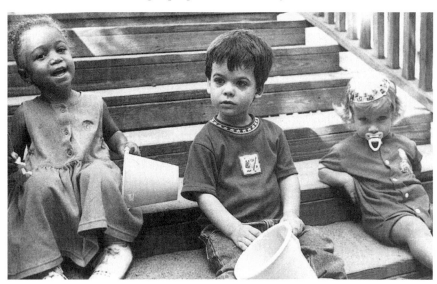

Children should see materials and books in the classroom that show people with different skin colors, hair styles, special holidays, clothing, abilities, and disabilities.

Respect means being given the opportunity to be seen as a unique individual rather than as a stereotypical caricature of some larger group. Underneath all the cultural and physical differences, we are all just people. We all put on our pants (or pantyhose) the same way: one leg at a time! We all want food, comfort, security, fulfillment, and most of all, the sense of belonging that comes with being loved and respected.

It is possible to urge children to better behavior and more functional habits while clearly letting them know that we accept and respect them as they are. Sometimes, adults label children by saying things like, "Vanessa, you are being so bad. Look how good Jeremy is." This sets an example for stereotyping people whose appearance or behavior is different. We can say instead, "Vanessa, hitting hurts. Use words instead of hitting, please." This way, an unacceptable behavior can be identified without lumping Vanessa into the category of "bad people."

By the age of three, children can recognize and identify different skin colors (Katz, 1982; Landreth & Johnson, 1953; Morland, 1972; Parrillo, 1985; Werner & Evans, 1971). They are very sensitive to subtle nonverbal as well as verbal indications from adults about the meaning and importance of differences in people. Adults may unconsciously show a more solicitous way of responding to people who are of similar ethnic and religious backgrounds, while at the same time, inadvertently snubbing those whose background is different.

Ethnicity and religion are not the only characteristics that generate prejudice. Some of us have difficulty showing warmth and respect for children whose parents behave in a way that is foreign to us, live a lifestyle we disapprove of, or are unappealing to us because of hygiene or style of dress. Some of us are obvious in our preference of girls over boys or boys over girls. We make comments such as, "The boys can go first because all the girls want to do is talk" or "You boys go on and find something to do. The girls just want to play by themselves without you causing trouble."

In order to provide a multicultural and nonsexist environment for young children, adults must consider all aspects of cultural exposure such as foods, books, toys, songs, rhymes, television shows, language, and clothing. Children can be helped to know and understand traditions of their own heritage as well as to know and honor the traditions of other cultures. They can be given dolls that are male and female as well as black, white, and brown. They can be exposed to books, songs, and television shows that show girls tackling adventurous challenges and boys expressing feelings. Dollhouse furniture can be combined with blocks and men's dress-up clothing can be mixed with dishes and doll beds.

Young children can be exposed to terms like *police officer*, *mail carrier*, and *repairperson* rather than *policeman*, *mailman*, and *repairman*. Teachers, doctors, nurses, and secretaries can be referred to as "he or she" rather than in a stereotypical way implying that all doctors are men and all secretaries are women. Children can learn nursery rhymes and songs in Spanish or Swahili as well as in English. Foods can be offered that sensitize children to regional and national dishes, ways of preparing foods, and food-related traditions and rituals.

THE ANTIBIAS CURRICULUM

The purpose of multicultural, nonsexist, and antidiscrimination exposure for children is not to force children into any specific mold, but rather to enhance their respect for others who are different, and to empower them to be whatever they have the talent and motivation to become. By fully appreciating differences in others and by recognizing that different does not necessarily mean inferior, children may become stronger in their own beliefs and traditions, and more resistant to peer pressure for conformity.

Children who have disgust for or fear of differences in others may be cruel in their treatment of children with special needs or ethnically different peers. They may also be very vulnerable in adolescence to popular peers who insist that anyone is a "nerd" who does not conform to group standards by smoking, drinking, taking drugs, participating in premarital sex, or driving at illegal speeds. Sometimes it takes a great deal of courage to be different and to know that being different is okay (Teaching Tolerance Project, 1997; Trawick-Smith, 1997).

TAKE TIME TO THINK BEFORE YOU JUDGE OTHERS

What to Consider

1. Do you find yourself having negative thoughts or feelings about a child or parent?

2. Does the parent have values, expectations, or communication styles different from your own? Does the child dress, speak, or behave in a way that seems unfamiliar or offensive to you? Examine your discomfort as objectively as you can. Could the differences be due to cultural backgrounds?

3. Ask whether the family members being served understand and relate to the values, assumptions, and philosophy of the early childhood program or school. Through parent meetings and one-on-one discussions, explore how parent views differ from those of the early childhood professionals. Listen, ask questions, and make a conscious effort to better understand their perspective. Just because someone's point of view is different, it is not necessarily wrong.

4. Are you proactive in providing an anti-bias learning environment? Are you setting a good example for children of tolerance and respect for others? Do you give domineering "I messages" to coworkers? Parents? Children? Are you diligent about putting into practice the principles of active listening? Are you willing to really listen to others and understand how things seem to them from

What to Do

1. Respect the uniqueness of each family system. Value every child and parent.

2. Remember that a family's cultural differences may relate to their race, ethnicity, religion, nationality, regional heritage, age, wealth, poverty, disability, gender preferences of parents, and many other factors. Individual perspectives evolve out of life experiences, upbringing, social status, and education.

3. Create a warm, respectful, collaborative relationship with families. Encourage parents to talk about their dreams for their child. Involve parents in school activities. Learn about different cultures. Make the curriculum culturally relevant by including books, activities, songs, and field trips intended to expand multicultural awareness. Find creative ways to use developmentally appropriate practice to achieve the goals parents have for their children.

4. Don't tell parents what is wrong with their views. Validate their values, prior experiences, and cultural knowledge. Use active listening, actively involve parents in the program, and always treat them with respect. Build on individual children's strengths. Consciously identify their strengths, and allow them opportunities for recognition and leadership that draw on their individual strengths. Help other children learn to understand

their perspective? Do you validate others' perspective, showing them that you understand and respect their view, even if you hold different views?

5. Have you taken steps to evaluate the effectiveness of your program's cultural sensitivity? Have children of certain background had difficulty fitting in? Have parents from some backgrounds tended to remove their children from the program at a higher rate than other families? (Seek information from the National Association for the Education of Young children (NAEYC) to locate effective early childhood evaluation tools and techniques.)

and appreciate cultural differences. Never allow hurtful teasing or bullying.

5. Take advantage of professional development for staff concerning multicultural curriculum development and cultural differences in kinship roles, beliefs, values, and communication styles. Read books and professional journals related to cultural sensitivity and multicultural teaching. Attend workshops, college classes, and discussion groups to expand knowledge and skill in this area. Observe highly regarded programs and respected early childhood professionals. Take notes, ask questions, and, mot important, have an open mind.

PHILOSOPHIES OF GUIDANCE

Culture plays an important role in shaping parents', teachers', and caregivers' philosophies about children and child rearing. A person's philosophy affects her perception of children, how they learn, what their intentions are, and why they behave as they do. Ideas about child guidance that immediately seem logical and appropriate or sound ridiculous have been filtered by the set of beliefs and assumptions that make up one's philosophy.

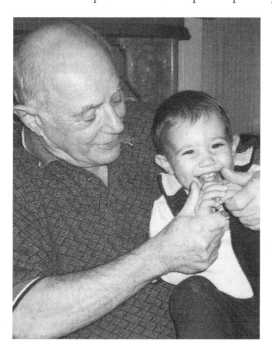

Our philosophy determines how we answer questions that have no right answer, and make decisions in situations that have no easy solution.

Although parents, teachers, or caregivers may think that they have no particular philosophy, it is likely that they simply have never really analyzed how their beliefs compare with those held by others. Some people may mistakenly assume that everyone in the world naturally shares their same underlying beliefs about how things should be and why they are as they are. The process of acquiring appropriate behavior is a learning process just as surely as the process of learning to read and write. It is, therefore, essential for us to explore various philosophies related to how and why learning takes place.

IS A CHILD'S PERSONALITY MOSTLY THE RESULT OF NATURE OR NURTURE?

One of the oldest debates related to children is the old nature versus nurture controversy. People who believe in "nature" believe that children become whatever they become based on heredity, inborn traits, and inner motivation. People who believe in "nurture" believe that children become whatever they become based on parental guidance, teaching effectiveness, television, and other external influences.

Whenever adults compare children, they can hardly resist venturing opinions about how children grow to be so different. Some will say, "Jennifer was born to be a little terror! She's just like her dad, never still for a minute" or "Rahul will undoubtedly be a talented musician. He has inherited musical ability from both sides of his family." These people emphasize the importance of children's internal nature in their development. They believe that children are predestined at birth to certain talents and personality traits because of genetic inheritance or inborn characteristics.

Others disagree. They say things like, "Of course Ming Li has become potty trained so early. Her child care teachers have trained hundreds of toddlers. They know how to do it" or "If that was my child, he wouldn't be whining and sucking his thumb. His parents must be overindulgent or he wouldn't behave that way." These people emphasize the importance of external nurturing in the development of children. They believe that children are all born pretty much the same, and their differences evolve because of differences in their treatment and teaching.

In past decades, cultural perceptions dictated that personality and potential were inborn. Some people even worried that an adopted child could carry a "bad seed." While human nature is such that we are often tempted to take credit for accomplishments and exemplary behavior, we have routinely blamed failures and unacceptable behaviors on either the inborn traits of the child or on her conscious choice to be bad.

As research into human learning has mushroomed over recent years, a dawning awareness has blossomed in parents and caregivers of the role of **environment** (everything and everyone the child encounters) in child development. The pendulum has swung to the extreme opposite direction from blaming fate for child behaviors to attempting to manipulate them artificially, speeding the process of development and even attempting to create "better babies."

In the early 1980s, a culturally popular trend began that has been referred to as the "superbaby phenomenon." As many parents had only one or two children well after both parents' careers were established, they began to place more and more emphasis on the optimum development of the child or children they had. People bought or made flashcards with abstract number concepts, names of famous composers, and anatomy terms to use in stimulating their infants. Some parents began to fear that their toddler would be left behind if she had not been enrolled in baby gymnastics, French tutoring, and violin lessons by the age of two. Guilt became a national pastime for trend-setting parents. Perhaps the pendulum will settle to a middle ground where popular culture encourages adults to recognize and appreciate the uniqueness of every individual child and her natural rate of development, and to take seriously the critically important role of play experiences and social interactions for the child's development to her fullest potential.

For example, cognitive stimulation is to psychic development much like food is to physical development. If enough food is not available, development will be stunted. However, forcing as much food as possible on a child is probably equally destructive. Making appropriate quantities of developmentally appropriate foods (or learning experiences) available while respecting the child's hunger (or readiness for learning) makes a great deal of sense (Elkind, 1997).

WHAT DO CURRENT EXPERTS SAY ABOUT THE ORIGIN OF INTELLIGENCE AND PERSONALITY?

Lately, educators have been placing more emphasis on the range of philosophies that underlie various theoretical explanations of the origin of human intelligence and personality. These experts trace the ancient nature versus nurture controversy and add a new interactionist point of view that assumes a reciprocal relationship between nature and nurture.

THE NATURE VERSUS NURTURE CONTROVERSY

If human thinking could be neatly separated into simple categories, we would find three contrasting views.
1. The **behaviorists**—those who believe that behavior and learning result from external forces such as reinforcement and punishment.
2. The **maturationists**—those who believe that behavior and learning hinge on internal processes such as physiological maturation and intrinsic motivation.
3. The **developmental interactionists**—those who believe that behavior and learning result from complex and dynamic reciprocal interactions involving both internal processes and external forces.

The Behaviorist Approach

The behaviorists incorporate the 17th-century tradition of John Locke who viewed the newborn's mind as a *tabula rasa*, or empty slate. These theorists—the behaviorists, positivists, and empiricists—believe that human learning comes from outside the learner. They believe that environment accounts for nearly all that a person becomes.

Watson (1930), Skinner (1953, 1974), and others have theorized that human beings are really products of their environments. People become scholars or cat burglars, not because of their genetic makeup or by choice, but because their environment has conditioned them to behave as they do. Subscription to this view has powerful implications for parents and educators. It implies that human beings can be molded or shaped by the controlling of environmental experiences. This view also shifts emphasis away from focus on human will and predisposition.

Behaviorists view the development of appropriate behavior as the responsibility of the adult. The adult is responsible for identifying and selecting specific behavior goals for the child. Then the adult observes the child and monitors any spontaneous behaviors that are slightly closer to the desired goal behavior, reinforcing each subsequent step closer to the desired goal by giving praise, treats, or **tokens** (that can be traded later for special prizes or privileges). The adult maneuvers the child's surroundings in order to **modify** (or change) specific behaviors in the child.

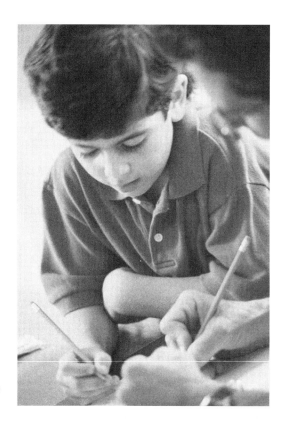

Nature lays the groundwork for a child's potential, but nurturing makes it possible for the child to achieve that potential.

Behaviorists leave nothing to chance. They choose goal behaviors, select reinforcers, and even plan a reinforcement schedule of when, how often, and under exactly what circumstances reinforcers will be given. Behaviorist views are all focused on the idea that learning is an external process, and that learning takes place in the child as a result of influences from the child's environment. Child guidance is seen as an adult-directed process.

The Maturationist Approach

From a point of view opposite to that of the behaviorists, the maturationists borrow from the tradition of Plato. These maturationists, innatists, and nativists believe that learning emerges from within. These educators and philosophers have theorized that human beings are born to be whatever they become; the human infant in this conception is like the rosebud, naturally unfolding into a preordained blossom as long as it is kept healthy. Well into the 1920s and the 1930s, Arnold Gesell, a researcher at Yale, maintained that children's external environment did not control developmental outcomes. He claimed that children's own genetic and biological characteristics determined their intelligence and personality (Gesell, Halvorson, Thompson, & Ilg, 1940).

The maturationists view the development of appropriate behavior as a natural process. They believe that as long as basic needs are met, the child will automatically develop the social skills, the intelligence, and the physical control necessary for the child to behave properly. They see the role of the adult as that of a facilitator. The adult studies children, carefully observing and monitoring their behaviors and abilities. When there is a problem, the adult steps in to help the child understand what has happened in a specific situation, and to help the child resolve the problem as independently as possible.

Maturationists perceive that learning comes from inside the child. They believe that the processes of learning cannot be rushed. Adults view themselves as role models, guides, and consultants. They believe children are ultimately responsible for their own decision to behave properly. Personality and growth traits inherited genetically and the child's own will power play an important role in the maturationists' views on how children learn to behave appropriately. The maturationists see the development of proper behavior as a child-directed process.

Obviously, this type of perception has broad implications for parents and educators concerned with guiding children. If early experiences are relatively inconsequential to one's later development, then adults need only be concerned with providing the basic necessities for safety and health—custodial care—in the earliest years. This view implies that growth and learning proceed according to internal rules of physiological growth, and as a result of personal decision-making, in spite of specific environmental circumstances.

The Developmental Interactionist Approach

Debate over the previous two contrasting view of human learning (the nature versus nurture controversy) has been complicated recently by a growing body of research compiled toward the end of the 20th century by the developmental interactionists who believe that human learning results from the interaction between the learner and her environment.

The work of Vygotsky (Berk, 1997; Gutek, 1997; Leong & Bodrova, 1996; Seefeldt & Barbour, 1998; Spafford, Pesce, & Grosser, 1998), Piaget (1952, 1962, 1963, 1970, 1983), Chomsky (1965), Kohlberg and DeVries (1987), Hunt (1976), Bloom (1964), Kagan and Moss (1962), Kagan (1971; Kagan, Kearsley, & Zelazo, 1978), and White (1975, 1995; White & Watts, 1973;

Children create their own learning; we are only their guides.

White, Kaban, & Attanucci, 1979) has made it clear that environmental factors influence human development. But the research also supports the importance of individual readiness, personal learning styles, and reciprocal interaction as a part of the process. This new stream of thought has gained scientific credibility and is now recognized to be neither a maturational nor a behaviorist view of learning. Piaget (1952), for example, termed himself a constructionist or cognitive interactionist (developmental interactionist). He asserted that infants are born with predispositions to certain kinds of thought and behavior but that they must create their own knowledge through stages of interaction with the environment. Play is the concept we use to refer to this early exploratory interaction with the environment.

Vygotsky, on the other hand, focused on the critical role adults and peers play in the child's creation of "mental tools." He believed that adults and peers challenge the child by presenting and modeling skills just outside the child's reach.

White (1975) said that newborn children come into the world with an internal structure that sets an upper limit to their potential, but that the internal structure is not a guarantee of any level of development or learning. The child is programmed to learn, but without stimulation and reinforcement from the environment, no learning can take place (Petersen, 1996). This way of thinking about young children creates pressure on parents and child care providers to produce high-quality early experiences so that optimum experiences can be made available. Chugani (1993) has further emphasized the importance of early environments by showing that a baby's

By analyzing what we know about child development in the context of day-to-day observations of the children in our care, we strive constantly to match the right activities and materials to the emerging abilities that we identify in each child.

brain uses information from sensory experiences to design its own architecture. A kind of "mapping" takes place inside the brain with astounding rapidity as the number of synapses (or connections) among brain cells multiplies by the trillions in a very few months.

Lorenz (1966), Hess (1972), von Frisch (1974), and Lamb (1978, 1981) are ethologists (researchers who study behaviors in terms of natural processes and in natural settings). They have refined the idea of sensitive periods for learning in which environmental stimuli can have a maximum impact on a child's learning. Hunt (1976) described what he called the "match." He said that a match must be created between a child's level of readiness and the exact level of difficulty or discrepancy in a specific learning situation in order for optimum learning to take place.

If interactions in the environment are too difficult, children become frustrated and discouraged. If they are too easy, children become bored. Children actively seek out materials and activities that match their own level. They enjoy and learn well from an environment that offers a fairly wide range of difficulty in which they are allowed the freedom to choose toys, games, and interactions that are matched to their own ability level, as well as the freedom to reject materials or activities that seem too easy or too difficult.

In terms of child guidance, the interactionists believe that children can only learn to behave appropriately when they have inner maturity as well as suitable external influences. Adults must study children and plan carefully, but they must also focus on the child's own interests and abilities. Some areas of child guidance seem more responsive to external control and some areas to internal control. Mindless habits a child really wants to change can probably be treated quickly and effectively through behaviorist strategies. More general problems that seem to have deeply rooted emotional causes are usually best treated with maturationist support of the natural processes of development.

The interactionist approach integrates the processes for inner and outer development. Interactionists see child guidance not as an adult-directed or a child-directed process, but rather as an interaction in which either can lead or follow. It is like a waltz with give and take, leading and following. The adult respects the child's interests and abilities but is also not afraid to take control when necessary. The child feels free to express herself but also knows and respects clearly defined limits. The interactionist approach includes the best of both worlds: nature and nurture.

IF THERE ARE DIFFERENT VIEWS ABOUT HOW CHILDREN DEVELOP, HOW DO I KNOW WHICH PHILOSOPHY IS RIGHT?

Within any group of people who care for and teach young children, there will be many successful and effective adults who tend to lean a bit toward either a more maturationist or a more behaviorist view of early growth and development. Generally, however, a predominant view in the field of early childhood education revolves around the belief that early development results from the interaction between children's inner capacity and motivation and their external environment.

Two basic assumptions that build a foundation for the procedures throughout this book are the beliefs that:

- babies and children develop skills and concepts by interacting (playing and living) in a stimulating and supportive environment.

- the way children interact in their environment is triggered by their particular stage of development as well as their own interests and motives.

Wouldn't it be a better world if children grew up remembering to be kind, neat, health and safety conscious, respectful of the rights of others, and thoughtful in preserving the environment.

In other words, one might say that healthy, well-developed children come into the world pre-programmed to learn (Chomsky, 1965). They will automatically be motivated to explore the physical properties of the environment around them by using their senses, they will seek human social contact, and they will quickly absorb any language they hear. If these components of the environment are abundantly available, the interactions that ensue will foster development in a healthy and natural way. Children who come into the world without all of the five senses intact, with developmental delays, or with impaired motor capabilities, need special equipment, extra stimulation, and skilled teaching to reach their full potential for development. Children with disabilities do not usually learn as easily and naturally as their peers.

Tragically, however, even an infant who is perfectly healthy at birth may eventually suffer from the effects of a hostile or nonnurturing environment. Lack of a healthy emotional environment can cause:

• failure-to-thrive syndrome.

• **marasmus** (a severe condition of underweight and poor health).

• developmental delay.

• permanent mental retardation.

• death.

Any of these can afflict potentially normal, healthy children if they are deprived of the essential elements of a normal environment with nurturing human contact, a sense of being wanted and accepted, the opportunity to share thoughts and feelings in verbal or nonverbal communication with others, and exposure to interesting things to explore by seeing, touching, tasting, feeling, smelling, and moving around.

The development of an intelligent, responsible human being is not an automatic internal process that takes place in spite of environmental factors, and it is not an external process of molding a pliable child into a predetermined shape chosen by parents and teachers. It is a lively process of give and take in which children explore their boundaries and limits. Sometimes, they accommodate to adult expectations, and sometimes, quite naturally, they resist.

Children come equipped with individual personalities, likes, dislikes, interests, and motives. The role of the adult is to guide, assertively and respectfully, never forgetting that even the youngest child is truly a person with all the rights befitting any other human being (even the right to be negative and recalcitrant on occasion). In the developmental interactionist perspective, child guidance is intended to give children feedback about the realities of their world, to allow them choices within reasonable limits, and to help them confront the logical consequences of their own actions.

> *We mark our progress as a civilization by what we see as advances in hardware, and that criterion, assumed so readily by the population at large, blinds us to other possible values such as community, reverence, wisdom, the care and education of children, and the condition of the natural world.*
> *I would wish to be a member of a community that judged itself on the happiness of its children rather than on the unhindered flow of its mechanical inventions.*
>
> *Thomas Moore (1994)*

POINTS TO REMEMBER

- Parents who depend on help from others in rearing their children want to be assured that their children will receive proper guidance.

- Adults may have difficulty changing old habit patterns in dealing with children, but change is possible with motivation and practice.

- People from different cultural and economic backgrounds often hold starkly contrasting views about the parameters of proper child care.

- Honoring cultural differences involves recognition and respect for the appearances, customs, and beliefs of others.

PRACTICAL APPLICATION

BRINGING HOME A BABY BUMBLEBEE

In a medium-sized neighborhood child care center, a group of preschool-aged children cluster around their teacher and sing with her. They snatch invisible bumblebees out of the air and pretend to trap them in their clasped hands as they sing:

I'm bringing home a baby bumblebee. Won't my mommy be so proud of me? I'm bringing home a baby bumblebee—bzzz bzzz bzzz bzzz. Ouch! [slap] He stung me!

In another part of town, in a child care center located in a tiny, dilapidated building that is part of a low-income housing project, a group of children sit on chairs around long, wobbly tables as they enthusiastically sing:

I'm bringing home a baby bumblebee. Won't my mama be surprised of me? I'm bringing home a baby bumblebee—bzzz bzzz bzzz bzzz. Ouch! [slap] He stung me! I'm squashing up the baby bumblebee. Now there's bumblebee blood all over me. I'm wiping off the blood of the bumblebee. Now there's no more blood all over me.

In still another part of town, in a tastefully decorated private preschool, a third group of children sit cross-legged on the floor in a circle singing happily with their teacher:

I'm bringing home a baby bumblebee. Won't my daddy be so proud of me? I'm opening up the window carefully, so my bee can fly away free—bzzz bzzz bzzz bzzz. Bye bye, baby bumblebee.

DISCUSSION QUESTIONS

1. How do the words to each of these songs reflect the differences in perspectives and expectations of childhood in these different communities?
2. Do you think that songs and games parents and child care workers use simply to entertain children pass cultural perceptions from one generation to the next?
3. What are your own cultural perceptions of children? Do you see children as innocent and pure, to be protected from anything violent, scary, or disgusting? Do you see children as regular people who enjoy raucous humor and vicarious aggression? Do you see children as "born sinners" who sometimes can have evil or cruel impulses?
4. Compare versions of songs and stories you have heard. Do the different versions reflect cultural experiences of children?
5. Why do you think the third teacher in the example replaced the word *mommy* or *mama* with the word *daddy*?
6. Do you think that children growing up in inner-city slums might like different songs and games than other, more sheltered children who have not experienced the discomfort and fear associated with poverty?
7. How are songs and stories purposely used by adults to instill in children an awareness of cultural values?
8. Identify a song or story you would feel uncomfortable using with children. What would you do to change it? Why?

RELATED READINGS
RESPECTING CULTURAL DIFFERENCES

Alperson, M. (2001). *Dim sum, bagels and grits: A sourcebook for multicultural families.* New York: Farrar Straus & Giroux.

Including an extensive resource directory, this book outlines specific issues and concerns facing multi-ethnic families, along with strategies for dealing with them. Personal interviews strengthen discussions of the struggles and joys multicultural families experience.

Aoki, E. M. (1981). Are you Chinese? Are you Japanese? Or are you just a mixed-up kid? Using Asian American children's literature. *The Reading Teacher, 34*, 382–385.

Beaty, J. J. (1997). *Building bridges with multicultural picture books: For children 3–5.* Upper Saddle River, NJ: Merrill Education/Prentice-Hall.

Focusing on the common bonds among children, this book shows future teachers how to bring multicultural values and ideas into early childhood programs using appropriate picture books. In addition to providing criteria for selecting appropriate books, the author describes how to lead children into book-related activities, and eventually, how to create a more multicultural curriculum through picture books.

Bel Geddes, J. (1997). *Childhood and children: A compendium of customs, superstitions, theories, profiles, and facts.* Phoenix, AZ: Oryx Press.

Bishop, R. S. (1987). Extending multicultural understanding through children's books. In B. Cullinan (Ed.), *Children's literature in the reading program* (pp. 60–67). Newark, DE: International Reading Association.

Bishop, R. S. (1991). African American literature for today's children: Anchor, compass, and sail. *Perspectives, 7*, ix–xii.

Cárdenas, J. A. (1995). *Multicultural education: A generation of advocacy.* Needham Heights, MA: Allyn & Bacon.

José Cárdenas has brought together a compilation of articles that span the last twenty-five years, and seek insights into the history and development of multicultural education. The articles address the education needs of minority and disadvantaged students, with a special emphasis on Hispanic Americans.

Davis, M. D., Kilgo J. L., & Gamel-McCormick, M. (1998). *Young children with special needs: A developmentally appropriate approach.* Needham Heights, MA: Allyn & Bacon.

Proposes that children with disabilities are more like their peers without disabilities than they are different. Early childhood classes reflect increasingly more diverse children as time goes on. Child diversity in terms of race, culture, religion, experience, ability, family, and national origin is related to social and economic realities. Increasing emphasis on inclusion promises to add even more complexity to teachers' decision-making processes.

de Melendez, W., & Ostertag, V. (1997). *Teaching young children in multicultural classrooms: Issues, concepts, and strategies.* Clifton Park, NY: Delmar Learning.

This book addresses the historical, theoretical, and practical aspects of multicultural education as it relates to young children. It includes current and future trends, addresses the current as well as future directions of multicultural education, and provides practical classroom ideas for implementation.

Derman-Sparks, L. (1989). *Anti-bias curriculum: Tools for empowering young children.* Washington, DC: National Association for the Education of Young Children.

Elman, J., Bates, E. A., Johnson, M., Karmiloff-Smith, A., Parisi, D., & Plunkett, K. (1997). *Rethinking innateness.* Cambridge, MA: MIT Press.

Emberton, S. (1994, Fall). Do your cultural homework. *National Center for Family Literacy Newsletter 6*(3), 5–6.

Everett, C., & Everett, S. V. (1998). *Healthy divorce: For parents and children.* Hoboken, NJ: Jossey-Bass.

Feeney, S. S., Christensen, D., & Moravcik, E. R. (1996). *Who am I in the lives of children? An introduction to teaching young children* (5th ed.). Upper Saddle River, NJ: Merrill Education/Prentice-Hall.

The authors cover such topics as career development initiatives, changes in professional preparation, and the movement to increase developmentally appropriate practice in primary grades. This book focuses on the value of a professional code of ethics and encourages readers to compare and contrast the field's values with their own and select ways of teaching that are consistent with their own values.

Fluney-Stefano, E. (1996). Caregiver's corner. Discovery learning-about other races. *Young Children, 51*(4), 73.

A story about a young child's experience with race teaches us the importance of discovery and learning.

Folberg, J., (Ed.). (1991). *Joint Custody and Shared Parenting.* (2nd ed.). New York: Guilford Press.

Reviews research, literature, and law to present useful information gleaned from child developmental experts, therapists, mediators, researchers, economists, and lawyers.

Gutek, G. L. (1997). *Historical and philosophical foundations of education: A biographical introduction* (2d ed.). Upper Saddle River, NJ: Merrill Education/Prentice-Hall.

This book explores notable personalities and philosophies in education from a variety of areas and cultures by identifying leading contributors to educational thought in an international setting, developing key philosophies of education through the lives of those who developed them, and relating education to global trends that have helped shape human history.

Harris, V. (Ed.). (1993). *Teaching multicultural literature in grades K–8.* Norwood, MA: Christopher Gordon.

Hildebrand, V., Phenice, L. A., Gray, M. M., & Hines, R. P. (1996). *Knowing and serving diverse families.* Upper Saddle River, NJ: Merrill Education/Prentice Hall.

This book responds to the growing need for programs to work comfortably with all people, and to help solve critical societal problems of relating to today's people at home, in the community, the nation, and the world. It examines both ethnic and structural diversity in families in the United States.

Ingoldsby, B. B., & Smith, S. (Eds.). (1995). *Families in multicultural perspective.* New York: Guilford.

This book explores the diversity of the world's families in structure, processes, history, and social and environmental contexts. It covers contemporary Third World and Western families.

King, E. W., Chipman, M. F., & Cruz-Janzen, M. (1994). *Educating young children in a diverse society.* Needham Heights, MA: Allyn & Bacon.

This text presents information, techniques, strategies, and incentives needed to generate an awareness of cultural diversity including race, ethnicity, gender, and social class in very young children. It uses incidents in the lives of various people as examples to illustrate how early encounters with the forces of ethnic, social, and gender identification shaped their lives. The text clearly shows how cultural conditioning inherent in families or religious, linguistic, or ethnic groups may influence learning outcomes.

Konner, M. (1991). *Childhood: A multicultural view.* Boston: Little, Brown.

Lakey, J. (1997, May). Teachers and parents define diversity in an Oregon preschool cooperative-Democracy at work. *Young Children, 52*(4), 20–28.

Levy, D. L., (Ed.). (1993). *The best parent is both parents: A guide to Shared parenting in the 21st century.* Charlottesville, VA: Hampton Roads Publishing;

Reviews research on joint and sole custody, and argues that children need both of their parents in their lives.

Lynch, E. W., & Hanson, M. J. (1992). *Developing cross-cultural competence: A guide for working with young children and their families.* Baltimore: Paul H. Brookes Publishing Company.

Miller, D. F. (1989). *First steps toward cultural difference: Socialization in infant/toddler day care.* Washington, DC: Child Welfare League of America.

Miller-Lachmann, L. (Ed.). (1992). *Our family, our friends, our world: Annotated guide to significant multicultural books for children and teenagers.* New Providence, NJ: Bowker.

Ramirez, G., Jr., & Ramirez, J. L. (1994). *Multiethnic children's literature: A comprehensive resource guide.* Clifton Park, NY: Delmar Learning.

Ramler, M., & Rice, S. (1997, Summer). Looking beyond chronic illness: Helping children be children. *Texas Child Care, 21*(1), 12–15.

Salmon, M., & Akaran, S. E. (2001). Enrich your kindergarten program with a cross-cultural connection. *Young Children, 56*(4), 30–32.

Kindergarten children explore, write, draw, ask questions, research, and share information about the similarities and differences of their communities.

Silvers, J. (1997). Child labor in Pakistan. In E. N. Junn & C. Boyatzis (Eds.), *Annual editions: Child growth and development 97/98* (4th ed.). New York: McGraw-Hill. (Original work published in *The Atlantic Monthly*, February 1996.)

The exploitation of children as laborers illustrates the influence of economic and political factors on how children are viewed and treated in a society. Jonathan Silvers describes how Pakistan's recent laws limiting child labor are generally ignored, leaving an estimated 11 million children toiling in that country's factories.

Slapin, B., & Seale, D. (1992). *Through Indian eyes: The native experience in books for children.* Philadelphia: New Society.

Strickland, D., & Strickland, M. (1994). *Families: Poems celebrating the African-American experience.* Honesdale, PA: Boyds Mills Press.

Stroud, J. E., Stoud, J. C., & Staley, L. M. (1997, Summer). Understanding and supporting adoptive families. *Early Childhood Education Journal, 24*(4), 229–234.

Swick, K. J., Boutte, G., & Van Scoy, I. (1997). Families and schools: Building multicultural values together. In K. M. Paciorek & J. H. Munro (Eds.), *Annual editions: Early childhood education 97/98* (18th ed.). New York: McGraw-Hill. (Original work published in *Childhood Education*, Winter 1995/96.)

> *If families and teachers looked down the road thirty years and developed a list of qualities they would like to see in their children, they could begin to plan collaboratively the types of experiences needed today. A multicultural society requires all families to advocate and work together.*

United Nations. (1994). *International year of the family.* New York: Department of Public Information.

Wagoner, S. A. (1982). Mexican Americans in children's literature since 1970. *The Reading Teacher, 36,* 274–279.

Weis, L., & Fine, M. (Eds.). (1993). *Beyond silenced voices: Class, race, and gender in United States schools.* New York: State University of New York Press.

York, S. (1991). *Roots and wings: Affirming culture in early childhood programs.* St. Paul, MN: Redleaf Press.

HELPFUL WEB SITES

http://www-rcf.usc.edu/~cmmr/   USC Center for Multilingual, Multicultural Research is an organized research unit at the University of Southern California, facilitating the research collaboration, dissemination and professional development activities of faculty, students, and others across School of Education, university and outside organizational lines.

http://www.colorado.edu/education/BUENO/index.html   BUENO Center for Multicultural Education. Organized in the School of Education at the University of Colorado at Boulder, the Center strongly promotes quality education with an emphasis on cultural pluralism through a comprehensive range of research, training, and service projects. The Center is deeply committed to facilitating equal educational opportunities for cultural and language minority students.

http://www.scfn.org/   The Single and Custodial Father's Network. The network includes both single and custodial fathers and is open to anyone interested in supporting fathers in custodial parenting roles.

http://www.av.qnet.com/~rlewis3/   The Single Father's Lighthouse. Resources, information, good humor.

http://www.singleparentcentral.com/   Single Parent Central. Online resource for single parent families.

http://www.singlerose.com/   Single Rose—Resource for Single Mothers. An emotionally supportive site for divorced, widowed and never-married women raising children alone.

http://www.fathersworld.com/   Father's World. Information, resources, support and education for all types of fathers and their families.

http://www.singlemoms.org/ M.O.M.S. Dedicated to providing resources, support and information to all single parents.

http://www.singlemothers.org/index.html National Organization of Single Mothers. Offers single parents resources and parenting education materials including SingleMOTHER, 21 Ways to Avoid Single Mother Burnout, and Support Group Guide.

http://www.hec.ohio-state.edu/famlife/divorce/pguides/intro.htm Parent Guides to Help Children Deal with Divorce (Free on-line publications). These guides will help you teach children to use a problem-solving approach in their lives.

http://www.drheller.com/parenting_challenges.html Parenting Challenges During Marital Separation (Free online publication). Guidelines that address many common parenting questions and concerns related to separation.

http://www.parentswithoutpartners.org/ Parents Without Partners. Provides discussions, professional speakers, study groups, publications and social activities for families and adults. Groups throughout the country.

http://www.singlefather.org/ Responsible Single Fathers. Provides mentoring, support and referrals to dads to help them cope, parent, nurture, love, and emotionally and financially care for their children.

For additional information on positive child guidance, visit our Web site at
http://www.earlychilded.delmar.com

Appendix A
Children's Books Addressing Values and Feelings

Hands Are Not for Hitting
by Martine Agassi
Marieka Heinlen (Illustrator)
Free Spirit Publishing, Board Edition, April 2002.

Stimulates children to think and talk about alternatives to hitting and other forms of hurtful behavior. The repeated phrase "hands are not for hitting" is accompanied by suggestions for positive uses for hands such as waving, helping, drawing, and making music. (Ages 2 to 5)

Don't Despair on Thursdays! The Children's Grief-Management Book
by Adolph J. Moser
David Melton (Illustrator)
Nancy R. Thatch (Editor)
Landmark Editions (The Emotional Impact Series), 1998.

Useful resource for children experiencing grief. (Ages 5 to 9)

Don't Feed the Monster on Tuesdays! The Children's Self-Esteem Book
by Adolph J. Moser
David Melton (Illustrator)
Nancy R. Thatch (Editor)
Landmark Editions (The Emotional Impact Series), 1991.

Shows numerous ways children are critical of themselves. Before the list is over, kids are laughing and realizing the importance of self-esteem. (Ages 5 to 9)

Don't Pop Your Cork on Mondays! The Children's Anti-Stress Book
by Adolph J. Moser
Dav Pilkey (Illustrator)
Landmark Editions (The Emotional Impact Series), 1988.

Helps children explore the causes and effects of stress, and offers children practical approaches for dealing with stress in their daily lives. (Ages 5 to 9)

Don't Tell a Whopper on Fridays! The Children's Truth-Control Book
by Adolph J. Moser
David Melton (Illustrator)
Landmark Editions (The Emotional Impact Series), 1999.

Discusses the problems of lying and the importance of telling the truth. (Ages 5 to 9)

Don't Rant and Rave on Wednesdays! The Children's Anger-Control Book
by Adolph J. Moser
David Melton (Illustrator)
Nancy R. Thatch (Editor)
Landmark Editions (The Emotional Impact Series), 1994.

Describes common but inappropriate behaviors and suggests ways to control anger and express feelings appropriately. (Ages 5 to 9)

When Dinosaurs Die: A Guide to Understanding Death
by Marc Tolon Brown (Illustrator)
Laurie Krasny Brown
Little Brown & Co (reprint edition), 1998.

Answers very basic questions about death such as what it is and what it means, and explores emotions related to grief. More appropriate for home than school settings as questions of a religious nature will probably arise. (Ages 5 to 8)

Don't Fall Apart on Saturdays! The Children's Divorce-Survival Book
by Adolph J. Moser
David Melton (Illustrator)
Landmark Editions (The Emotional Impact Series), 2000.

Helps children understand what divorce is and why their parents are getting a divorce. (Ages 5 to 9)

It's Not Your Fault, Koko Bear: A Read-Together Book for Parents & Young Children During Divorce
by Vicki Lansky
Jane Prince (Illustrator)
Minnetonka, MN: Book Peddlers, 1998.

This book provides a reassuring message to children that their feelings are natural, that their parents still love and will care for them, and that the divorce is not their fault. Each page includes endnotes for parents with information and advice about what children are experiencing, and tips for handling each issue as it arises. (Ages 3 to 7 and parents)

Dear Mr. Henshaw
by Beverly Cleary
Paul O. Zelinsky (Illustrator)
Scott Foresman (Reprint Edition) 2000.

This award-winning book by Beverly Cleary will be appreciated by any youngster who feels lonely and troubled during the difficult transition into adolescence. (Ages 8 to 12)

How Tia Lola Came to Stay
by Julia Alvarez
Andrea Cascardi (Editor)
Knopf, 2001.

Miguel and Juanita Guzman and their mother have moved from New York City to rural Vermont. Left behind is their beloved Papi, a painter whom their mother is divorcing. To ease the transition and to help with baby-sitting, Mami has sent for her aunt from the Dominican Republic who creates a delightful whirlwind in their home. The story ends with a holiday trip to the Dominican Republic where the children meet their mother's family for the first time, and begin to accept that home is where love is.

Vicki Lansky's Divorce Book for Parents: Helping Your Children Cope with Divorce and Its Aftermath
by Jeanie Franz Ransom
Kathryn Kunz Finney (Illustrator)
Magination, 2000.

Story of a young girl whose parents have just told her they are getting a divorce. The narrative then goes through the range of the child's possible emotions, as the adults suggest how she might be feeling and she imagines herself to be an animal that would adequately express her emotions. (Ages 5 to 8)

What Children Need to Know When Parents Get Divorced
by William L. Coleman
Bethany House (revised & updated edition), 1998.

This practical guide from a licensed family counselor is designed to be read with elementary age children facing the agonizing trauma of divorce. When read with a caring adult, this book can be the first step in bringing children of divorce toward much-needed emotional healing. (Ages 6 to 12)

How It Feels When Parents Divorce
by Jill Krementz
Knopf (reprint edition), 1988.

A culturally diverse group of boys and girls, ages seven to sixteen, share their feelings about their parents' divorce. (Ages 7 to 16)

Help! A Girl's Guide to Divorce and Stepfamilies
by Nancy Holyoke
Scott Nash (Illustrator)
Pleasant Company Publications, 1999.

An appropriate resource of stories shared by other girls to open the doors of communication about divorce and provide comfort. (Girls ages 7 to 12)

The Fall of Freddie the Leaf: A Story of Life for All Ages
by Leo F. Buscaglia
Holt Rinehart Winston, 1983.

A warm, wise, beautiful and simple story about a leaf named Freddie. Freddie and the other leaves change with the seasons, finally falling to the ground with winter's snow. (All ages)

Sad Isn't Bad: A Good-Grief Guidebook for Kids Dealing with Loss
by Michaelene Mundy
R. W. Alley (Illustrator)
Abbey Press, 1998.

Written by a school counselor, this book helps comfort children facing loss. (Ages 5 to 8)

Grandmother's Song
by Barbara Soros
Jackie Morris (Illustrator)
Barefoot Books, 2000.

A girl learns to pass on the wonderful lessons she learned from her late grandmother. (Ages 7 to 10)

Play Lady: LA Senora Juguetona
by Eric Hoffman
Suzanne Tornquist (Illustrator)
Carmen Sosa Masso (Translator)
Redleaf Press, 1999.

When her mobile home is vandalized, neighbors come to the aid of their friend, Senora Jugue-tora. The children who visit to play with her are of many cultures and colors, and one, Kayla, is in a wheelchair. The children enlist their parents' help in repairing the Play Lady's house and yard. The illustrations express the feelings of the characters, enhancing the book's message of accepting diversity. (Ages 3 to 7)

Bright Eyes, Brown Skin
by Cheryl Willis Hudson
Bernette G. Ford (Contributor)
George Cephas Ford (Illustrator)
Just Us Books, 1990.

Four African American children interact with one another in a preschool environment, and in so doing, explore their facial features, skin tones, activities, personalities, and how they learn from and appreciate each other. (Ages 3 to 5)

Uncle Jed's Barbershop
by Margaree King Mitchell
James Ransome (Illustrator)
Aladdin Paperbacks (reprint edition), 1998.

Sarah Jean's favorite relative is her great-uncle Jed, who is the only black barber in the county. Great-uncle Jed travels from house to house cutting hair. His dream is to have his own barber shop. Unfortunately, segregation and the depression present huge obstacles, and he puts aside his dream to pay Sarah Jean's hospital bill. When he finally opens his own shop on his 79th birthday, a grown up Sarah Jean and the whole community share the joy of his dream come true. (Ages 4 to 8)

Nappy Hair
by Carolivia Herron
Joe Cepeda (Illustrator)
(reprint edition), Random House, 1998.

At the family picnic, Uncle Mordecai calls out the story of Brenda's hair—the nappiest hair in the world—while everyone else chimes in with "Yep," "You said it,'" and "Ain't it the truth." The traditional African American call and response style, and Cepeda's vibrant, folk-art paintings capture children's imagination and hold their attention. (Ages 3 to 9)

In Daddy's Arms I Am Tall: African Americans Celebrating Fathers
by Javaka Steptoe (Illustrator)
Lee & Low Books, 2001.

This award-winning book creates a beautiful series of images in mixed media—torn and cut paper, found objects, and color—to illustrate short poems about fathers. (Ages 9 to 12)

My Dream of Martin Luther King
by Faith Ringgold (Illustrator)
Dragonfly Books, 1998.

The author looks at the life of Martin Luther King, Jr. to narrate a dream story in which King is a child who must go to a segregated school and hear his daddy called "boy." He watches police on horseback beat up protesters, and is taken to prison where his grandmother holds him and tries to explain segregation. The book teaches about King's life through an impressionistic dream sequence. (Ages 6 to 9)

Virgie Goes to School with Us Boys
by Elizabeth Fitzgerald Howard
Earl B. Lewis (Illustrator)
Simon & Schuster Juvenile Books, 2000.

This family story is about five brothers and one little sister growing up in Tennessee just after the Civil War. Virgie, the daughter, wants to learn to read and write like her older brothers. But the boys have to walk seven miles to Jonesborough each Monday morning, carrying their clothes and enough food for the week in a tin pail. They sleep all week at the school and walk home on Friday evening. Although her parents are frightened about letting her go to school with her brothers, she begs until her father finally gives in. He says, "All free people need learning. Old folks, young folks . . . small girls, too." (Ages 5 to 10)

My Man Blue
by Nikki Grimes
Jerome Lagarrigue (Illustrator)
Toby Sherry (Editor)
Dial Books for Young Readers, 1999.

Through a series of poems, an African American boy living in a tough neighborhood tells about his friend Blue. Damon and his mother have just moved to a new apartment when an old friend of the mother's named Blue befriends Damon. Blue lost one boy to the streets and is determined to keep Damon on the right track. Blue shoots hoops with Damon, listens to him, and shares laughs and hot dogs. Blue always stands steadfast in Damon's corner and keeps him headed in the right direction. (Ages 7 to 10)

Danitra Brown Leaves Town
by Nikki Grimes
Floyd Cooper (Illustrator)
Harpercollins Juvenile Books, 2001.

When best friends Zuri Jackson and Danitra Brown are split up for summer vacation, Danitra goes off to the country to visit relatives and Zuri is stuck in the city. They write letters to each other all summer—in richly descriptive poetry—sharing their feelings and experiences. We met these two unforgettable best friends in the Coretta Scott King Honor Book Meet Danitra Brown (1994). (Ages 4 to 8)

Night Golf
by William Miller
Cedric Lucas (Illustrator)
Lee & Low Books, 1999.

Before 1961, golf courses were closed to people who were not white. James finds a rusty old golf club and becomes interested in golf. Barred from the course except as a caddy, he is befriended by an older black caddy who invites him back into the golf course after the sun goes down so he can practice. (Ages 7 to 12)

A Pig Is Moving in
by Claudia Fries (Illustrator)
Orchard Books, 2000.

Doctor Fox, Henrietta Hen, and Nick Hare see a pig moving into their cozy apartment building, and quickly jump to the conclusion that he will be "messy and dirty and sloppy." They assume that every mess they encounter was left by this pig, but discover that they were wrong. The pig was cleaning up their own messes. Their tidy pig neighbor turns out to be a clever and generous neighbor. (Ages 4 to 7)

Jack & Jim
by Kitty Crowther
Hyperion Press, 2000.

Jack, a blackbird, decides to venture out of his forest home to explore the nearby ocean. He makes friends with a dashingly handsome seagull named Jim. Unfortunately, the other white gulls aren't so hospitable. In spite of Jim's efforts to defend his friend, the village gulls can't seem to get beyond Jack's different appearance until they discover he has a talent none of them have. Jack reads funny stories to them from an old box of books that has washed up onto the shore. Finally, he wins the admiration and friendship of the narrow-minded gulls. (Ages 4 to 7)

Sister Anne's Hands
by Marybeth Lorbiecki
K. Wendy Popp (Illustrator)
Joy Peskin (Editor)
Dial Books for Young Readers, 2000.

This touching story about a black nun in the early 1960s and the lessons she imparts is based on the author's own childhood experiences. From the first day of second grade, Sister Anne lights up Anna's classroom. But it's the early '60s and not everyone in Anna's small town is ready to accept Sister. How she deals with prejudice and the profound impact she has on her students is at the heart of this beautiful, timeless story about tolerance, and how a devoted teacher can change a child's life. (Ages 8 to12)

Companeros De Equipo
by Peter Golenbock
F. Isabel Campoy, Alma Flor Ada (Translators)
Libros Viajeros (reprint edition), 2002.

In a time of racial inequality, two teammates overcome boundaries and learn they are brothers despite the color of their skin. The story focuses on standing up for one's own beliefs, fighting injustice, and respecting the rights of others. (Ages 8 to 12)

Pelitos/Hairs
by Sandra Cisneros
Terry Ybanez (Illustrator)
Random House, 1997.

This bilingual story describes differences between family members' hair. It helps children celebrate the experience of differences even within their own family. Classroom discussion can be extended from children's own family traditions, similarities and differences, and encourages them to write their own stories. (Ages 3 to 7)

My Very Own Room/Mi Propio Cuartito
by Amada Irma Pérez
Maya Christina Gonzalez (Illustrator)
Children's Book Press (bilingual edition), 2000.

The eight-year-old telling this touching family story shares a noisy, crowded little room with her five brothers. She wishes she had her own room where she could write in her diary, read, and dream undisturbed. She claims a tiny storage closet behind a flour-sack curtain and imagines that she has a bedroom with her own bed, table, and lamp. The whole family pitches in to help her empty the closet and piece together her very own little room. (Ages 5 to 9)

Carlos and the Cornfield/Carlos Y LA Milpa De Maiz
by Jan Romero Stevens
Jeanne Arnold (Illustrator)
Patricia Davison (Translator)
Rising Moon, 1995.

Before Carlos plants seed corn, his papa warns him, "Remember, 'Cosechas lo que siembras': You reap what you sow." Carlos is so excited about earning money to buy a new red pocketknife that he plants all of the seeds in the first few rows, leaving no seed to plant in the last rows. He gives up his beloved knife to buy more seed corn for the empty rows. When the corn is harvested, the error of his ways is discovered: the last rows turn out to be blue rather than yellow corn, so mama serves blue corn cakes for breakfast. Bilingual and complete with a recipe for blue corn pancakes, this beautifully written sequel to *Carlos y la Planta de Calabaza / Carlos and the Squash Plant* (1993) presents a valuable lesson on being responsible for one's own actions. (Ages 5 to 8)

Chato's Kitchen
by Gary Soto
Susan Guevara (Illustrator)
Paper Star (reprint edition), 1997.

This award-winning book tells the story of Chato, a sly, mustachioed "cool cat" from an East Los Angeles barrio. Five mice the color of gray river rock move next door. Chato promptly invites the mice over for dinner, unfortunately, as the main course. Instead of the gruesome outcome you might expect, the author creates a delightfully surprising ending. (Ages 4 to 8)

Too Many Tamales
by Gary Soto
Ed Martinez (Illustrator)
Putnam Publishing Group, 1993.

In preparation for a family Christmas fiesta, Maria and her parents are busy making tamales. Maria can't resist trying on her mother's diamond ring, but she forgets all about the ring until she realizes it has disappeared. Maria is sure the ring must be inside a tamale, so she talks her cousins into eating all 24 to help her find it. The overstuffed cousins are greatly relieved to discover that the ring really isn't lost after all. Child readers empathize with mischievous Maria and appreciate this playful reminder about the importance of forgiveness. (Ages 4 and older)

Goin' Someplace Special
by Patricia C. McKissack
Jerry Pinkney (Illustrator)
Atheneum Press, 2001.

This 2002 Coretta Scott King Illustrator Award Winner is about 'Tricia Ann's first solo trip out of her neighborhood. 'Tricia Ann is confronted by the segregation of Nashville in the 1950s, but her confidence, intelligence, pride in her heritage, and sense of self-worth make this a victorious journey for her as she searches for truth. The story is based on the author's own experiences and the many indignities she encountered during that troubling period. (Ages 7 to 10)

Markita
by Alissa Nash
Doby London (Illustrator)
African American Images, 1997.

Nice stories about beautiful flowers in a colorful human bouquet offer little comfort to a young girl who never feels as special as her lighter complexioned cousins. This book offers a compassionate look at diversity and self-esteem. (Ages 6 to 9)

Oliver's High Five
by Beverly Swerdlow Brown
Margot J. Ott (Illustrator)
Health Press, 1998.

Oliver Octopus has only five arms, but he doesn't mind. Young children with any kind of disability or difference will enjoy reading about Oliver's adventures above the sea. Through determination and a positive attitude, he changes the way others think about his uniqueness. (Ages 3 to 9)

Harry and Willy and Carrothead
by Judith Caseley
Greenwillow, 1991.

Harry, born without a left hand, is a lively, confident, and lovable child. His physical difference doesn't keep him from becoming a good baseball player. His red-headed friend Oscar is not so self-assured and is hurt by taunts of "carrot head." Harry stands up to Oscar's tormentor, Willy, and soon the three are best friends. (Ages 3 to 9)

If the Shoe Fits
by Gary Soto
Terry Widener (Illustrator)
Putnam Publishing Group Juvenile Press, 2002.

As the youngest son in a large Mexican American family, Rigo often gets stuck wearing worn out hand-me-downs. He's thrilled to receive a pair of brand new penny loafers for his ninth birthday, but when a neighborhood bully makes fun of his fancy shoes, Rigo hides the shoes in his closet. A few months later, he tries to wear the shoes to a party, but they no longer fit. Rigo's disappointment helps him see hand-me-downs in a new light. He thoughtfully gives the almost new shoes to Uncle Celso, who needs good shoes for his new job as a waiter. (Ages 5 and up)

Dancing in the Wings
by Debbie Allen
Kadir Nelson (Illustrator)
Dial Books for Young Readers, 2000.

Though tall and lanky for a ballerina, African American Sassy loves to dance and dreams of performing on stage. She is hurt by teasing from classmates about her long legs but encouraged by her uncle's belief that she is beautiful. A Russian ballet master believes in her and she finally finds herself on stage, in the spotlight, partnered by an even taller young man. (Ages 5 to 8)

Simon's Hook: A Story About Teases and Put-downs
by Karen Gedig Burnett
Laurie Barrows (Illustrator)
GR Publishing, 1999.

This book helps children learn appropriate ways to respond to teasing. Through the use of a fishing analogy, Burnett shows children how to "swim free" from feeling helpless, trapped, stuck, or powerless. The book teaches alternatives to hitting back. (Ages 6 and up)

The First Strawberries: A Cherokee Story
by Joseph Bruchac
Anna Vojtech (Illustrator)
Puffin (reprint edition), 1998.

This native Cherokee folktale reminds people to be kind to each other. In this creation story, the first man and woman have an angry quarrel that is forgotten when they share delicious strawberries she has discovered. (Ages 5 to 10)

La mujer que brillaba aún más que el sol/The Woman Who Outshone the Sun
by Rosalma Zubizarreta, Harriet Rohmer, David Schecter, & Alejandro Cruz Martinez
Fernando Olivera (Illustrator)
Scott Foresman, 1994.

This retelling of a legend from the Zapotec Indians of Oaxaco, Mexico, is about a beautiful stranger, Lucia, whose odd ways arouse suspicion among the other villagers. When the young people chase her away, the river goes dry, creating a desert. After the elders urge the young people to apologize, Luchia returns and all is well. (Ages 5 to 8)

Coyote: A Trickster Tale from the American Southwest
by Gerald McDermott
Voyager Books (reprint edition), 1999.

Coyote, the trickster in this native legend, is rude, boastful, vain, and always in trouble. Young children will identify with this foolish but very human character who has a nose for trouble and always manages to find it. (Ages 2 to 5)

Dumpling Soup
by Jama Kim Rattigan
Lillian Hsu-Flanders (Illustrator)
Little Brown & Company (reprint edition), 1998.

This story about Marisa, a little girl who lives in Hawaii, describes the traditional New Year celebration by her family. Her relatives enjoy foods from many of the cultures represented in her family that includes Japanese, Chinese, Korean, Hawaiian, and haole (Hawaiian term for Anglo persons). (Ages 4 to 8)

Kids Like Me in China
by Ying Ying Fry and Amy Klatzkin
Brian Boyd and Terry Fry (Photographers)
Yeong & Yeong, 2001.

This touching, enlightening, and entertaining book provides children an opportunity to see China through a child's eyes. Ying Ying tells her own story as readers learn about ordinary life in China (schools, homes, and families). (Ages 7 to 12)

I Love You Like Crazy Cakes
by Rose A. Lewis
Jane Dyer (Illustrator)
Little Brown & Company, 2000.

This simple, touching love story describes an American mother's adoption of her beautiful Chinese baby. It is told in a way that even very young children can understand. (Ages 3 to 6)

A Day I'll Never Forget: A Keepsake to Help Children Deal with the September 11th, 2001 Attack on America
by Latania Love Wright
Jack West (Illustrator)
Hastings House Publishing, 2001.

Appropriate for parents whose children were affected by the September 11th crisis. Usually not suitable for school use because of the sensitive nature of the content. (Ages 5 to 10)

Lucy and the Liberty Quilt
by Victoria London
Angela Liang (Illustrator)
A Gifted Girls Series, Book 1; Sparklesoup Studios, 2001.

Combines lessons in life, history, and culture to provide positive themes for girls growing up today. (Ages 9 to 12)

Frankie Wonders . . . What Happened Today?
by Yvonne Conte
Amsterdam-Berwick Publishing, 2001.

Appropriate for parents to read to children to help them understand the events of September 11th. (Ages 4 to 8)

Come and Abide (We Are All The Same Inside)
by Timothy D. Bellavia
Randi Cannata's 4th Grade T.A.G. @ P.S. 175 Q. District 28 N.Y.C. (Collaborator)
T.I.M.M.-E. Company, Inc. (Tolerance in Multi Media Education), 2002.

Come and Abide, a result of the author's collaboration with 26 4th graders, helps children better understand tolerance and diversity.

Comanche Peace Pipe
by Patrick Dearen
Alan McCuller (Illustrator)
Lone Star Heroes, Book 1; Republic of Texas Press, 2001.

These tales of Texas history, lore, and legend (supplemented with the history behind the stories) describe the attempts of two young boys trying to prevent a battle between Comanches and an Anglo wagon train in 1867. (Ages 8 to 12)

Somewhere Today: A Book of Peace
by Shelly Moore Thomas
Eric Futran (Photographer)
Shelley Moore Thomas and Abby Levine (Editors)
Albert Whitman & Company, 1998.

This simple, readable picture book reminds children how to behave positively rather than aggressively. (Ages 4 to 8)

Something Beautiful
by Sharon Dennis Wyeth
Chris K. Soentpiet (Illustrator)
Dragonfly Books (reprint edition), 2002.

A small African American girl living in a very scary neighborhood searches for something beautiful. She sees garbage, broken glass, angry graffiti, and a homeless woman sleeping under plastic covers. The little girl manages, however, to find beauty and warmth in unlikely places. (All ages.)

Five Minutes' Peace
by Jill Murphy
Paper Star, 1999.

A humorous book about a mother searching for five minutes' peace. Unfortunately, chaos follows her around the house. (Ages 4 to 7)

Appendix B
Resources for Responding to Special Needs and Interests

Adoptive, Foster, and Biological Parents of FAS/FAE Children
A support network for adoptive, foster, and biological parents of children affected by fetal alcohol syndrome or prenatal drug use.

Ronnie Jacobs
Adoptive, Foster, and Biological Parents of FAS/FAE Children
Bergen County Council on Alcoholism and Drug Abuse Inc.
P.O. Box 626
Paramus, NJ 07653
Telephone: (201) 261-2183 or (201) 261-1450

Allergy and Asthma Network, Mothers of Asthmatics, Inc. (AAN-MA)
An international, nonprofit organization dedicated to educating families dealing with asthma and allergies. Members of AAN-MA receive a monthly newsletter that includes information on medical research, current treatments and therapies, new products, and coping techniques.

Allergy and Asthma Network
Mothers of Asthmatics, Inc.
3554 chain Bridge Road, Suite 200
Fairfax, VA 22030
Telephone: (703) 385-4403 or (800) 878-4403
Fax: (703) 352 4354
E-mail: aanma@aol.com
http://www.podi.com/health/aanma/

American Academy of child and Adolescent Psychiatry
Professional organization for child and adolescent psychiatrists conducting research, and diagnosing and treating psychiatric disorders of children, adolescents, and their families. It publishes "Facts for Families," a series that includes over 50 informational sheets on topics such as the depressed child, suicide, discipline, and child sexual abuse.

Terri Baxter
Deputy Director of Research Development
3615 Wisconsin Avenue, NW
Washington, DC 20016
Telephone: (202) 966-7300
Fax: (202) 966-7300
E-mail: 74003.264@Compuserve.com
http://www.aacap.org/web/aacap/

The Arc of the United States

The country's largest voluntary organization committed to the welfare of all children and adults with mental retardation, and their families.

The Arc of the United States
500 east Border Street, Suite 300
Arlington, TX 76010
Telephone: (817) 261-6003
Fax: (817) 277-3491
TDD: (817) 277-0553
E-mail: thearc@metronet.com
http://The Arc.org/welcome.html

Association of Birth Defect Children (ABDC)

A charitable organization that provides free telephone information to parents and professionals about birth defects. ABDC sponsors the National Birth Defect Registry, a birth defect prevention project that provides information on possible links between specific birth defects and their causes (e.g., exposures to chemicals during the Gulf War). Members of ABDC receive publications (e.g., fact sheets), special reports, and a newsletter.

The Association of Birth Defect Children, Inc.
Telephone: (407) 245-7035

Association for the Care of Children's Health (ACCH)

A network of individuals, programs, and organizations whose vision is to humanize health care for children and families through education, dissemination of resources, research, and advocacy. ACCH publishes resources that address the psychological, emotional, social, and spiritual needs of children and their families, and maintains an information clearinghouse for infants with disabilities and life-threatening conditions.

Association for the Care of Children's Health
7910 Woodmont Avenue, Suite 300
Bethesda, MD 20814
Telephone: (301) 654-6549 or (800) 808-ACCH (2224)
Fax: (301) 986-4553
http://Look.net/ACCH/

Association for Special Kids, Inc. (A.S.K.)

A financial planning organization dedicated to helping parents of children with disabilities to protect their children's future. Counselors work individually with parents, and with a network of qualified attorneys and accountants to set parent' plans into action. There is no fee for these services. Most of the counselors are parents of children with disabilities.

A.S.K.
107 West Hill Street
Baltimore, MD 21230
Telephone: (800) 832-0467

ASPIRA Association, Inc.: An Investment in Latino Youth

A national, nonprofit organization serving Puerto Rican and other Latino/a youth and their families through leadership and education. (ASPIRA is taken from the Spanish word "aspirar" with means to aspire to something greater.) It provides bilingual publication at low cost related to Hispanic health, education, violence, and the like.

ASPIRA Association, Inc.
1444 I Street, NW, Suite 800
Washington, DC 20005
Telephone: (202) 835-3600
Fax: (202) 835-3613
E-mail: aspira1@aol.com
http://www.incacorp.com/aspira/

Asthma and Allergy Foundation of America (AAFA)

An organization supporting families by providing a bimonthly newsletter with practical articles on asthma and allergies. AAFA also maintains a clearinghouse of current and affordable educational materials, funds medical research, and sponsors a nationwide network of affiliated AAFA chapters.

Asthma and Allergy Foundation of America
1125 Fifteenth Street, NW, Suite 502
Washington, DC 20005
Telephone: (202) 466-7643 or (800) 7-ASTHMA (727-8462)
Fax: (202) 466-8940

Attention Deficit Disorders Association—Southern Region (ADDA Southern Region)

An independent, nonprofit organization providing a resource network for parents, educators, and health care professionals in Texas, Louisiana, Arkansas, Oklahoma, and New Mexico. ADDA (Southern Region) keeps the public informed about ADD/ADHD through a newsletter and referral service, monthly meetings, educational programs, parent support services, conferences, and workshops.

Attention Deficit Disorders Association—Southern Region
12345 Jones Road, Suite 287
Houston, TX 77070
Telephone: (713) 955-3720

Center for Child Welfare (CCW)

An organization dedicated to promoting and advancing interdisciplinary knowledge and policy in child, youth, and family welfare with a focus on Hispanic/Latino children, youth, and families at risk in Latin America and the United States. CCW conducts interdisciplinary comparative research; integrates research knowledge into existing and developing programs; disseminates papers, resource manuals, and curriculum guides; and provides training to increase knowledge and skills in child, youth, and family welfare issues to individuals from Latin America and the United States.

Ruth E. Zambrana
Center for Child Welfare
College of Nursing and Health Science
George Mason University
4400 University Drive MS 2E8
Fairfax, VA 22030-4444
Telephone: (703) 993-1051
Fax: (703) 993-1970

Child Attention Deficit disorder/Attention Deficit Hyperactivity Disorder (CH.A.D.D.)
Support organization for families coping with ADD/ADHD.

CH.A.D.D.
S499 Northwest 70th Avenue, Suite 101
Plantation, FL 33317
Telephone: (800) 233-4050
http://chadd.org/

Children's Hospice International
A nonprofit organization providing medical, psychological, emotional, and spiritual support to seriously ill children and their families, as well as to families recovering from the loss of child.

Children's Hospice International
Alexandria, VA 22301
Telephone: (703) 684-0330 or (800) 24-CHILD
Fax: (703) 684-0226

The Council for Exceptional Children (CEC) and
ERIC Clearinghouse on Disabilities and Gifted Education
CEC provides information through its library and datatbase of professional literature to those concerned with the education of children who are gifted and have special needs. CEC also convenes conferences, assists lawmakers, and effects coordination of the North American Political Action Network.

The Council for Exceptional Children
1920 Association Drive
Reston, VA 20191-1589
Telephone: (800) 328-0272

Education for Parents of Indian children with Special Needs (EPICS)
A national project providing parent training and information for Native American families with special needs children.

Indian Children with Special Needs
P.O. Box 788
Bernalillo, NM 87004
Telephone: (505) 867-3396 or (parents only): (800) 765-7429

Educators for Social Responsibility
Develops curricula and trains teachers with a particular focus on conflict resolution.

ESR
23 Garden Street
Cambridge, MA 02138
Telephone: (617) 232-1595

Families Anonymous
A national group that provides support for individuals who are concerned about drugs and drug-related behavioral problems of friends and relatives.

Families Anonymous
P.O. Box 3475
Culver City, CA 90231-3475
Telephone: (800) 736-9805 or (310) 313-5800
Fax: (310) 313-6841

Family Service America, Inc. (FSA)
An international, nonprofit association that assists individuals and families through education, services, and advocacy. The FSA network helps families solve problems related to parenting skills, parent-child tensions, teenage pregnancy, child abuse and neglect, family violence, and work-related problems.

Family Service America, Inc.
11700 west Lake Park Drive
Milwaukee, WI 53211

Family Violence and Sexual Assault Institute (FVSAI)
A nonprofit, international resource center functioning as a clearinghouse on all aspects of family violence and sexual abuse. Information and materials are reviewed and information is disseminated in the Family Violence and Sexual Assault Bulletin. FVSAI also works with crisis centers, agencies, and counseling clinics to develop treatment programs for spouse/partner abuse and sexual abuse. The FVSAI Book Club offers *Flip Flops: A Workbook for Children Who Have Been Sexually Abused* (Ages 7–9).

Family Violence and Sexual Assault Institute
1310 Clinic Drive
Tyler, TX 75701
Telephone: (903) 595-6600

Federation for Children with Special Needs
A center for parents and parent organizations to work together on behalf of children with special needs and their families.

Federation for Children with Special Needs
95 Berkely Street, suite 104
Boston, MA 02116
Telephone: (617) 482-2915 or (800) 331-0688 (in MA)
E-mail: fesninfo@fcsn.org

Federation of Families for Children's Mental Health

A national organization, run by parents, that focuses on the needs of children and youth with emotional, behavioral, or mental disorders, and their families.

Federation of Families for Children's Mental Health
1021 Prince Street
Alexandria, VA 22314-2971
Telephone: (703) 684-7710
Fax: (703) 836-1040
E-mail: ffcmh@crosslink.net
http://www.crosslink.net/pub/users/f/ffcmh/enghome.htm

National Association for Visually Handicapped

A private, nonprofit organization serving visually impaired—not totally blind—children, their parents, and professionals who work with them, as well as adults with vision loss. The organization provides large-print visual aids, a newsletter, and brochures with information about commercially manufactured optical aids.

National Association for Visually Handicapped
22 West 21st Street
New York, NY 10010
Telephone: (212) 889-3141
Fax: (212) 727-2931

National Black Child Development Institute (NBCDI)

An organization providing community and direct services to African American children, families, and advocates.

National Black Child Development Institute
1023 15th Street, NW, Suite 600
Washington, DC 20005
Telephone: (202) 387-1281
Fax: (202) 234-1738
http://www.nbcdi.org

National Burn Victim Foundation (NBVF)

A program providing advocacy and services to burn victims and their families at no charge. NBVF provides burn-related information, referrals, and community burn-prevention resources. It also conducts seminars on how to determine if a child's burns are a result of child abuse.

National Burn Victim Foundation
246A Madisonville Road, P.O. Box 409
Basking Ridge, NJ 07920

Telephone: (908) 953-9091
Fax: (908) 953-9099
E-mail: NBVF@intac.com
http://www.nbvf.org

National Clearinghouse for Alcohol and Drug Information (NCADI)

Serves as the world's largest resource for current information and materials concerning substance abuse prevention. NCADI has an information services staff equipped to respond to the public's alcohol, tobacco, and illicit drug inquiries. The program is a service of the Center for Substance Abuse Prevention, Substance Abuse and Mental Health Services Administration, U.S. Public Health Service, U.S. Department of Health and Human Services.

National Clearinghouse for Alcohol and Drug Information
P.O. Box 2345
Rockville, MD 20847-2345
Telephone: (800) NCADI-64 (622-3464)
Fax: (301) 468-6433
http://www.health.org/index.htm
"Just for kids"
http://www.health.org/kidsarea/index.htm

National Clearinghouse on Child Abuse and Neglect

A clearinghouse providing resources for professionals related to the prevention of child abuse and neglect. It is a service of the National Center on Child Abuse and Neglect (NCCAN), Administration on Children, Youth and Families, Administration for Children and Families, U.S. Department of Health and Human Services.

National Clearinghouse on Child Abuse and Neglect
P.O. Box 1182
Washington, DC 20013-1182
Telephone: (703) 385-7565 or (800) FYI-3366 (394-3366)
Fax: (703) 385-3206
E-mail: nccanch@calib.com
http://www.calib.com/nccanch/

National Latino Children's Institute (NLCI)

Promotes and implements the National Latino Children's Agenda, which is a statement of principles essential for the healthy and complete development of Latino children. NLCI identifies and recognizes "best practice" in the areas of children's health, environment, economic, and educational conditions that are respectful of Latino cultural values and language.

National Latino Children's Institute
320 El Paso Street
San Antonio, TX 78207
Telephone: (210) 228 9997
Fax: (210) 228-9972
E-mail: nlci@nlci.org
http://www. nlci.org

National Organization of Parents of Blind Children (NOPBC)

Facilitates the sharing of experience and concerns among parents of blind children and visually impaired children, to provide information and support, and to develop resources for them. NOPBC conducts seminars and workshops, and publishes free or low-cost brochures.

Mrs. Barbara Cheadle, President
National Organization of Parents of Blind Children
1800 Johnson Street
Baltimore, MD 21230
Telephone: (410) 659-9314
Fax: (410) 685-5653

The Stuttering Foundation of America (SFA)

Maintains a toll-free Hotline on Stuttering. Call for free information, brochures, and a nationwide referral list of speech-language pathologists who specialize in stuttering. SFA has also produced *Stuttering, and Your Child: A Videotape for Parents*, which is offered free of charge to public libraries. Provide you local library with the toll-free telephone number below and ask that they obtain a copy of the video for their collection. The video is geared toward parents, teachers, child care professionals, and others interested in helping a child who stutters.

Stuttering Foundation of America
3100 Walnut Grove, Suite 603
P.O. Box 11749
Memphis, TN 3811-0749
Telephone: (800) 992-9392 or (901) 452-7343
http://www.stuttersfa.org/index.html

The Women's Educational Equity Act (WEEA) Resource Center

A federal program dedicated to reducing educational disparity for women and girls.

Women's Educational Equity Act (WEEA)
Education Development Center
55Chapel Street
Newton, MA 02158-1060
E-mail: weeapub@edc.org
http://www.edc.org/CEEC/WEEA

Appendix C
Bilingual Children's Books Affirming Cultural Differences

All the Colors of the Earth
Author: Sheila Hamanaka

From the "whispering golds of late summer grasses" to "the roaring browns of bears and soaring eagles," children come in all colors. The author likens different skin colors and hair textures to things found in nature, and in the process, affirms the beauty of every child.

Morrow Junior Books
1350 Avenue of the Americas
New York, NY 10019
Telephone: (800) 237-0657
http://www.williammorrow.com

All the Colors We Are/Todos los Colores de Nuestra Piel
Author: Katie Kissinger

This book uses simple language to explain how we get skin color. Photographs by Wernher Krutein present a diverse array of skin hues.

Redleaf Press
450 N. Syndicate, Suite 5
St. Paul, MN 55104-4125
Telephone: (800) 423-8309
Fax: (800) 788-3123

Black Is Brown Is Tan; Black, White, Just Right!; and Real Sisters
Author: Arnold Adoff

These stories were written especially to address the needs of children of multiracial families, but they are appropriate for helping all children respect and understand ethnic differences.

Great Owl Books
33 Watchung Plaza
Montclair, NJ 07042-4111
Telephone: (800) 299-3181
Fax: (201) 783-5899

Bread, Bread, Bread; Shoes, Shoes; Houses and Homes; and Loving
Author: Ann Morris

This series of books is focused on the way different people all around the world meet the universal human needs of food, clothing, housing, and love. Photographs from around the globe foster a respect for individual differences.

William Morrow & Company
10 East 53rd Street
New York, NY 10022
(212) 207-7000

My Song Is Beautiful: Poems and Pictures in Many Voices
Editor: Mary Ann Hoberman

This collection of poems from different cultures celebrates childhood. The illustrations reflect the cultural diversity of the various poems.

Little, Brown & Company
200 West Street
Waltham, MA 02154
Telephone: (800) 759-0190

Multicultural Connections—Provides a selection of children's books written with Spanish and English appearing side by side. These books introduce bilingual skills, increase language and learning abilities, and positively heighten awareness of many cultures. This publisher also makes available musical and language-learning tapes and games that depict multicultural images in an affirmative manner.

Bilingual Books for Kids, Inc.
Libros Bilingües para Niños
P.O. Box 653
Ardsley, NY 10502
Phone/Fax: (800) 385-1020
E-mail: bilingualbooks@mindspring.com.bonnie.arons@armriskmanagers.com
http://secure2.hispeed.net/cgi-bin/cgiwrap/bilingualbooks/Make-a-Store.cgi

Bastante grande/Big Enough

Author: Ofelia Dumas Lachtman

Everyone in this story discovers that although Lupita is too little for some tasks, she is just the right size for others.

Diez Deditos/Ten Little Fingers and Other Play Rhymes and Action Songs from Latin America

Selected, arranged, and translated by Jose-Luis Orozco

Children can sing, chant, clap, wiggle, wave, and dance to more than thirty finger rhymes and action songs adapted from the traditional to the new. The bilingual lyrics, background notes, and simple pictographs show the children how to move. Guitar and piano music included.
Audiotape and compact disc also available.

Esos desagradables detestables sucios completamente asquerosos pero . . . invisibles germanes/Those Mean Nasty Dirty Downright Disgusting but . . . Invisible Germs

Author: Judith Anne Rice

Through playful and colorful illustrations, this book tells about the germs that cause illness and the importance of hand-washing to good health.

Esos sucios pegajosos olorosos causantes de caries pero . . . invisibles germenes/Those Icky Sticky Smelly, Cavity-Causing but . . . Invisible Germs

Author: Judith Anne Rice

This companion to the above selection is intended to help children develop good toothbrushing habits. Lively, colorful illustrations tell about the germs that cause cavities and demonstrate how important brushing is to good dental health.

Fiesta!

Author: Sesame Street

Sesame Street presents a fiesta, complete with floats, costumes, and Elmo's favorite new dance: The Conga-Wiffle. All the songs are in English and Spanish. It presents familiar characters such as Maria, Gabi, Rosita, and their Sesame Street friends, as well as special performances by Linda Ronstadt and Celia Cruz.
Audiotape and compact disc also available.

Hola Amigos

Trio of VHS recordings with Paco and his friends presented in a series of bilingual adventures designed to introduce the Spanish language. In his first adventure, Paco and his sister Lupe learn about numbers with Pepe the Clown. In Volume 2, Paco starts in the kitchen and travels throughout his house learning about letters. In Volume 3, Paco and his friends go to a farm, to the city, and to Monkey Island.

La lagartija y el sol/The Lizard and the Sun

Author: Dr. Alma Flor Aida

Traditional folktale of ancient Mexico. Youngsters will enjoy the story of the brave little lizard who, after the sun disappeared, would not rest until she brought back the light and warmth to everyone. (Dr. Flor Aida is an authority on bilingual and multicultural education.)

Pepita y el color rosado/Pepita Thinks Pink

Author: Ofelia Dumas Lachtman

Pepita likes every color but pink, so she just cannot bring herself to make friends with her new neighbor, Sonya, a little girl in a pink dress with pink balloons. Pepita soon learns, however, that the things that make people different from one another are the very things that make a friendship special.

Thinking Stories

Author: Jackie Scott

Series of three books, each containing four stories presented in bilingual format. The stories promote inductive and deductive reasoning, flexibility of thought, and predictive strategies, and increase confidence in problem-solving. Teacher's guides, lesson plans, discussion questions, and follow-up activities are presented at the end of each selection to promote categorization and associative thinking objectives.

Un regalo de Papa Diego/A Gift from Papa Diego

Author: Benjamin Alire Saenz

Little Diego loves his grandfather, but does not see him often because Papa Diego lives in Mexico. Diego asks for a Superman outfit for his birthday because he wants to fly across the border to Mexico to be with his grandfather. Includes author notes, a glossary, and claymation illustrations.

Glossary

A

active listening—A form of attentive listening in which one concentrates on what is being said, then reflects the ideas to the speaker to show an understanding of what the speaker is feeling and saying.

anarchy—Absence of any form of control; chaos and disorder.

antisocial—Behavior that detracts from the welfare of others or has a generally negative effect on persons with whom one comes in contact. Antisocial personality behaviors are typically marked by lack of ethical restraint, lack of moral control, impulsiveness, and an inability to experience feelings of guilt.

apnea—Transient cessation of breathing.

appropriate—Suitable for the occasion and the person affected, nonexploitative, and having no concealed intention.

auditory physiology—The physical makeup of the ear that enables hearing. Sounds are channeled through the external auditory canal to the tympanic membrane (ear drum) and the middle ear (ossicles), and then through the auditory nerve to the brain for interpretation of what has been heard. Auditory perception encompasses the ability to understand what has been heard.

autocracy—Control by a single person having unlimited power.

B

behaviorists—Those holding the view that the environment is the primary determinant of human behavior and that objectively observable behavior constitutes the essential psychological makeup of a human being.

biases—One's own set of beliefs, values, perceptions, and assumptions that develop from one's upbringing, past experience, and personal philosophy of life.

bonding—The process of becoming emotionally attached to another.

C

cephalocaudal—The process of developing in a pattern from the head downward toward the feet (head to toe).

child-directed—Learning activity instigated by the child's natural curiosity and desire to learn rather than by the adult's manipulation or coercion.

classical conditioning—Training in which a neutral stimulus produces an expected response; a learned association between a stimulus and a response. This term derives from an experiment originally performed by Ivan Pavlov in which a bell was rung just as food was offered to a hungry dog. Soon, the dog would salivate at the sound of the bell whether or not food was offered, demonstrating how this association becomes learned.

community of learners—A group of people who share ideas, talk about and solve problems together, help each other, and cooperate as a team to learn new information and develop new skills. Community of learners is a model for cooperative rather than competitive learning.

concept—An idea, understanding, or belief formed by organizing images or mental pictures from specific occurrences and experiences.

concrete operational—The third stage of cognitive development in Jean Piaget's theory that begins with the ability to analyze thoughts concerning a concrete idea (as opposed to an abstract idea).

cues—Words, facial expressions, or gestures that trigger certain behaviors. A technique used to help children remember what is expected by giving them a specific signal.

cultural pluralism—The peaceful coexistence of numerous distinct ethnic, religious, or cultural groups within one's community or society.

D

delay gratification—The process of putting off something desired until a later time. This skill can be learned gradually during early childhood by children who develop a strong sense of trust that their essential needs will be met.

democracy—The principles of social equality and respect for the individual within a cohesive community.

developmental interactionists—Those holding the Piagetian view that, rather than only passively absorbing information or emerging into a predestined form, a human being's essential psychological makeup derives from a dynamic interactive process, based on both innate cognitive structures and external experiences.

dysfunctional—Inappropriate or self-destructive behavior not serving any positive or productive function in a child's life.

E

egocentric—Seeing oneself as the center of the universe; self-centered; selfish. This point of view is a perfectly normal development characteristic of babies and very young children.

egocentrism—The inability to view reality from the standpoint of another person that is an intellectual limitation of children in the preoperational stage of cognitive growth in Piaget's theory.

emotional growth—Learning to understand the feelings that affect how we behave.

empathy—The ability to understand or have concern for someone other than oneself, marked by identification with and understanding of another's situation, feelings, and motives.

environment—The physical surroundings or conditions around a child that influence his growth, development, and learning. The young child's environment can be described as everything the child sees, hears, touches, and experiences.

ethologists—Scientists who study the behavior of animals living under normal conditions. Ethology is the scientific study of animal behavior. (Ethnology is the science of depicting the character or disposition peculiar to a particular culture.)

expressive language—The ability to communicate with others by oral or written language.

external environment—A term that refers to one's physical surroundings experienced through the senses, including daily routines and patterns of interactions.

F

functional—Appropriate actions or behaviors that serve some productive or positive function in a child's life.

H

habituated—The process of becoming accustomed to something by frequent repetition or pattern of behavior.

hyperactivity—Also called *hyperkinesia* or *attention deficit disorder*, a behavior disorder marked by excessive physical activity at inappropriate times. Typically, the child cannot sit still, fidgets compulsively, and shows a persistent lack of attention or focus on the task at hand.

I

industry—One's motivation to work constructively; to be diligent and productive.

inferiority—The process of feeling incapable, having a pervasive sense of inadequacy, and experiencing a tendency toward self-diminishment.

inferring meaning—The act of drawing conclusions from evidence perceived by one's senses or through communication.

intermittent reinforcers—The presence of a reinforcer after some, but not all, occurrences of a particular behavior. This process tends to result in an increase in the specific behavior that is reinforced, even if the reinforcement is only sporadic.

internal sensations—The feelings sensed by one's own body such as hunger or fear.

internalize—The process of taking in experiences and absorbing learning, then making them part of one's own behavior or belief.

L

learned behavior—The process of learning to repeat an action that has produced a favorable response in the past. A behavior that is taught by the reinforcing response of another person.

M

manipulative—Using trickery to coerce another person into doing something that she really does not want to do.

marasmus—A disease associated with inadequate or inadequately assimilated nutrition that affects infants and causes a wasting away of the child's body. Also referred to as *failure to thrive syndrome*, this condition can result from prolonged absence of emotional nurturance as well as from malnutrition. Affected infants typically evidence delays in motor and intellectual development.

maturationists—Those holding the view that internal predisposition, physiological characteristics, or inherited traits account for the essential psychological makeup of a human being.

metacognition—The ability to reflect or evaluate one's own behavior or actions.

mirror—Reflecting the feelings expressed by someone else; repeating what you understood *See also* Active listening.

modeling—The process of following a guided example or imitating a role model. In positive child guidance, the adult demonstrates appropriate behavior, teaching by providing an example of appropriate or desired behaviors.

modify—The process of bringing about a change. In behavior modification, modifying is the process of changing a specific behavior through external reinforcement of some kind.

moral affect—The ability to feel guilt or shame; feelings associated with a guilty or clear conscience.

moral reasoning—The thinking processes that guide people in deciding what is or is not moral behavior.

N

negotiate—The process of settling disputes through interactive verbal exchanges rather than by physical force.

Nonverbal communication—Communicating ideas without the use of speech through such cues as gesture, tone of voice, facial expression, or body posture.

O

object permanence—The knowledge that something hidden from view is not gone forever, but rather is in another location at that time and likely to reappear.

osmosis—A gradual, often unconscious mental process of assimilating ideas or absorbing information that resembles the tendency of fluids to gradually flow through an absorbent material.

P

perceive—To become aware of something by directly using one's senses; to notice or to understand in one's own mind.

pluralistic culture—*See* Cultural pluralism.

preoperational—The second stage of cognitive development in Jean Piaget's theory that begins with the achievement of object permanence. This stage is typified by imaginative play, egocentricity, the inability to take another person's point of view, and the belief that the number or amount is changed when objects are rearranged.

prosocial—Behavior that improves the welfare of others or has a generally positive effect on persons with whom one comes in contact.

proximodistal—The process of developing in a direction from closest to the body's trunk to the farthest, such as controlling the muscles of the trunk, and then learning how to control the muscles down the arms and finally, in the hands (close to far).

R

receptive language—The ability to understand written or spoken communication expressed by others.

redirection—The process of offering a substitute focus to distract the child from a current undesirable one. For example, a child may be offered a developmentally appropriate water play activity to refocus his or her inappropriate interest in pouring milk from a cup onto the floor.

replaces—Substitutes one action for another when both cannot be done at the same time, so that an undesired behavior must be given up or suspended for the new action to take place.

rescued—A situation in which one has been removed from experiencing the logical consequence of an inappropriate behavior. Typically, a child has acted improperly without any negative results because an adult has intervened to extricate the child from a precarious situation she has created.

respect—The process of showing regard for the rights and needs of another; to display polite expressions of consideration for another.

S

self-concept—One's own perception of oneself in terms of personal worth, life and school successes, and perceived social status.

self-esteem—Seeing oneself as a worthwhile individual.

social growth—Learning to understand and function appropriately in one's social environment; learning how to effectively interact with others.

stimuli—Things taken in through the senses that might incite activity or thought; things seen, smelled, heard, felt, or tasted; incentives for action.

T

tokens—Objects (e.g., stars, points, stickers) given to children for performing specified behaviors that are then exchanged at prearranged times for their choice of activities or items from a "menu" of rewards (e.g., toys, special food treats, field trips).

U

unconscious reactions—Actions that are unplanned; devoid of forethought.

References

A

Adams, G., & Rohacek, M. (2002, February). Child care and welfare reform. WR&B Policy Brief #14. Washington, DC: Brookings Institution.

Adlam, D. (1977). *Code in context.* London: Routledge & Kegan Paul.

Adler, A. (1931). *The pattern of life.* London: Kegan, Paul, Trench, Tutner and Company.

Adler, A. (1964, originally published 1931). Compulsion neurosis. In H. L. Ansbacher & R. R. Ansbacher (Eds.), *Superiority and social interest: A collection of later writings.* Evanston, IL: Northwestern University Press.

The AFL-CIO Working Women's Department. Bargaining for child care: Fact sheet. *Labor Project for Working Families and the AFL-CIO Working Women's Department.* This fact sheet was prepared by the Labor Project for Working Families and the AFL-CIO Working Women's Department. Washington, DC (Original available at http://www.aflcio.org/women/equalpay.htm, viewed July 2002.)

The AFL-CIO Working Women's Department. Working together for kids. *Labor Project for Working Families and the AFL-CIO Working Women's Department.* This online document was prepared by the Labor Project for Working Families and the AFL-CIO Working Women's Department. Washington, DC (Original available at http://www.aflcio.org/women/kids.htm, viewed August 2002.)

Aidman, A. (1997). *Television violence: Content, context, and consequences.* Champaign, IL: ERIC Clearinghouse on Elementary and Early Childhood Education.

Ainsworth, M. D. S. (1973). The development of the infant-mother attachment. In B. M. Caldwell & H. N. Ricciuti (Eds.), *Review of child development research, 3*, 1–94. Chicago: University of Chicago Press.

Allinsmith, W., & Greening, T. C. (1955). Guilt over anger as predicted from parental discipline: A study of superego development. *American Psychologist, 10*, 320.

Altenor, A., Kay, E., & Richter, M. (1977). The generality of learned helplessness in the rat. *Learning & Motivation, 8*, 54–61.

Amato, P. R. (1997). Life-span adjustment of children to their parents' divorce. In E. N. Junn & C. Boyatzis (Eds.), *Annual editions: Child growth and development 97/98* (4th ed.). New York: McGraw-Hill. (Original work published in *The Future of Children*, Spring 1994.)

American Academy of Pediatrics. (1995). *Caring for your school-age child: Ages 5–12.* New York: Bantam Books.

Anyon, J. (1983). Intersections of gender and class: Accommodation and resistance by contradictory sex-role ideologies. In S. Walker and L. Barton (Eds.), *Gender, class and education* (pp. 21–37). London: Falmer.

Aries, P. (1962). *Centuries of childhood.* New York: Random House.

B

Bagley, C., Verma, G. K., Mallick, K., & Young, L. (1979). *Personality, self-esteem and prejudice.* Westmead, Farnborough, Hants, England: Saxon House.

Baillargeon, R. (1997). How do infants learn about the physical world? In E. N. Junn & C. Boyatzis (Eds.), *Annual editions: Child growth and development 97/98* (4th ed.). New York: McGraw-Hill. (Original work published in *Current Directions in Psychological Science*, October 1994.)

Bandura, A. (1977). *Social learning theory.* Englewood Cliffs, NJ: Prentice-Hall.

Banich, M. T. (1997). *Neurology: The neural bases of mental function.* Boston: Houghton Mifflin.

Barko, N. (1997). Labeled for life? In K. M. Paciorek & J. H. Munro (Eds.), *Annual editions: Early childhood education 97/98* (18th ed.). New York: McGraw-Hill. (Original work published in *Parents*, September 1996.)

Barnett, R. C., & Rivers, C. (1998). *She works he works: How two income families are happy, healthy and thriving.* Cambridge: Harvard University Press.

Baumrind, D. (1971). Current patterns of parental authority. *Developmental Psychology Monographs, 4*(1), 1–103.

Baumrind, D. (1978). Parental disciplinary patterns and social competence in children. *Youth and Society, 9*(3), 239–276.

Baumrind, D. (1980). New directions in socialization research. *Psychological Bulletin, 35*, 639–652.

Beaty, J. J. (1997). *Building bridges with multicultural picture books: For children 3–5.* Upper Saddle River, NJ: Merrill Education/Prentice-Hall.

Beck, R. (1973). White House conferences on children: An historical perspective. *Harvard Educational Review, 43*, 4.

Begley, S. (1997a). Your child's brain. In K. M. Paciorek & J. H. Munro (Eds.), *Annual editions: Early childhood education 97/98* (18th ed.). New York: McGraw-Hill. (Original work published in *Newsweek*, February 19, 1996)

Begley, S. (1997b). The IQ puzzle. In E. N. Junn & C. Boyatzis (Eds.), *Annual editions: Child growth and development 97/98* (4th ed.). New York: McGraw-Hill. (Original work published in *Newsweek*, May 6, 1996.)

Begley, S., & Springen, K. (1997). Life in a parallel world. In E. N. Junn & C. Boyatzis (Eds.), *Annual editions: Child growth and development 97/98* (4th ed.). New York: McGraw-Hill. (Original work published in *Newsweek*, May 13, 1996.)

Bentzen, W. R. (1997). *Seeing young children: A guide to observing and recording behavior* (3rd ed.). Clifton Park, NY: Delmar Learning.

Berk, L. E. (1997). Vygotsky's theory: The importance of make-believe play. In E. N. Junn & C. Boyatzis (Eds.), *Annual editions: Child growth and development 97/98* (4th ed.). New York: McGraw-Hill. (Original work published in *Young Children*, November 1994.)

Berkowitz, M. W., & Grych, J. H. (1998). Fostering goodness: Teaching parents to facilitate children's moral development. *Journal of Moral Education, 27*(3), 371–391.

Berkowitz, M. W., & Gibbs, J. C. (1983). Measuring the developmental features of moral discussion. *Merrill-Palmer Quarterly, 29*, 399–410.

Berlak, A., & Berlak, H. (1981). *Dilemmas of schooling: Teaching and social change.* London: Methuen.

Berndt, T. J. (1997). *Child development* (2d ed.). New York: McGraw-Hill.

Billman, J., & Sherman, J. A. (1997). *Observation and participation in early childhood settings: A practicum guide, birth through age five.* Needham Heights, MA: Allyn & Bacon.

Blau, F. (1998, March). Trends in the well-being of American women, 1990–1995. *Journal of Economic Literature, 36*, 112–165.

Bloom, B. S. (1964). *Stability and change in human characteristics.* New York: John Wiley & Sons.

Bodrova, E., & Leong, D. J. (1996). *Tools of the mind: The Vygotskian approach to early childhood education.* Englewood Cliffs, NJ: Prentice-Hall.

Bond, J. T., Galinsky, E., & Swanberg, J. E. (1998). *The 1997 national study of the changing workforce.* New York: Families & Work Institute.

Bowlby, J. (1958). The nature of the child's tie to his mother. *International Journal of Psychoanalysis, 39*, 350–373.

Boyatzis, C. (1997). *Annual editions: Child growth and development 97/98.* New York: McGraw-Hill.

Brazelton, T. B. (1985). *Working and caring.* Reading, MA: Addison-Wesley.

Brazelton, T. B., Koslowski, B., & Main, M. (1974). The origins of reciprocity. In M. Lewis & L. Rosenblum (Eds.), *The effect of the infant on its caregiver.* New York: Wiley-Interscience.

Bredekamp, S., & Copple, C. (Eds.). (1997). *Developmentally appropriate practice in early childhood programs* (rev. ed). Washington, DC: National Association for the Education of Young Children.

Bremner, R. H. (Ed.). (1974). *Children and youth in America: A documentary history* (vols. 1–3). Cambridge, MA: Harvard University Press.

Bretherton, I., & Waters, E. (1985). Security in infancy, childhood and adulthood. *Monographs of the Society for Research in Child Development, 50*(1–2).

Brewer, A. (1998). *Introduction to early childhood education: Preschool through primary grades* (3d ed.). Needham Heights, MA: Allyn & Bacon.

Bronfenbrenner, U., & Morris, P. A. (1998). The ecology of developmental processes. In W. Damon (Series Ed.) & R. M. Lerner (Vol. Ed.) *Handbook of child psychology: Theoretical models of human development* (vol. 1, 5th ed.) (pp. 993–1027). New York: Wiley.

Brooks, R., & Goldstein, S. (2001). *Raising resilient children: Fostering strength, hope, and optimism in your child.* Lincolnwood, IL: Contemporary Books

Bruner, J. (1978a, September). Learning the mother tongue. *Human Nature, 1*, 43–48.

Bruner, J. (1978b). Learning how to do things with words. In J. S. Bruner & A. Garton (Eds.), *Human growth and development: Wolfson College lectures.* Oxford: Clarendon Press.

Bruns, D. A., & Corso, R. M. (2001). *Working with culturally and linguistically diverse families.* Champaign, IL: ERIC Clearinghouse on Elementary and Early Childhood Education.

Bullock, J. R. (1997). Children without friends. In E. N. Junn & C. Boyatzis (Eds.), *Annual editions: Child growth and development 97/98* (4th ed.). New York: McGraw-Hill. (Original work published in *Childhood Education*, Winter 1992.)

C

Cairns, R. B. (1979). *Social development: The origins and plasticity of interchanges.* San Francisco: Freeman.

Cantor, J. (1998). *Mommy, I'm scared: How TV and movies frighten children and what we can do to protect them.* Fort Washington, PA: Harvest Books.

Cárdenas, J. A. (1995). *Multicultural education: A generation of advocacy.* Needham Heights, MA: Allyn & Bacon.

Center for Policy Alternatives. (2002). *Kids count data book: State profiles of child well-being.* Washington, DC: Center for Policy Alternatives.

Charlesworth, R. (2004). *Understanding child development* (6th ed.). Clifton Park, NY: Delmar Learning.

Child Care Bureau. (1997, May). *Using research to improve child care for low-income families.* Washington DC: Child Care Bureau, U.S. Department of health and Human Services.

Children's Defense Fund, & Edelman, M. W. (2000). The state of America's children: Yearbook 2000—A report from the Children's Defense Fund. Boston: Beacon Press.

Children's Defense Fund. (1999). Overview of child care, early education, and school-age care. Washington, DC (Original available at http://www.childrensdefense.org/pdf/99_overview.pdf, viewed August 2002).

Chomsky, N. (1965). *Aspects of the theory of syntax.* Cambridge, MA: MIT Press.

Chugani, H. (1993, June). Positron emission tomography scanning: Applications in newborns. *Clinics in Perinatology, 20*(2), 398.

Clark, L., DeWolf, S., & Clark, C. (1992). Teaching teachers to avoid having culturally assaultive classrooms. *Young Children, 47*(5), 4–9.

Clarke, J. I. (1978). *Self-esteem: A family affair.* New York: Winston Press.

Clarke-Stewart, A. (1978). Popular primer for parents. *American Psychologist, 33,* 359.

Cole, L. (1950). *A history of education.* New York: Rinehart.

Collins, W. A., & Gunnar, M. R. (1990). Social and personality development. *Annual Review of Psychology, 41,* 387–416.

Condon, W. S., & Sander, L. (1974). Neonate movement is synchronized with adult speech: Interactional participation and language acquisition. *Science, 183,* 99–101.

Cook-Gumperz, J. (1973). *Social control and socialization.* London: Routledge & Kegan Paul.

Coontz, S. (1997). Where are the good old days? In K. M. Paciorek & J. H. Munro (Eds.), *Annual editions: Early childhood education 97/98* (18th ed.). New York: McGraw-Hill. (Original work published in *Modern Maturity*, May/June 1996)

Coopersmith, S. (1967). *The antecedents of self-esteem.* San Francisco: W. H. Freeman.

Copeland, M. L., & McCreedy, B. S. (1997, January–February). Creating family-friendly policies: Are child care center policies in line with current family realities? *Child Care Information Exchange, 113,* 7–10, 12.

Corsaro, W. A. (1981). Friendship in the nursery school: Social organization in a peer environment. In S. R. Asher and J. M. Gottman (Eds.), *The development of children's friendships.* New York: Cambridge University Press.

Costley, D., & Todd, R. (1987). *Human relations in organization* (3d ed.). New York: West.

Cotton, N. (1984). The development of self-esteem and self-esteem regulation. In J. E. Mack and S. L. Ablon (Eds.), *The development and sustaining of self-esteem in childhood.* New York: International Universities Press.

Couture, L. A. (2001). Corporal punishment: Society's remaining acceptable violence. Condensed essay based on unpublished Master's Thesis by L. A. Couture, Evidence against the efficacy of corporal punishment.

Cowan, C. P., & Cowan, P. (1992). *When partners become parents.* New York: Basic Books.

Crockenberg, S. (1997). How children learn to resolve conflicts in families. In E. N. Junn & C. Boyatzis (Eds.), *Annual editions: Child growth and development 97/98* (4th ed.). New York: McGraw-Hill. (Original work published in *Zero to Three*, April 1992.)

Cunnington, P., & Buck, A. (1965). *Children's costume in England.* New York: Barnes & Noble.

Curran, D. (1985). *Stress and the healthy family.* Minneapolis, MN: Winston Press.

D

Dale, S. (1993, Winter). Spanking as an addiction, *Mothering, 69,* 31–35.

Daly, K. (1996). *Families and rime: Keeping pace in a hurried culture.* Thousand Oaks, CA: Sage.

Daly, K. (200). *It keeps getting faster: Changing patterns of time in families.* Guelph, Ontario, Canada: Va??? Institute of the Family, University of Guelph.

Damon, W. (1988). *The moral child: Nurturing children's natural moral growth.* New York: Free Press.

Day, R., Peterson, G., & McCracken, C. (1998). Predicting spanking of younger and older children by mothers and fathers. *Journal of Marriage and the Family, 60,* 79–94.

Dean, A. L., Malik, M. M., Richards, W., & Stringer, S. A. (1986). Effects of parental maltreatment on children's conceptions of interpersonal relationships. *Developmental Psychology, 22,* 617–626.

DeCasper, A. J., & Fifer, W. P. (1980). Of human bonding: Newborns prefer their mothers' voices. *Science, 208,* 1174–1176.

deMelendez, R., & Ostertag, V. (1997). *Teaching young children in multicultural classrooms: Issues, concepts and strategies.* Clifton Park, NY: Delmar Learning.

Denby, D. (1997). Buried alive. In E. N. Junn & C. Boyatzis (Eds.), *Annual editions: Child growth and development 97/98* (4th ed.). New York: McGraw-Hill. (Original work published in *The New Yorker*, July 15, 1996.)

Dennis, R. E., & Giangreco, M. F. (1996). Creating conversation: Reflections on cultural sensitivity in family interviewing. *Exceptional Children, 63*(1), 103–116

Dennis, W. (1960). Causes of retardation among institutional children: Iran. *The Journal of Genetic Psychology, 96*, 47–59.

Dennis, W. (1973). *Children of the creche.* New York: Appleton-Century-Crofts.

deSales, F., & Ryan, J. (1972). *Introduction to the devout life by St. Francis deSales* (reissue ed.). New York: Image Books.

DeVries, R., & Zan, B. (1994). *Moral classrooms, moral children: Creating a constructivist atmosphere in early education.* New York: Teachers College Press.

Dewey, J. (1966). *Experience and education.* New York: Collier.

Dinkmeyer, D. C., & McKay, G. D. (1982). *The parent's handbook: Systematic training for effective parenting.* Circle Pines, MN: American Guidance Service.

Dinnebeil, L. A., & Rule, S. (1994). Variables that influence collaboration between parents and service providers. *Journal of Early Intervention, 18*(4), 349–361.

Dreikurs, R., & Cassel, P. (1972). *Discipline without tears* (2d ed.). New York: Hawthorn Books.

E

Eddowes, E. A., & Ralph, K. S. (1998). *Interactions for development and learning: Birth through eight years.* Upper Saddle River, NJ: Merrill Education/Prentice-Hall.

Edwards, C. H. (1997). *Classroom discipline and management* (2d ed.). Upper Saddle River, NJ: Merrill Education/Prentice-Hall.

Eisenberg, R. B. (1976). *Auditory competence in early life.* Baltimore, MD: University Park Press.

Eisenberg-Berg, N. (1979). Development of children's prosocial moral judgment. *Developmental Psychology, 15*, 128–138.

Elkind, D. (1981). *The hurried child.* Reading, MA: Addison-Wesley.

Elkind, D. (1997). School and family in the postmodern world. In E. N. Junn & C. Boyatzis (Eds.), *Annual editions: Child growth and development 97/98* (4th ed.). New York: McGraw-Hill.

Elman, J., Bates, E. A., Johnson, M., Kaemiloff-Smith, A., Parisi, D., & Plunkett, K. (1997). *Rethinking innateness.* Cambridge, MA: MIT Press.

Erikson, E. (1963). *Childhood and society* (2d ed.). New York: W. W. Norton.

Erikson, E. (1982). *The life cycle completed: A review.* New York: W. W. Norton.

Erikson, E. H. (1959). Growth and crises of the healthy personality. *Psychological Issues, 1*, 50–100.

Erikson, E. H. (1971). A healthy personality for every child. In Robert H. Anderson and Harold G. Shane (Eds.), *As the twig is bent.* Boston: Houghton Mifflin.

Everett C., & Everett, S. V. (1998). *Healthy divorce: For parents and children.* Hoboken, NJ: Jossey-Bass.

F

Faegre, M., & Anderson, J. (1930). *Child care and training* (3d ed.). Minneapolis, MN: University of Minnesota Press.

Fantuzzo, J. W., Rohrbeck, C. A., Hightower, A. D., & Work, W. C. (1991). Teacher's use and children's preferences of rewards in elementary school. *Psychology in the Schools, 28*(2), 175–181.

Feeney, S. S., Christensen, D., & Moravcik, E. R. (1996). *Who am I in the lives of children? An introduction to teaching young children* (5th ed.). Upper Saddle River, NJ: Merrill Education/Prentice-Hall.

Ferguson, T. J., & Rule, B. G. (1982). Influence of inferential set, outcome intent, and outcome severity on children's moral judgments. *Developmental Psychology, 18*, 843–851.

Field, T. M. (1982). Affective and physiological changes during manipulated interactions of high-risk infants. In T. Field & A. Fogel (Eds.), *Emotion and early interaction.* Hillsdale, NJ: Lawrence Erlbaum Associates.

Fields, M. V., & Boesser, C. (1998). *Constructive guidance and discipline: Preschool and primary education* (2d ed.). Upper Saddle River, NJ: Merrill Education/Prentice-Hall.

Finkelhor, D., & Dziuba-Leatherman, J. (1997). Victimization of children. In E. N. Junn & C. Boyatzis (Eds.), *Annual editions: Child growth and development 97/98* (4th ed.). New York: McGraw-Hill. (Original work published in *American Psychologist*, March 1994.)

Finkelstein, N. W., & Ramey, C. T. (1977). Learning to control the environment in infancy. *Child Development, 48*, 806–819.

Fleming, R., Baum, A., & Singer, J. E. (1984). Toward an integrative approach to the study of stress. *Journal of Personality and Social Psychology, 46*(4), 939–949.

Flynn, C. (1996). Regional differences in spanking experiences and attitudes: A comparison of northeastern and southern college students. *Journal of Family Violence, 11*(1), 59–80.

Francke, L. B. (1983). *Growing up divorced.* New York: Fawcett Crest.

French, L. (1996). "I told you all about it, so don't tell me you don't know." *Young Children, 5*(2), 17–20.

Friedman, E. H. (1990). *Friedman's fables.* New York: Guilford Publishing.

Froebel, F. (1887). *The education of man: The art of education, instruction and training.* New York: D. Appleton and Co.

Furth, H. G. (1970). *Piaget for teachers.* Englewood Cliffs, NJ: Prentice-Hall.

G

Gaetano, Y. D., Williams, L. R., & Volk, D. (1998). *Kaleidoscope: A multicultural approach for the primary school classroom.* Upper Saddle River, NJ: Merrill Education/Prentice-Hall.

Gallo, N. (1997). Why spanking takes the spunk out of kids. In E. N. Junn & C. Boyatzis (Eds.), *Annual editions: Child growth and development 97/98* (4th ed.). New York: McGraw-Hill. (Original work published in *Child*, March/April 1989)

Galston, W. (1993, Winter). Causes of declining well-being among U.S. children. *The Aspen Institute Quarterly, 5*(1) 52–77.

Gartrell, D. (1997). Misbehavior or mistaken behavior? In K. M. Paciorek & J. H. Munro (Eds.), *Annual editions: Early childhood education 97/98* (18th ed.). New York: McGraw-Hill. (Original work published in *Young Children*, July 1995.)

Gartrell, D. (2003). *A Guidance approach for the encouraging classroom* (3rd ed.). Clifton Park, NY: Delmar Learning.

Gazda, G. M., Asbury, F. S., Balzar, F. J., Childers, W. C., & Walters, R. P. (1990). *Human relations development* (4th ed.). Boston: Allyn & Bacon.

Gerbner, G., & Gross, L. (1980). The violent face of television and its lessons. In E. L. Palmer and A. Dorr (Eds.), *Children and the faces of television: Teaching, violence, selling.* New York: Academic Press.

Gershoff, E. T. (2002). Corporal punishment by parents and associated child behaviors and experiences: A meta-analytic and theoretical review. *American Psychological Association, 128*(4), 539–579.

Gesell, A., Halverson, H. M., Thompson, H., Ilg, F. L., Castner, B. M., Ames, L. B., & Matruda, C. S. (1940). *The first five years of life: A guide to the study of the preschool child.* New York: Harper & Row.

Gestwicki, C. (1999). *Developmentally appropriate practice.* Clifton Park, NY: Delmar Learning.

Gibbs, N. (1997). The EQ factor. In E. N. Junn & C. Boyatzis (Eds.), *Annual editions: Child growth and development 97/98* (4th ed.). New York: McGraw-Hill. (Original work published in *Time*, October 2, 1995.)

Glubok, S. (Ed.). (1969). *Home and child life in colonial days.* New York: Macmillan.

Gonzalez-Alvarez, L. I. (1998). A short course in sensitivity training: Working with Hispanic families of children with disabilities. *Teaching Exceptional Children, 31*(2), 73–77.

Gonzalez-Mena, J. (1998a). *The child in the family and in the community* (2d ed.). Upper Saddle River, NJ: Merrill Education/Prentice-Hall.

Gonzalez-Mena, J. (1998b). *Foundations: Early childhood education in a diverse society.* Mountain View, CA: Mayfield Publishing Company.

Gordon, A., & Browne, K. W. (1996a). *Guiding young children in a diverse society.* Needham Heights, MA: Allyn & Bacon.

Gordon, A., & Browne, K. W. (2004). *Beginnings and beyond* (6th ed.). Clifton Park, NY: Delmar Learning.

Gordon, T. (1970). *Parent effectiveness training.* New York: Peter Wyden.

Gough, P. B. (1993). Dealing with diversity. *Phi Delta Kappan, 75*(1), 3.

Green, V., & Stafford, S. H. (1997). Preschool integration: Strategies for teachers. In K. M. Paciorek and J. H. Munro (Eds.), *Annual editions: Early childhood education 97/98* (18th ed.). New York: McGraw-Hill. (Original work published in *Childhood Education*, Summer 1996.)

Greenenough, W. E., Black, J. E., & Wallace, C. S. (1993). Experience and brain development In M. Johnson (Ed.), *Brain development and cognition: A reader* (pp. 290–322). Oxford: Blackwell.

Gronlund, G. (1997). Families and schools: Bringing the DAP message to kindergarten and primary teachers. In K. M. Paciorek & J. H. Munro (Eds.), *Annual editions: Early childhood education 97/98* (18th ed.). New York: McGraw-Hill. (Original work published in *Young Children*, July 1995.)

Grossman, D., Degaetano, G., & Grossman, D. (1999). *Stop teaching our kids to kill: A call to action against TV, movie and video game violence.* New York: Random House.

Grusec, J. E., Kuczynski, L., Rushton, J. P., & Simutis, Z. (1979). Learning resistance to temptation through observation. *Developmental Psychology, 15,* 233–240.

Gudykunst, W. B., Ting-Toomey, S., & Nishida, T. (1996). *Communication in personal relationships across cultures.* Thousand Oaks, CA: Sage.

Gutek, G. L. (1997). *Historical and philosophical foundations of education: A biographical introduction* (2d ed.). Upper Saddle River, NJ: Merrill Education/Prentice-Hall.

Grych, J. H., & Fincham, F. D. (1990). Marital conflict and children's adjustment: A cognitive-contextual framework. *Psychological Bulletin, 108,* 267–290.

Grych, J. H., & Fincham, F. D. (1993). Children's appraisals of marital conflict: Initial investigations of the cognitive-contextual framework. *Child Development, 64,* 215–230.

H

Hamburg, D. A. (1992). *Today's children.* New York: Times Books.

Harding, C. G., & Golinkoff, R. M. (1979). The origins of intentional vocalizations in prelinguistic infants. *Child Development, 50,* 33–40.

Harlow, H., & Zimmerman, R. (1959). Affectional responses in the infant monkey. *Science, 130,* 421–432.

Harms,T., & Clifford, R. (1998). *Early childhood environment rating scale* (rev. ed.). New York: Teachers College Press.

Harrison, A. O., Wilson, M. N., Pine, C. J., Chan, S. Q., & Buriel, R. (1990). Family ecologies of ethnic minority children. *Child Development, 61,* 347–362.

Hartshorne, H., & May, M. A. (1928). *Studies in the nature of character* (vol. 1). New York: Macmillan.

Heineman, R. V. (1998). *The abused child psychodynamic: Understanding and treatment.* New York: Guilford.

Hernandez, D. J. (1997). Changing demographics: Past and future demands for early childhood programs. In K. M. Paciorek & J. H. Munro (Eds.), *Annual editions: Early childhood education 97/98* (18th ed.). New York: McGraw-Hill. (Original work published in *The Future of Children,* Winter 1995.)

Hess, E. (1972). Imprinting in a natural laboratory. *Scientific American, 227,* 24–31.

Hess, R., & Shipman, V. (1967). Parents as teachers: How lower and middle class mothers teach. In C. S. Lavatelli & F. Stendler (Eds.), *Readings in child behavior and development* (3d ed.) (pp. 436–446). New York: Harcourt Brace Jovanovich.

Hildebrand, V. (1997). *Introduction to early childhood education* (6th ed.). Upper Saddle River, NJ: Merrill Education/Prentice-Hall.

Hildebrand, V., Phenice, L. A., Gray, M. M., & Hines, R. P. (1996). *Knowing and serving diverse families.* Upper Saddle River, NJ: Merrill Education/Prentice-Hall.

Hochschild, A. R. (1997). *The time bind: When work becomes home and home becomes work.* New York: Henry Holt and Company.

Hoffman, L., & Manis, J. D. (1979). The value of children in the United States: A new approach to the study of fertility. *Journal of Marriage and the Family, 41,* 583–596.

Hoffman, M. L. (1979). Development of moral thought, feeling, and behavior. *American Psychologist, 34,* 958–967.

Hoffman-Plotkin, D., & Twentyman, C. T. (1984). A multimodal assessment of behavioral and cognitive deficits in abused and neglected preschoolers. *Child Development, 55,* 794–802.

Hoffman, M. L., & Saltzstein, H. D. (1967). Parent discipline and the child's moral development. *Journal of Personality and Social Psychology, 5,* 45–57.

Honig, A. S. (1986, July). Stress and coping in children (Part 2): Interpersonal family relationships. *Young Children, 41*(5), 47–60.

Honig, A. S., & Wittmer, D. S. (1997). Helping children become more prosocial: Ideas for classrooms. In K. M. Paciorek & J. H. Munro (Eds.), *Annual editions: Early childhood education 97/98* (18th ed.). New York: McGraw-Hill. (Original work published in *Young Children*, January 1996.)

Howard, G. R. (1993). Whites in multicultural education: Rethinking our role. *Phi Delta Kappan, 75*(1), 36–41.

Hunt, J. (1976). The psychological development of orphanage-reared infants: Interventions with outcomes (Teheran). *Genetic Psychology Monographs, 94,* 177–226.

I

Ingrassia, M., & McCormick, J. (1997). Why leave children with bad parents? In E. N. Junn & C. Boyatzis (Eds.), *Annual editions: Child growth and development 97/98* (4th ed.). New York: McGraw-Hill. (Original work published in *Newsweek*, April 25, 1994.)

J

Jackson, B. R. (1997, November). Creating a climate for healing in a violent society. *Young Children, 52*(7), 68–70.

Joe, J. R., & Malach, R. S. (1998). Families with Native American roots. In E. W. Lynch & M. J. Hanson (Eds.), *Developing cross-cultural competence: A guide for working with young children and their families.* (pp. 127–164). Baltimore: Paul H. Brookes Publishing Company.

K

Kagan, J. (1984). *The nature of the child.* New York: Basic Books.

Kagan, J. (1971). *Change and continuity in infancy.* New York: Wiley.

Kagan, J., Kearsley, R. B., & Zelazo, P. R. (1978). *Infancy: Its place in human development.* Cambridge, MA: Harvard University Press.

Kagan, J., & Moss, H. (1962). *Birth to maturity.* New York: Wiley.

Kagan, S. L. (1997, May). Support systems for children, youths, families, and schools in inner-city situations. *Education and Urban Society, 29*(3), 277–295.

Kalyanpur, M., & Harry, B. (1999). *Culture in Special Education: Building reciprocal family-professional relationships.* Baltimore: Paul H. Brookes Publishing Company.

Kantrowitz, B., & Wingert, P. (1997). How kids learn. In E. N. Junn & C. Boyatzis (Eds.), *Annual editions: Child growth and development 97/98* (4th ed.). New York: McGraw-Hill. (Original work published in Newsweek, April 17, 1989.)

Katz, L. G. (1999, December). *Curriculum disputes in early childhood education.* ERIC Digest. Champaign, IL: ERIC Clearinghouse on Elementary and Early Childhood Education. (ERIC Document No. ED436298.)

Katz, L., & McClellan, D. (1997). *Fostering children's social competence: The teacher's role.* Washington, DC: National Association for the Education of Young Children.

Katz, P. A. (1982). Development of children's racial awareness and intergroup attitudes. In L. Katz (Ed.), *Current topics in early childhood education* (vol. 4). Norwood, NJ: Ablex.

Kaye, K. (1982). *The mental and social life of babies.* Chicago: University of Chicago Press.

Keirsey, D. (1984). *Please understand me II: Temperament, character, intelligence* (5th ed.) Costa Mesa, CA: David Prometheus Nemesis Book Co.

Kempe, R. S., & Kempe, C. H. (1978). *Child abuse.* Cambridge, MA: Harvard University Press.

Knowlson, J. (1996). *Damned to fame: The life of Samuel Beckett.* New York: Simon & Schuster.

Kochanek, T. T., & Buka, S. L. (1998). Influential factors in the utilization of early intervention services. *Journal of Early Intervention, 21*(4), 323–338.

Kochanska, G. (1997). Mutually responsive orientation between mothers and their young children: Implications for early socializaton. *Child Development, 68,* 94–112.

Kochanska, G., & Aksan, N. (1995). Mother-child mutually positive affect, the quality of child compliance to requests and prohibitions, and maternal control as correlates of early internalization. *Child Development, 66,* 236–254.

Kohlberg, L. (1969). Stage and sequence: The cognitive-developmental approach to socialization. In D. Goslin (Ed.), *Handbook of socialization theory and research.* Skokie, IL: Rand-McNally.

Kohlberg, L. (1976). Moral stages and moralization: The cognitive-developmental approach. In T. Lickona (Ed.), *Moral development and behavior.* New York: Holt, Rinehart & Winston.

Kohlberg, L., & DeVries, R. (1987). *Constructivist early education: Overview and comparison with other programs.* Washington, DC: National Association for the Education of Young Children.

Kohn, A. (1990). *The brighter side of human nature: Altruism and empathy in evryday life.* New York: Basic Books.

Kohn, A. (1993). *Punished by rewards: The trouble with gold stars, incentive plans, A's, praise, and other bribes.* Boston: Houghton Mifflin.

Kohn, A. (1994). *The risks of rewards.* ERIC Clearinghouse on Elementary and Early Childhood Education. Urbana IL: Document #ED376990. Available online at http://www.ed.gov/databases/ERIC_Digests/ed376990.html.

Kokenes, B. (1974). Grade level differences in factors of self-esteem. *Developmental Psychology, 10*, 954–958.

Krogh, S. (1995). *The integrated early childhood curriculum* (2d ed.). New York: McGraw-Hill.

Krupinski, E., & Weikel, D. (1986). *Death from child abuse and no one heard.* Winter Park, FL: Currier-Davis.

Kuhl, P. K. (1981). Auditory category formation and developmental speech perception. In R. Stark (Ed.), *Language behavior in infancy and early childhood.* New York: Elsevier.

L

Ladd, R. E. (Ed.). (1996). *Children's rights revisioned: Philosophical readings.* Belmont, CA: Wadsworth Publishing.

Lamb, M. E. (1978). Infant social cognition and "second-order" effects. *Infant Behavior and Development, 1*, 1–10.

Lamb, M. E. (1981). *The role of the father in childhood development* (2d ed.). New York: Wiley.

Lamb, M. E., Gaensbauer, T. J., Malkin, C. M., & Schultz, L. A. (1985). The effects of child maltreatment on security of infant-adult attachment. *Infant Behavior and Development, 8*, 35–45.

Landreth, C., & Johnson, B. (1953). Young children's responses to a picture inset test designed to reveal reactions to persons of different skin color. *Child Development, 24*, 63–80.

Leach, P. (1996, July 9). *Spanking: A shortcut to nowhere* [WWW document]. http://cnet.unb.ca/orgs/prevention_cruelty/spank.htm.

Lefkowitz, M. M., & Tesiny, E. P. (1980). Dejection and depression: Prospective and contemporaneous analyses. *Developmental Psychology, 20*, 776–786.

Leland, J. (1997). Violence, reel to real. In E. N. Junn & C. Boyatzis (Eds.), *Annual editions: Child growth and development 97/98* (4th ed.). New York: McGraw-Hill. (Original work published in *Newsweek*, December 11, 1995.)

Leong, D., & Bodrova, E. (1996). *Tools of the mind: A Vygotskian approach to early childhood education.* Upper Saddle River, NJ: Merrill Education/Prentice-Hall.

Levine, M. (1998). *See no evil: A guide to protecting our children from media violence.* New York: Jossey-Bass.

Lickona, T. (1983). *Raising good children.* New York: Bantam Books.

Lindjord, D. (1997, November–December). Child care: The continuing crisis for working families and child care teachers. *Journal of Early Education and Family Review, 5*(2), 6–7.

Lorenz, K. (1966). *On aggression.* New York: Harcourt, Brace & World.

Lubeck, S. (1985). *Sandbox society: Early education in black and white America.* London: Falmer.

Lynch, E. W., & Hanson, M. J. (Eds.). (1998). *Developing cross-cultural competence: A guide for working with children and their families* (2nd ed.). Baltimore: Paul H. Brookes Publishing Company.

M

Majors, R., & Billson, J. M. (1992). *Cool pose: The dilemmas of black manhood in America.* New York: Touchstone.

Marose, N. R. (1997, November). Successful toilet learning: At a child's pace. *Young Children 52*(7), 81.

Marshall, R. (1991). *The state of Families: 3. Losing direction, families, human resource development, and economic performance.* Milwaukee, WI: Family Service America.

Maslow, A. H. (1943, July). A theory of human motivation. *Psychological Review, 50,* 370–396.

Maslow, A. H. (1970). *Motivation and personality* (2nd ed.). New York: Harper & Row.

Maslow, A. (1993). *The farther reaches of human nature* (Esalen Book reprint ed.). Manhattan Beach, CA: Arkana.

Mathur, A. K., & Straus, M. A. (1996). *Social Changes and trends in approval of corporal punishment by parents from 1968 to 1994.* Durham, NH: University of New Hampshire.

McAlister, B. G. (1997, Spring). Growing up in a violent world: The impact of family and community violence on young children and their families. *Topics in Early Childhood Special Education, 17*(1), 74–102.

McCloskey, C. M. (1997). Taking positive steps toward classroom management in preschool: Loosening up without letting it all fall apart. In K. M. Paciorek & J. H. Munro (Eds.), *Annual editions: Early childhood education 97/98* (18th ed.). New York: McGraw-Hill. (Original work published in *Young Children*, March 1996.)

McGraw, M. (1941). *The child in painting.* New York: Greystone Press.

McLean, M. E., Bailey, D. B., Jr., & Wolery, M. (1997). *Assessing infants and preschoolers with special needs* (2d ed.). Upper Saddle River, NJ: Merrill Education/Prentice-Hall.

McLoyd, V. C. (1990). The impact of economic hardship on black families and children: Psychological distress, parenting, and socioemotional development. *Child Development, 61,* 311–346.

McMillan, M. (1930). *The nursery school.* New York: E. P. Dutton.

Meece, J. (1997). *Child and adolescent development for educators.* New York: McGraw-Hill.

Miller, D. (1986). *Infant/toddler day care in high, middle, and low socio-economic settings: An ethnography of dialectical enculturation and linguistic code.* Unpublished doctoral dissertation, University of Houston, Houston, TX.

Mindes, G., Ireton, H., & Mardell-Czudnowski, C. (1996). *Assessing young children.* Clifton Park, NY: Delmar Learning.

Montessori, M. (1968). *Reconstruction in education.* India: Theosophical Publishing House.

Montessori, M. (1971). *Peace and education.* Adar, Chennai, India: Theosophical Publishing House.

Montessori, M., & Hunt, J. M. (1989). *The Montessori method.* New York: Schocken Books.

Mooney, C. G. (2000). *Theories of childhood: An introduction to Dewey, Montessori, Erickson, Piaget & Vygotsky.* Saint Paul, MN: Redleaf Press.

Moore, T. (1994). *Care of the soul: A guide for cultivating depth and sacredness in everyday life* (reprint ed.). New York: Harper.

Morland, J. (1972). *Racial acceptance and preference in nursery school children in a southern city.* In A. R. Brown (Ed.), Prejudice in children. Springfield, IL: Charles C. Thomas.

Mussen, P. H., & Eisenberg-Berg, N. (1977). *Roots of caring, sharing and helping.* San Francisco: Freeman.

N

National Association for the Education of Young Children (NAEYC). (1993). Enriching classroom diversity with books for children, in-depth discussion of them, and story-extension activities. *Young Children, 48*(3), 10–12.

National Commission on Children. (1991). *Speaking of kids: A national survey of children and parents.* Washington, DC: National Commission on Children.

National Committee to Prevent Child Abuse. (1998). *Child abuse and neglect statistics.* Chicago: National Committee to Prevent Child Abuse.

O

Ohtake, Y., Santos, R. M., & Fowler, S. A. (2000). It's a three way conversation: Families, service providers, and interpreters working together. *Young Exceptional Children, 4*(1), 12–18.

Oliner, S. P., & Oliner, P. M. (1988). *The altruistic personality: Rescuers of Jews in Nazi Europe.* New York: Free Press.

Osborn, D. (1980). *Early childhood education in historical perspective.* Athens: Education Association.

Owen, R. (1958). *Life of Robert Owen written by himself.* New York: Augustus M. Kelley.

P

Paley, V. (1992). *You can't say you can't play.* Cambridge, MA: Harvard University Press.

Papousek, H. (1967). Conditioning during postnatal development. In Y. Brackbill & G. G. Thompson (Eds.), *Behavior in infancy and early childhood* (pp. 259–284). New York: Free Press.

Parents and Teachers against Violence in Education (PTAVE). (2002). *Project NoSpank.* Alamo, CA: PTAVE.

Parrillo, V. N. (1985). *Strangers to these shores: Race and ethnic relations in the United States/Vincent N. Parrillo* (2d ed.). Boston: Houghton Mifflin.

Parke, R. D., & Slaby, R. G. (1983). The development of aggression. In E.M. Hetherington (Ed.), *Handbook of child psychology: Socialization, personality and social development* (4th ed.) (vol. 4, pp. 537–643). New York: Wiley.

Petersen, E. A. (1996). *A practical guide to early childhood planning, methods and materials: The what, why and how of lesson plans.* Needham Heights, MA: Allyn & Bacon.

Peterson, L. (1983). Influence of age, task competence, and responsibility focus on children's altruism. *Developmental Psychology, 19*, 141–148.

Phillips, C. B. (1988). Nurturing diversity for today's children and tomorrow's leaders. *Young Children, 43*(2), 42–47.

Phillips, D., Scarr, S., & McCartney, K. (1987). dimensions and effects of child care quality: The Bermuda study. In D. Phillips (Ed.), *Quality in child care: What does research tell us?* Washington, DC: NAEYC.

Piaget, J. (1952). *The origins of intelligence in children.* New York: International University Press.

Piaget, J. (1962). *Play, dreams, and imitation in childhood.* New York: W. W. Norton.

Piaget, J. (1963). *The origins of intelligence in children.* New York: W. W. Norton.

Piaget, J. (1968). *On the development of memory and identity.* Barre, MA: Clark University Press.

Piaget, J. (1970). *Science of education and the psychology of the child.* New York: Orion Press.

Piaget, J. (1983). Piaget's theory. In P. H. Mussen (Ed.), *Handbook of child psychology* (4th ed.), and W. Kessen (Ed.), *History, theory, and methods* (vol. 1). New York: John Wiley & Sons.

Pitzer, R.L. (1997, November 9). *Corporal Punishment in the Discipline of Children in the Home. Research Update for Practitioners presented at the National Council on Family Relations Annual Conference*, Washington DC.

Poussaint, A. F., & Linn, S. (1997, Spring/Summer). Fragile: Handle with care. *Newsweek* [Your Child: From Birth to Three, Special Issue], *33*.

Power, F. C., Higgins, A., & Kohlberg, L. (1989). *Lawrence Kohlberg's approach to moral education.* New York: Columbia University Press.

Powers, S. I. (1982). *Family interaction and parental moral development as a context for adolescent moral development.* Unpublished doctoral dissertation, Harvard University.

Pransky, J. (1991). *Prevention: The critical need.* Springfield, MO: Burrell Foundation and Paradigm Press.

Prothrow-Stith, D., & Quaday, S. (1995). *Hidden casualties: The relationship between violence and learning.* Washington, DC: National Health & Education Consortium and National Consortium for African American Children, Inc.

Provence, S., & Lipton, R.C. (1967). *Infants in institutions: A comparison of their development during the first year of life with family reared infants.* Madison, CT: International Universities. Press.

R

Randy, L., Hoover, R. L., & Kindsvatter, R. (1997). *Democratic discipline: Foundation & practice.* Upper Saddle River, NJ: Merrill Education/Prentice-Hall.

Roberts, P. (1997). Fathers' time. In E. N. Junn & C. Boyatzis (Eds.), *Annual editions: Child growth and development 97/98* (4th ed.). New York: McGraw-Hill. (Original work published in *Psychology Today*, May/June 1996.)

Rosenblith, J. F., Sims-Knight, J. (1985). *In the beginning: Development in the first two years.* Monterey, CA: Brooks/Cole.

Rosenthal, R., & Jacobson, L. (1968). *Pygmalion in the classroom: Teacher expectations and pupils' intellectual development.* New York: Holt, Rinehart & Winston.

Rousseau, J. (1893). *Emile: Or treatise on education.* New York: Appleton.

Rutter, M. (1976). Family, area, and school influences in the genesis of conduct disorders. In L. Hersov, M. Berber, & D. Shaffer (Eds.), *Aggression and antisocial behavior development.* Oxford: Pergamom Press.

S

Salk, L. (1992). *Familyhood.* New York: Simon & Schuster.

Sameroff, J. J., & Cavanagh, P. J. (1979). Learning in infancy: A developmental perspective. In J. D. Osofsky (Ed.), *Handbook of infant development* (pp. 344–392). New York: Wiley.

Santrock, J. W. (1997). *Children.* New York: McGraw-Hill.

Schwartz, W. (1995). *A guide to communicating with Asian American families: For parents/about parents.* New York: ERIC Clearinghouse on Urban Education.

Sears, R. R., Maccoby, E. E., & Lewin, H. (1957). *Patterns of child rearing.* Evanston, IL: Row & Peterson.

Seefeldt, C., & Barbour, N. (1998). *Early childhood education: An introduction* (4th ed.). Upper Saddle River, NJ: Merrill Education/Prentice-Hall.

Shore, R. (1997). *Rethinking the brain: New insights into early development.* [Executive Summary]. New York: Families & Work Institute.

Silvers, J. (1997). Child labor in Pakistan. In E. N. Junn & C. Boyatzis (Eds.), *Annual editions: Child growth and development 97/98* (4th ed.). New York: McGraw-Hill. (Original work published in *The Atlantic Monthly*, February 1996.)

Simons, R., Johnson, C., & Conger, R. (1994). Harsh corporal punishment versus quality of parental involvement as an explanation of adolesent maladjustment. *Journal of Marriage and the Family, 56*, 591–607.

Skinner, B. (1953). *Science and human behavior.* New York: Macmillan.

Skinner, B. (1974). *About behaviorism.* New York: Knopf.

Skolnick, A. (1991). *Embattled paradise: The American family in an age of uncertainty.* New York: Basic Books.

Slaby, R.G., Roedell, W.C., Arezzo, D., & Hendrix, K. (1995). *Early violence prevention: Tools for teachers of young children.* Washington, DC: NAEYC.

Solomon, D., Watson, M., Battistich, V., Schaps, E., & Delucchi, K. (1992). Creating a caring community: Educational practices that promote children's prosocial development. In F. K. Oser, A. Dick, and J. L. Patry (Eds.), *Effective and responsible teaching: The new synthesis.* San Francisco: Jossey-Bass.

Spafford, C. S., Pesce, A. I., & Grosser, G. (1998). *The cyclopedic education dictionary.* Clifton Park, NY: Delmar Learning.

Sroufe, L. A. (1996). *Child development: Its nature and course.* New York: McGraw-Hill.

Sroufe, L. A. (1979). Socioemotional development. In J. Osofsky (Ed.), *Handbook of infant development.* New York: Wiley.

Steinberg, L. (1995). *Childhood.* New York: McGraw-Hill.

Stengel, R. (1997). Fly till I die. In K. M. Paciorek & J. H. Munro, *Annual editions: Early childhood education 97/98* (18th ed.). New York: McGraw-Hill. (Original work published in *Time*, April 22, 1996.)

Stern, D. N. (1974). Mother and infant at play: The dyadic interaction involving facial, vocal and gaze behaviors. In M. Lewis & L. Rosenblum (Eds.), *The effect of the infant on its caregiver.* New York: Wiley-Interscience.

Stevenson, H. W., Chen, C., & Uttal, D.H. (1990). Beliefs and achievement: A study of black, white and Hispanic children. *Child Development, 61*, 508–523.

Stevenson, H. W., & Lee, S. (1990). Contexts of achievement. *Monograph of the Society for Research in Child Development, 55*, 1–2.

Stott, L. H., & Ball, R. S. (1957). Consistency and change in ascendance-submission in the social interaction of children. *Child Development, 28*, 259–272.

Straus, M. (1995). *Beating the devil out of them: Corporal punishment in American families.* New York: Lexington Books.

Straus, M.A. (1994). *Beating the devil out of them: Corporal punishment in American families.* San Francisco, CA: New Lexington Press

Straus, M. A. (2001). *Beating the devil out of them: Corporal punishment in American families and its effects on children.* (2nd ed.). New Brunswick, NJ: Transaction Publishers.

Straus, M. A., & Gelles, R. J. (Eds.). (1990). *Physical violence in American families: Risk factors and adaptations to violence in 8,145 families.* New Brunswick, NJ: Transactions.

Straus, M. A., & Mathur, A. (1996). Social change and change in approval of corporal punishment by parents from 1968 to 1994. In D. Frehsee, W. Horn, & K. D. Bussman (Eds.), *Family violence against children.* Berlin: Walter deGruyter.

Straus, M. A., Sugarman, D.B., & Giles-Sims, J. (1997). Spanking by parents and subsequent antisocial behavior of children. *Archives of Pediatrics and Adolescent Medicine, 151*, 761–767.

Strassberg, Z., Dodge, K. A., Pettit, G. S., & Bates, J. E. (1994). Spanking in families and subsequent aggressive behavior toward peers by kindergarten students. *Development and Psychopathology, 6*, 445–461

Stringer-Seibold, T., et al. (1996, Fall). Strengths and needs of divided families. Research Highlights. *Dimensions of Early Childhood, 24*(4), 22–29.

T

Teaching Tolerance Project. (1997). *Starting small: Teaching tolerance in preschool and the early grades.* Montgomery, AL: Southern Poverty Law Center.

Thomas, A., & Chess, S. (1977). *Temperament and development.* New York: Brunner/Mazel.

Thomas, A., Chess, S., & Birch, H. G. (1970). *The origin of personality. Scientific American, 233*, 102–109.

Thorne, B. (1997). Girls and boys together but mostly apart. In E. N. Junn & C. Boyatzis (Eds.), *Annual editions: Child growth and development 97/98* (4th ed.). New York: McGraw-Hill. (Original work published in *GenderPlay: Girls and Boys in School*, Rutgers University Press, 1993.)

Thorpe, K., & Daly, K. (1999). Children, parents and time. The dialectics of control. In Sheehan (Ed.), *Through the eyes of the child: Revisioning children as active agents of family life.* New York: JAI Press.

Toner, I. J., Parke, R. D., & Yussen, S. R. (1978). The effect of observation of model behavior on the establishment and stability of resistance to deviation in children. *Journal of Genetic Psychology, 132*, 283–290.

Toner, I. J., & Potts, R. (1981). Effect of modeled rationales on moral behavior, moral choice, and level of moral judgment in children. *Journal of Psychology, 107*, 153–162.

Trad, P. V. (1986). *Infant depression: Paradigms and paradoxes.* Berlin, Germany: Axel Springer Verlag.

Trad, P. V. (1987). *Infant and childhood depression: Developmental factors* (Wiley Series in Child and Adolescent Mental Health). Hoboken, NJ: John Wiley & Sons.

Trad, P. V. (1991). *Interventions with infants and parents: The theory and practice of previewing.* Hoboken, NJ: John Wiley & Sons.

Trad, P. V. (1994). *Infant depression.* St. Northvale, NJ: Jason Aronson, Inc.

Trawick-Smith, J. (1997). *Early childhood development in multicultural perspective.* Upper Saddle River, NJ: Merrill Education/Prentice-Hall.

Trehub, S. (1973). Infants' sensitivity to vowel and tonal contrasts. *Developmental Psychology, 9*, 81–96.

U

Ulich, R. (1954). *Three thousand years of educational wisdom.* Cambridge, MA: Harvard University Press.

U.S. Department of Health and Human Services (1995, April). A nation's shame: Fatal child abuse and neglect in the United States. Washington, DC: A Report of the U.S. Advisory Board on Child Abuse and Neglect.

V

von Frisch, K. (1974). Decoding the language of the bee. *Science, 185*, 663–668.

von Goethe, W. (1995). Conversations of German refugees: Wilhelm Meister's journeyman years, or the renunciants (J. Van Heurck, trans.). In J. K. Brown (Ed.), *Goethe's collected works* (reprint ed.) (vol. 10). Princeton, NJ: Princeton University Press.

W

Walker, L. J., & Taylor, J. H. (1991). Family interactions and the development of moral reasoning. *Child Development, 62*, 264–283.

Wallach, L. B. (1997). Breaking the cycle of violence. In K. M. Paciorek & J. H. Munro (Eds.), *Annual editions: Early childhood education 97/98* (18th ed.). New York: McGraw-Hill. (Original work published in *Children Today, 23*[3], 1994–1995.)

Wang, C. T., & Daro, D. (1998). *Current trends in child abuse reporting and fatalities: The results of the 1997 annual fifty state survey.* Chicago: National Committee to Prevent Child Abuse.

Watson, J. (1930). *Behaviorism* (2d ed.). Chicago: University of Chicago Press.

Watson, J. (1973). Smiling, cooing and "the game." *Merrill-Palmer Quarterly, 18,* 323–339.

Weiser, M. (1982). *Group care and education of infants and toddlers.* St. Louis, MO: Mosby.

Weiss, C. D., & Lillywhite, H. S. (1976). *Communicative disorders: A handbook for prevention and early intervention.* St. Louis, MO: Mosby.

Werner, E. E. (1987). Vulnerability and resiliency in children at risk for delinquency: A longitudinal study from birth to adulthood. In J. D. Burchard & S. N. Burchard (Eds.), *Primary prevention of psychopathology: Prevention of delinquent behavior* (vol. 10, pp. 16–43). Newbury Park, CA: Sage.

Werner, N. E., & Evans, I. M. (1971). Perception of prejudice in Mexican-American preschool children. In N. N. Wagner & M. J. Haug (Eds.), *Chicano: Social and psychological perspectives.* St. Louis, MO: Mosby.

Wertsch, J. V. (1988). *Vygotsky and the social formation of mind.* Boston: Harvard University Press.

White, B. L. (1975). *The first three years of life.* New York: Avon.

White, B. L. (1995). *The new first three years of life* (rev. ed.). New York: Simon & Shuster.

White, B., Kaban, B., & Attanucci, J. (1979). *The origins of human competence: The final report of the Harvard preschool project.* Lanham, MD: Lexington Books.

White, B., & Watts, J. (1973). *Experience and environment: Major influences on the development of the young child* (vol. 2). Upper Saddle River, NJ: Prentice-Hall.

Williams, B. F., & Port, P. D. (2000). *Very young children with special needs: A formative approach for the 21st century.* V. F. Howard (Ed.) (2nd ed.). Upper Saddle River, NJ: Prentice Hall.

Wittmer, D. S., & Honig, A. S. (1997). Encouraging positive social development in young children. In K. M. Paciorek & J. H. Munro (Eds.), *Annual editions: Early childhood education 97/98* (18th ed.). New York: McGraw-Hill. (Original work published in *Young Children,* July 1994.)

Wolff, P. (1963). Observations on the early development of smiling. In B. M. Foss (Ed.), *Determinants of infant behavior* (vol. 2). London: Methuen.

Y

Yarrow, A. (1991). *Latecomers: Children of parents over 35.* New York: Free Press.

Z

Zahn-Waxler, C., Radke-Yarrow, M., & King, R. A. (1979). Child rearing and children's prosocial initiations towards victims of distress. *Child Development, 50,* 319–330.

Index